Praise for
Night after Night: New Zealanders in Bomber Command

'Wonderful'
former bomber pilot Jack Hardie

'A very rewarding book'
Gisborne Herald

'Truly a must read'
Iain Duffy, *Northern Advocate*, Whangarei

'A crisp compelling read'
Daily Post, Rotorua

'*Night after Night* is a classic'
Tom Empson, former Mosquito pilot

'A cracker'
Waikato Times

'What a magnificent job Lambert has done ...'
Christchurch Star

Praise for
Day after Day: New Zealanders in Fighter Command

'A remarkable book'
Matthew Wright, *Listener*

'An excellent companion to *Night after Night*'
Paul Harrison, *NZ Aviation News*

'A fine addition to New Zealand's historical aviation'
Roger Moroney, APN Regional Newspapers

'A wonderful tribute to the men of Fighter Command'
RSA Review

'An exceptional work of research'
Oliver Riddell, *Otago Daily Times*

Also by Max Lambert and published by HarperCollins:

Night after Night
Day after Day

VICTORY
NEW ZEALAND AIRMEN AND
THE FALL OF GERMANY

MAX LAMBERT

HarperCollins*Publishers*

HarperCollins*Publishers*

First published in 2014
by HarperCollins*Publishers* (New Zealand) Limited
Unit D1, 63 Apollo Drive, Rosedale, Auckland 0632, New Zealand

Copyright © Max Lambert 2014

Max Lambert asserts the moral right to be identified as the author of this work.
All rights reserved. No part of this publication may be reproduced, stored in a retrieval system or transmitted in any form or by any means, electronic, mechanical, photocopying, recording or otherwise, without the prior written permission of the publishers.

HarperCollins*Publishers*
Unit D1, 63 Apollo Drive, Rosedale, Auckland 0632, New Zealand
Level 13, 201 Elizabeth Street, Sydney, NSW 2000, Australia
A 53, Sector 57, Noida, UP, India
77–85 Fulham Palace Road, London W6 8JB, United Kingdom
2 Bloor Street East, 20th floor, Toronto, Ontario M4W 1A8, Canada
10 East 53rd Street, New York, NY 10022, USA

A catalogue record is available for this book from the
National Library of New Zealand

Cover design by HarperCollins Design Studio
Cover image © IWM
Typeset in Bembo Std by Kirby Jones

*To all New Zealand aircrew who served in the European theatre,
especially those who lost their lives*

CONTENTS

Chapter 1:	The eve of D-Day	1
Chapter 2:	D-Day – the door to Fortress Europe is prised open	14
Chapter 3:	Bomber Command at war	62
Chapter 4:	Sinking the U-boats	100
Chapter 5:	Operations most secret	121
Chapter 6:	On the run in Occupied Europe	145
Chapter 7:	Air Sea Rescue	176
Chapter 8:	Falaise	186
Chapter 9:	Arnhem – Montgomery's folly	195
Chapter 10:	Flying Mosquitoes and other aircraft	236
Chapter 11:	The Rhine Crossing – 24 March 1945	257
Chapter 12:	Friendly fire	266
Chapter 13:	Wrecking Germany's petroleum industry	271
Chapter 14:	The last weeks	294
Appendix:	The battle against the U-boats	308

Acknowledgements	366
Bibliography	370
Abbreviations	373
Index of New Zealand aircrew (and selected others)	374
General index	380
About the author	391

CHAPTER 1

The eve of D-Day

On Sunday, 4 June 1944, two days before thousands of Allied troops waded ashore on the beaches of Normandy, New Zealand air gunner Des Reevely whacked golf balls around at RAF Tarrant Rushton in the peaceful Dorset countryside. The base, built in 1943 and home to 38 Group squadrons 298 and 644, was sealed off for the imminent invasion of France – no private phone calls in or out, no outward mail, no visitors, no one allowed off-field. Six Halifaxes, three from each squadron, would haul gliders carrying the first Allied troops into battle on D-Day. The 6th Airborne Division men chosen for the key operation, the capture in Normandy of what's now known as Pegasus Bridge, and another nearby, were tough infantry from the Oxford and Buffs. They'd been working with the squadrons for weeks.

Reevely, down to fly in one of the 298 aircraft, wrote in his diary that the game and the occasion 'reminds me very much of Francis

Drake and Plymouth Hoe'. Reevely also wrote the Halifax crews had been briefed the day before on their role 'in the big drop'. They had expected to take off late in the evening of 4 June but in the face of predicted strong winds, Allied Supreme Commander Ike Eisenhower put the invasion back to the following morning. So Reevely and his fellow aircrew loafed around and had their second 'last and final briefing' some hours before the Halifaxes, bombers converted to the airborne role, were due to lift off.

Meanwhile, sixty miles north in the Cotswolds at RAF Fairford, in the southeast corner of Gloucestershire, New Zealanders in 190 and 620 Squadrons prepared for their part in the invasion's airborne assault. Their big Stirlings and those of other squadrons in 38 Group were earmarked to take off from 11.15 p.m. on 5 June in Operation Tonga, to drop 6th Airborne paratroopers near Caen and then back the next day, this time 'tugging' gliders packed with troops and guns, in Operation Mallard. On 5 June these crews had little to do. Their planes had been serviced to perfection and only one needed a final air test. Months of practice drops and glider-towing flights were over. Among the New Zealanders readying for the late-night lift off was 22-year-old Flight Sergeant Edward Harry Atkinson. Nominally he was the bomb aimer but these Stirlings dropped paras, supplies and equipment. So Atkinson had become a map reader, the navigator's eyes, up in the nose of the plane, key in guiding the aircraft to the correct spot to drop paratroopers, release a glider or drop supplies to Resistance groups. He also helped his pilot if needed. Atkinson would die in Normandy, just hours before the first troops hit the beaches, his aircraft a victim of German flak and, perhaps, a German fighter. He was the first of two New Zealanders to lose their lives on D-Day.

THE EVE OF D-DAY

*

The second was navigator James Chalmers (21) from Invercargill, shot down and killed with two others flying an 88 Squadron Boston, laying smoke to mask the British beaches and incoming landing craft. Chalmers was based at RAF Hartford Bridge in Hampshire. The squadron shared the base with 342 (Lorraine) Squadron, a French-crewed unit also operating Bostons, and 226 Squadron on Mitchells. The three operated as 137 Wing. The light-bomber Bostons were adapted with smoke canisters installed in the bomb bays and outlet vents poking through holes punched in the bomb-bay doors. British 88 Squadron navigator George Louden, who flew on D-Day morning, remembered years later in the BBC's written archive of World War II memories 'WW2 People's War' that all the mess bars were closed at 6 p.m. on 5 June and crews ordered to have an early night. When he looked for friends at the tented site the squadron occupied he encountered a strange silence. 'I went to the field latrines ... and found almost everyone discussing the situation, those not "sitting" standing in front of those who were ... No one slept much and crews were up again at 1 a.m. for the breakfast fryup, final briefing and takeoff.'

In East Anglia at RAF Mildenhall, a pre-war air base where aircrew lived in some comfort, New Zealander Jim Insull, a navigator on 622 Squadron, a heavy bomber unit, was called to a briefing at 10 p.m. on 5 June, his fourth in the past few days. The previous three had been for targets in France but the planned ops had been scrubbed – poor weather. Ears pricked up at the late evening briefing when the target was announced as gun emplacements on the French coast at Ouistreham. Insull wrote in his diary:

We pricked up our ears even higher when the CO warned us to keep clear of certain areas west of the Greenwich meridian 'because the Navy will be there and they don't like aircraft, not even Allied. Aircraft recognition is unknown to them.' We were to take off at 3 a.m. and Zero hour was fixed for 0505 hours [and we were to] drop our load (11 x 1000 pounders and three x 500 pounders) between 0505 and 0509. No bombing was to take place on any consideration after 0513. So this was it!

One New Zealand airman was already at sea on the way to France. Ned Hitchcock (25), from Christchurch, was fast asleep on a Landing Craft Tank headed for Omaha. His trip to the battlefield as part of a mobile RAF radar team was a last-minute arrangement. Hitchcock was at work in his office at 60 (Signals) Group's headquarters at Leighton Buzzard, Bedfordshire, and looked up when a colleague poked his head round the door. 'Want to go in on the invasion, Hitch?'

Hitchcock couldn't have imagined what he was letting himself in for – his team landed at Omaha, where American troops met the fiercest German resistance and suffered awful losses. Omaha was not the place to be on D-Day.

Bob Spurdle, DFC and bar, mention in dispatches, was a great fighter pilot and great character, who called a spade a spade. He was also a survivor. A Battle of Britain veteran in South African Sailor Malan's 74 Squadron, he flew five tours for an astonishing 564 sorties. A Short Service Commission pilot, he was RAF during the war. Loaned to the RNZAF for a year from December 1942, he flew his fourth tour in the southwest Pacific, scoring two of his ten 'kills'. Back in England in March 1944, he served briefly with 130 Squadron before joining the Detling Wing as a flight commander in 80 Squadron at the invitation of fellow New Zealander and friend, Wing Commander 'Hawkeye' Wells. In 1940 they'd been on the same ship to Britain, where Wells predicted Spurdle would have his own squadron. In late July he sewed a third ring on his uniform.

When Spurdle was posted to 80 Squadron, it was led by Norwegian Bjorn Bjornstad and based in Hertfordshire at RAF Sawbridgeworth. The squadron was just back from Egypt, Greece, Libya, Palestine and Italy, where it had been stationed since May 1938, and was at Detling for D-Day. On 5 June the CO drew Spurdle aside and told him to organise a strong team for the morning and see they got to bed early. Spurdle wrote in *The Blue Arena*:

> All night heavy planes droned overhead – we'd never heard anything like it before. It was ON! Invasion! ... We were awakened well before dawn by excited batmen, scoffed hurried breakfast and tore off to dispersal. We waited and waited. The CO was almost beside himself with frustration and pestered Ops for a job for our squadron. But everything had been planned and planned again. Our job was to standby and be ready for any special job that might crop up. We were being held in reserve!

On the afternoon of 5 June flying boat skipper Les Baveystock of 201 Squadron pulled his big Sunderland off the calm waters of Milford Haven, a long indent on the southwest coast of Wales. Several cylinders had been replaced and the plane needed testing. 'We took off to the west and climbed clear of the coast [and] saw an amazing spectacle,' he wrote in *Wavetops at My Wing*:

A few miles out was an armada of naval ships of every type and size. They stretched as far as the eye could see from north to south … This could mean only one thing: the Invasion Fleet was under way, and D-Day for the landings would be 6 June. We returned to base full of exhilaration at the prospect of the great news that would burst upon the world the following morning.

Baveystock was a Londoner but immigrated to New Zealand four years after the war. By the time of that 5 June test flight, Baveystock was a flight lieutenant, one of 201 Squadron's most experienced pilots and holder of a DFC and DFM. Thirty-six hours later he would have a bar to his DFC for sinking a U-boat, in the first post-Normandy landings.

A frustrated Rex Daniell cooled his heels the night of 5 June, livid that he wasn't in the air. Daniell (23), from Masterton, a decorated veteran with almost four years war service, had reported to Dakota-flying 48 Squadron at Down Ampney, Wiltshire, in March 1944. Years later in *What Did You Do in the War, Poppa Rekka?*, he remembered a lukewarm reception when he arrived at 48's Gloucestershire base from India. The wing commander had little to say apart from telling him he would command 48's C flight.

After a couple of days' leave after intensive late-May training, Daniell returned to his base in early June to find briefings under way for crews flying on the night of 5 June – and that he wasn't wanted. The CO had him down to lead the squadron's glider effort on D-Day's afternoon. Daniell protested that none of the C flight crews had his experience in dropping paras at night. 'Surely I should be allowed to have a go,' he told his boss. 'I was furious when he would not budge ... and I made up my mind to find an alternative posting as soon as something could be arranged.' He subsequently moved to 233 Squadron, another Dakota unit in 46 Group.

Daniell remembered 5 June as the longest possible day. 'No one knew how to pass the time when the bars remained closed. It was a "nothing" day with the guys shovelling away at the "shove halfpenny board" or throwing a few darts or getting down to a game of cards with little concentration.'

Eventually the waiting was over and Daniell watched the paratroops clamber into their Horsa gliders. 'One soldier ... had his pet crow with him and a colonel arrived complete with a rugby ball decorated with luminous white paint. He was going to boot it out the door just before he jumped in the hope it might distract the chaps down below!' Hugely disappointed, Daniell watched the Dakotas and their gliders lift into the air and was back on the field at 3 a.m. as the planes returned. His turn was coming.

Aircraft engines began coughing into life in the hour between 11 p.m. and midnight on 5 June at two RAF heavy bomber fields. The planes warming their engines carried no bombs, and would fly only a short distance – to the Channel. Lancasters of 617 Squadron – the Dambusters – and 218 Squadron Stirlings were being prepared for special twin operations designed to fool the Nazis. At Woodhill Spa 617 was readying its aircraft for Operation Taxable while at Woolfox Lodge 218 was about to dispatch its aircraft on Operation Glimmer.

After its stunning raid on the Ruhr dams in May 1943, 617 Squadron stole the limelight, and its role in Taxable's deception has been widely documented. Not so well known is the part played by 218 Squadron flying Glimmer. Both involved the dropping of vast quantities of 'window', or 'chaff' as it was also known – narrow, 30 cm aluminium-backed paper strips designed to swamp enemy radar. First used by Bomber Command on the July 1943 firestorm raids on Hamburg, it caused multiple and trick images on German radar. Though the Germans developed counter measures, window remained effective.

Flying precise moving circuits at two points in the English Channel, crews hurled out countless packages of window. The aircraft would work in tandem with a number of small ships flying balloons coated with material which also created myriad signals on enemy radar. Together the radar patterns and phoney radio chatter would create the false impression of two convoys at sea, one heading for Cap d'Antifer, on the French coast north of Le Havre, the other making for Boulogne not far from the Channel's narrowest point. Because of the demanding requirements of piloting and navigation plus the continuous dropping of window, all the aircraft carried double crews.

The elaborate hoax was one of the final planks in the long-running Allied plan to convince Germany the Invasion would occur in the Pas de Calais region. This subterfuge played on the already-strong German belief the Allies would pick the region closest to England. While 617 and 218 were flying on 5–6 June 1944, the real invasion force was at sea, steaming for the beaches of Normandy. For some days after 6 June the Nazi hierarchy continued to believe Normandy was a feint and the real thrust would come in the Pas de Calais, with Hitler delaying permission to move armour south.

Veteran New Zealander skipper Les Munro played a key role in Taxable, his squadron CO, Wing Commander Leonard Cheshire, flying with him as second pilot. Munro, then 23, was one of two New Zealand pilots on Taxable. The other was West Coaster Terry

Kearns (24), who flew with his long-time navigator, John Barclay (23), Dunedin.

Three of the eight captains on 218 that night were New Zealanders: Arnold King (21) from Wellington, Ian Lock (20), a farmer from Okaihau in the Bay of Islands, and Trevor Knapman (21) from New Plymouth. All flight lieutenants, just out of their teens. King was chosen as one of the six skippers for Glimmer. Lock and Knapman would orbit the South Coast as backups, in case they were needed.

King, flying EF207, HA-F (for Freddie), was the last off from Chedburgh, forty-three minutes into D-Day. The others had started taking off before midnight. King was nearing the end of a 34-ops tour. He had five of his regular crew with him, including South Islander Geoff Robb. Almost 32, Robb was King's bomb aimer but on Glimmer was one of the men doing the physically demanding job of heaving window. King had a soft spot for Robb, a lowly aircrafthand when they met at Harewood in 1942, when King was learning to fly. One day King vomited in the cockpit and Robb offered to clean up the mess. A year later when King was sorting out a crew at 11 Operational Training Unit (OTU) Westcott near Oxford, he spotted Robb and instantly signed him on. Robb flew every one of King's thirty-four ops. He dropped the bombs in the right places and King brought them home safely.

617 put up two flights of eight aircraft each, with Munro leading and lifting his Lancaster into the air shortly after 11 p.m. The first of 218's Stirlings was up at 11.29 p.m. King's, the last, was somewhat later, while Lock and Knapman were in the air at 11.50 p.m.

*

Mosquito pilot Roy Le Long and his English navigator John 'Mac' McLaren took their aircraft up for a test flight at RAF Manston on the southeast tip of England, as 5 June began to wane. They wanted to be sure it was in top shape for their night's work – patrolling German airfields in Normandy. They rolled down the runway, powerful Merlins lifting them into the night sky at nine minutes before midnight, one of thirteen Mosquitoes of 605 (County of Warwick) Squadron bound for similar targets. Their goals were bases at Evreux, about 40 miles south of Rouen, and nearby St Andre-de-l'Eure.

Le Long, a mature 26-year-old, was in home territory. His father, born in Guernsey in the Channel Islands, arrived in New Zealand with two brothers in the early 1900s and a bit further back the family hailed from Nehou, a small Normandy village in the heart of the Cherbourg Peninsula.

After earning his wings in Canada in September 1942, Le Long spent a year as an instructor at Moncton, New Brunswick, surviving a nasty crash. His Anson, with two student pilots, hit tree tops in snowy hill country in poor weather, before plunging to the ground. All survived but faced a hellish eight-mile journey through forest thick with snow. Le Long, head and face covered with clotted blood from deep scalp wounds and hampered by a groin injury, spent a month in hospital. He reached England in November 1943 and was posted to 605, based at Bradwell Bay on the Essex coast. The squadron moved to Manston two months before D-Day. As he took off just before midnight on the fifth, he was unaware he was about to create RAF history.

No New Zealander was more experienced at glider-towing than Cromwell man Basil Bretherton. He'd been on 295 Squadron as a rookie pilot in April 1943 and the following month was up for the first time with a glider in tow. One year to the day before D-Day he was on a Halifax towing a Horsa from Portreath, Cornwall, to North Africa. Seven times he made the 1600-mile run to Sale, Morocco, with a more senior captain. On three occasions he hauled a glider to Sousse in Tunisia, another 1600 miles. The long trip to Sale was dangerous. German fighters shot down three Halifaxes and five Horsas as the tugs crossed the Bay of Biscay. But 295 delivered twenty-seven Horsas to Tunisia in time for the July 1943 landings in Sicily, and later operations and reinforcements in that theatre. The gliders supplemented Wacos, their American counterparts. The Wacos could carry thirteen troops, the British Horsas double that.

As 1943 ebbed, Bretherton was posted to 298 Squadron at Tarrant Rushton as it began taking delivery of Hamilcars, the next generation of British gliders. All wood, their wingspan was six feet greater than the four-engined Halifax towing it. Bretherton pulled his first Hamilcar off the ground on Armistice Day 1943 and on the second-last day of the year made his mark in RAF records by taking off with the first fully-loaded Hamilcar. The glider's all-up weight reached 36,000 pounds (16 tons). Bretherton wrote:

> In a normal takeoff the glider always became airborne first but on this occasion we had used up the full 2000 yards of runway and the glider hadn't shown any sign of lifting. As we had sufficient flying speed and no runway left we became airborne and simply pulled the glider off after us.

Bretherton didn't get far on Tonga. Now with 644 Squadron, also at Tarrant Rushton, he hauled a Horsa off at 1.25 a.m. He was over Worthy near Winchester, 35 miles northeast of his base, as the fleet of tugs and gliders formed up and readied for their first turn toward France – then disaster. Bretherton wrote in his log the simple letters DNCO (duty not carried out). Nothing more. The squadron's Operations Record Book (ORB) says the tow-rope came out of the glider's sockets and the Horsa force-landed near Worthy Down. Doug Wood in his book *A Noble Pair of Brothers* also says the glider cast-off because of an imminent collision with another combination. A disappointed Bretherton landed back at base 1 hour 30 minutes after takeoff with nine containers of supplies still in his aircraft's bomb bays.

At least two New Zealand fighter pilots were already on the ground in France on 5 June, one at large in Normandy since the previous October, another further north since December. For Jim Mortimer, a member of 485, the New Zealand Spitfire Squadron, and Joe Helan, a Typhoon pilot on 486 (NZ) Squadron, the invasion would mean eventual freedom. A third New Zealander, 75 (NZ) Squadron bomber pilot Ron Clark, shot down on 28 May on his first op as he flew with another crew for experience, was dodging the Gestapo in Belgium, dashing back and forth from a safe house to a dugout in the chickencoop. With the help of the Resistance he was at large until August, when he ended up in a POW camp.

Another New Zealand pilot was in France involuntarily, operating on sabotage missions with the Resistance southeast of Bordeaux in support of the famous Wheelwright network, run by Englishman George Starr. Les Brown (26), a South Island school teacher, took off in his 620 Squadron Stirling from Tarrant Rushton the night of 11–12 April, bound for a drop zone inland from Bordeaux. Not far short of their target and flying low, Brown's plane was hit by flak, setting both port engines afire. Despite his inexperience, Brown crash-landed successfully and all but one of the six men got out alive. Three headed for a farmhouse to seek aid and were betrayed, but Brown and his 'elderly' rear gunner, 35-year-old Briton George Griffin, skedaddled into the forest and linked up with the Resistance. Griffin eventually fell into enemy hands but his Kiwi colleague's adventures climaxed with a full-scale battle in June, followed by escape to England over the Pyrenees. And a Military Medal, a rare award for air crew.

CHAPTER 2

D-Day – the door to Fortress Europe is prised open

It was an amphibious landing on a grand scale – an operation such as the world had never seen. On 6 June 1944, more than 5000 ships, from the biggest and most powerful battle wagons to the smallest naval units, combined in Operation Overlord, putting 200,000 British, Canadian and American troops ashore in Normandy. The assault on Hitler's Fortress Europe had begun, four long years after the German armies rolled out of the Ardennes Forest to subdue France, Belgium, Holland, and Britain at Dunkirk. Stalin had pressed for the second front for two years, the Americans had wanted it a year earlier. Sensibly, after Churchill's arguments, it had been delayed.

By June 1944 the Allies had thousands of aircraft in their arsenal, ranged against the German Luftwaffe, already a shadow of what it once was. The Germans had been swept from the skies over

Normandy, their numbers decimated, airfields blitzed and radar-control stations smoking ruins. German plans to hurl the invaders back failed. Tank and infantry columns moving up to counter-attack ground to a halt, battered and bruised by fighters, bombers, artillery and naval gunfire. Remnant German naval surface units sank a handful of Allied ships but were ineffective and easily chased off – U-boats fared no better.

German forces couldn't prevent the Allies landing their men on the coast of the Calvados department of Normandy, on a 61-mile coastline. Omaha Beach, where the US 1st and 29th Infantry Divisions waded ashore and the fiercest fighting and heaviest casualties were sustained, was one of five assault areas – the longest, at almost 20 miles. The shortest, at six miles, was Juno Beach, one of the three British sectors. The others were Gold, on Juno's right flank, and Sword on its left. Gold, Juno and Sword were at the eastern side of the landing coast, Omaha and Utah, the other American beach, to the west. Three of the five Omaha sectors were subdivided into smaller areas – the landing beaches Dog, Easy and Fox, totalling four miles. In turn these were split again and targeted by units of the 1st and 29th and battalions of Rangers – Dog Green, Dog White, Dog Red and so on. The story of the bloody landings on Omaha needs no retelling. Elsewhere, on Utah and the British and Canadian beaches, casualties and resistance by German defenders weren't as severe.

Offshore powerful naval support fleets, a western task force (US) and a matching eastern group (British) covered the men going ashore. They pounded enemy positions and fired heavy shells at German gun batteries all along the coastline, until the enemy stopped replying. Some destroyers ran dangerously close to the shoreline, pouring fire at the dug-in guns shelling assaulting troops. The western force included several Royal Navy cruisers, including HMS *Black Prince*, loaned post-war to the RNZN. Another cruiser in the fleet was HMS *Ajax*, one of the heros of the Battle of the River Plate.

Clay Blair in *Hitler's U-Boat War* writes that the Allied maritime forces and aircraft assigned to the seaborne phase of Operation Overlord 'were enormous beyond imagining' with 1213 warships and 4126 transports and landing craft, and almost 6000 fighters and bombers. 'It was little wonder Allied pilots were astonished by the D-Day armada of ships streaming back and forth across the Channel, the greatest line-up of vessels in history.'

Fighter pilots who might have expected the biggest battle of the war with an all-out effort by the Luftwaffe were disappointed. Most of the German air resources were tied up defending the Fatherland from day and night bombing or on the Eastern Front. Fighter units based in coastal France and nearby Belgium had pulled back, driven off by relentless bombing of their airfields and the overwhelming swarms of Allied fighters. The few German aircraft daring to poke their noses into the air on D-Day were promptly shot down.

New Zealander Johnnie Houlton, flying with 485 (NZ) Squadron, is credited with the first enemy aircraft, a Ju 88, shot down over the battlefield. He blasted the bomber's starboard engine and watched the crew bale out. Three other squadron pilots joined him to down a second. Naval anti-aircraft fire was the fighters' biggest problem. The navy didn't give a damn for the white invasion stripes painted on Allied aircraft, showing they were friendly, firing at anything in the air within range. New Zealander Johnny Checketts' Spitfire wing was often driven off by naval gunfire. 'Lots more bloody flak from our ships [than the Germans],' he wrote in his logbook.

Though there had been some doubt during the day that the landings would succeed, especially during the worst hours on Omaha, it was clear by evening the Allied armies were ashore to stay. Next day the bridgehead was secured, expanded and naval gunfire and deadly rocket-firing Typhoons crippled attempts by German armour to counter-attack. The door to Fortress Europe had been well and truly prised open.

Des Reevely's D-Day log-book entry was short and to the point: 'Operations – Coup de Main. Loaded Horsa, tow-high release followed by bombing raid on factory near Caen. 3hrs 30m.'

French for a swift, surprise attack, Coup de Main was the perfect name for the operation to capture two key bridges just in from the Normandy coast, in order to protect the left flank of invading British troops, and block German reinforcements. Widely used, the phrase appeared in the written orders given to Major John Howard, the man who led the bridges assault in the early hours of D-Day.

Reevely, a rear gunner with above-average night vision, had been in England since September 1940, thrown into operations with thirty hours' flying – only seven of those at night. Ten of his draft of twenty-one never came home. Posted to 149 Squadron at Mildenhall in Suffolk, a 3 Group unit on Wellingtons, two hours into New Year 1941 he flew his first op to Lille. His tour of thirty-three ops lasted 15 months, its end prolonged by gunnery and other courses and 149's conversion from twin-engined Wellingtons to Stirlings.

The odds of completing a tour weren't good and Reevely experienced his share of terror as 149 visited Berlin, Kiel, Bremen and Wilhelmshaven, the Ruhr Valley cities, Hanover, Frankfurt and targets on the French Atlantic coast. In his diary Reevely wrote on 31 December 1941, 'I never thought I would be spared to finish this diary.' Tour over in March 1942, the 24-year-old Aucklander began almost two years as an instructor in Scotland. He tried to get a posting to Coastal Command in early 1944 but was ordered back to Bomber Command – 51 and 76 Squadrons and three more ops – before appointment as gunnery leader of 298 Squadron at Tarrant Rushton ten days before the invasion.

Crew lists for the six Halifaxes from 298 and 644 Squadrons charged with landing gliders alongside the Caen Canal and Orne River bridges show 298's LL335-K carrying seven men with Flt Lt WD Reevely, RNZAF as 2nd gunner. In effect, the squadron's new gunnery boss was a supernumerary and the only New Zealander among the six crews. His aircraft, Horsa glider in tow, took off with the other five just before 11 p.m. Safely in the air, the tug-glider combinations, led by RAF Wing Commander Derek Duder, gained height and headed for Normandy. They flew at about 7000 feet, high above the clouds cloaking the huge fleet on its way to unleash the invasion. Fractionally after midnight, they reached France, crossing the coast at Cabourg, a town at the mouth of the River Dives.

The moment they were over land the ungainly Horsas, with two men from the Glider Pilot Regiment in each cockpit and 20-odd heavily armed 6th Airborne Division soldiers in the body of the gliders, cast off from their tugs. The gliders, losing height, headed for their targets – three for the bridge over the Caen Canal at Benouville, the others for its twin, half a mile to the east over the Orne, both about five miles inland. The pilots knew the layouts inside out after studying drawings, maps, photographs and mock-ups for weeks. The co-pilots, grasping stopwatches and course instructions, ordered sweeping turns bringing them over the canal and river.

So began the capture of what became known as Pegasus Bridge, named after the mythical winged horse, the Airborne's emblem. The troops who stormed the bridge emerged shaken but largely uninjured from the rough landing on a small patch of turf, 100 yards from the bridge – astonishing accuracy. At 12.15 a.m. the three of them landed, a minute or so apart. Holes dug in the grass ready for wooden anti-invasion poles – 'Rommel's Asparagus' – were still empty.

Staff Sergeant Jim Wallwork, at the controls of the first glider, was catapulted through the shattered cockpit canopy as the Horsa shuddered to a halt – and became the first Allied soldier on French soil on D-Day. He survived his rude introduction to Normandy and his Horsa was followed in by the one released from Reevely's Halifax.

The 80 glider soldiers from platoons of the 2nd Battalion, Oxfordshire and Buckinghamshire Light Infantry (Ox and Bucks) were the first Allied unit in action on the ground on D-Day, the first to suffer casualties – two dead, five wounded – and the first to inflict casualties. The bridge was in their hands in a few minutes, the German fire haphazard, the light opposition soon overwhelmed. Most of the fifty defenders, there to man machine-gun posts, a pillbox and an anti-tank gun, were asleep in bunkers and trenches honeycombing the area. The bridge itself was wired for demolition but explosives weren't in place. The major in charge was said to have been absent – an affair of the heart.

British soldiers trying to rouse one German found sleeping in a bunker near the bridge were told to 'fuck off'. The man turned over and went back to sleep according to American author Stephen Ambrose in *Pegasus Bridge – June 6, 1944*, thinking his mates were playing games. Ambrose also wrote about an English lieutenant who tried to interrogate an English-speaking prisoner. The German kept interrupting, demanding to know, 'Who are you? What is going on? Where did you come from?' His reaction wasn't surprising. Stormy weather in the past day or two had ruled out an invasion in German minds and in the dark the gliders arrived silently, while aircraft overhead muffled the sound of the bridge landings.

The troops faced no opposition from the two sentries on duty, but the brilliance of their gliders' navigation and landings was offset by the errant plotting of the sixth Horsa's pilots, who mistook the Dives River for the Orne and set down far from the targets.

Capture of the bridges, the only ones over the canal and the Orne between the sea and Caen, was vital to protect the left flank of the British landings and advance from Sword Beach. Realising the bridges' significance, German troops stationed nearby launched a quick counter-attack. But the German tank or half track leading them was knocked out and the attackers pulled back, uncertain of what they were facing. The Ox and Bucks were soon reinforced by other air-dropped units of 6th Airborne, now landing in droves east and west of the canal, and a little later by guns, Jeeps and troops borne in by the gliders towed by 298 and 644 Squadrons. Further to the west in the early-morning darkness, hundreds of aircraft were delivering two American airborne divisions inland of the Normandy beaches where soon so much American blood would be shed. The paras' hold on the bridges was strengthened late in the day by the arrival of troops who had landed on Normandy beaches at daybreak.

German commanders who wanted to deliver immediate attacks to retake the bridges and head for the coast were frustrated, forbidden to move. Hans von Luck, who commanded a regiment of the reconstituted 21st Panzer Division – destroyed in North Africa – laagered on both sides of the town and port of Caen, fumed about the delay. When finally ordered to attack in the morning, it was too late. His units were beaten back by paratroopers, gunfire from navy units off the beaches and constant harassment by RAF fighter bombers.

After seeing the gliders cast off, the Coup de Main Halifaxes droned on the short distance to Caen, aiming a couple of bombs each on a cement factory. But when bomb-flattened Caen finally fell weeks later, the factory was the only building still standing.

Back safely after the 3 hours 30 minutes flight, Reevely noted in his diary, 'We are told that the bridges were captured intact; a successful operation.' And the next day: 'Our final glider pilots arrived back from France … also another crew who ditched off the coast.' Reevely flew on three 298 Secret Operations Executive (SOE) ops to France after D-Day and crewed on a Halifax towing a Horsa on Arnhem's second day. After that he was group gunnery leader at 38's headquarters.

Reevely kept a comprehensive diary during his first couple of years in Britain but his writing tailed right off in late 1943 because he had something more important on his mind – Primrose Hodge. They met during 1943 in Scotland and became engaged on Christmas Day. She 'is really the loveliest Christmas present one could ever have,' his diary says. They were married in Fort William, Perthshire, on 1 August 1944. The diary never recovered.

The crews of 190 and 620 Squadrons epitomised the old, loyal Empire. Both units mustered twenty-three aircraft at Fairford, Gloucestershire, for the late-night takeoff carrying paratroopers for

Operation Tonga. Fourteen of the twenty-three pilots rostered on 190's battle orders board wore Commonwealth shoulder tags – six Canadians, five New Zealanders, three Australians. Regrettably the compiler of 620's ORB didn't specify crew nationalities, but four of the captains were New Zealanders and bomb aimer Ted Atkinson's skipper, Bill Pettit, was a Canadian.

The New Zealand pilots flying with 190 the last pre-invasion night were Brian Bebarfald (22), Bill Brain (25), Len Kilgour (24), Larry Siegert (21) and Noel Sutherland (23). The New Zealand skippers on 620 were Bill Bell (31), Frank Cox (25), John Kay (22) and Ted Robinson (21). Other New Zealanders were on the Normandy-bound crews, among them Malcolm Yarwood (33), oldest of them all, and Bebarfald's navigator, who would die with him at Arnhem three months later. New Zealanders were sprinkled on other tug-glider squadrons within 38 Group

At 93, Sutherland remembers how they'd all been finely trained for this historic operation. 'We'd dropped paras and towed gliders in exercises large and small for several months in preparation. We were really tuned up for it.' Each member of the crew – six of them – was called to final 'trade' briefings on the 5th, one for the pilots, one for the navigators. 'We were ready.' Sutherland had pretty much an Anzac crew: two New Zealanders, navigator Colin Rouse (24) and rear gunner Reg Vincent, plus two Australians, bomb aimer Dave Bertram and wireless operator Ian 'Nix' Nixon. English flight engineer Eric Algar completed the six.

Sutherland, his compatriots and Nixon, had been together since crewing up at Pennfield Ridge, New Brunswick in May 1943, flying Venturas for two months before shipping to England and more training on Mitchells, before a posting to 299 Squadron at Stony Cross,

Hampshire. There it was back to the deficient Ventura. Finally they learned to fly the Stirling at 1665 HCU at Tilstock, Shropshire, joining 190 twelve weeks before D-Day. They immediately began day and night glider-towing exercises, dropping paratroopers and supply containers. On 7 May the Sutherland crew took off from Fairford at 11 p.m. on their only operation before D-Day – a supply drop to Resistance forces near Poitiers, southeast of Nantes – an SOE drop code named Mongrel II.

Sutherland remembers the landing craft in the Channel on 5–6 June and the dust on the ground during the Tonga drop:

> There were so many landing craft they churned up the sea, making it look like Cook Strait in a strong northwester; they extended as far as the eye could see. Bomber Command and the US Air Force had pounded the Normandy sea coast and the dust and grime generated, together with a slight on-shore breeze, meant we couldn't see a thing on the ground [the drop zones were only a few kilometres back from the sea]. At briefing we were told, 'If you don't drop on the first run there is no going round again.' With less than 10 miles distance even at slow speed we were about to give it away when Bertie called out 'Left but quick.' He had just spotted a pin point through the murk which showed us to be about half a mile astray. A quick turn and we finished up just near the DZ.

Near enough had to be good enough. The paras disappeared through the big hole in the floor. Twenty-three 190 Stirlings left Fairford that night carrying 426 paratroops to Normandy. All returned safely after delivering 408 troops. One aircraft with eighteen paras flew home, unable to recognise the DZ.

Hit by flak as it flew in over the French coast, 620 Squadron Stirling EF295, one perhaps two engines aflame, began to go down. In the nick of time, a handful of paratroopers jumped – one, two, then a third … five in all. Four landed safely, three to become POWs, one to evade capture. The fifth man died, his chute on fire. The remaining twelve paras and all the crew were still inside when the plane hit the ground. The crash and fire killed New Zealander Ted Atkinson (22) and three other up-front crew. Only two crew lived – wireless operator Bob Kebbell, at the back of the aircraft at the time as para dispatcher, and rear gunner Bert Pryce.

Dennis Williams, author of *Stirlings in Action with the Airborne Forces*, quotes Pryce's son saying his father said the aircraft was also attacked in one pass by a Ju 88, whose fire shattered his turret and sprayed the wings and fuselage. Williams also notes a French farmer claiming he saw the Stirling in a shallow dive. Approaching the ground the starboard wing hit a large tree and the plane crashed in a flash of fire. Both wings disintegrated, the shattered fuselage cracking open just aft of the wings.

Amazingly the majority of the paras in the body of the plane survived. Only two were killed outright, while a third died of injuries. As the plane was going down, Kebbell apparently heard over the intercom that Canadian pilot Bill Pettit was wounded in the neck and Atkinson was trying to help him fly the plane.

All but two of the paras aboard EF295 when it took off from Fairford at 11.45 p.m. on 5 June were sappers of 591 (Antrim) Parachute Squadron, Royal Engineers. The other pair were Major Andy Wood, 591 CO, and his intelligence officer, Lieutenant John Shinner. Each of the sappers carried plastic explosives in bicycle inner tubes wrapped around their bodies like a sausage string, dangerous material in an aircraft under attack. In an account of what happened that night, written in 1994 for the *Royal Engineers Journal*, Shinner said he watched the ripples of the water on the Channel as the plane flew toward Normandy. Right on time, with three minutes to go before the planned 1 a.m. drop, he could see surf and a strip of sand as the aircraft crossed into France at about 1000 feet. A moment or two later flak began to pepper the Stirling, the sky full of vivid flashes and orange streaks. 'Suddenly there was a flash and a burst of flame inside the aircraft, astern of where I stood. In a matter of seconds the whole of the inside of the aircraft was blazing.'

Shinner said he and others closest to the front were forced further forward while five of the paras, including Wood, managed to take to their chutes from the rear drop hole. At least one of the port engines was on fire. Then the nose dipped …

> There was a horrendous rending and crashing and I had the sensation that we were being rolled over and over. It seemed to go on for an awfully long time … when all the movement stopped … there was a fierce fire burning in the forward part of the aircraft … I couldn't move of my own accord because I was hanging upside down, by one leg on my static [parachute drop] line, which had become entangled with the roof of the aircraft … If I didn't do something I was going to cook in the immediate future.

A para who survived the crash slashed the line with his knife and he and Shinner scrambled out from the fractured fuselage. The two men and a couple of others still on their feet helped several injured men to safety but could do nothing for the crew up front. Shinner described the crew area as a raging furnace. Atkinson, Pettit, the flight engineer and navigator all died. Ironically, Pettit had won an OBE for rescuing the crew of a crashed and burning aircraft earlier in the war. He also had a DFC for bravery over Berlin the previous winter.

The Stirling plunged to earth three miles from the coastal town of Dives-Sur-Mer, about 500 yards from the elegant three-storey Chateau Grangues. Ploughing across the corner of an orchard and then a meadow, it shed its tail and left a trail of burning wreckage. Two hundred yards away another 620 Stirling already lay blazing furiously, blasts from its ammunition and explosives shattering the night. All nineteen paratroops aboard, most from the 7th Light Infantry Parachute Battalion, and the entire crew perished.

Shinner, one arm injured, was captured by Germans from a unit stationed in the grounds of the chateau, taken away for questioning and became a POW. He was one of the lucky ones. Dazed para survivors, staggering to safety, were soon rounded up. Seven were executed in cold blood several hours later by the leader of the chateau detachment, who couldn't be found after the war. Atkinson, one of the first Allied casualties on D-Day action, lies in a collective grave with the rest of his crew in Ranville War Cemetery, near Pegasus Bridge. Born in Kaponga, Atkinson was working as a plasterer when he enlisted. The paratroop drop was his third op, his first two special duties flights dropping SAS troops or equipment to French Resistance groups between exercises and preparations for the invasion.

620 Squadron lost three aircraft that night, the third falling close to Dives-sur-Mer. Everyone aboard died. All three may have been slightly off course, perhaps mistakenly picking the Dives River as their landmark, running parallel about five miles to the west, which

led to the intended drop zone. All up the ten squadrons of 38 group lost five Stirlings and one Halifax while dropping slightly more than 3000 paras into the battle area to support troops who'd captured the bridges. The 46 Group Dakotas carried paras to two other landing zones (LZs).

The paras of 3rd and 5th Brigades of the 6th Airborne who tumbled out of the fleet of planes were scattered far and wide, as much as 20 miles from their DZs, some drowning when they landed in low-lying areas the Germans had flooded. The paras were slow finding and forming up into their units and many groups met German resistance and counter-attacks. But they held their ground, supporting the troops who'd captured the Orne bridges until strengthened on D-Day afternoon by forces who'd come ashore on the Normandy beaches – and then in the evening by the men and guns landed from Operation Mallard gliders.

Like Noel Sutherland on 190 Squadron, other New Zealand captains had flown only limited ops before Normandy, but Frank Cox (25), from Christchurch, had flown with 620 on bombing raids before the squadron switched to 38 Group. Among his parachute passengers on Tonga was BBC correspondent Guy Byam, who leapt with the troops. In his broadcast in 'War Report', a programme launched by the BBC on D-Day, Byam recounted his experience:

> We're over the enemy coast now … and the [timing] has started … one minute … thirty seconds [to go] …. red light, green light, out … out … get on, get out … get out … outside into the clear night … out, out into the air over France. We know the dropping zone is obstructed … nothing in fact but fields covered with poles … but I

hit my chute and lower my kit bag which suspends on the end of a 40-foot rope to my harness ... and then the ground comes up to hit me and and I find myself in the middle of a cornfield.

Ron Reader was lucky. Twice the rear gunner survived ordeals that could have cost him his life. Early on D-Day, flying with 298 Squadron in Operation Tonga, his Halifax was hit by flak over Normandy and caught fire. Reader baled out. Two months later, still with 298, he survived a violent crash-landing in the French countryside, which killed his pilot. Injured and in hospital, he became a POW for a few days, his flying career over. Enough was enough. Reader had a tough early life. His father died when he was six, his mother five years later. He was then fostered, and had two years at high school. Jobs were hard to find in the Depression and he was working as a labourer in Riwaka, near Motueka, when he enlisted in July 1941, just short of his 21st birthday.

Like many young servicemen about to leave New Zealand, Reader was given a final-leave sendoff – and a small cheque – at a sing-song staged by the Patriotic Committee in Brooklyn, a tiny rural community outside Riwaka. Buried in a newspaper account of the evening was the name KJ Holyoake, one of a group who 'contributed vocal and dance items'. Holyoake, a future New Zealand prime minister, was back on his farm after losing his Motueka seat in the 1938 election.

Reader sailed for Canada and gunnery training in August 1941, then went on to England where the RAF applied the finishing touches at a gunnery school. He was posted to 76 Squadron on Halifaxes, where his skipper and navigator were both South Islanders – pilot Ron Perks, from Greymouth, and navigator Clem

Strang (22), from Winton. Perks, a few months short of 30, who was old for a tyro pilot but survived a demanding period with 76, including the Ruhr Valley raids, was rewarded with a DFC, and went on to fly a second tour with another squadron.

Strang was on his sixty-fifth op the night of 27 June 1944 when he died, unable to get out of a 692 Squadron Mosquito hit at 25,000 feet in remarkable shooting by a German 88 mm battery. Strang was buried in Germany but postwar an American graves registration unit moved his remains to Holland, where they were reinterred in a British cemetery, as those of an unknown airman. As positive ID wasn't possible then, Strang is remembered at Runnymede.

On 21 July 1943 *New Zealand Truth* ran an item from London staff reporter Henry Bateson, which began: 'One of the greatest thrills which can come the way of a Bomber Command pilot is a mid-air collision.' He qualified such nonsense by saying the thrill was a 'nasty' one. Bateson reported Perks' shakiest 'do' occurred on the home-bound leg of a mine-laying trip on a dark night [28 April 1943] and quoted him: 'I was flying along at 800 feet over the sea when suddenly what must have been an enemy aircraft coming up from underneath crashed into us. It carried off our starboard outer engine and bomb doors. We lost height but I managed to regain control of the aircraft ... and we managed to make base on three engines.' Bateson noted Reader and Strang among Perks' crew.

None of the New Zealanders mentioned this frightening incident in their log books. Reader and Strang, the epitome of brevity, both wrote: 'Operations, Mining.' But Perks, who frequently made lengthy and lively comments in his log, wrote: 'Minelaying. Baltic Sea. Good trip. 1000 ft. No opposition encountered.' There's a good chance they drank with Bateson in a London pub and spun him a line. There were precedents. New Zealand pilot Arnold King, who flew with 218 Squadron, has a nice yarn in a family memoir about a couple of New Zealand bomber boys telling whoppers to *Truth*'s Eric Baume in a London boozer and seeing their mythical tale spread over a full page.

Reader spent a year instructing after leaving 76 and in December 1943, he was commissioned, joining 298 at Tarrant Rushton six weeks before the invasion. On the night of 5 June the airfield was relatively quiet after the six Horsas towed by 298 and 644 Halifaxes had taken off on their Coup de Main task. But shortly before 1.30 a.m. engines on thirty-four other Halifaxes, seventeen from each squadron, shattered the stillness. After picking up their tow lines and gliders, they accelerated down the runway. They gradually gained height and order, heading for Normandy. Carrying mainly anti-tank guns, they followed behind the earlier squadrons to give sappers and other troops time to clear any anti-glider obstacles on the big landing zone near Ranville.

This last act of Operation Tonga, carried out in rain and low cloud over Normandy, cost 298 an aeroplane – Halifax LL407-K, captained by Canadian Charles Anderson, with Reader in the rear turret. The aircraft was hit heavily in the port wing after releasing its glider and was seen on fire by other Halis. Reader left no written record of what happened but the crew had time to jump before the plane crashed in flames. All survived, landing in areas where paras were already in control. Reader, back at Tarrant Rushton six days later, was unharmed.

London-born Vic Beckett, a New Zealander for a long time now, had just turned 21 and was newly commissioned the night he flew on

Operation Glimmer, as mid-upper gunner. He was on skipper Robert Chaplin's 218 Squadron Stirling as it lifted off the runway at 11.39 p.m. on 5 June. 'First off, last down at 5.10 a.m.' The big Stirling had thirteen aboard, as had all the other Stirlings and 617's Lancasters flying the parallel Operation Taxable. 'We had two pilots and two navigators, plus the rear gunner and me from our regular crew,' Beckett says. 'Our bomb aimer was stand-in front gunner. The rest were busy chucking out the window that played havoc with German radar, kidding the enemy that two fleets were at sea headed for the Pas De Calais.'

Perched atop the Stirling in his turret, Beckett had a 360-degree view. 'I could see the other five aircraft following each other around the circuit at about 5000 feet, 200 or 300 yards apart. And I could see the tiny flotilla of the small ships below.' The little vessels floated balloons emitting radar signals to further confuse the Jerries. 'The coastal guns were firing at the flotilla.' The circuits gradually shifted toward the French coast to create the illusion of moving ships. He also remembers the tension and excitement involved in Glimmer and the 'fantastic sight' flying home at 10,000 feet watching the aircraft below. 'It seemed as if every aeroplane in Britain was flying.' Beckett's Brownings didn't fire a shot that night – they never saw an enemy fighter.

Because 218 hadn't been so heavily involved in bombing since the Stirlings were ordered off the battle order for Germany in the late autumn of 1943, because of their height and bomb-load deficiencies and unsustainable casualties, it had the chance to become highly proficient in the use of the blind bombing aid G-H. First used in October 1943, it was a development of the Oboe radio navigation system. Where Oboe could direct one aircraft at a time, G-H could handle up to eighty. Writing about Glimmer, Steve Smith, 218 historian, says 218 was chosen in early May 1944 to supplement 617's role on D-Day. The squadron trained hard to perfect the precision flying required, choosing eight senior crews – six in the main role, the other two as backup. New Zealander Arnold King was one of the six. Fellow countrymen Ian Lock and Trevor Knapman had the boring but necessary task of circling off the South Coast while the group out in the Channel. Also among them was King, with an Australian as his second pilot.

King, Lock and Knapman and their crews arrived on 218 squadron about the same time, late September–early October 1943. They survived the war with a dollop of luck. King's aircraft, on a mine-laying op on the night of 17–18 April 1944, beat off a determined night-fighter attack on the west coast of Denmark, south of Esbjerg. The combat report was short and to the point: 'Rear and mid-upper turrets made u/s [unserviceable], fuselage riddled with mg and cannon fire. Rear gunner wounded in leg.'

On 12 December 1943 Lock used up another slice of luck. Homebound from a mining trip to the southwest coast of France, his Stirling ran into shocking weather, knocking out their navigation aids and causing excessive petrol consumption. Out of fuel, Lock tried to land at St Eval, a Cornish airfield with which he was unfamiliar, in darkness with poor visibility and driving rain. The Stirling crashed near the base boundary, wrecked beyond belief. The plane had been in the air for 9 hours 20 minutes but with empty gas tanks didn't burn. Amazingly the crew escaped. The accident report said no blame was attached to the crew for the crash and 'the pilot did well'.

Munro led the 617 Lancasters and when he returned described Taxable in his log book, tongue-in-cheek, as 'the most hazardous, difficult and most dangerous operation ever undertaken in the history of air warfare. Involved flying within at least nine miles of the French coast without fighter cover, in bright moonlight at a height of not more than 3000 feet – open to attack by the deadliest of all weapons – light flak. Believed successful.'

617's CO, Wing Commander Leonard Cheshire, soon to have a Victoria Cross, flew with the New Zealander, sharing the controls. He signed the log and wrote: 'Certified that S/L Munro is still in possession of most of his faculties after completing the operation described on this page.'

Twenty-nine minutes into D-Day pilot Roy Le Long and navigator Mac McLaren's Mosquito roared across the French coast at Ault, south of the Somme Estuary, then turned south-southeast for Evreux and St Andre airfields south of Rouen. Visibility was good with broken cloud when they reached their targets and they began cruising out from them so their plane wasn't apparent. At 1.30 a.m. St Andre's flare path was lit up and Very lights were seen. Seven minutes later, just as they were about to bomb the field, the Germans doused all lights but the attackers went ahead, unloading two 500 pounders and two 250 pounders.

They turned now for Evreux. Moments later searchlights came on, forming a canopy over the field, and more Very lights showed. At 1.47 a.m. Le Long spotted what he'd been hunting – an aircraft at 1000 feet. The aircraft had no lights showing – Le Long and McLaren had to be certain. From behind and at a distance the plane could have been another Mosquito. His combat report said steady search lights, the moon and the plane's silhouette against cloud helped him identify the prey as an Me 410, the twin-engined heavy fighter, successor to the failed Me 210:

[We] then flew in a steady climb to just underneath the a/c and confirmed it as an Me 410, then throttled back and pulled up to dead astern and at a range of 150 yards opened fire with a 1-1/2 second burst at about 900–1000 feet above ground level. Strikes were seen around the cockpit area and the aircraft then burst into flames, in the light of which it was without doubt confirmed as an Me 410. It then lost height slowly in a spiral dive and finally crashed about 7 miles SE of Evreux airfield.

Le Long fired thirteen shells from each of his four cannons, a nearly equal mix of semi armour-piercing incendiary rounds and high explosive incendiaries. The German plane's two-man crew presumably perished, as Le Long made no reference to seeing parachutes. The Mosquito flew over the wreck taking photos as it burned on the ground. Five minutes after the crash the fighter exploded. They left the scene a few minutes later for St Andre, where lights had come back on, but saw no activity and at 2.15 a.m. turned for home. At one point on their way back to the coast 'meagre' light flak was fired but nothing came near them. The Mosquito crossed the coast at Ault, landing at Manston at 3.25 a.m. just forty minutes later. Le Long had just shot down the first German aircraft destroyed on D-Day.

Bomber Command dispatched 1211 aircraft the night of 5–6 June 1944, a new high for the war. Most took off in the early-morning hours of D-Day to attack the coastal defence batteries on the Normandy coast. The great majority were Lancasters and Halifaxes but Mosquitoes were also in action and more than a hundred bomber support planes flew out of Britain to jam and confuse German communications. The bombers dumped about 5000 tons of bombs on their targets, setting another new mark for the war.

Of the hordes of British aircraft in the air that night, only ten were lost. One of the handful of downed Lancasters was piloted by New Zealander Malcolm Steel (31), an experienced skipper from Auckland. His 101 bomber support squadron plane took off from Ludford Magna on the Lincolnshire Wolds at 10.27 p.m. on a special duties patrol. From October 1943 the squadron carried radio-jamming transmitters and a normal load of bombs on its raids, with an eighth German-speaking crew member. The boffins called it ABC for Airborne Cigar, a code word itself. The extra crew member listened for German voices broadcasting instructions to night fighters. Once heard, he would switch one of his powerful transmitters to the same frequency, pulsing out a strong jamming warble to blot the German signal. Each Lancaster carried three transmitters so if the three-flight squadron had twenty bombers on a raid it had the potential to wash out sixty German transmissions. The enemy tried all manner of counter devices, even having sopranos sing messages to night-fighter pilots.

Steel's D-Day support op ended in the choppy waters of the English Channel. Two hours after takeoff the constant speed unit on one engine began to give trouble. As Steel and his flight engineer tried to feather the propeller, both inner engines failed. The bomber turned for home but Steel couldn't maintain height. Realising the aircraft wouldn't make England, he ordered crash stations. With top hatches open for a quick get-out, the plane neared the sea. Steel kept the tail down to hit first and made a skilful landing. The crew scrambled clear into their dinghy, which popped out of the wing. Distress and position calls had been sent by the wireless operator before the ditching, 20 miles south of Beachy Head on the South Coast. The dinghy bobbed round for slightly more than an hour before His Majesty's destroyer *Orwell* loomed up. If a plane had to ditch, 5–6 June was the night to do so – the Channel was alive with ships. In moments Steel and his crew were in warm dry clothes, wrapped in blankets and being plied with hot drinks.

Sadly, their crew story doesn't have a happy ending. Twelve weeks after D-Day, on 25–26 August, their Lancaster went down over Luxembourg with just one survivor. It wasn't Steel.

Navigator Jim Insull (35), a married man from Napier, had only another five ops to complete his tour when he took off from RAF Mildenhall in his 622 Squadron Lancaster at 3.11 a.m. on D-Day. For many reasons – crashes, hopeless pilots, hospital stays, lost crews – he'd done his tour at snail's pace, flying his first op as long ago as 24–25 July 1943, the opening firestorm raid on Hamburg. Back on duty at last in April 1944, Insull joined a 622 crew minus its sick navigator. 'All Brits except Hutch, a Canadian.'

Before D-Day they'd raided Karlsruhe and Friedrichshafen in Germany and then, as Bomber Command turned its sights on key railway yards, airfields and gun emplacements in France and Belgium in the run-up to the invasion, bombed Chambly, Nantes, Cape Gris Nez, Louvain, Boulogne and Angers. After a late-night briefing on 5 June and warnings about navy fire, Insull wrote in his diary:

> We roared into the air at 3.01 a.m. and climbed to 12,000 feet before setting course for Hastings on the South Coast at 0405 and out over the English Channel in the direction of our target. We came down to 8000 feet to make sure of being able to see our aiming point without

the odd patch of cloud interfering. At 0505 both Alex and Frank reported that the markers had appeared ahead of us. I looked out. Four searchlights were groping in the half-light with just a sprinkle of flak here and there. Frank called 'Bombs gone' at 0508 after we had made an orbit to give a better run-up on our aiming point. We turned sharply to port to avoid Caen marked by more searchlights and flak – and after a short run eastwards, turned north and crossed the mouth of the Seine just east of Le Havre. By 0530 we were back over the Channel heading for base. Dawn was well advanced and we were flying at 9000 feet above large patches of fluffy clouds … away over on our port, probably forty or more miles off, I caught sight of the white wakes of hundreds of ships … as they sped towards the French coast we had just left.

C-Charlie, Insull's Lancaster, landed at Mildenhall at 6.26 a.m. and the crew headed for their beds after debriefing. Insull finished off his diary for the day. 'It is now 2 p.m. We have slept, bathed and lunched … and the BBC has just announced that landings have been made on the French coast.'

Fate dealt cruelly with James Chalmers. He joined the RNZAF in July 1941 from a clerk's job at an Invercargill sawmill, and was posted to 214 Squadron flying Stirlings from Chedburgh, Suffolk. In early February 1943 he did his first two ops, mine-laying flights which passed off uneventfully. The third was altogether different.

Chalmers' Stirling, captained by fellow New Zealander John Rundle, also on his third trip, took off three minutes after six on the night of 17 February with mines targeted for the Gironde Estuary, the long, wide inlet leading to Bordeaux. The crew released the mines successfully, parachuting them into the sea, then almost immediately the Stirling was attacked by a night fighter. The two gunners drove off the enemy, though gunfire damaged the aircraft. More damage was inflicted as the now low-on-fuel Stirling strayed over heavily defended Portsmouth and copped friendly anti-aircraft fire. Heading north for an emergency landing at RAF Odiham near Reading, the big plane was still ten miles short of the field when fuel-starved engines stuttered, then quit. Rundle ordered the crew out and followed. The crew's parachutes opened and all landed uninjured – except for Rundle, struck by one of the windmilling propellers. Rundle (24), left a wife and daughter.

It's not known whether Chalmers attended his captain's funeral; he probably did. But his leap from a doomed aircraft and the loss of his captain would have been traumatic. Such events were common and he was back on the squadron's battle order board for a raid on Munich on the night of 9–10 March. The old Rundle crew were still together, with a replacement captain – a Canadian called Moore.

The flight to Munich was short. Disaster struck as the Stirling lifted off at 8.39 p.m. when, according to Bill Chorley's book, *Bomber* Command Losses, the Stirling's port undercarriage leg failed to retract and the still-low bomber clipped a tree and a house then crashed a mile from the airfield, bursting into flames, fanned by a full load of fuel, the crew petrified by the threat of the bomb load exploding.

The mid-upper gunner was trapped, his life saved by the gallantry of Moore and the rear gunner, who braved the flames to drag their mate to safety. Both men were awarded the George Medal. Amazingly the entire crew survived the horror crash, staggering away from the fiery scene, but all were burned and Chalmers sustained second- and third-degree damage to his face and hands. He was treated for almost a month in hospital but didn't need skin grafts. After leave he was passed fit for flying in late May but he'd had enough of Stirlings. One medical report said he distrusted the bombers and a doctor noted his 'disinclination' to fly in Stirlings again, adding that 'after his recent crash this reluctance cannot be dismissed as altogether unreasonable'. The doctor said Chalmers remained keen on flying and had no other symptoms of illness, anxiety or lack of confidence. 'I asked him if he would refuse to fly if ordered to do so in a Stirling. He replied, "Well, of course I should hate to be stripped [of his sergeant's stripes] and should obey orders."'

A medical board recommended a transfer to another type of aircraft and Chalmers bade farewell to 214 Squadron. He flew with an OTU from September 1943, was commissioned in March 1944 and the following month posted to 2TAF's 88 Squadron on Bostons, twin-engined light bombers designed and built in the United States. Ironically he may have lived had he stayed with his old crew, all of whom survived the war. But the die was cast.

88 was a busy unit, making many mostly daylight trips across the Channel. In the two months he was with 88, Chalmers posted no fewer than twenty-eight ops, among them ten attacks on flying bomb sites in France, a dangerous task. Raiding aircraft invariably faced concentrated flak and often suffered damage. One such attack punctured Chalmers' aircraft with thirty-eight holes. Among other targets were marshalling yards, engine sheds, airfields, gun positions.

On D-Day morning 88 and 342, its sister French squadron, were tasked with laying smoke to screen landing craft approaching the British beaches, 88 on the eastern flank, the French unit on the west. After a 1 a.m. breakfast and a final briefing, the 88 crews began engine warm-ups and at about 4.30 a.m. started taking off. The Bostons flew across the Channel at wave-top level, taking fire from British battleships as they neared the coast, despite the fact the planes 'were painted like a humbug [with] the black and white [invasion stripes] applied overnight on wings and fuselage, the markings of 2TAF,' said one airman.

The eighteen Bostons of 88 Squadron went in one after the other from 5 a.m. at carefully planned ten-minute intervals, the thick smoke billowing from the canisters in their bomb bays. Flying out, their jobs done, most of the aircraft turning for home found themselves near or over the port entrance to Le Havre being pasted by the port's guns and German E-boats. Fire from one of these sources claimed BZ243-N, Chalmers' aircraft, piloted by Briton Alan Boyle. It plunged into the sea about 7.30 a.m. killing its three crew. The body of the wireless operator/air gunner was recovered and buried inland at Rouen. The bodies of Chalmers and Boyle weren't found and they are remembered at Runnymede. The French squadron also lost an aircraft to flak, and another from 88 was damaged by ground fire and crashed on return to base, killing the navigator.

Spitfire pilot John Clouston was another New Zealand D-Day casualty, though he died later, killed on the ground as a POW. On 6 June the 25-year-old, flying as a squadron leader supernumerary with 65 Squadron on a Rodeo, a fighter-only offensive over enemy territory, ganged up with three other Spits and shot down an enemy fighter near Lorient. Clouston's petrol tank was riddled by coastal flak on the homeward flight and he had to bale out at 8000 feet. He landed in the sea off the northern coast of Brittany and was rescued by the Germans, to become a POW. Fifteen days later Clouston, a skilled pilot with about 330 ops behind him, was dead, killed by friendly fire from American P-38 Lightnings. The POWs had been moved by stages to Tours and were on a truck nearing Chartres, when the vehicle broke down. The Germans were trying to repair it when the twin-engined fighters swooped. Guards and prisoners raced for roadside ditches. After the attack Clouston was found dead on the road, killed instantly. He lies today in Pont-du-Cens Communal Cemetery in Nantes.

Ned Hitchcock couldn't resist an invitation to the Normandy landings. But at 9 a.m. on D-Day he probably wished he'd said 'no' as his LCT neared Omaha. 'We could see clearly that it was not yet captured. The men ashore were taking cover from enemy fire, there was a vehicle burning and as we watched an explosion blew a figure high into the air.'

Hitchcock was in the third year of an engineering course in Christchurch when the war began. The following year, he emerged with a degree and was called up by the army. And passed – fit for garrison duty in the tropics! But when Britain sought Commonwealth volunteers to work on the coastal radar stations, which had a major impact on the outcome of the Battle of Britain, Hitchcock was there by September 1941, as a radio mechanic training for radar duties. He trained with Arthur C Clarke, postwar a famous sci-fi author. Soon Hitchcock was involved with aircraft electrics and posted to RAF Swanton Morley, Norfolk, in charge of electrical and instrument sections of three squadrons of 2 Group's medium bombers – Bostons. But the Air Ministry had other plans and he found himself at 60 (Signals) Group, the unit responsible for ground radar in Britain.

Radar, Hitchcock wrote in later life, had begun as a defence mechanism but as the pattern of the war changed, development work on mobile radar units quickened to provide mobile Ground Controlled Interception (GCI) for the RAF. The mobiles were 'self-contained units with their own cooks, tented accommodation and power supplied by truck-mounted 20kVA diesel generators [and] four different types of radar, each with its own variety of turning gear and aerial systems'.

Hitchcock received his Normandy invite after returning to group headquarters from urgent radar maintenance on the Devon coast. His unit was scheduled for Omaha because the Americans didn't yet have a fully operational system. Two or three days before D-Day Hitchcock joined Radar Unit 15082, already ensconced among thousands of American GIs on the South Coast. They were to land at H-hour plus five, about full tide, on Dog Red sector of Omaha. They were told they would enter via a cleared lane and a beachmaster would direct them to an exit from the beach.

> Our vehicles were lined up on the road outside the camp, and we had special permission to inspect and check waterproofing. The engines were well covered with green paste. Air intakes carried up to roof level inside the cab. Memories of precautions when fording rivers in Canterbury back country surfaced … remove the fan belt to stop the fan pelting the engine [with water] and extend the exhaust above water level to stop rapid cooling sucking water back in. But it was too late to raise such questions.

Hitchcock's LCT sailed for France late in the afternoon of 4 June, due to be off the beaches at dawn. But the landings were postponed twenty-four hours because of bad weather and Hitchcock woke to find the ship back in English waters. 'We pottered about that day, borrowed a dinghy and rowed around among the ships. That afternoon we set off again and woke to grey skies and a hardly visible French coast.' About 9 a.m. Hitchcock's LCT headed straight in, leading others, and the men could see what was happening ashore. Aboard with the RAF was a sensible US observer who'd been at Pantelleria, an Italian island in the Mediterranean between Sicily and Tunisia, invaded in an amphibious assault and captured by the Allies in June 1943.

> We heard he had assessed the situation, concluded the last thing needed ashore at this stage was a collection of technicians armed with radar aerials, and, rather relieved, we turned seaward with landing next day presumed. We stood off while naval guns pounded the shore. Mercifully, we knew nothing of the desperate battle by the American infantry to gain a foothold on Easy Green [the beach east of Dog Red where the RAF radar unit landed] … by about 4 p.m. we had concluded that it would be useless to land then, no chance of working that night. Suddenly, in we go … Then followed the debacle! The unplanned landing at low tide, instead of full, had disastrous results. Some vehicles like ours, were landed on sandbars and stalled as they drove into deeper water. Others sank in patches of soft sand on the long run up the beach and were immersed as the tide rose. Those reaching the shoreline found the wire and earth barriers had not yet been breached and there was no way off the exposed beach. They became sitting targets for enemy shellfire, and shrapnel-punctured diesel oil drums fed flames. On our LCT, the ramp splashed down as the vessel grounded, the vehicles roared down

the ramp, the water rose steadily around our waists, the engines gave up … and we sat.

Hitchcock waded ashore to the unit's Diamond-T crane, dragged a cable from it and groped under water to hook on. By the time he realised the rising tide had embedded the wheels too deep for retrieval, the water had risen to cab-top level. Back on the beach after his full-kit swim he staggered, exhausted, up the sand. 'There seemed no one, no beach-master, no medics, just dead and wounded and abandoned vehicles.' It seemed best to save what equipment he and others could.

> Flames threatened an undamaged truck. I managed to pull out a wounded GI from his somewhat doubtful shelter underneath and drove my first-ever heavy transport clear of the flames. Then a bulldozer cleared a way off the beach and our group seemed to come together again, rescuing what vehicles could be driven up to a field in the narrow valley and collecting wounded for evacuation. We had suffered heavy casualties – two dead, 40 wounded.

Max Hastings in Normandy, his book about the campaign, says by nightfall on 6 June the RAF party of 158 had lost eight killed, thirty-five wounded and twenty-eight of their thirty-five vehicles.

Hitchcock borrowed a blanket and slept in his sodden clothes under a hedge in the grounds of a seaside villa. In the morning he persuaded a bulldozer to rescue the unit's Type-14 transmitter. The truck carrying it popped out of the sand 'like a cork out of a bottle'. The New Zealander and his RAF team were pleased to see American tanks rumbling in from Easy Beach and listened to the

BBC saying the invasion was a success. Men and material were now pouring ashore. In the next couple of days an operational site was chosen, replacement men and gear arrived and Radar Unit 15082 was on the air. On the night of D+4 the first enemy aircraft were shot down, the first GCIs from the American beachhead.

Hitchcock worked on a couple of other mobile radar sites, then hitched a ride on an American LCT from Utah beach back to Portland on the South Coast. As they passed Omaha he spotted and saluted the Union Steam Ship Co's trans-Tasman liner *Monowai* among the array of ships standing offshore. She had just delivered 1800 British commandos to Gold Beach. 'It was good to see an old friend,' Hitchcock wrote.

Rex Daniell, denied a place among the 48 Squadron Dakota flight crews on the 5 June trip to Normandy, was on hand at 3 a.m to welcome the planes home as they touched down. He watched as medics carried a wounded man to a waiting ambulance. Only one aircraft was missing from the flight he commanded and it soon reported in from a Kent airfield where it had landed with a flak-damaged engine. He wrote in his war autobiography that it seemed many crews had failed to find their dropping zones (Dzs) – only half had been successful. The Americans also had problems, their airborne troops scattered over the Cotentin Peninsula. Daniell led 48 Squadron's 4 p.m. takeoff on 6 June on Operation Mallard:

> For both the tug and glider pilots it became a job of solid manual labour just keeping to the correct heading at 90 mph. The turbulence worsened in the middle of the 'stream' as we slowly forged our way south over Tangmere on the South Coast. Knowing that evasive

action was impossible we were reassured as dozens of escorting fighter planes arrived to provide cover during the crossing. By this time it was a sunny afternoon with broken cloud and a surface wind of 20 to 25 knots, judging by the white caps in the Channel.

The armada of tugs and gliders crossed into Normandy over the British beaches, crews watching the enormous ship numbers below, some loading, some waiting while a bit further out warships belched shells at targets ashore. Then it was time for tug-glider tow lines to be cast off.

> A few miles in from the coast, I picked up the mike saying [to the glider pilots] 'Thirty seconds to go to release point, matchbox, good luck [tug pilots called their gliders matchboxes].' The reply: 'Thankyou tug, cheerio' followed by a great surge forward as the plane, freed of its burden, picked up normal speed.

Light flak and small arms fire from the ground hit some aircraft and nearby a Dakota's starboard engine flamed. The damaged aircraft peeled away to make a safe belly landing among the gliders scattered all over the LZs. Daniell dived to gain speed as he flew out to sea, spotting two gliders and a Stirling in the water. Back at base plaudits were being handed out. The entire 46 Group operation was deemed to be a success of the first order.

Ray Bretherton, down at Tarrant Rushton just before 3 a.m. on D-Day after 'losing' his glider, was back in his cockpit sixteen hours later readying his Halifax for takeoff on Operation Mallard, 644 Squadron's second run to Normandy, to the same area near Caen to ferry in more troops, armaments and supplies for the men fighting on the ground. This time he hauled the big Hamilcar and in its belly was a seven-ton Tetrarch light tank. The British-designed armoured vehicle was built in low numbers, with twenty flown to Normandy by Hamilcars, where they performed poorly. However, the tank was useful against German machine-gun posts, as Bretherton discovered.

He was in the air at 7.30 p.m., the sun still shining, for what turned out to be a 3 hours 5 minutes round flight. The squadron launched fifteen Halifax/Hamilcar combinations and one Halifax towing a Horsa. Bretherton, writing about his war for his family, remembered the D-Day evening flight:

> The daylight trip was much more interesting as one was able to see the hundreds and hundreds of tow and glider combinations in the air. That day the sky seemed a very full place, particularly when we began to converge on the glider landing zones. With all those aircraft up over the Channel it was amazing to see so many launches in the water below. For various reasons a small number of gliders and aircraft went down and we could witness the launches speeding to the rescue. I remember seeing one particular glider going down to ditch and two of these speedy little craft circling the approximate place of landing. One glider [crew] unfortunate enough to ditch reported that not even their feet got wet.

At the LZ allotted to 644 the main resistance came from one machine-gun post on the perimeter. The tank from Bretherton's Hamilcar began spouting fire the moment it clanked on to ground, attacking the chattering German machine gun. 'The … post was soon silenced by the tank from our glider.' Bretherton was chuffed.

We had just begun the return journey when the rear gunner reported something black hosing past his turret. It was oil from one of the port engines. It was then we realised our plane too had passed through the sights of that lone machine-gun. The plane immediately on our left suddenly dropped back and seconds later was seen to settle on the water. We later learned from its crew that this plane was on fire inside. Fortunately our own position did not alter and apart from having one engine out we were ourselves still happy.

Another Halifax returned on three engines, one had a burst tyre from flak and a third suffered holes in a fuel tank. But no one was hurt and no gliders were lost.

The Hamilcar and the Tetrarch must have been new to defence correspondents as *The Times* unveiled both post-D-Day. The paper said most of the success of the fighting inland of the Normandy beaches had been due to the Hamilcar, 'a secret motorless aircraft'. The gliders carried a fast light tank, the paper added, started up by its crew while still airborne and 'goes into action as soon as the glider touches down … the nose of the glider swings back and the fuselage sinks to the ground allowing the tank to run out free.'

New Zealander Des Scott, still only 25 but already a group captain leading 84 Group's 123 Wing of 198 and 609 Squadrons, flew over the Normandy battlefield late on D-Day. He watched the gliders landing alongside the Orne. 'They ploughed on down into the fields … like a flock of exhausted swans. Some skimmed along the ground and finished up in a cloud of yellow dust. Others hit the ground at too steep an angle and burst open like paper bags.' The tanks emerging from Hamilcars fascinated him. 'I was surprised how quickly the tanks left their winged carriers. No sooner had one touched down than out crawled a tank like a crustacean hurriedly vacating its shell.' Scott described the beachhead as 'a huge, fire-rimmed boiling cauldron'.

Bretherton flew a supplemental supply trip to Normandy on 11 June but took his load back to base when heavy cloud obscured the DZ. He also operated the first two days at Arnhem in September, flying a Horsa and a Hamilcar to the battle zone without incident.

Through the morning and well into the afternoon of D-Day, 80 Squadron and its B-flight commander Bob Spurdle waited for the call to arms. And waited. He wrote in *The Blue Arena* that just when the pilots despaired they were called and ran to their Spitfires.

> We took off to join a glider 'train' of Albemarles towing Horsa gliders at 6000 feet. Then a group of giant Stirling night-bombers black and menacing hove in sight lugging huge Hamilcar gliders to join our group [The tugs and gliders were flying in Operation Mallard]. Below, stretching as far as one could see, were rows of ships of all sizes. Some towed silver barrage balloons which floated along in the air like kids' toys. We weaved back and forth riding 'shotgun' for the otherwise almost defenceless 'train'. Loaded ships heading for the beach-heads kept in huge lanes while emptied craft steamed back to England for reloading in separate channels. We could see towering clouds of smoke from fires on sea and land. Destroyers laid more screens of smoke as myriad tank and infantry landing barges shuttled back and forth from the transports lying offshore.

Spurdle watched the tugs and gliders part company as they neared their target landing grounds and then, down low at 2000 feet, he and his section attacked a Jerry tank without effect, bullets and 20 mm shells bouncing off the thick steel hull, 'but at least it would scare the shit out of the bastards'.

New Zealander 'Kiwi' Saunders must have been among the last people in Britain to hear the invasion was under way. Saunders, flying from Shoreham-on-Sea on the South Coast with 277 Squadron, an Air Sea Rescue unit, had done a long, unsuccessful 3 hours 45 minutes search for a downed pilot in the English Channel on the morning of 5 June. Back ashore he began a 24-hour leave, visiting his wife. He had married Rebecca Green on 20 November the previous year, a day before she turned 21. She was the youngest of sixteen and still living nearby with her parents. On the morning of 6 June something unusual happened. Her father, for some unknown reason, didn't turn on the radio.

A spruced-up Saunders and his wife went to an 11 a.m. wedding in Brighton, the bride a close friend. They took their seats without talking to anyone. When the priest urged everyone to 'say a prayer for our boys this special day', Saunders was puzzled. He couldn't go to the reception, as he had to get back to the base by 1 p.m. He boarded the local train for the short ride back to Shoreham, where he saw the white invasion stripes painted on all their aircraft and realised. D-Day. He'd watched the huge build-up of Allied forces and shipping for weeks patrolling the South Coast, seen hordes of gliders flying in training and watched the massive cross-Channel aircraft movements. But his father-in-law didn't switch on the radio that morning.

There wasn't much to do for 277 Squadron that day ... or the day after. 'There were so many ships in the Channel they really didn't need us much. If a pilot was going to ditch and could see a ship, he always ditched as close as he could to that ship.' Saunders, who was nearing the end of a long tour with 277, didn't fly on D-Day afternoon and made only one short search the following day. He already had the United States' Air Medal for finding or rescuing American aircrew and would be awarded the DFC in July 1944, the citation noting in particular his rescue of a ditched Spitfire pilot two months earlier. Altogether he was involved in the rescue of almost forty aircrew.

The depth charges fell precisely, the sea geysered in a series of explosions and the U-boat vanished from the radar screen in the big Sunderland circling overhead. The radar had done its job, picked up the contact a few minutes before midnight as D-Day ended.

U-955, a type VIIC submarine, the sturdy workhorse unit of the German underwater fleet, went down in the Bay of Biscay, almost home from a long weather-reporting patrol in the Atlantic. None of her 50-man crew survived. She was the first U-boat sunk after the Normandy landings, victim of the 201 Squadron flying boat skippered by Les Baveystock, decorated with a bar to his Distinguished Flying Cross (DFC) for this success. Baveystock was a Londoner, who immigrated to New Zealander after the war with his family.

The Sunderland, based at Pembroke Dock in southwest Wales, lifted off the calm water of Milford Haven at 7.42 p.m., with a crew of twelve. Baveystock added the squadron intelligence officer, who wanted to be able to tell his grandchildren he'd flown on D-Day. Baveystock gave him a lookout's job in the astrodome. About 11.30 p.m. the flying boat reached its patrol area northwest of Gijon, midway along the coast of northern Spain. On a Creeping Line Ahead (CLA) search pattern, the Sunderland began its hunt for *U-955*. The crew knew they were seeking a particular submarine, though they didn't know its number. The sub had been attacked by an aircraft on 5 June and had been kept submerged since then by other planes, which saturated the entire bay. Intelligence expected *U-955* would have to surface, desperate to charge batteries, during Baveystock's patrol. So it proved. The eastern end of the English Channel was easily protected from the entry of U-boats, mainly by mines, but the far wider western approaches were a different story. Overlord planners divided 20,000 square miles into rectangles patrolled by anti-sub aircraft from the many squadrons available in the lead-up to D-Day. *Hitler's U-Boat War* says the entire area would be covered every thirty minutes. 'This dense coverage would almost certainly prevent most U-boats from surfacing to charge batteries or to refresh their air and would catch any U-boat on the surface attempting to carry out these routines.' The air offensive was named Cork – a 'cork in the bottle' – and the aircraft were backed up by dozens of ships.

The Sunderland crew settled into the rhythm of its search pattern. Baveystock in his wartime years autobiography *Wavetops at My Wingtips* says:

> [We crept] back and forth across and progressively along the estimated course of the U-boat. Each leg was about fifteen miles, first to the north and then to the south, with the legs about ten miles apart. In this way, our radar coverage would normally have ensured that if the U-boat was on the surface we would pick it up on our PPI [Plan Position Indicator] screen; and pick it up we did, just before midnight.

Baveystock closed on the contact. Was it their hoped-for prey or just a harmless Spanish fishing trawler? Powerful flares dropped from the Sunderland at 300 feet lit the surface like day and there was the proof. A white swirl, just ahead and a little to the right of their path. The U-boat had picked up an approaching aircraft and crash-dived.

The Sunderland climbed away, crew disappointed. Baveystock signalled what had happened and added two words: Am baiting. 'Group would know that we would stay in the area until either the U-boat surfaced, or we ran short of fuel.' The crew marked the spot where the U-boat disappeared with a bright, long-burning flame-float and a cat-and-mouse game began. Baiting required the plane to fly north, south, east and west legs of four miles out from the flame float and back, upping the distance to 8 miles after an hour, 12 miles after two. From time to time a new flame-float was dropped. Baveystock talked it over with his men, deciding the U-boat had only just surfaced. Had it been up longer it would have shown on the radar of other searching Sunderlands, one so close it almost rammed Baveystock's plane as it climbed away after the sub's crash-dive. The U-boat would need two hours on the surface to recharge batteries and with dawn at 6 a.m. the Brits figured the boat had to be up by about 3 a.m.

At 2.44 a.m. the intercom crackled – a radar contact 11 miles off. Baveystock knew it had to be the U-boat. The other Sunderland had gone home and their relief wasn't due until 4.15 a.m. This time as they closed there was no crash-dive. Gunfire from *U-955* greeted them. Their flares lit the scene and Baveystock wrote: 'There was our U-boat, fully surfaced about half a mile away ...' Their own guns blazed, knocking out the U-boat gun crews. 'Our final few seconds of attack were unopposed. At just the right moment I pressed the bomb tit and our stick of six depth charges fell clean cross his hull, just forward of the conning tower.'

As the Sunderland pulled away columns of water exploded from the sea around the submarine and the blip on the radar vanished. Baveystock flew the Sunderland around for twenty minutes but saw nothing and turned for home. *U-955* had gone down at 45.13 North, 3.30 West with her entire complement.

Baveystock was a flight lieutenant and one of 201's most experienced pilots. He flew the night they sank *U-955* knowing his father had died that morning of lung cancer. He couldn't be spared but before he took off he learned he had leave to attend the funeral. During his few days in London he was dismayed to learn of the loss of his crew, who'd gone out on another patrol and not returned. The aircraft had signalled a contact and its intention to attack. Nothing more was heard. A Catalina flying nearby saw flares, tracer and an explosion as though something had hit the water. 'That their WOp had not sent out even the briefest SOS was almost certain proof their end had been sudden and violent,' Baveystock wrote.

He was particularly upset by the death of his friend and navigator Peter Hunt, whose parents had now lost three of their four sons, all serving in the RAF. One died bombing Germany, a second was hit and killed by a spinning propeller after returning from a raid. The fourth son, still training, was banned from operations after the loss of his navigator brother. The stand-in pilot on his crew's last op was flight commander 'Babe' Ruth who'd done two tours with Bomber Command and then volunteered for Coastal Command, because he couldn't bear the dull life of an instructor.

Baveystock returned to Pembroke Dock from his father's funeral, his missing crew heavily on his mind, to find notification of the bar to his DFC. His two lost radar operators had also been decorated, with the Distinguished Flying Medal (DFM). 'It was one of the few occasions that a wild party did not follow an award to a member of the squadron.'

Baveystock's first DFC, an immediate award, was for his part in the Boxing Day 1943 sinking of the the German blockade runner *Alsterufer* as she made for a French Atlantic coast port. He found her in the Bay of Biscay, a needle-in-the-haystack job, but the fuses on his bombs had been wrongly set, thwarting any low-level attack. The flying boat was without a bomb sight, so dropping them from a safe height was futile. Baveystock's position reports brought reinforcements swarming. Rockets and bombs from a 311 (Czech) Squadron Liberator set the ship afire and she was abandoned by her crew. Two 86 Squadron Liberators sank her four hours later. The Royal Navy unleashed a pair of nearby cruisers, which sank three of the German destroyers sent out to escort the *Alsterufer*.

Earlier, Baveystock won the DFM after a Victoria Cross drama in the air and an escape from occupied Europe. On the night of 30–31 May 1942 on the one-thousand bomber raid on Cologne, Baveystock, then a raw second pilot on Bomber Command's 50 Squadron, sat alongside Pilot Officer Leslie Manser. Their two-engined Manchester was coned by searchlights approaching the target and hit by flak. They survived the run in to drop their bombs but the damaged port engine burst into flame as they climbed away.

Manser delayed the 'jump' order, trying to get clear of Germany and see if the fire would burn itself out. It didn't and Manser told the crew to go. Baveystock, last out at 700 feet, tried to clip his skipper's parachute on but Manser knocked his hands away shouting, 'For Christ's sake, get out! We're going in.' Baveystock wrote Manser knew that once he let go of the controls the aircraft would drop its 'dead wing' and roll over into a spin. Diving out of the forward escape hatch, Baveystock pulled his rip cord instantly. Seconds later the Manchester plunged to earth 100 yards ahead and blew up. Baveystock, down safely seconds later, found himself thrashing about in an icy stream, water up to his chest.

Manser died in the crash but succeeded in getting the bomber inside Belgium. With incredible luck and life-risking help from Belgian and French patriots, Baveystock was whisked to safety, fed into an escape line and crossed the Pyrenees into Spain, eventually reaching Gibraltar. He was home in England on 9 July, a speedy evasion. Baveystock's testimony praising Manser's heroism and selfless actions was backed by others of his crew who also evaded capture and on 20 October 1942 the lost pilot was awarded a posthumous Victoria Cross.

Flight Lieutenant George Mervyn Kennedy, a 23-year-old Aucklander, was the first Bomber Command New Zealander to lose his life after D-Day. He was one of no fewer than 350 who fell while serving in the command between 1 June 1944 and 8 May 1945. The pathfinder pilot and all but one of his crew died when their 83 Squadron Lancaster was shot down by a night fighter just outside Caen in the early hours of 7 June. Their plane was one of 337 aircraft – 195 Halifaxes, 122 Lancasters and twenty Mosquitoes – targeting road and railway communications in France. 83 Squadron Lancs were given a target close to the battle lines – Caen. Crippled by a night fighter over the target, Kennedy's bomber crashed just south of the city, with only the rear gunner surviving.

When Kennedy enlisted in September 1941 he was a clerk. After flight training in Canada, he served as an instructor before sailing for England in May 1943. On 7 January 1944 he joined 83 Squadron at Coningsby, Lincolnshire. By the time he was killed he had flown 1048 hours, a total due largely to his year in Canada, been awarded the pathfinder badge three weeks before his death and completed twelve ops. His 13th was indeed an unlucky one. Kennedy lies in Banneville-la-Campagne Military Cemetery, five miles east of Caen.

The RAF paid a high price for its attacks on rail targets the night of 6–7 June. *The Bomber Command War Diaries* notes that 8.5 percent of the raiding forces was lost – seventeen Lancasters and eleven Halifaxes. 'The targets were mostly more distant from the battle front ... and German night fighters had more time to intercept the bombers.'

Bruce Barton and Bob O'Kane met for the first time the day they enlisted as RNZAF wireless operator-air gunners at the Initial Training Wing, Levin, on 2 November 1941. Born in Wanganui in September 1922, Barton served in the territorials in Auckland for a year. O'Kane was born in Balclutha but his family moved to Te Kuiti. O'Kane was fifteen months older than Barton, not a great difference. They became firm mates and were able to stay together. They sailed for Canada on the same ship in December 1941, graduated as sergeants after their wireless and gunnery courses nine months later and flew their first op together, an anti-sub patrol from a Hudson OTU on the east coast of Canada. They embarked for England in late January 1943 with identical postings. In late July 1943 they teamed up in a 53 Squadron Liberator crew skippered by Englishman George Crawford, flying more than 30 ops on this noted squadron.

On 13 December 1943 the Crawford Liberator, with both New Zealanders aboard, sank *U-391* during a night attack in the Bay of

Biscay. Six months later, on the night of 6–7 June, their tour almost complete, Barton and O'Kane died together, perishing with the rest of the crew. Their plane was shot down off the Britanny coast by an unknown submarine in a night of confused action between aircraft and U-boats in the western approaches to the English Channel. The Crawford crew were part of the successful Allied campaign blocking attempts by the German subs to get among the invasion fleet. The price that night was three Liberators.

Crawford's Liberator, BZ778-M, lifted off 53's base at St Eval on the Cornish coast three minutes before midnight on D+1. Its last flight ended some hours later on the 7th, O'Kane's 23rd birthday, as it smashed into the sea in the Bay of Douarnenez, south of Brest. Eleven days later the sea yielded O'Kane, his body washing ashore from the Atlantic in a coastal cove near Kerandraon, a hamlet set among fields on the coastal cliffs. O'Kane was the only one of the crew found. The nine others are remembered at Runnymede. O'Kane's body was carried to a barn in Kerandraon where locals kept vigil. Then it was moved to Poullan-sur-Mer, a bigger village a mile or so away and big enough to have a cabinet maker, who produced the coffin.

Nickee Sanders, an Auckland woman, struck up a pen-pal friendship with Frenchman Corentin Claquin, whose father and grandfather made the coffin. Claquin, a boy of five in 1944, 'more curious than obedient,' hid himself behind the curtains in the family's living room and watched as the two men finished the coffin before putting O'Kane's body in for burial. Few people attended the graveside service. The invasion had begun, there were many heavily armed German soldiers about and the mayor didn't want trouble. O'Kane is the only New Zealander buried in the Poullan cemetery, his last resting place well cared for, villagers regularly placing flowers at the foot of his headstone. Claquin wrote:

> In November every year, for many years, I went with my grandfather to the grave of this young [airman] who died for Peace, far from his native country not even threatened by this war. A [small] act to honour his sacrifice.

New Zealand wireless operator Perce Burgess waved his arms and hailed a wary British soldier on the Normandy battlefield two mornings after D-Day. The soldier was astonished to be confronted by air force battledress but speechless when he learned the airman, one of the crew of a downed RAF Stirling, had sixty German prisoners.

Two or three weeks later Burgess talked to Alan Mitchell, the New Zealand Press Association man in London. 'High Adventure in Normandy' was one newspaper headline in Burgess's hometown, Christchurch. Another: 'City Airman Takes Bag of 60 Prisoners'.

His adventure began at 7.30 p.m. on D-Day when Canadian Gordon Thring, a peacetime school teacher, opened the throttles of his 620 Squadron Stirling and took off from RAF Fairford on Operation Mallard. Burgess sat at the wireless console. The previous night, just before midnight, they'd headed away from Fairford with a load of paratroops, who jumped on drop zones near Normandy's capital of Caen. Though 620 lost three Stirlings on the night of 5–6 June, Thring's plane came home safely. On this second flight to the Caen area the Stirling was towing a glider with equipment and men of the 6th Airborne.

The trip to the target area, in bright daylight, was uneventful. The glider released, the tow rope dropped and the Stirling turned away. But as it headed for home at 9.20 p.m. it was hit by machine-gun fire from the ground and flames sprouted from the port wing. Thring told interrogators later that because the 'dinghy [carried in the wing] was on fire and the sea near the coast was crowded with shipping, I decided it was inadvisable to ditch.' He put about and in a masterful crash-landing got the big plane down in one piece in a wheat field on the edge of the village of Periers-sur-le-Dan, three miles from the coast. The stunned crew scrambled from the blazing wreck not quite believing they had all survived. They hid in the field until dark, then walked openly in an attempt to reach their own lines but were seen by Germans, challenged and taken prisoner.

Burgess described how four officers in the crew were made to carry a wounded German on an improvised stretcher while the flight engineer pushed a motorcycle.

> I was given a bicycle on which was a heavy radio. We marched all that night, taking frequent rests and were thankful when a German tank took the wounded man aboard. At dawn on June 7 we arrived at a chateau that had been shelled rather badly. We were put into a barn with baled hay and given a meal of very hard black bread and sausages. And a bottle of French champagne stamped, 'to be consumed by German officers only.' We also had a pot of coffee and plenty of real butter so managed to make a good meal.

Their captors, elements of the Herman Goering Division, treated them well and shared the day with them in the chateau, and in slit trenches when shells from both sides were flying overhead. At night they shifted to the chateau's basement. NZPA quoted Burgess:

Things were pretty hot as lots of bombs fell in addition to British naval shells. The whole place seemed to have gone mad and sleep was impossible. At last daylight came but we were pretty miserable. [So, apparently, were their captors. The senior German officer asked Burgess to take him and his men prisoners and scout around for a British soldier to take their surrender.] Though our advance had passed on, it was still dangerous as the place was rotten with German snipers but after one or two exciting moments, the navigator and [I] managed to find a Tommy. He had a great surprise seeing us, but received a bigger one when I told him we had 60 prisoners for him.

The enemy tramped off to captivity while the men from the Stirling made for the beach and the tank landing ship that carried them home. Before he left the chateau, Burgess snaffled a bottle of the champagne. He managed to get it home to New Zealand in November 1944, and the following month popped the cork on his wedding day.

Burgess didn't fly after Normandy, choosing repatriation following more than three years overseas. He sailed from New Zealand in April 1941 in a draft of naval airmen for training as Fleet Air Arm pilots. He didn't make the grade and switched to the RAF (and later the RNZAF) and signals training, which eventually turned him into a wireless operator. He was posted to the short-lived 513 Squadron and then on to 620 Squadron in November 1943. Thring, awarded a DFC after his skilful crash-landing on D-Day, and the rest of the crew, sans Burgess, survived three flights to Arnhem and the war.

CHAPTER 3

Bomber Command at war

Twenty-six New Zealanders died raiding rail targets in France and Belgium before D-Day, another twenty-five in the weeks after the invasion, before the Allies broke German resistance in Normandy and poured across France and into Belgium. The bombing campaign ended when the Allied armies overran the railway yards and junctions which had been their goal.

On the night of 10–11 April 1944 four New Zealand aircrew on three different aircraft perished bombing key French rail points – the first of fifty-one killed. Bomber Command began mounting the attacks the previous month when 261 Halifaxes and six Mosquitoes unloaded on the yards at Trappes, just southwest of Paris.

Martin Middlebrook, in *The Bomber Command War Diaries*, says the initial attack on 6–7 March took place in good visibility, with later photographs showing enormous damage to railway tracks, rolling stock and installations. The campaign proper – the command's switch from non-stop area bombing of German cities to focus on heavy raids in support of invasion preparations – started in early April. The majority of attacks hit the rail network but bombers were also pitted against other specialised targets. Middlebrook notes raids on military camps, ammunition depots, aircraft and armaments factories and, just before the invasion, radio and radar stations and coastal gun batteries.

Attacks on German cities didn't stop entirely but the focus was now on the invasion. The disastrous late winter-early spring trips to Berlin and Nuremberg, when losses reached catastrophic levels, stretched the command's resources and shook morale. Crews welcomed the change to short not-so-stressful operations, though mutiny was in their minds when the hierarchy decreed near-at-hand targets would count as only one-third of an op. After dreadful casualties on the 4–5 May attack on German tanks and troops at Mailly-le-Camp, command realised the short hops across the Channel could be every bit as dangerous as Berlin and the contentious rule was abandoned.

Air Marshal Sir Arthur Harris, Bomber Command's gruff and gritty leader, detested anything that deflected his bombers from the destruction of Germany's cities which he believed could win the war. He saw anything else as a 'panacea'. Middlebrook says Harris had reservations about his orders to bomb railway yards and other military targets in France and Belgium. Those reservations involved the ability of his force to hit the many small targets allocated without killing too many friendly civilians. Despite his doubts, 'Harris gave full and loyal support to the directions he received, both in the preparations for the invasion and in support of the first weeks of the land battle.' Middlebrook says Bomber Command 'was more successful in attacking the small, sensitive targets … than anyone had ever hoped,' adding the use of a Master Bomber became a standard feature.

The series of pre-invasion raids also introduced low-level marking of targets by 617 Squadron Mosquitoes, flown by Leonard Cheshire and some of his pilots, among them New Zealander Terry Kearns, who was accompanied by his compatriot and long-time navigator John Barclay. Such marking introduced greater accuracy and minimised civilian deaths.

Bomber Command aimed to make such a mess of the railways behind the French and Belgian coastlines that the movement of trains carrying German infantry, tanks and guns to combat the invaders after D-Day would be enormously difficult. The American Eighth Air Force and the light day bombers of the 2nd Tactical Air Force (2TAF) played a full role in the campaign, providing round-the-clock raids on key choke points on lines, junctions and yards. Working on the railways in France and Belgium in the early summer of 1944 was hazardous. Though the Germans repaired key facilities amazingly quickly and the RAF needed to return to some targets several times, Bomber Command's railway attacks helped stifle the movement of German forces.

As part of the plan to reinforce the Nazi leadership's belief the invasion would probably occur in the Pas de Calais region at the narrowest point of the Channel, Allied air forces dropped heavy bomb tonnages on railways in western Belgium in the run-up to D-Day.

The four New Zealanders who lost their lives on the night of 10–11 April were 158 Squadron pilot Leonard Neil Couchman (31), from Wanganui, 103 Squadron pilot John Armstrong (28), from Albany, his mid-upper gunner Michael Dillon (26), from Cambridge, and Aucklander William Green, at 20 by far the youngest. He was a 625 Squadron Lancaster pilot, commissioned just four days before his death. With the exception of Dillon who was on his second tour, all were newcomers to ops. Couchman was on his second, Armstrong about his fifth and Green on his seventh. Dillon had begun operational flying in November 1942 and was on his 37th trip. He had flown a full tour with 196 Squadron, instructed in his 'rest' break and then joined 103 at Elsham Wolds in Lincolnshire.

Three of the four were farmers. Armstrong and his fellow crewman Dillon worked on their fathers' farms, while Couchman was a farm manager at Rapanui. Bomber Command dispatched 739 aircraft to five rail centres – Ghent in Belgium on 9 April and on 10 April four in France: Tours, Tergnier, Laon and Aulnoye-Aymeries. Civilian casualties were light during the campaign but at Ghent bombs aimed at yards on the main line to Brussels fell off-target and 428 Belgians died. Many more were injured in flattened and blazing buildings. The Halifaxes and pathfinder Mosquitoes which attacked Ghent escaped loss, but nineteen aircraft fell over the other four targets. Tergnier, about 50 miles southeast of Amiens, cost ten Halifaxes, Aulnoye seven Lancasters, the other two targets a Lancaster apiece. Night fighters got among the bombers at Tergnier and 158 Squadron suffered severely, losing four aircraft. Of the twenty-eight men aboard all but three died, the tiny group of survivors all coming from one plane.

Bob Chorley in *Bomber Command Losses* says Couchman's Halifax was shot down by a night fighter and Errol Martyn in *For Your Tomorrow* adds it exploded in mid-air. But Couchman's son Barry believes otherwise. Family research leads them to believe the plane was hit by flak, one engine set on fire. Couchman crash-landed successfully but in doing so ran into a high earth berm or bank and broke up, killing all the crew. His son has seen the field, although the berm had gone by the time of his visit. He talked to French farmers who remembered the crash and the bodies laid out beside the wreck – some of whom clearly had shrapnel wounds.

Couchman says his father volunteered because he wanted to go. One brother was serving in the army overseas, another left New Zealand in March and served in the Royal Navy. Both survived the war. When he joined the RNZAF in May 1942, Couchman was married with two young children. He learned to fly at Bell Block and Wigram, sailing for England in April 1943, where he finished his training at 1663 Heavy Conversion Unit in Yorkshire before his posting in late March 1944 to 158 at Lissett, also in Yorkshire. Two weeks later he was dead, killed on his first op with the squadron. Earlier he had flown one op as a second pilot, to Leipzig on 3–4 December 1943, an attack costing twenty-four Lancasters and Halifaxes. The New Zealander and his crew are buried at Poix-de-Picardie, a cemetery renamed in 1965 as Poix-de-la-Somme. Almost 150 Commonwealth aircrew, eight of them New Zealanders, lie in the graveyard of the 16th-century Church of St Denis.

Armstrong, Dillon and Green died attacking Aulnoye, an important rail junction 80 miles northeast of Amiens near the Belgian border. Armstrong's aircraft fell on the home-bound leg but it's not clear whether Green's Lancaster was caught before or after dropping its bombs. The aircraft went down near Amiens, where the seven crew are buried.

Six months after Dillon's death his parents learned exactly what took place – something many parents of air force dead never discovered, and for which they were grateful. The Dillons opened a letter dated 6 October from Tonbridge, Kent, from Alex Drage, the navigator in their son's crew. He wrote: 'I thought that you would like to have a first-hand account of what happened.'

> We'd experienced no trouble on our dozen or so flights to the big German targets and it was our first flight to the comparatively soft French targets. Soon after leaving the target [at about 10,000 feet], we were hit by heavy flak ... I think the shell burst a few feet below the aircraft. It blew a smallish hole in the aircraft floor, several feet in front and below Mick's position in the mid-upper turret. It started a small fire on the floor of the fuselage. We reported this at once to John Armstrong, the captain. He made up his mind immediately and gave the order to abandon aircraft. Before he had finished speaking the petrol tanks exploded and caught fire. Immediately the skipper had finished speaking, Mick called out, in his usual matter-of-fact way, 'OK John' and switched off his microphone ... Owing to Armstrong's great promptness I estimate that the four of us who managed to leave the aircraft had done so [from the front escape hatch] within 40/50 seconds of the shell burst. When I left, third, with the wireless operator waiting behind me, there was no sign of flames inside the aircraft (except for the small fire on the floor half way back – no petrol flames) and Armstrong still had the aircraft under control. When I landed, however, the burning aircraft was less than a quarter mile from me [on the ground]. At the height at which I baled out, I think that my parachute would have drifted but little and from this I deduced that the aircraft must have gone straight down out of control a very few seconds after I left it.

Drage judged the plane hit the ground a fraction of a minute after he jumped and said Dillon would have died instantly. Armstrong,

Dillon and the rear gunner were killed, the other four got down safely, all able to get out quickly. Drage and the bomb aimer evaded capture but the other two became POWs.

The Lancaster crashed near Meharicourt, a small town twenty miles southeast of Amiens, where the three bodies were taken from the wreckage and buried in the local cemetery. Forty-one World War II Commonwealth aircrew rest in the brick-walled graveyard, the Cross of Remembrance standing behind the headstones. The two New Zealanders lie side by side, among the six Australians, twelve Canadians and twenty-one Britons.

In his letter to the Dillons, Drage said the crew appreciated Dillon's 'good-natured friendliness to us all, his unfailing good humour, the skill and experience which he commanded, his enthusiasm for the work we were doing, the way in which he was able to take each raid as just the job for the day without any excitement and his complete coolness over Germany.'

Many Elsham Wolds fliers lost their lives during the war. 103 Squadron flew from the station from July 1942 until war's end, operating Halifaxes in the early stages, then Lancasters. It suffered fearful losses, some of them documented by Don Charlwood, an Australian 103 navigator, in *No Moon Tonight*, one of the best books to emerge from the bomber war.

Dillon was born in Dacca in 1917, his father a captain and engineer in the Royal Irish Regiment. The family returned to England, then migrated to New Zealand. Armstrong was born in Exeter, England, in 1915 and arrived here in 1924 as a small boy.

The death of New Zealander Fraser Barron on the 19 May raid on the railway hub of Le Mans was a particular loss – to his squadron and New Zealand. From sergeant and sprog pilot to wing commander with the DSO and bar, DFC and DFM, Barron's career was spectacular. He flew two tours of 61 ops with 15 and 7 Squadrons before being compulsorily rested. High Commissioner Bill Jordan took him to lunch after King George pinned the DSO and DFC on Barron's chest at Buckingham Palace on 25 May 1943. He then wrote to Barron's parents, telling them he was a 'fine lad'. Still only twenty-two, Barron was short, slight and good looking. Jordan added, 'He is certainly one of New Zealand's most distinguished sons. We trust that all will go well with him and that he will return safely to you.'

Barron was bored instructing and itched to get back on ops. In early January 1944 he was posted back to pathfinder 7 Squadron, now on Lancasters. Barron had a charmed run on his third tour and twice he took temporary command of 7 Squadron when its wing commanders were killed. He was Master Bomber on three railway raids in France, including Le Mans on 19–20 January, his job to tell the main force where and when to bomb. Ironically, flak or night fighters didn't kill him. Instead he died in a mid-air collision with his deputy, a deadly smash that perhaps involved a third Lancaster from 115 Squadron. The three Lancasters plunged to earth without survivors, Barron's and the 115's in the same area, the deputy Master Bomber some distance away. Twenty-three men dead. Fellow New Zealander Jack Walters (23), Barron's wireless operator, who was on his 51st op, had done a full tour on 75 Squadron before joining him. Barron and four of his crew were buried at Le Mans but Walters is remembered at Runnymede.

7 Squadron's dual losses over Le Mans were compounded by the destruction of a third Lancaster, taking part in an attempt to knock out a radar station at Mont de Couple, two miles inland

from the Channel coast in the Cape Gris-Nez area. Hit by flak, ND736 exploded, the pilot the only survivor, thrown out by the force of the blast. Among the dead was mid-upper gunner William MacDonald (21), a Wanganui farmer's son. Four months short of his 22nd birthday, he had already completed a tour with 75 Squadron, and was a Flying Officer.

75 (NZ) Squadron, in the process of converting from Stirlings to Lancasters, did three rail-bombing trips in late March after flying on seven nights that month to drop supplies to French Resistance cells, and a bout of minelaying. The squadron, and others in 3 Group still using Stirlings, were called in to supplement the work of the regular SOE units as the invasion loomed and more guns, ammunition and other supplies were needed. Just one aircraft was lost over the seven nights.

The first time 75 operated Lancasters on ops, the night of 9–10 April, fifteen of the new aircraft took off from Mepal, the squadron's Cambridgeshire base, to attack yards at Villeneuve in the southeast suburbs of Paris. The next night when Couchman, Armstrong, Dillon and Green were killed, 75 was up again, raiding rail installations at Laon, midway between Saint Quentin and Reims. The squadron stepped up its rail attacks in May and continued after the invasion into July and August, its last on 11 August, against marshalling yards at Lens, an industrial city in the Pas de Calais region.

75 Squadron's overall losses attacking rail installations were not heavy but on 10–11 June two of the twenty-four Lancs dispatched to Dreux in Normandy didn't return. The aircraft, skippered by Lester Bonisch of Christchurch and Tom Donaghy of Wanganui, were brought down by German defence – the former's aircraft twice

hit by flak over the target area then exploding. Donaghy fell victim to a night fighter, a few miles from Dreux. The mid-upper gunner, taken prisoner, was the sole survivor of Bonisch's crew while only the rear gunner on the other aircraft lived. Twelve men dead.

Bonisch, halfway through his tour, was just a couple of weeks short of 22. Donaghy (33) was the only New Zealander in his Lancaster but two fellow countrymen died in the Bonisch plane – navigator John McKenzie (27) from Levin, and bomb aimer James Miller (33), another 'elderly' flier.

Both McKenzie and his father lie in French graves. *For Your Tomorrow* notes that John Murdock McKenzie, an NZEF member in the Wellington Regiment, is buried in the Anzac cemetery at Sailly-sur-la-Lys, near Armentieres. His son, John Murdoch Thomas McKenzie, was born three months after his father's death. (Both spellings of their respective middle names are correct, by the way.) He and his five crew are buried at Bayeux in Normandy.

The next night when 75 Squadron was up again, bound for the marshalling yards at Nantes, Australian bomb aimer Alex Hurse won the rare Conspicuous Gallantry Medal (CGM) after his New Zealand pilot Cyril McCardle was severely wounded by a light flak shell bursting in the cockpit of their Lancaster. Hurse, a farmer from western Victoria, bounded up the steps from the nose to the flight deck, hearing calls to bale out and found a bloodied McCardle clutching the stick to his chest. The flight engineer, normally the man to take over the controls in an emergency, was also hurt. Though Hurse's piloting experience was virtually nil, he had seen and heard enough to have a fair idea what to do. He wrenched the stick away from McCardle and got the bomber, dangerously nose up and close to stalling, back to level flight. McCardle had taken the plane down below cloud level to bomb visually but as they emerged into clear air searchlights locked on to them and flak hit the aircraft.

Much later, Hurse explained: 'I felt the aircraft start to climb and we were back in the cloud. I yelled out to them to put the nose down. They yelled back we were going to crash and for us to get out of the aircraft.' Hurse had other ideas. He dropped the 18 x 500 pound bomb load in a flash, then scampered up top. He pushed the stick forward, the plane responded and levelled out. All four engines beat strongly and Hurse headed the Lancaster away from the target area. With New Zealand navigator Rob Zillwood plotting the course, Hurse turned for home.

McCardle, hit in the head, chest and legs, was lifted out of his seat, put on the rest bed and given morphine. The wireless operator signalled base they'd been hit, had wounded aboard and the bomb aimer was piloting. The plane was instructed to head for RAF Boscombe Down in Wiltshire and its long main runway, and as they flew over England searchlights pointed the way. The skipper, in no condition to land the plane, urged his mates to jump when they reached England but Hurse, described by someone who knew him as a typical Australian – 'loud, competent and confident' – had no intention of doing so. He put the plane down safely.

His major worry wasn't the actual landing, but halting the big bomber once it was down. He figured in the worst case they could pull up the undercarriage and run on the belly to slow up. They didn't need to – the Lancaster touched down at 150 mph, way too fast, but though she bounced wildly and threatened to loop, Hurse kept her rolling straight enough and she ground to a halt. Ambulances and fire trucks paced the plane along the runway and

McCardle and the engineer were whisked off to hospital. Both Hurse and Zillwood were awarded immediate decorations, the Australian a CGM, next best to a Victoria Cross, Zillwood a DFC. Their citations said they had shown 'exceptional coolness [and] great determination'. McCardle was later honoured with a mention in dispatches.

McCardle (27), Zillwood and Hurst (24), were all near the end of their tours and didn't fly operationally again. They'd done enough and were screened as tour expired, spending the rest of the war as instructors – McCardle after twelve weeks in hospital. The Australian returned to his farm at Carisbrook, northwest of Melbourne, and McCardle and Zillwood to the Wairarapa and Wellington. McCardle and Zillwood were cousins and had made a pact that if the opportunity ever arose they would fly together. They bumped into each other at a London pub and, unlikely as it might seem, came together as pilot and navigator. Hurse wasn't in the original crew but joined early on as a replacement bomb aimer. Zillwood sources say his name caused plenty of black humour among a superstitious crew. Fortunately Hurse proved more of a guardian angel than a jinx.

Bomber Command sent its aircraft off on their last rail attacks on 11 August, daylight operations to four targets in France, and to Givors in south central France that night. Cruelly, the last New Zealand casualty of all was attributed to 'friendly fire'. Bomb aimer Harold Crampton (27) of Cheviot was in the nose of his 514 Squadron Lancaster on the bombing run over Lens when a bomb dropped from above crashed into the plane's nose. Crampton was thrown out. His parachute failed to deploy, because he was either already dead or knocked out. He is buried in Loos British Cemetery in France, the last resting place of thousands of British World War I dead. No one else in the crew, including New Zealand navigator Keith Stafford (26), from Wellington, and wireless operator Ron Collender (21), from Christchurch, was hurt. English pilot Bill Brickwood flew the badly damaged Lancaster back to England for a straight-in landing at Woodbridge, the big Suffolk coast emergency field. The plane never flew again.

Crampton's crew mourned his loss but a new bomb aimer was drafted in and they were soon flying again in a new aircraft. A month later attacking Frankfurt their Lancaster was shot down. Ironically, the fresh bomb aimer was one of two survivors. The two New Zealanders died.

The RAF suffered its worst losses of the railway campaign during a series of raids on Revigny-sur-Ornain, a small township of about 3000 in northeast France, 150 miles east of Paris, 50 miles southeast of Reims. Battered in World War I, it was damaged again in the German Blitzkrieg of 1940 when many of the RAF's squadrons were based in this region.

Revigny lay astride the east-west Paris-Strasbourg line, a major link. With virtually no industry, there was nothing to attract Bomber Command — except the railway yards. In July 1944 its marshalling yards and locomotive depot were an important cog in the movement of German troops and equipment. The RAF attacked Revigny three times in a week — on the nights of 12–13 July, 14–15 July and 18–19 July. It had little to show and the cost was awful — forty-one Lancasters and 231 aircrew. Just fifty men from the doomed aircraft reached the ground alive. The dead included seven New Zealand aircrew. They were among the casualties killed on four aircraft that crashed to earth without survivors.

Oliver Clutton-Brock, in his 1994 book *Massacre over the Marne*, says that collectively the raids failed. 'The target was a small one and for that reason alone would always be difficult to destroy. With the hopeless weather conditions on the first two raids and the severe attacks of the Luftwaffe on the third, the chances of success were further reduced.' The Revigny yards emerged virtually unscathed from the first two attacks. The third cratered the complex, destroyed some lines and exploded wagons on an ammunition train. But the Germans, masters at quick repairs, ordered the male inhabitants of Revigny to work the morning of the 19th and the main through-line was open in a few hours.

Clutton-Brock reasons it would be easy to blame the planners for the heavy losses, noting that St Dizier airfield, barely fifteen minutes from Revigny, was the base of an experienced night-fighter unit. He adds the target should have been destroyed the first night but as bomber chief Arthur Harris had promised Allied HQ it would be destroyed, RAF Bomber Command had to keep at it. 'Poor weather and the Luftwaffe saw to it that a heavy price was extorted. Revigny was just another name, another place, another time for dying.'

Raid number one, by 100 Lancasters of 1 Group, was thwarted by several factors – cloud over the target, malfunctioning H2S radar aboard the Master Bomber's aircraft and a breakdown in communications. Attackers circling the target waiting to bomb couldn't hear instructions. Eventually the raid was called off and fewer than half bombed. The extraordinarily long route to and from the target on the first two raids – into France over Brittany, southeast to the country's centre, then northeast to Revigny – meant near ten-hour flights. Crews of two fuel-exhausted aircraft baled out over England and a third plane crash-landed across a runway, the pilot yanking up his undercarriage and grinding to a halt.

The confused situation over Revigny the first night caused mayhem. Some crews bombed early, others didn't hear the 'go home' order and unloaded. Some of the planes in the circuit bombed burning wrecks, certain the fires were red target indicators. One aircraft joined in another raid on the way back to England. Clutton-Brock: 'With the plan falling apart at the seams and aircraft coming and going on many different headings, the almost inevitable happened. At 0155 hours two Lancasters orbiting in opposite directions were seen to collide.' No survivors. New Zealander Walter Boocock (29) from Ngapara, North Otago, was flying LL796 of 550 Squadron when it slammed into a 103 Squadron bomber. By the time Boocock was killed he was an experienced captain, on op number twenty-three. His navigator and compatriot Morris Eckhold (26) had done twice as many. He was on his 50th, about half flown while he was stationed with a squadron on the east coast of Canada. He was also a North Otago man, a Mackenzie Country telephone exchange clerk. On the way home another two Lancasters mistakenly shot each other down and a third was lost homebound in a collision with a Lancaster on another raid. The other Lancasters were victims of night fighters, which arrived as the raid ended. The smoking wreckage of ten Lancasters lay over the French landscape. Seven more crashed on the second attack and an appalling twenty-four on the third.

1 Group provided 106 Lancasters for the second attack, but again poor bombing conditions undid them. Fog obscured the target for the Master Bomber, who radioed 'Sugar Plum', an early and

controversial call cancelling the bombing when only a handful of Lancasters had let their bombs go. Night fighters began arriving as the Lancs turned for home. First victim was the aircraft flown by 550 Squadron's popular commander, Wing Commander PEGG Connolly. No survivors. Next down was the deputy Master Bomber's Lancaster, a 156 Squadron pathfinder. The pilot and bomb aimer lived, the rest of the crew perished. As the Lancasters began the long route home they were hunted by night fighters. Another five were shot down, two from 103 Squadron.

The one New Zealander lost on this second raid was Alan Rodgers, a 21-year-old freshly posted to 166 Squadron at Kirmington in Lincolnshire, and on his first op, flying as second pilot. Clutton-Brock says his aircraft, ND621, was the last to be shot down. 'This was a doubly tragic loss, for not only was there a 'second dickey' aboard [Rodgers] … but also the crew were on their 29th operation. Just one more and they would have been tour expired, with every expectation of surviving the war.' Rodgers, from Palmerston North, lies with his seven companions in a collective grave at Lusigny-sur-Barse, 10 miles southeast of Troyes.

The disastrous third raid on 18–19 July claimed four New Zealanders – the captain and bomb aimer in two crews, one from 619 Squadron based at Dunholme Lodge, the other from 49 Squadron at Fiskerton, both in Lincolnshire. Fourteen men perished. Their aircraft were among almost 1000 dispatched by the RAF that night against targets in France and Germany. No. 5 group was chosen to raid Revigny and 109 Lancasters began taking off from their bases while it was still light, Clutton-Brock writing that ND797, the first aircraft into the air at 10.36 p.m., was in the hands of 'F/L G. Joblin, 630 Squadron' – Flight Lieutenant George Joblin (24), from Hawera.

He was one of the lucky ones. 630 lost four of the dozen Lancasters it sent off, a number matched by 49's four and exceeded only by the five missing from 619 Squadron.

Joblin and others on his squadron were on their second op of the day. Such was probably the case with crews from other squadrons on the Revigny raid, as Bomber Command had launched almost 1000 aircraft that morning against targets in Caen, in support of General Bernard Montgomery's Operation Goodwood. 630 sent seventeen aircraft on the daylight Caen raid and then the group for Revigny. 630's ORB shows that seven of the ten crews that flew across the Channel to the Normandy battlefield early on 18 July flew to Revigny later in the day.

The RAF was asking a lot of its young crews to fly two ops inside twenty-four hours and it's possible this contributed to losses at Revigny. Crews needed to be alert to ward off night fighters and at least some of the aircrew doing double 'shifts' might not have been quite so vigilant on the second op.

When Joblin lifted his Lancaster from East Kirkby he and his crew would have been awakened two or three hours earlier. Their undamaged Lancaster had returned from Caen at 7.25 a.m., a flight of 3 hours 35 minutes. Then debriefing, breakfast and bed and what sleep was possible in high summer. Later that afternoon they would have been up again and the rigmarole for another op would have begun. Joblin was airborne for Revigny in daylight and safe home again at 3.52 a.m., a run of almost five and a half hours and his 26th op. It would have been a tough night. Night fighters harried the Revigny Lancasters from the time they crossed the French coast, this time just west of the Somme Estuary, the change in route taking the force in a straight line to Revigny with the exception of a sharp

90-degree plus turn not far short of the target. The German radar and radio plotters, expert at their jobs after four years at war, had the aircraft in their sights early.

One 467 Squadron skipper quoted by Clutton-Brock said, 'From enemy coast [the] inward track was marked by enemy with green changing to white flares. Fighters seemed very busy the whole way.' Alerted night fighters found and stayed in the bomber stream. The initial sighting of a fighter was reported at 12.40 a.m. and twenty minutes later the first Lancaster, from 619 Squadron, went down about 35 miles northeast of Paris. The night fighters prowled in the area where 619 happened to be and four of the first five Lancs to be shot down carried 619's code. The four were all victims of German guns in the space of fifteen minutes. New Zealander Norman Donnelley (32) from Auckland flew the fourth 619 Squadron machine lost. The plane crashed at Ussy-sur-Marne, a little town on the north bank of the Marne. The entire crew is buried there. Donnelley and his bomb aimer, fellow New Zealander Donald Grant (33), a North Otago farmer, formed an experienced team. There was a measure of revenge. The Lancaster's two gunners poured a stream of fire into their attacker before they crashed and died and the fighter was seen to go down.

Fighters found three more Lancasters as the force made the final turn for the run-in to Revigny and two more New Zealanders died. Pilot William Green (28) and his bomb aimer Merv Hollard (21) were killed with the rest of their 49 Squadron crew on JB178 when it crashed near Herbisse, midway between Reims and Troyes. Herbisse, a tiny village where the flyers are buried, is close to the scene of the 3–4 May 1944 disastrous raid on the military camp at Mailly-le-Camp, which cost the RAF forty-three Lancasters.

Says Clutton-Brock: 'It was probably the demise of JB178 that was witnessed at 0130 hours by another unidentified Lancaster – "Lanc dead astern 800 yards own height [7800 ft] seen to burst into flames and crash ... cause unknown".' There were no survivors, and no mention of tracer or air-to-air firing suggests that yet again schrage musik [German aircraft's upward-firing cannon] had triumphed.

Green had done twenty-eight ops, Hollard twenty-four. Green, a hairdresser in Adelaide, came home to New Zealand in 1941 to enlist. Hollard, born and raised in Opotiki, was working as a storeman, the two meeting at 28 OTU in August 1943. Green was awarded the DFC after his death but was already in line for his bravery the previous month during a raid to the Ruhr, when his aircraft drove off one night fighter approaching the target then survived another attack. Though the plane was damaged and one engine knocked out, Green flew on, dropped his bombs and struggled back to base on three engines.

Clutton-Brock tallies an astonishing seventeen Lancasters lost and 105 men dead before the target was reached. The other seven bombers were lost over Revigny or on the way home, one hit by ground fire as it fled west. 630 Squadron's ORB says '... considerable fighter activity on the outward route and near the target, decreasing if anything on the return route.'

The Germans lost three fighters for certain and two probables during the night battles but they had scored a notable victory. Herbert Altner claimed five victories (he ended the war with twenty-one) in half an hour. Using his SN2 radar he picked up each Lancaster's blip, followed it to visual sighting distance, slipped unseen under his target and pressed his schrage musik guns. He aimed between the two port engines each time and closed his eyes as his deadly cannon opened up. His crew watched as the shells pumped into the Lancaster and told him when it caught fire. Like many German pilots he tried to spare the RAF crews, setting planes afire on the wing to give crew a chance to jump. Clutton-Brock quotes Altner, 'After the fifth I'd had enough and flew home.' When Altner landed he was unable to light his cigarette – his flight mechanic kept him supplied until he calmed down.

Nothing is known of Joblin's flight to and from Revigny. He would have seen combats between aircraft, watched other Lancasters go down, explode and burn on the ground. He and the rest of the squadron would have been shaken by 630's losses – four planes missing, four crews gone. Friends lost. Some pilots and crewmen routinely wrote comments in their logs about what happened. Logs didn't have much space but some are crammed. Ron Perks, a New Zealander who did a tour with 76 Halifax Squadron from January to June 1943, flew to Berlin on 1 March, a scary 8 hours 20 minutes flight. He wrote in his log: 'Operations BERLIN – Nightmare trip, numerous S/L's [searchlights], coned twice, shot at by all and sundry. 19,000 ft. Numerous large fires seen. ME 109 sighted.' In contrast, Joblin never wrote more than necessary. All he said was: 'Ops. Revigny (Rail Yard).'

Stuttgart was one of the few 'lucky' German cities of World War II – if the word can be used to describe a city subject to major air raids. In southwest Germany sixty miles east of the Rhine, it was a tempting target, with automotive and aviation plants. Stuttgart was, and continues to be, the headquarters of Mercedes-Benz.

While the city suffered, it escaped the destruction inflicted on most German cities because of its topographical layout. Martin Middlebrook says in *The Bomber Command War Diaries* that its location 'spread out in a series of deep valleys consistently frustrated the Pathfinders, and the shelters dug into the sides of the surrounding hills had saved many lives.' He adds almost 70 percent of the city's blocks of flats and houses were destroyed but quotes local historian Heinz Bardua as putting Stuttgart's wartime death toll at 4562, of whom 770 were POWs or foreign workers (slave labour), a fraction of the dead in other cities.

The first RAF bombs fell on Stuttgart on the night of 24–25 August 1940 when Bomber Command sent 68 Wellingtons and Whitleys to five targets in Germany. The RAF had yet to learn to concentrate its slender resources. Middlebrook notes four people died in Stuttgart when bombs dropped in the suburbs 'hit some houses and a garage'. The last bombs fell on the city on 17–18 March 1945 when two Mosquitoes attacked. Neither raid counted as 'major'.

What did count was the last major attack on 28–29 January 1945 when 602 Lancasters, Halifaxes and Mosquitoes descended on Stuttgart in two waves, three hours apart. Just time for the shelters to empty and people not bombed out to get to bed before the sirens sounded again. Middlebrook says the target area was mostly cloud-covered and the bombing on sky-markers was scattered.

He quotes Bardua again, writing about the commander of a flak battery just south of a decoy fire, where the Germans fired dummy target-indicator rockets to confuse the bombers. Lancasters zeroed in on the decoy and the commander 'thought the raid was directed at his battery ... He ignored regulations about conservation of ammunition and shot his entire stock at the radar echoes of the attacking bombers. 2 Lancasters and a Halifax crashed in the immediate vicinity, much to the relief of the officer, who feared a court martial because of his prodigious use of ammunition.'

Stuttgart took its worst pounding of the war in late July 1944 when it was hit by Bomber Command three times in five days. The first raid, on the night of 24–25 July, was followed by another the next night and again on 28–29 July. Middlebrook writes that the only report from city sources is a composite saying the three raids caused the most serious damage of the war in the central districts, where the majority of public and cultural buildings were destroyed. The middle raid was the most successful for the RAF and the worst for the city, costing 1171 lives and leaving 1600 injured.

As usual Bomber Command paid a heavy price.

Raid 1: 461 Lancasters, 153 Halifaxes took part with 3.4 percent losses – 17 Lancasters and 4 Halifaxes.

Raid 2: 412 Lancasters, 138 Halifaxes and 10 Mosquitoes took part with 2.1 percent losses – 8 Lancasters and 4 Halifaxes.

Raid 3: 494 Lancasters and 2 Mosquitoes took part with 7.9 percent losses – 39 Lancasters.

Losses on the first two raids were acceptable, those on the third raid bearable only because aircraft and aircrews were being produced in great numbers.

Three hundred and seventy-seven aircrew died over the three raids, 208 of them on the last night. This numbing total included fourteen New Zealanders, nine on the first raid, five on the third. Eighty-two crewmen became POWs and sixty-six evaded capture. Aircrew numbers here will not tally with lost aircraft – some aircraft had eight men aboard, two or three were written off after crash-landings in England and some parachuting crew landed among Allied forces in the Normandy battle zone and were not considered evaders. Because routes to and from the target were for the most part over France, many of the downed bombers fell in French territory and many of the men who jumped safely were helped by French civilians.

On 28 July New Zealand pilot Ian Herbert and his crew arrived at 630 Squadron's base, East Kirkby, Lincolnshire. He found the battle-order blackboard and spotted the name of skipper George Joblin. When Herbert went to bed that night he thought to himself, 'Well, that's someone I know I can ask what things are really like'. He had been at night school in Hawera with Joblin when both were studying for the RNZAF. Returning aircraft wakened him the next morning and aircrew heading for bed stomped into his hut. The first thing he heard one of them say was 'Jobby hasn't come back.' Joblin was dead, the wreck of his bomber lying on a hill near Stuttgart.

It always seemed deeply unfair when men like Joblin lost their lives on their last op, when they would have been safe back at base in another three or four hours, celebrating. But many deaths seemed unfair. On the opening Stuttgart raid, Eric Houghton (22), working in a Christchurch bank when he enlisted, died when his 15 Squadron Lancaster was downed over France the first time he flew to war. He climbed onto the plane as second pilot to gain experience before beginning ops with his own crew. No survivors. Two and a half years in training, preparing for this night, his life snuffed out the first time he ventured over hostile territory. Peter Vercoe (22) from Nelson and Doug Pepper (22) from Wellington, pilot and navigator, respectively, of a 622 Squadron Lancaster, were also at the beginning of their tours. They were lost when their bomber exploded over the outskirts of Nancy in northeast France. Pepper's brother Terence, a Hurricane pilot, died in August 1942 while flying a night exercise over the North Sea. Their parents, like another 100 New Zealand couples, lost two sons in the air force.

On 24–25 July, 75 (NZ) Squadron was still recovering from its horrifying losses four nights earlier when no fewer than seven of its Lancasters were shot down attacking an oil refinery in the Ruhr – record losses. 75's bad run continued with Stuttgart. The squadron contributed strongly on each of the three raids, twenty-one, fourteen and twenty-two, respectively. Two aircraft failed to return the opening night and two more the third night. No survivors the first night, fourteen men dead, four of them New Zealanders. Pilot Keith Whitehouse (23) from Wellington and wireless operator Keat Dudding (25) from Te Kuiti died in one Lancaster; pilot James McRae and his bomb aimer Tom Potts, both 27 and from Invercargill, in the other.

The other two New Zealand victims of the 24–25 July raid were Sydney Davies (23) and George Sinclair (29). Dunedin-born Davies crossed the Tasman in 1938 and was working in a Melbourne bank when he joined the RAAF in mid-1942. He was a bomb aimer on Australian 466 (Halifax) Squadron based at Driffield, Yorkshire, when he was killed over Stuttgart. Sinclair, the mid-upper gunner on 622 Squadron, died when his Lancaster crashed near Nancy.

Three other New Zealand pilots were flying on 630 Squadron at the same time as George Joblin – Roy Calvert, Doug Hawker and Joe Lennon. All survived the war.

Calvert, a squadron leader from Cambridge, and one of the two 630 flight commanders, came home with a DFC and two bars and a reputation as an outstanding pilot. He received his first DFC early on his opening tour with 50 Squadron, when he flew a badly damaged Manchester home from the Cologne thousand-bomber raid in May 1942, the second five months later when he wrestled a Lancaster back to England with heavy flak damage suffered over Hamburg, one crew member dead, another wounded, himself peppered with flak fragments. He then instructed for a year before a posting to 630 where he earned his third DFC. Hawker, from Christchurch, and Northlander Lennon were awarded DFCs on 630. Both had a single New Zealander in their crews – bomb aimer Colin Griffin (35) from Morrinsville with Hawker, and Bruce Reese, born in Marlborough, as Lennon's navigator.

Hawker totalled thirty-five ops, his tour extended by five because of heavy losses, and succeeded Calvert as flight commander when the latter was promoted to temporary command when their wing commander was killed. Hawker had gone from raw pilot officer to a veteran and flight commander in nine weeks. His story is in *Night after Night*.

Lennon, born in the Whangarei area in 1913, was a dairy farmer. Years after the war, his flight engineer, Londoner Harry Parkins, remembered his red-haired skipper, known inevitably as 'Bluey', as a skilful, excellent pilot. Parkins said of navigator Reese: 'A tall young man, a racehorse owner. He had an eye for the girls and a favourite saying, "she's got her good points". He had a habit of keeping his collar turned up, for which he was always being reprimanded.' Their mid-upper Joe Malloy, a bookmaker, hailed from Liverpool. Parkins said he'd pin a picture of Hitler on the darts board and take wagers on who'd put the darts in Hitler's eyes. 'We were a super crew, great comrades, one for all and all for one, and all a bit crazy.'

630's crews were worked hard in the last days of July – with good settled late summer weather there was no reason to scrub ops. On 23–24 eight Lancasters went to Kiel, Joblin among them. The next night another eight to Stuttgart, first of the three raids, but no New Zealanders on the battle order. One aircraft came back early, another went missing over France. Four evaders, one POW, two dead. The same night seven planes flew a six-hour trip to an oil dump near St Nazaire on France's Bay of Biscay coastline, including Joblin, Hawker and Lennon. Twelve flew to Stuttgart 25–26 July, Hawker among them. No losses. The next night, a long haul to marshalling yards at Givors in southern France, with Joblin and Lennon in the eight detailed. One aircraft lost, the crew all dead. And two nights later the third raid to Stuttgart. Thirteen aircraft on the battle order, eleven took off, ten bombed – and Joblin missing. He and all but one of his crew dead.

This is how it was. Constant operations, constant death, those who lived through a tour the lucky ones. The missing were mourned but new crews appeared and the bombing continued. 630 went to a target in the Normandy battle zone on 30 July, a daylight raid, but unexpectedly bad weather battered the area, and the planes carried their bombs home. Hawker was on the battle order again on the last day of July as 630 attacked a flying bomb site and railway yards across the Channel.

75 (NZ) Squadron lost two Lancasters and four men on the last raid to Stuttgart. Three died on ND756 – skipper Ian Blance (21) from New Plymouth, wireless operator Fred Climo (22) from Timaru, and mid-upper Fred Jenkins (30), also from New Plymouth, all believed to be on their 3rd op. The Lancaster went down in flames over France but three of the crew jumped safely – Aubrey Kirk (21), from Christchurch, lived with Resistance forces until getting back to England in September 1944, while navigator Colin Greig, born in Paeroa, was captured immediately.

The other 75 bomber, piloted by Noel Stokes (25), from Christchurch, a veteran of twenty-eight ops, crashed near the village of Yevres, about 70 miles southwest of Paris. Over the years legends have developed around Stokes; revered as a hero in Yevres, he is believed to have steered the aircraft away from the village. His Lancaster was shot up by a night fighter, hunting between Chartres and Orleans. Stokes, like hundreds of skippers throughout the war, held his burning plane up long enough for the crew to jump – one died during the attack – and then was unable to get out himself, all control gone the moment he lifted his hands from the stick. Four of his crew and a 2nd dickey pilot, all New Zealanders, jumped and survived.

George Joblin had come a long way by the time he joined 630 Squadron on 21 March 1944, almost two years from the day he'd quit as a storeman in Hawera. It must have seemed a glamorous move. Joblin was the fourth child in a family of ten from a dairy farm at Kakaramea. He enlisted on 16 May 1942 as a prospective wireless operator/air gunner but remustered as a pilot. He soloed at Harewood, then sailed to Canada for more intensive training, graduating with wings and a commission. His crew arrived at East Kirkby, 630's field in Lincolnshire, on 21 March 1944 presumably pleased to be finished their long training regime, ready for the real thing. But also apprehensive – aware of the odds they faced against finishing their tour, odds that gave them an excellent chance of being killed. This new crew, especially at danger in their first five or ten ops, needed several things – a good skipper, good teamwork and above all a huge dose of luck. Joblin was a good pilot and skipper and their teamwork helped them survive. Luck deserted them at the very end, when all but one died.

East Kirkby, built on the edge of the Lincolnshire fens, was completed just before 57 Squadron moved in from Scampton in

August 1943 when Scampton's runways were being concreted. Three months later 57's B-flight was hived off to create the nucleus of 630, which remained at East Kirkby for the rest of the war.

Two days after reaching East Kirkby, Joblin had his first outing on 630, a 1 hour 10 minutes check with Calvert, his B-flight commander. The next night, 24–25 March, he was on the battle order, flying second pilot for experience. To Berlin. 630 didn't believe in easy introductions.

Joblin also wasn't one for writing much in his log book. His entry for 24 March 1944 reads simply, 'Ops. Berlin', with 7.15 in the hours and minutes column. Joblin would have had plenty to think about. The raid that night was the RAF's last major attack of the war on the German capital. The losses were awful. Flak batteries and night fighters claimed seventy-two British bombers – forty-four Lancasters, twenty-eight Halifaxes, almost nine percent of the attacking force. Strong winds scattered the stream and bombs fell willy-nilly. Middlebrook reports housing destroyed in Berlin's southwest suburbs but no important industrial concerns.

With nothing much else to do other than watch from the flight engineer's pop-up seat, Joblin would have been mesmerised by the bomb bursts and fires on the ground, powerful searchlights, flak bursts and burning and exploding bombers, their funeral pyres on the ground. When his Lancaster landed safely at East Kirkby about 2 a.m. five were missing – two from 57 Squadron, three from 630. Three of them were shot down on the homeward run.

Six days later the RAF suffered its worst night of the war with ninety-five bombers lost on the failed raid to Nuremberg. More crashed on return to England. Night fighters got amongst the stream soon after it crossed into Belgium and in bright moonlight hacked down eighty-two raiders. East Kirkby was hit again – this time 57 lost one aircraft, 630 another three. But they got off lightly. 101 Squadron lost seven, two squadrons lost six and several others chalked 'missing' against four.

Joblin flew his first op with his own crew on the night of 5–6 April on LE-W (for Willie), serial number ND797, the aircraft on which he would die, and the one he seemed to fly more than any other. That night the aircraft of 5 Group dropped their bombs with remarkable accuracy on an aircraft factory at Toulouse, 617 squadron CO Leonard Cheshire marking the plant at low level in his Mosquito.

Over the weeks that followed, Joblin and his crew became an experienced team, coming safely through their early ops. They flew to targets in France in the lead-up to the invasion – railway yards, airfields, flying bomb sites and military installations including Mailly-le-Camp on 3–4 May, where so many others were shot down. They dropped mines in Danzig Bay and Kiel Bay, and bombed Brunswick, Schweinfurt, Munich and Kiel. There's no indication in Joblin's log book of any attacks by night fighters. He scribbled on 23 May – the one and only note in his entire log – after raiding Brunswick – 'Flak. BA's panel', meaning flak splinters smashed into the bomb aimer's control panel.

On 28–29 July Joblin's Lancaster rolled down the runway at 9.53 p.m. and off, two minutes after Roy Calvert. The Met people had forecast cloud over France on the way to Stuttgart. They were wrong. The ORB put it drily: 'The anticipated cloud cover was not met with on the outward route and fighter activity was intense from about 05 [degrees] E to the target. Moderate heavy [88 mm] flak was experienced at the target.' The moonlit sky was ideal for night fighters. They found and wove into the stream over France and set about destroying the bombers.

Joblin avoided the attackers on his way to Stuttgart but Chorley says the Lancaster was hit by a fighter about 2.30 a.m. between Magstadt and again at 2.30 a.m. near Sindelfingen, just west of the city. Martyn also says a night fighter downed the aircraft, as does the RAF loss card for ND797. Three jumped but only Flying Officer Charles Beeson, the English bomb aimer, landed safely. The loss card quotes him, 'I lost my top teeth when I baled out'. He said their Lancaster was hit in the tail by flak. It's possible that Beeson, in the very front of the plane, may have been mistaken about being hit by flak at the rear, unaware a fighter had attacked them. German night-fighter pilots lodged twenty-one claims for destroying Lancasters that night and one by Benno Kranz over Sindelfingen at 5200 metres (17,060 feet) would seem to match. Beeson says his aircraft was at 17,000 feet when hit. In an account for his family he said:

> We were four minutes late arriving and being in the last wave of the raid were open to predicted flak. On approaching the target many aircraft were seen to be hit by the flak which was very heavy and concentrated … the target was shrouded by 10/10 low cloud but fire could be seen through it. When we were hit it didn't at first appear that the aircraft had been seriously damaged but the rear gunner reported the tail was on fire … the skipper … put the aircraft into a steep dive in an endeavour to force the fire out. He then called, 'Get out, the aircraft is out of control.' During the dive I had great difficulty in opening the escape hatch but after a few seconds I was able to jettison it. I then baled out. The engineer was waiting to follow me. When first hit we were flying at 17,000 feet and I estimate we were at 15,000 feet when I jumped.

Beeson's parachute opened instantly and as he floated down he watched 'our plane going down very quickly, still on fire.' He survived a 'violent' landing, crashing to the ground through trees 'which gave me a very bad shaking.' He covered his parachute with branches snapped off as he plunged through the trees, studied his escape maps and found he was 70-odd miles from the Swiss frontier. 'I decided I would make for Switzerland.' After walking through woods for an hour he struck a road junction and a sign telling him he was two miles from Sindelfingen. During that day, a Saturday, he kept to the woods, eating a few wild berries, and milk tablets from his escape kit, drinking water from ditches. He slept all night. Sunday Beeson climbed a succession of wooded 600-foot ridges and was drenched in a thunderstorm. Exhausted, he went down to an open valley to try to determine his position, ignored by passing soldiers but eventually rumbled by civilians. By 3 September he was at Dulag Luft, the POW-holding pen outside Frankfurt, for the inevitable interrogation lasting several days. Then he was off to start life as a POW at one of the Sagan camps. But he was alive.

On 29 July, the squadron's ORB noted simply: 'Flight Lieutenant Joblin is missing.' Postwar when the British Missing Research Enquiry Units spread over Europe trying to determine the fate of missing airmen, they questioned authorities and inspected graves in an area where ND797 was reported to have crashed. MREU Section 13 officers reported in March 1947 they'd talked to the wartime and current mayors of Maichingen, a village close to Sindelfingen, site of a major Mercedes-Benz plant. The officers were told that on the night of 29 August 1944 at 2 a.m. an aircraft crashed on a hill about a mile east of the village and burned out. The wartime mayor reported the police were at the scene before he got there and were recovering the bodies of two of the airmen from near the crash site and another two from the aircraft. The four were buried without ceremony in the village cemetery the following day – the two complete bodies in separate coffins, the two from the plane, both burned, in a third coffin. The grave site, covered with greenery when the MREU men visited it, was surrounded by a six-inch high concrete wall and a brown wooden cross inscribed:'Here lie four English airmen'.

The report added: 'As it was known that the aircraft must have had a crew of seven men, a search was instituted for the three remaining members … fourteen days later the decomposing parts of two human bodies were found in a forest near the village of Magstadt.' The remains were buried in separate coffins in Magstadt a mile north of Maichingen, the white cross on the graves noting, 'Here lie two unknown English fliers'. The MREU said it considered the two grave sites commemorated the crew of ND797 – 'the coincidence of date and other gen given by the witnesses leave little doubt as to the crew involved.' The bodies of Joblin and his crew were later reinterred in Durnbach War Cemetery just south of Munich.

The night George Joblin died attacking Stuttgart, James Archibald, another New Zealand pilot on the same raid, survived – flung out of his Lancaster as the bomber exploded. His crew perished. Archibald floated down under his parachute, landing high in a tree in forest-clad country near Epinal, a town now of 35,000 on the Moselle in northeast France.

Archibald never wrote about that night, though he did talk about his return to Epinal in 1960 on a tape recording he sent to his family in New Zealand, and opened up to his son, also James, as he grew older. Jim says his father 'remembered hearing bullet and shell strikes on the wings and then nothing more until he woke up in a tree, parachute tangled and torn in the branches above. He had no recollection of pulling the ripcord to open the chute.'

Archibald's 576 Squadron Lancaster, still on its way to Stuttgart, was shot down by a night fighter about 2.30 a.m. and was one of four the squadron lost that night. Sister squadron on Elsham Wolds, 103, also had four not return, five counting the badly damaged bomber that crash-landed in a South Coast field.

Shocked, dazed and in pain from a fractured pelvis, shoulders and arms bleeding with painful Perspex shards embedded in his flesh after he was blasted into the cold night air through the cockpit roof, Archibald hung from his parachute harness. He didn't know how far he was from the ground so didn't hit the release mechanism – airmen died falling to the ground in similar circumstances. Drifting in and out of consciousness, he came round to hear guttural voices and barking dogs, and saw torches flashing in the dark. Germans were out looking for survivors. The searchers didn't find him and it was after daybreak when a French farmer spotted him. The man returned with help, retrieved Archibald with a ladder and carried him to a farmhouse. There they tended his wounds and put him to bed.

The rescuers' plans to involve the Resistance went poof when German troops surrounded the farmhouse a few hours later. The enemy treated him well but when his stretcher was being loaded into a vehicle to be taken to hospital, they arrested a young Frenchman who embraced him, planted kisses on both cheeks and wished him well. The youngster, accused of passing secret information, was hustled off to prison. Archibald was held in Epinal Hospital until 4 August then transferred to a hospital in Nancy before being taken by rail to Paris five days later. While lying on a stretcher on a station platform, a uniformed German soldier opened his flies and urinated all over him, whereupon an officer rounded on the soldier and gave him an almighty dressing down. On 27 August, still in hospital, Archibald was liberated by the Americans as the Germans fled. Recuperating in England, Archibald took part in a scheme for airmen to visit hospitals. The inevitable happened. He met a Welsh nurse called Evelynn Morgan at Cardiff Infirmary, who became his wife. Archibald later wrote to the wife of his English navigator, John Kearney:

> Dear Betty – I must tell you what happened and I hate to do it as it will take away the scrap of hope you may have. You know what a happy bunch we were Betty, there wasn't one of those boys that I didn't love like a brother. I would have done anything to save them but there wasn't anything I could do. We were shot down without warning by a German fighter. I didn't hear anything from Wee Alec or Terry [the gunners] and by the time I realised we were attacked, the plane was out of control and the intercom out of action. I called out to them to abandon aircraft but got no reply. Johnny Cuthbert [the flight engineer] and I were struggling with the controls but something must have gone for the plane started to turn over and over. Then there was an explosion and I found myself falling … The French people who found me found your Johnny, Johnny Cuthbert, Pete and Les. They must have died instantly when the explosion occurred. There is nothing more I can say Betty, I can't offer sympathy or cheer; I can only say my heart bleeds for you both and them. There was a time in hospital when I wished I had gone too. Every little thing reminds me of them and for you it must be so much worse.

Born in 1915 in Alloa, a Scottish town on the upper reaches of the Firth of Forth, Archibald arrived in New Zealand with his parents and younger brother Daniel in 1927 and lived in Wanganui. The brothers became school teachers and enlisted 27 January 1942. Their service numbers were NZ42785 (Daniel) and NZ42786 (James). They sailed from New Zealand for Canada in October 1942 and graduated as pilots in Dunnville, Ontario. After they reached England they split up, James to 576 Squadron in Lincolnshire, Dan to 159 Squadron in India, flying Liberators.

On 11 September 1944, after 'missing' messages their father was told his injured son James was safe in England and in hospital. Two months later he was informed 'he is now walking'. An English orthopedic specialist said in a medical report the young New Zealander was 'an excellent type, a bit shaken by a bad experience'. Archibald was home in mid-February 1945, and his brother before year's end.

In 1960 James went to France to try to find where his crew were buried. His Lancaster, PB253 UL-A2, plunged down in a forest just southwest of Epinal in an area known as Renauvoid. One eyewitness wrote later to the parents of the plane's Canadian bomb aimer Peter Biollo:

> We heard a vague sound of cannon grape shot and we saw several rockets blazing. We ran to our homes and instinctively bent down our heads under the thundering noise that passed over our houses. We went out again to hear and see the most terrible of all explosions, the ground, the walls etc, were all shaking terribly. We were all hoping that it was a German plane as we watched the flames shooting up to the sky. Alas, next morning … I learned that it was an English plane, one of 'ours'.

The crash and explosion levelled a large area in woods bordering open country, snapping off the tops of trees and leaving fire-blackened trunks and branches among the wreckage. The bodies lay scattered. A seminarian, hurrying to the site in the morning hoping to find signs of life, was disappointed. 'The first had died immediately, partly burned. Another had been crushed by an engine ... another was headless.' The rear gunner was found dead, still in his turret.

Archibald found his crew's graves in the village of Chaumousey, a few miles away, saluting the men with whom he had trained and flown, wondering why he had been spared.

Malcolm Steel survived the night before the D-Day landings when he successfully ditched his Lancaster in the English Channel, twenty miles off the South Coast. He and his 101 Squadron crew were picked up by a destroyer after an hour in their dinghy. All but one of the same crew perished over Luxembourg in the late summer of 1944, flying home from a bombing run. Four hundred and twelve Lancasters headed for Russelsheim, a small city near the confluence of the Main and Rhine rivers on the night of 25–26 August. Their target – the Opel motor factory. Errant bombs had fallen on Russelsheim two years before during a raid on Frankfurt but the first specific raid on this city didn't occur until 12–13 August 1944 – a failure when most of the attackers' bombs landed in open country to the south. The results of the second August raid were patchy at best and fifteen Lancasters were lost – Steel's among them.

The sole survivor was Steel's rear gunner, a man called More. In late January 1945 his story was relayed to Wellington from RNZAF headquarters in London. Steel's Lancaster took off from Ludford

Magna about 10 p.m. on a moonless night and in good weather. Russelsheim was reached and bombed without incident. The plane flew lower after leaving the target area, gradually losing height until it was at 15,000 feet over Luxembourg.

More suddenly heard several thuds and saw flames erupt from the starboard wing and pour back past his turret. He saw neither fighter nor flak but believed the bomber was attacked from below by an enemy fighter. The Lancaster turned down into a steep dive and More heard someone say 'out'. He called up on the intercom but there was no response and he heard nothing further. More ripped off his helmet, clipped on his chute and tried to rotate his turret to get out. It wouldn't move. Desperate, he climbed head first out of the clear-vision panel above his half-inch machine guns. Halfway out he pulled the rip cord – it billowed at once and dragged him clear. Flaming petrol streaming over his face burned and partly blinded him. Keeping his eyes closed on the way down, he didn't see the Lancaster crash. He reported a normal descent and landed in a field without further injury. The bomber crashed near the tiny village of Limpach, just southwest of Luxembourg's capital.

Steel and his crew were buried locally, transferred to an American cemetery postwar and finally moved to Choloy near Nancy, the same war cemetery where New Zealand fighter pilot ace Cobber Kain lies, along with fourteen New Zealand Bomber Command crew.

Despite his burns and eye injuries, More avoided capture in the few days before the Americans rampaged into Luxembourg, captured the capital and rescued the airman. More was soon back in England, his successful jump from the stricken Lancaster earning him membership of the Caterpillar Club and his return home a place in the 'Late Arrivals' club.

101 Squadron lost a second Lancaster on the Russelsheim raid, this one without survivors. Seventeen men from 101 died – each Lancaster carried a second pilot that night – as well as the special operators. 75 (NZ) Squadron also lost two planes, and grieved for five dead New Zealanders. Two more died in other downed Lancasters from other squadrons. The New Zealand toll for the night rose to nine when bomb aimer and DFM holder James Williams (30), from Gisborne, died, baling out from a crashing 83 Squadron Lancaster over Darmstadt. He was on his 44th op, having previously flown a tour in 1942–43 with 57 Squadron. This attack was the first serious RAF attempt to pound Darmstadt and rated a failure. However, the RAF returned on a clear night the following month to destroy much of the city, in the words of Martin Middlebrook, an 'outstandingly accurate and concentrated raid'. Between 8000 and 10,000 people died in the firestorm created by the bombing.

CHAPTER 4

Sinking the U-boats

A long-term ban on attacking U-boats in Norwegian coastal waters because of the presence of Royal Navy submarines was lifted in the run-up to D-Day and the Germans, previously safe running along the shoreline, were stunned by a torrent of depth charges. They lost seven U-boats to aircraft between 1 May and 3 June. Five more were damaged.

A New Zealand *Truth* headline writer and Australian war correspondent Keith Hooper reported the story of Christchurch pilot Jack MacDonald's part in the 24 May 1944 sinking of *U-675*, one of the last submarines destroyed before D-Day.

'Avenging Death was Winged,' screamed the page-wide header in the issue of 7 June, followed by the sub-head: 'U-Boat Suffered End Meant for Prey.' Hooper's opening sentence was classic *Truth*: 'Another of Admiral Doenitz's steel sharks – his vaunted "unterseebooten" – found a watery grave in the chill waters of the North Atlantic ocean from the shattering compression of depth charges released by a Sunderland piloted by Warrant-Officer Jack McDonald (sic).' Hooper, who filed his story by 'Beam Radio and Cable', quoted MacDonald saying he considered himself one of the luckiest fellows in England as the submarine was 'pranged' on his first operational flight as captain.

MacDonald, born in Christchurch in 1914, sailed for England in March 1942. He spent fourteen months at various training units before ferrying a Catalina to join 490 (NZ) Squadron, flying anti-submarine patrols off the West African coast. During his year with 490 and a largely New Zealand crew, he was promoted to captain. He and his men flew back to England for conversion on to Sunderlands at a Coastal Command Operational Training unit at Alness in northeast Scotland. His course ended just after the clash with *U-675*.

Hooper described MacDonald as the skipper of the Sunderland on 24 May – maybe journalistic licence for a New Zealand audience, or maybe he didn't check. He certainly misspelt the New Zealander's name. Australian Flying Officer Peter Frizell was in charge, his log entry for that day noting he was first pilot with MacDonald second pilot. The U-Boat Attack Assessment report, signed by Royal Navy captain DV (Dudley) Peyton-Ward, an expert in the anti-submarine field, and countersigned by an Air Staff Air Commodore, also lists Frizell as captain. MacDonald and his men were 'trainee' crew. Frizell, in an account which his family still has, says he hopped into the captain's seat 'which had been occupied by the trainee captain'. It's clear Frizell was in command of Sunderland ML 736, but MacDonald shared in the kudos and it was one of his gunners who sighted the U-boat. Frizell believed it was one of only two occasions in the war when a sub was sunk by a crew under training. Frizell was instructing at Alness after earlier flying Sunderlands with 201 Squadron and a full tour with 423 (RCAF) Squadron. He tallied sixty-three ops with the Canadians – but no U-boat sinking.

On a day when the cloud base was 3000 feet, the sea moderate and visibility more than 30 miles, they spotted *U-675* five miles away running on the surface at 8–10 knots. The aircraft was patrolling off the big southern bulge of western Norway when the U-boat was seen, within sight of the coastline.

U-675 made no attempt to submerge, obviously intent on scrapping. She was powerfully armed with a big gun on the conning tower. The Sunderland started two attacks before unloading her depth charges on the third. On the first, the electrically operated starboard system failed and the depth charge rack on that side had to be wound out by hand as the plane continued to circle. Once the 'bombs' were in place the Sunderland closed again but the submarine increased speed, turning to port to keep its tormentor on its beam – and opened fire. Frizell turned away. 'I had always sworn I would not waste precious depth charges on a bad approach.'

According to the attack report, during the third and final attempt 'the captain seized an opportunity to go into the attack downwind.' The Sunderland began 'undulating heavily, as much as 300 feet, and the U-boat's fire, though continuous, failed to score a hit ... At one mile, 20 mm fire was experienced all round the aircraft, black puffs and tracer appeared.' Frizell:

> I ... called for the rear gunner and others to announce the instant they could see a flash from the [big] gun. I figured light travels much

faster than a shell and thus climbed, dived or turned each time he fired, and managed not to be there when a shell arrived.

The Sunderland roared in at its target just 20 feet above the sea. Frizell triggered the depth charge release and five shallow-depth-set Torpex-filled depth charges plunged down. The sixth didn't release. They fell fifty to sixty feet apart, one bouncing off the sub's deck into the water. The attack assessment noted that as the huge plumes of water erupted from the depth charges explosions subsided:

> The U-boat's bows lifted in the air until they were very nearly vertical; as the U-boat sank an explosion occurred, apparently in the U-boat itself, and it disappeared from view. Large mushrooms of bubbles appeared in the resulting swirl and merged into one patch whose centre was coloured red. Wreckage was clearly seen … oil drums, planking … bodies, parts of bodies and clothing.

None of the U-boat's complement of fifty-one survived. The submarine was on its first patrol and had sailed just six days earlier, headed for the North Atlantic. The Sunderland didn't linger. Its port outer engine was giving trouble and Frizell feared a chase by enemy fighters. 'We had sent out a sighting report as no doubt the U-boat had.' He circled for just six minutes, then turned for home and safety. Frizell's log entry was brief and to the point: 'A/S patrol to Norway – Ops. U/Boat sighted, attacked & sunk.'

Peyton-Ward interviewed Frizell for his assessment. He called it 'an exceedingly accurate attack' and Air Commodore Ivor Lloyd praised it as 'a perfect attack in the face of intense fire'. Frizell, awarded an immediate DFC for the sinking, had one regret. He had finished a full tour with his crew who were sitting in the Mess looking disconsolate the night he returned from Norway. 'They had been with me for so long out over the Atlantic and the Bay [of Biscay], and had never had a success, and on this day had not been with me. Such is Fate.'

Frizell was promoted flight lieutenant (later squadron leader) in June 1944 and posted home to Australia while his crew flew out to West Africa. MacDonald and his crew reached 490 on 5 July 44 – *sans* Sunderland. The delivery trip ended in the sea off the west coast of Africa near the edge of the Sahara Desert. Fire blazed in an engine and could not be put out. The crew took to a dinghy after a sea landing and hoisting its weather-protection sheets as sails reached shore in five hours. A rescue plane looking for them signalled for help to a group of Arabs, French camel-mounted desert troops who arrived on the beach next morning. 'They thought we were Germans at first and pointed rifles at us,' one crew member said later, 'but we said "Anglais, Anglais" and then they were most friendly.' A French patrol vessel soon arrived and took them aboard.

The margin between life and death in the anti-submarine war was slim, for both aircraft and U-boat crews, luck and chance playing a big part; nowhere more so than in the merciless Arctic waters, even at the height of summer when the sun shone twenty-four hours a day.

In a one-on-one encounter between an aircraft and a U-boat, the odds may have been in favour of the aircraft and its powerful, destructive depth charges – but the boat often won. Attacks in the face of heavy well-aimed flak from U-boats cost countless men and aircraft. Crews of aircraft plunging straight into the sea, shot down by U-boats, rarely survived the impact. Crews who ditched from planes crippled by gunfire faced three hurdles. First they had to survive a shattering landing – from flying speed to zero in an instant – which often broke the plane apart. Then they had to find dinghies and clamber into them – if they didn't, immersion in the cold Arctic with or without life jackets was a death sentence. Aircraft sinking U-boats frequently reported large numbers of German sailors in the water, but if there were no ships nearby those sailors died. Finally, aircrew afloat in rubber dinghies, pinpricks in a vast heaving sea, depended on luck – lots of it – to be found and picked up. Aircraft flashed position reports and 'we are attacking' messages so stations ashore knew fairly well where a plane was. If it didn't report in after an engagement, air searches were begun immediately and pursued relentlessly by own-squadron planes and other aircraft.

The stories of two New Zealanders on Coastal Command Liberators involve many of these elements. Both navigators serving on 86 Squadron at Tain in a remote part of Scotland, they manned the front gun during attacks on U-boats off Norway. One lived and won the DFM, one died.

Des Carter, two months short of his twenty-first birthday, cleared the deck of *U-317*'s gun crews with sustained accurate fire from the single half-inch machine gun in the nose of his aircraft on 26 June 1944, playing a major role in the sinking of the submarine off the Norwegian coast. The sub's flak damaged the big bomber but she limped home safely. Graham Richardson, much older at 32, was also in the nose on the gun when his Liberator attacked *U-968*, off Norway's west coast on 18 July. The Liberator twice zeroed in on the sub, dropping depth charges which missed their mark, and each time Richardson's gun jammed. *U-968* put up a devastating veil of flak that smashed into the aircraft. Streaming fire with a wing about to burn off, the Liberator ditched. Richardson died and two others of the nine-man crew lost their lives. Three days later the others were found by a Catalina, bobbing about in a white-capped sea, near death.

Carter, who grew up in Wellington, was learning accountancy when he enlisted. In early September 1943 he joined 489 (NZ) Squadron at Wick in the far northwest of Scotland. He'd done four ops flying Hampdens on convoy escort and anti-sub patrols when 489 began its conversion to Beaufighters. Some of the navigators, idle as their pilots learned to fly the new aircraft, were posted elsewhere. Carter joined 86 Squadron at Ballykelly on the northwest coast of Ireland in January 1944 and had his first flight in a Liberator on the 16th. He flew a couple of ops with different pilots then joined up with a crew led by English pilot Geoff Parker. In late March 86 Squadron flew to Reykjavik, a five-hour flight from Ballykelly, with its uncertain weather, to begin operations from Iceland.

Richardson was about six months behind Carter on his training schedule. A country boy, he was born in Eketahuna. He enlisted in April 1942, a farmer in a protected industry, with no requirement to serve. He volunteered anyway. He trained in Canada, and the Bahamas where he flew two ops on Mitchells, searching for subs in tropical waters. Richardson reached England in the last days of January 1944 and within a month was with an 86 detachment operating out of Tain.

Tain lies on the far northeast coast of Scotland on the south side of Dornoch Firth, one of the inner firths of the enormous Moray Firth. An ancient Scots town, Tain has a connection with New Zealand – just five miles away, the village of Fearn was the birthplace of Prime Minister Peter Fraser.

The Parker crew flew nine ops from Reykjavik without incident, before returning to Scotland. A week later in the Atlantic they got a sniff. Carter's log records a U-boat sighting. It was only five miles away but the sub must have spotted them early because it had submerged before they could attack. Another four ops without incident followed but on the fifth, on 26 June, Carter's log specifies a Creeping Line Ahead anti-U-boat patrol and the stark outcome: 'Sank U/Boat 62N-01.45E. 1st attack 5 DCs. 2nd attack 3 DCs. Oil patch, 15 survivors. No. 3 engine hit. Diverted to Stornoway [Isle of Lewis, Outer Hebrides].'

One hundred and twenty-five miles off coastal Norway, Liberator FL916-N found *U-317*. They'd taken off at 8.40 p.m. and not quite three hours later the radar picked up a submarine as they flew in and out of cloud at 500 feet – the sea calm and rippled, visibility 10 miles. Binoculars latched on to the VIIC-type U-boat and the crew went to action stations. Carter, the No. 2 navigator, went to the machine gun in the nose. The attack assessment report written by navy staff, said the boat was greyish-black with no guns forward of the conning tower but about six on the bandstand aft.

Parker broke cloud two miles from *U-317* and dived steeply to attack, using undulating evasive action. 'The U-boat opened fire at once, using light AA [flak] with red tracer, and commenced a tight turn to port.' At 900 yards Carter began to loose off a stream of fire, making hits on and in the region of the conning tower. Five depth charges hurtled down but were short of their target, the nearest exploding 17 yards dead astern.

Parker climbed the Liberator into cloud, circling to make a bow attack. Foiled by U-boat skipper Peter Rahlf who cleverly circled to port, keeping stern on, Parker accepted the challenge and four minutes later attacked again from astern, releasing his last three depth charges. Carter opened fire at 800 yards. The U-boat traded shots with the Liberator at 500 yards but Carter's machine gun silenced the submarine gunners and the flak stopped abruptly when the aircraft was 300 yards away. This time the depth charges fell in exactly the right place, entering the water alongside the starboard hull. The attack report:

> On exploding a large piece of metal from the conning tower was blown fifty feet in the air. The U-boat heeled over almost ninety degrees to port and had completely disappeared from view before [the] plumes subsided. 1-1/2 minutes later, when aircraft returned to the scene, a large oil patch, 150 yards by 50 yards, was observed with 15 survivors in the middle.

Despite Parker's jinking approach the Liberator had taken flak, damaging the port inner engine's oil and fuel tanks. It was shut down and the captain decided to return to base. The Liberator flew from the scene twelve minutes after the second attack by which time the oil slick had spread. Rahlf and all his crew, on their first patrol out from Norway, perished. Parker diverted to Stornoway, and put the plane down five hours thirty minutes after takeoff.

The navy assessment:

> A very determined second run (after good manoeuvring in cloud) in face of intense flak which was smothered by excellent gunnery from aircraft. A perfect up-track attack was delivered which put all three depth charges close up alongside U/B's starboard side and destroyed it. Excellent photographs confirm all the evidence. [Air Staff added:]

This crew is congratulated on the excellence of their final attack with the resulting destruction of the U/Boat which it merited.

Parker was awarded the DFC and Carter the DFM. The New Zealander's award was immediate, the citation saying he'd replied to the Germans' flak with 'deadly effect and completely subdued the enemy's fire'. It added that Carter 'displayed a high degree of skill, courage and resolution'.

On 18 July 1944 at 2.02 p.m. Richardson's Liberator, captained by Squadron Leader Reg Nelms, lifted off from Tain on its last patrol. The aircraft had reached 68 North and was about 100 miles west of the Lofoten Islands when it spotted a sub. The Lofotens stretch in a long chain down Norway's northwest coast, the wide inside channel between them and the mainland leading to the fjords that end just beyond ice-free Narvik, an important port and U-boat base. The sea was alive with aircraft and U-boats in mid-July – a powerful British fleet had left Scapa Flow in the Orkney Islands for a carrier-borne attack on the German battleship *Tirpitz*, hidden in Norway's fjords. The strike was cancelled when the attack fleet was well on the way because of bad weather but the U-boats were still directed to do what damage they could to the Royal Navy ships, and Coastal Command was doing its best to stop them.

Six hours after takeoff at 8 p.m. and 1000 feet up Nelms and second pilot Australian Slim Sommerville spotted *U-968*, eight miles ahead. By the time the Liberator reached the spot the sub had crash-dived. Englishman Ralph Barker, himself RAF aircrew in World War II, wrote a detailed account of the patrol and ditching of the Liberator in his book *Survival in the Sky* after talking to Nelms. He says *U-968* skipper Otto Westphalen had seen the Liberator early and thought it was going to fly on. The moment it turned toward him he knew he'd been seen and dived. The frustrated Lib crew dropped a sea marker to fix the U-boat's dive position and settled down to wait it out. Nelms began a square search, lengthening the sides of the square each time to try to keep the enemy enclosed in the search area, hoping to be in the right place when the sub surfaced.

At 10 p.m. and just when they thought they'd lost the U-boat they sighted her – on the surface. Rear gunner Dennis Cossey shouted, 'Skipper, I can see her! She's right behind us!' The navigator began sending attack and position reports to base. They were acknowledged. 'In the front turret, Richardson … was lining up his single .5 [inch] machine-gun on the deck of the U-boat. It would be up to him to silence the U-boat's guns,' Barker adds, noting there was a weight trade-off on long range Liberators – extra fuel tanks carried to prolong flight times meant stripping most heavy machine guns and ammunition. With no starboard or port waist guns and only one gun in the front turret, the only protection was the rear turret guns, which couldn't fire forward in an attack.

The Liberator was heavily outgunned by the U-boat and its cannons – 20 mm and 37 mm, and machine guns – and it would fight, not submerge. Gunners streamed out of the conning tower to pour flak at the approaching Liberator. They knew what they were doing and even before the Liberator was fully into its attack run, the German shells were uncomfortably close. Richardson began firing at 1200 yards but almost immediately his gun jammed. Somehow as Nelms guided his aircraft in from 500 yards at 50 feet on a steady line, the Liberator emerged safely from the storm of U-boat fire. The six depth charges were off target.

Richardson cleared the gun stoppage as Nelms climbed away and came around for another attack with his final two depth charges. Richardson's gun had barely begun firing on the run in when, disastrously, it jammed again. Flak began hitting the Liberator, shells smashing into the inner starboard engine, starboard wing and rear sections. Flames streamed from the wing of the stricken plane as Nelms feathered the inner engine. He turned for home but within a minute or two it was obvious the plane was doomed.

The attack assessment says Sommerville put out the engine fire and the engineer doused a fire in the rear compartment. 'Fire in main plane [wing] very intense and was burning through the structure and into the bomb bay … as wing in danger of burning off or petrol tanks exploding, captain decided to ditch.' Barker:

> Nelms eased her down towards the water and looked behind him to see if everyone on the flight deck was ready. The engineer was getting out the Very pistol so they would have something to signal with from the dinghy. The wireless operator was also in position. Richardson had come back from the front turret and was sitting at a table, bracing himself, arms raised to protect his head. Gray [1st nav] had come up from the bomb-aimer's position, and as Nelms looked around he caught his eye. Gray had been sole survivor of a Sunderland crash, and the look on his face said that he didn't expect his luck to hold a second time.

Gray survived, as did five others. Richardson, Cossey and William Daly died. The Liberator broke up on impact, the tail unit snapping off, the hood of the cockpit and the roof of the flight deck torn away, throwing the men up front straight out. All except Nelms, who went down with the sinking plane and had a huge struggle to free himself and pop to the surface. Richardson was killed on impact and the survivors found him floating in the water. Cossey and Daly floated away, the survivors uncertain if they were dead but unable to reach them. Richardson and Cossey are remembered at Runnymede but Daly's body was recovered and buried at Tromso.

The six survivors crammed into three single-man dinghies, two to a dinghy, which they tied together. (The Liberator's large dinghies, supposed to come out of wing pockets and inflate automatically, were nowhere to be seen.) They were hopelessly small and the men were wet and cold. But it was better than being in the water. Just an hour or to into the new day another 86 Squadron Lib came within half a mile but didn't spot them despite the survivors firing off most of their Very cartridges. They knew their chances were slight but a determined search was under way and all aircraft on anti-sub patrols were asked to check the area. A Catalina flew close late on the 19th but not close enough for Nelms to fire off the last Very cartridge.

According to Barker, Coastal Command HQ called off the search, saying no more time could be spared, but the order was ignored closer to the scene. Two Liberators from Tain, one from 120 Squadron, the other from their own squadron, were dispatched in a last desperate effort. The 120 aircraft spotted them – three tiny half-submerged dinghies and six exhausted, sodden, starving, dehydrated men suffering from exposure. Their last Very flare was sighted by the Liberator and the big aircraft swooped over them.

A precise location report led a 210 Squadron Catalina straight to them. It picked up the men and took off at 9 a.m. on the 21st. Missing messages to families of the nine men aboard were followed, in the case of the survivors, by word their men were safe.

It's not clear now how close to *U-968* Nelms ditched his plane. Barker says it went down 'some distance' away and Westphalen didn't know if there were survivors. But he realised his location would be known and he had to get away from the area swiftly. He also had one dead and several wounded. *U-968* was attacked again the next day by another 86 Squadron Liberator and though also surviving this attack, suffered damage serious enough to force her back to base for repairs.

Hitler's U-Boat War says RAF aircraft sank four submarines and damaged six, including *U-968*, in supporting Royal Navy and Fleet Air Arm operations against the *Tirpitz* in the last two weeks of July. It adds Coastal Command had every reason to walk tall. 'During 77 days in May, June and July it knocked out 37 boats in Norwegian waters – 17 sunk and 20 forced to abort [the navy got two others]. It disorganised U-boat operations in the area and, of course, prevented the transfer of many U-boats to the English Channel.'

U-968 and her skipper led a charmed life in perilous times for German submarines at the tail end of the war. Both survived. In early 1945, sailing against Arctic convoys, Westphalen sank the Royal Navy sloop *Lark* and wrecked another, the *Lapwing*, plus two Liberty ships and a Norwegian tanker. He was rewarded with a Knights Cross, or Ritterkreuz. On 9 May 1945 Westphalen surrendered his boat and crew at Narvik.

Just ten weeks after Les Baveystock sank *U-955* on 7 June, he destroyed another submarine, the famous *U-107*. The Sunderland skipper thus became one the few airmen to account for two U-boats in World War II, for which he was awarded the DSO.

U-107 was a legend in the German submarine service. Built in Bremen and launched 2 July 1940, just as the Battle of Britain was about to begin, the U-boat is credited with the greatest tonnage of shipping destroyed on a single patrol. That she survived until the last year of the war is remarkable, given her number of patrols. In all she sank thirty-nine Allied ships for a tally of 217,768 tons.

In 1937, Gunther Hessler, her first skipper, married submarine chief Karl Donitz's daughter Ursula. Hessler took *U-107* out of Wilhelmshaven on 24 January 1941 on her first war patrol, the first of thirteen the submarine made, and sank four ships in the Atlantic, west of Britain and south of Iceland. Four was a good beginning but Hessler and *107* were celebrated for their second trip, starting from Lorient on 29 March 1941. Back in port ninety-six days later the submarine had tallied fourteen more ships for 86,699 tons, a single-patrol tonnage figure which stood for the rest of the war. Hessler's victims were sunk off the Canary Islands south to Freetown, Sierra Leone. Among the ships sent to the bottom was the New Zealand Shipping Company's *Piako*, bound for Liverpool from Australia with a cargo of frozen food and zinc.

Hessler sank another three ships on his third and final patrol. In December 1941 he handed over to Harald Gelhaus, who commanded the U-boat for almost 18 months and six patrols from Lorient, sinking a total of eighteen ships, including the Port Line's *Port Victor*, sailing for Britain from Argentina. Gelhaus also survived the war.

Volker Simmermacher, 27, skippered *U-107* for a year and three patrols from July 1943 without sinking anything – pickings had become lean. The Allies had the measure of U-boats with an overwhelming concentration of convoy escorts, hunter-killer surface groups, huge numbers of aircraft and enormous advantages in technological and weapons systems. From mid-1943 getting across the Bay of Biscay to or from patrols had become a terrifying experience, fraught with tension and constant stress for U-boat skippers and crews. Simmermacher had to fight off aircraft the day after leaving Lorient on his first patrol in July 1943 and in January 1944, crossing the bay, *U-107* was attacked unsuccessfully from the air on the 3rd. Again, on the 7th she somehow survived attacks lasting more than an hour. *U-107*'s luck finally ran out on 18 August 1944 when Les Baveystock's 201 Squadron Sunderland crew found her in the Bay of Biscay, headed for La Pallice under Karl-Heinz Fritz (23), on his first trip as commander. Because Simmermacher was away in Germany, Fritz, his first lieutenant, was named to skipper the boat when it was rushed to sea to carry a cargo of snorkels to La Pallice. The U-boat bases on the French Atlantic Coast – Brest, Lorient, St Nazaire, La Pallice and Bordeaux – were doomed the moment the invasion succeeded. Once the Americans broke out of their Normandy beachhead, and invaded southern France in mid-August, the bases were cut off. They began to be evacuated, serviceable U-boats fleeing to Norway, carrying what fuel and equipment they could, the rest decommissioned or destroyed.

Bordeaux, in the south on the heavily mined Gironde, was abandoned by the submariners in late August; Brest, the most northerly of the bases, in September. German forces were ordered to defend the other three to the last man but the Allies simply bypassed them, their bomb-proof concrete pens empty and useless. Their garrisons didn't surrender until the end of the European war. La Pallice, the industrial harbour for La Rochelle, claims to be the last French city liberated in World War II and its still-standing pens were used during the 1981 filming of the German U-boat epic *Das Boot*.

The squadron had teamed Baveystock with a crew whose pilot had finished his tour. Among them was a New Zealander, navigator Ian Riddell from Wellington. The skipper and Riddell became good friends, Riddell often urging Baveystock to migrate to New Zealand.

Riddell joined the RNZAF in July 1941, qualifying as a navigator in Canada before crossing the Atlantic and undergoing another year of intensive training. He'd been at Canterbury University studying engineering the year war broke out and volunteered for service with the army as an engineer. Too short for the army, he ended up in the RNZAF.

Riddell reached RAF Turnberry, a Coastal Command training field on a headland on the eastern side of the Firth of Clyde, on 26 August 1942 and that evening met New Zealand sergeant pilot Alf Knewstubb, from Dunedin. Knewstubb was looking for a navigator and he and Riddell agreed to fly together. They found two wireless operator-air gunners, a Canadian and an American. For the next eight months they trained together on Beauforts and Hampdens – air firing, bombing, dropping torpedoes and flying long-range exercises which tested them all, especially Riddell, whose job it was to get them safely from one spot on the map to another, mostly over open ocean.

The Hampden was a torpedo-carrying, pencil-slim aircraft with twin tail fins. It was a sweet aircraft to fly but cramped. Crew could only change places, or escape, with extreme difficulty, posing problems in emergency. Riddell was to operate one with Knewstubb after their posting to 489 (NZ) Squadron in May 1943. Hampden deliveries to the RAF began in September 1938 and by the time war began the ten squadrons of 5 Group, Bomber Command, flew them.

Inadequate as bombers and defensively hopeless in daylight ops, by September 1942 all the Hampdens had gone to Coastal Command, mostly for use as torpedo bombers. 489 got its cast-offs in March 1942 and flew them until October 1943 when they were replaced by Beaufighters.

Riddell and Knewstubb had their first flight with 489 at Wick, a base in the far north of Scotland, on 17 May 1943 and two days later flew their initial op, a navigation and anti-submarine patrol of almost six hours. In the next six months (the squadron moved further south to Leuchars in October 1943) they did 14 ops – Rover patrols, anti-sub, air sea rescue and convoy escort – to Norway, Denmark and Iceland. They never tangled with the enemy but the endless Atlantic and bad weather posed daily dangers.

The pair parted in November 1943 as 489 began converting to Beaufighters, a crackerjack of a plane. 489's pilots had to learn to fly the new aircraft, while their navigators were idle for some weeks. Riddell flew two ops with 455 squadron, 489's Australian twin, also at Leuchars, and then early in the New Year joined 201 Squadron on Sunderlands at Castle Archdale on Loch Erne in Northern Ireland.

201 was the start of an intense phase of flying for Riddell, which included the D-Day period and lasted until the end of September 1944, when his tour expired. He did eighteen ops with a number of pilots before teaming with Baveystock, first flying ops with him on 26 June, a fourteen hours, five minutes day-night trip on a Cork patrol. At a pinch fuel-laden Sunderlands could go close to 15 hours in the air on long-range patrols but were two or three hours short of the very long-range Liberators.

By the time they sank *U-107*, Riddell had flown eight times with Baveystock and the crew had melded well with their new skipper.

The eight trips were all Cork patrols, hunting subs, preventing them interfering with cross-Channel traffic. On 19 August when they got *U-107*, Riddell let fly with an unaccustomed flourish in his log:

> 11 crew (3 pilots, 3 WOps, 2 FEs, 2 gunners [and 1 navigator]). Patrol, Bay of Biscay. Periscope sighted 1710 at 46.46 North-03.39 West. Attacked port beam. Perfect straddle. [Sub] disappeared. Debris, oil, compressed air, German charts and wood. Homed escort groups [to the scene]. Sunk. Daylight flight of 8.35.

Baveystock also let fly – he was sitting on the dunny when the alarm hooters in the Sunderland sounded three short blasts, signalling a U-boat sighting. The Sunderlands were luxurious compared with most wartime aircraft and were later turned into comfortable passenger planes. They were big and spacious; two deckers with companionways and a bridge (cockpit). In some ways they were Navy rather than Air Force. The aircraft had an anchoring winch, a small machine shop for in-flight repairs, six bunks on the lower deck and a galley with a twin kerosene pressure stove. *And*, believe it or not, a flushing porcelain toilet – a step up from the Elsan cans most larger aircraft carried. Baveystock:

> I was sitting quietly when I was shaken out of my wits. I literally leapt to my feet and snatched up my trousers, pulling braces over my shoulders. With my shirt-tails flying, I tore up the companionway to the bridge, where Ian Riddell shouted that we has just passed a submarine that was clearly showing its periscope ... [Second pilot Brian] Landers had it under observation through the binoculars.

Baveystock jumped into the second pilot's seat, one of the crew plonking his flying helmet on him and plugging him into the intercom. Depth charges run out, release mechanism checked, stick spacing set, Landers banked the Sunderland, positioning it perfectly for the attack. 'I gave Landers the thumbs up and took over,' Baveystock said. Now he could see the periscope, its long feathery wake trailing behind. 'The lookout on the periscope must have been blind not to see us. I can only imagine that he had been searching the horizon for surface ships (we had destroyers in the area) and had neglected the sky above.'

At fifty feet Baveystock pressed the release button and held the aircraft steady as the stick went down. 'Ian was watching from the astrodome and, together with our mid-upper and rear gunners, clearly saw the stick drop across the U-boat's track, three on each side.

> As we turned to port, the rear gunner shouted excitedly that the U-boat was attempting to surface ... [but] ... I believed that he was not trying to surface but had been lifted by the force of the explosions ... The sea was boiling with the vast amount of compressed air that was coming to the surface, and was white over an area fully one hundred feet in diameter. As we passed over it, taking photographs from the galley hatch, the sun shining deep down into the dense rising column of air bubbles caused it to take on a brilliant light green appearance. This eruption of escaping air continued for the best part of twenty minutes, bringing up thick oil and debris that spread out over an ever-widening circle.

Finally the eruption of air and debris slackened, leaving two locations, about fifty feet apart, from which two thinner streams of air bubbles continued to surface. 'This made us believe that the third DC in the stick had actually split the U-boat into two sections.' Baveystock flew home to acclaim and within a few days a DSO. The veteran *U-107* lay broken on the floor of the Bay of Biscay, her complement of 58 all dead. She had sunk thirty-nine ships in her long career. Now it was her turn. Later, Baveystock remembered: 'This attack was just too easy … an easy target.'

Baveystock and Riddell each flew their last op with 201 on 29 September, Riddell clocking up twenty with the squadron to complete his tour – and his war. He and his skipper went down to London together on leave. Wrote Baveystock:

> Ian, not a very strong person at the best of times, had become an absolute cot case. There was only one navigator in a Sunderland crew, and he worked with his head down on every trip. He had to keep a continuous DR [Dead Reckoning] plot, take a wind check every fifteen minutes, and work out our new position each time. This was not too difficult perhaps when flying from A to B but on patrol when we were flying a pattern with continuing changes of course having to be worked out, he was as busy as a one-armed paper hanger. The squadron doctor had ordered Ian into hospital for a few days' rest. Instead I persuaded the doc that I should invite him to spend his leave with Betty [his wife] and me in London.

Riddell logged just under 1000 hours of flying, more than 500 on operations. Tour over he was repatriated, arriving home in February 1945. Baveystock eventually immigrated to New Zealand.

CHAPTER 5

Operations most secret

Flying at low level over the French countryside, anywhere really in occupied Europe, on moonlight nights, crew searching for signals showing a Resistance reception party was ready and waiting at the Drop Zone was a dangerous business. Getting to the right dropping place at the right time was important for the people on the ground, who couldn't hang around long – groups were conspicuous. The bomb aimer lay in the nose of the aircraft map-reading the way to the DZ, aiding the work of the navigator doing the basic work. The route was planned in advance but the crew needed to be on course and the bomb aimer carefully following his maps and the ground below, tracing their path by what he could see below – roads, train tracks, villages, cathedrals, chateaus, rivers, canals and other geographic features. Moonlight was essential so the best time for SOE flights meant good weather and the period as the moon approached full and for some days after. Unexpected cloud added greatly to the hazards faced by planes and their crew. Airmen knew what a vital role the Maquis played and that they couldn't operate without supplies. Pilots were reluctant to fly home with their loads still aboard and often gambled, venturing below safe heights in cloud to find DZs. Sometimes they killed themselves and their crews.

Reception teams used signal lamps, torches or lit fires to identify DZs but as 1944 wore on the Resistance began to make greater use of the remarkable British Eureka-Rebecca system, whose signals could be picked up by aircraft 120 miles away. Scientists had designed the portable, easily assembled, ground-operated Eureka, and the aircraft-borne Rebecca direction finder to identify DZs in occupied Europe and help accurate air-drop deliveries – a step up from bonfires and torches. Sutherland remembers with gratitude the Eureka impulses transmitted by a South African agent from a Norwegian ice cave on one long trip. 'A Godsend to receive them on our Rebecca set 90 miles out from land after flying across the North Sea for one and a quarter hours at 250 feet above the sea.' The impulses from the Eureka ground transmitters played on to a screen in the aircraft through external aerials on either side of the cockpit.

The Stirlings and Halifaxes employed on the SOE flights were packed with goodies for the Maquis – everything from Brens, Stens and other weapons to petrol, boots, ammunition, bicycles, motor bikes. They even dropped Jeeps, slung under four parachutes, for SAS use in France. Sutherland grins recalling the night he carried a container of lacy underwear for women of the French Resistance. Late in 1944 the New Zealander tackled the new chief of 38 Group, Air Vice-Marshal James Scarlett-Streatfield. Normally tight secrecy surrounded the cargoes the planes were carrying. 'They wouldn't tell us what was in the containers,' Sutherland says. So I talked to

Scarlett-Streatfield and told him, "this is not a fair go, because if there's ammunition or petrol in there instead of boots it's a different kind of cargo and I think that in an emergency at least the skipper of the aeroplane should know what we are carrying." I got that past him and after that they told the skipper what was in the cargo.'

Sutherland, in the early stages of studying for a science degree in Christchurch, joined the RNZAF in April 1942 after trying for the army. 'You've got flat feet, don't waste our time,' he was told, so it was the air force. After getting his pilot's wings in Canada Sutherland was posted to 34 OTU at Pennfield Ridge on the Bay of Fundy, New Brunswick, to convert to Venturas. 487 (RNZAF) Squadron, operating Venturas, would need crew and Pennfield Ridge would provide them. The pilots at 34 formed complete crews and it was there that Sutherland and the nucleus of the men who would fly with him for the rest of the war came together – navigator Colin Rouse from Christchurch, gunner Reg Vincent from New Plymouth and Australian wireless operator, Ian 'Nix' Nixon. The plan for Pennfield Ridge crews to serve with 487 (NZ) Squadron and other Ventura squadrons fell apart when the American-designed light day-bomber proved unsuccessful. 487's attack on an Amsterdam power station on 1 May 1943 cost eleven of twelve aircraft dispatched, with heavy crew losses.

The RAF was loath to break up trained crews so although a few Ventura pilots and navigators eventually went to Mosquito squadrons, many, like Sutherland's, ended up on 38 Group Stirlings flying SOE/SAS operations and taking part at Normandy, Arnhem and the Rhine crossing. When the Sutherland crew arrived in England they flew Mitchells for a month at an OTU before postings in November 1943 to 299 Squadron at Stoney Cross in Hampshire –

on Venturas. But they and other New Zealanders on 299 were soon on their way to 190 Squadron at East Leicester via 1665 Heavy Conversion Unit, at an airfield called Tilstock in Shropshire. Here they learned to fly the big four-engined Stirlings and picked up the fifth and sixth members of their crew – bomb aimer Dave 'Bertie' Bertram, another Australian, and English flight engineer Eric Algar. This largely Anzac crew called their Stirling at 190 *It's Easy Cobber*, with nose art of a flying kiwi with a bomb in its beak and a 'roo with a container in its pouch.

They arrived at 190 at East Leicester in mid-March 1944 and before month's end were at Fairford. They immediately took part in concentrated glider-towing, para- and container-dropping training in preparation for the invasion. They towed gliders for the big army ground operations at Normandy, Arnhem and the Rhine crossing, interspersed with SOE and SAS flights to France and, after the Germans were evicted from most of France in August 1944, to Holland and Norway.

The log books of Sutherland and Rouse show two major SAS drops in France, Houndsworth and Bulbasket, both aimed at blocking German reinforcements bound from southern France to Normandy, and disrupting German communications. Both were ordered by Supreme Headquarters Allied Expeditionary Force (SHAEF). Houndsworth, centred around Dijon in central eastern France with troops of A Squadron, 1 SAS, began on 6 June with the dropping of a reconnaissance group and ended three months later, a huge success.

Bulbasket, operated by B Squadron, 1 SAS, over the same time frame east of Poitiers, ended in disaster. Betrayed, the group's hideout was surrounded and attacked by the Germans. Thirty-three SAS troops were captured and executed. Another three were murdered in hospital and a number of Maquis also killed. French civilians were lined up and shot.

Sutherland and his crew dropped sixteen SAS troops and fourteen containers of weapons and supplies for Houndsworth the night of 21–22 June and on their next flight over enemy territory on 3–4 July dropped twenty-four containers and four panniers of supplies for the Bulbasket team.

On one long flight into the depths of France to drop paras, their Stirling was hit by fragments from an 88 mm shell burst right in front, as it crossed the coast. The windscreen in front of Sutherland shattered so he jumped into the second pilot's seat and with difficulty pulled the plane out of a steep dive close to the ground. Several instruments failed but he pressed on with his shaken paras. At low level the team found their DZ but Sutherland spotted an enemy truck convoy, lights dimmed. 'The paras would have been shot before they reached the ground.' The French leader, an officer, objected to Sutherland's decision not to let the troops jump, saying his men would sooner face almost certain death rather than go through the chance of flak damage and the big dive again.

> Very reluctantly, the officer calmed his men down and we turned for home. On the return trip as we climbed over Le Havre one motor failed, a broken con rod, and as we came up to the UK coast we were told a blanket of fog covered our base and we were to land at the first clear drome we found. So we went in at Ford, a fighter field on the South Coast, with strict instructions that crew and paras were NOT to talk to anyone. Early in the afternoon a small convoy of Humber Super Snipes from MI5 picked up the French and were gone. I learned the paras did jump successfully about two weeks later.

Five 190 Squadron Stirlings flew on SAS operations the night of 22–23 July 1944, delivering paras on Operations Gain, Wash and Rupert. Two of the five skippers were New Zealanders; Watty Brain (26) from Oamaru, and Danny Kilgour. Dennis Williams, in Stirlings with the Airborne Forces, says Brain – dead four months later on a training flight – came home to a message from France saying he and another pilot had made 'impeccable' drops at Wash DZ, and a congratulatory note from Air Vice-Marshal Les Hollinghurst, 38 Group chief.

Kilgour was another story. Williams says Kilgour's aircraft was to drop Rupert's advance party of two officers and four men of 2 SAS plus two signallers. These men plus the crew of six and two dispatchers made sixteen on the plane. The paras, commanded by a major, spearheaded a group planning to disrupt rail transport around Metz in northeast France.

Williams records that the Stirling crew failed to see any signals at the primary DZ and was on its way to another when it crashed into high ground near the village of Graffigny-Chemin about 40 miles southeast of Nancy. Three men survived the impact: two crewmen, the navigator and rear gunner, and one paratrooper. With French help the gunner evaded. The other two were captured. Navigator Joe Vinet is quoted by Williams:

> A stick of eight paras was to be dropped near Chaumont, but by deciding to nip in between the cloud base and the ground we clipped the forest and ploughed in. Our air gunner, Paul Bell, wasn't injured so the French moved him into Paris and back to the squadron … The one para and I were carried off and hidden, but were hospital cases, so the local doctor dictated, and we were sent via Chaumont military hospital to internment.

Bell was quoted in a letter from Air Secretary Tom Barrow in Wellington to Kilgour's distressed father in March 1945, when he was trying to find out more about the loss of his son. Bell described his experience surviving the crash on a wooded hill just over a mile west of Graffigny: 'I know very little of what happened because at one moment we were flying along smoothly and the next thing I knew was that I was picking myself up in a very dazed condition from the wreckage of the aircraft which was burning.' Bell couldn't hear anyone else, crawling off into the trees to be found by the French.

Kilgour, known as Danny but officially Leonard Alfred Arthur, was born in Palmerston North just before Christmas 1919. When he enlisted in mid-1942 he was working as a telegraphist. It's not known how many ops he'd flown before his death but he had completed several successful SOE/SAS drops and flew in the Normandy landings.

He was one of only two New Zealanders lost on SOE/SAS operations in July 1944 despite the huge number of flights as the RAF gave the French Resistance and their own SAS men on the ground a rising tide of weapons, ammunition and supplies to create increasing mayhem behind enemy lines in actions to support British and American troops on the Normandy battlefronts. The only other New Zealander killed in July while dropping supplies was Wesley Hunniford (24) from Pukekohe, bomb aimer on a 296 Squadron Albemarle lost without trace on the night of the 11–12. Hunniford is remembered at Runnymede.

Early August signalled a tough time for New Zealanders flying on SOE trips to places with fancy code names, eight men losing their lives in the space of four nights. The bad run began on the night of 4–5 when two crashes left four New Zealanders dead. Navigator Ian Blaikie and wireless operator Ken Morgan died when their 161 Squadron Halifax crashed southeast of Reims, and pilot Ted Robinson and his bomb aimer Ihaia 'Ike' Trainor were killed when their 620 Squadron Stirling was hit by flak and went down in Normandy. The next night when Ron Reader escaped death by the skin of his teeth as his 298 Squadron Halifax crash-landed in France, 299 Squadron pilot Henare Uru and his navigator Robert Braddock died in the wreck of their Stirling, another flak victim, in a village on the edge of Quiberon Bay on France's Atlantic coast. Three nights later on 8–9 August, a fighter caught pilot Graham Paterson's 138 Squadron Halifax over France as it returned from a drop in Belgium and shot it down. Paterson (22), from Invercargill, his bomb aimer Lewis Searell (20), from Wellington, and the rest of the crew were killed – except the rear gunner, Frank Evans, who was sheltered by the French and soon back in England.

If anyone deserved to survive the war it was Blaikie. The Napier landscape gardener left New Zealand in February 1941 at the age of 22, did a long tour on Wellingtons in the Middle East earning himself a DFM, and ferried aircraft between Britain and the Middle East. He returned to England to instruct before joining 161. It's thought he was on his twenty-sixth op with 161 and would have finished with a tally of about eighty ops. He was part of a vastly experienced crew. The pilot, an RAF flight lieutenant, held a DFC and New Zealander Ken Morgan, still only 21, had completed no fewer than forty-five ops with 161, first on Hudsons and then Halifaxes. An old boy of Mt Albert Grammar in Auckland, he was commissioned less than four months earlier. Errol Martyn says the Hali went down near the village of Huiron, three miles from the town of Vitry-le-Francois. An RAF dispatcher was the sole survivor and evaded capture. Martyn adds the plane carried a 'substantial' amount of money for the Resistance.

Robinson (21), from Wellington, and Trainor (32), from Rotorua, were both married but neither had children. Trainor, like Uru, was Maori. Maori served and died in Britain in the air force, flying in the entire range of trades from pilot to gunner, but the deaths of two just a day apart was unusual. Their Stirling was carrying supplies for British SAS troops on the ground around Dijon in central eastern France but was far short of its target when it was caught by a flak burst and crashed in Normandy, seven miles west of Lisieux.

Frank Evans, the sole survivor of the crashed 138 Squadron Halifax skippered by Graham Paterson (22), from Invercargill, told his story in *Night after Night*. The Halifax, which had dropped supplies to a Resistance group in Belgium, was hit and shot down by a fighter near Troyes in northeast France as it began a big circular swing south to head for the Channel. Evans, in the rear turret, remembered the plane in a shallow dive then an explosion in the forward part of the aircraft. He heard Paterson calling urgently, 'Bale out, bale out!' then shot back over the intercom, 'What about you, skipper?' Paterson responded, 'Don't worry about me … go, go.' Evans clipped on his chute, shed his helmet and intercom leads, swung the turret and, hanging half out, pulled the ripcord. The chute snapped open, jerking him clear. A few minutes later, dazed and bruised, he woke up on the ground, the Halifax wreckage blazing fiercely 300 yards away.

Another New Zealander was lost on an SOE trip on the night of 30–31 August, the last such casualty for four months. Aucklander Robert Macduff, 26, a navigator, died when his 298 Squadron Halifax failed to return from a trip to a DZ near Diest in eastern

Belgium. *For Your Tomorrow* records how another aircraft reported seeing a Halifax thought to be Macduff's shot down by ship's flak off the Dutch coast. The New Zealander, who'd been on 298 for five months and flown fifteen ops, is remembered at Runnymede with the rest of the crew.

Ray McGregor (24), another Aucklander, also had fifteen SOE ops behind him when the 138 Squadron Stirling he captained was lost in similar circumstances on 30–31 December 1944. The plane was carrying supplies for a drop in the interior of Norway at a spot 150 miles northwest of Oslo. Flying up the Skagerrak to approach the DZ from Norway's eastern coast, it was caught by flak fired by a ship off Arendal. *For Your Tomorrow* says the crew of another plane on a similar op saw flak and a 'terrific flash'. The lost crew's names are remembered at Runnymede.

She is Beatrice 'Robbie' Shearer now – and has been for sixty-five years, a happy wife, grandmother, great grand-mother. But she still mourns the death of Ted Robinson, the young New Zealand pilot she married. They met at a YWCA dance in late 1943 in Leicester, the east Midlands city where Beatrice lived with her parents. Robinson had just joined 620 Squadron at Leicester East, a new RAF base close to the city. They married on 15 April 1944. He had turned twenty-one the month before, the skipper of a Stirling crew training for glider towing and paratroop and supply dropping. She was just eighteen. The bride wore white, the bridegroom handsome in his pilot officer's blues. Robinson's bomb aimer, 'Ike' Trainor, was his best man. The rest of the crew watched from the pews. Robinson had leave from 620 Squadron, now based at RAF Fairford in Gloucestershire, and he and his new wife spent their honeymoon at Colwyn Bay, Wales. When it was over he returned to duty, she to her parents' home and job. In 1944 married couples didn't live on base.

The Robinson crew came safely through Normandy. They dropped paras near Caen on the night of 5–6 June and returned to the same area in late daylight on D-Day with a glider in tow. Then they went back to training and to SOE flights on moonlight nights. Robinson and his new wife snatched whatever time together they could; just an occasional twenty-four hours' leave pass and his seven days off every six weeks. They were married not quite four months when he was killed. Robinson, Trainor and the rest of the crew plus a second bomb aimer and two army dispatchers perished the night of 4–5 August as their aircraft crossed Normandy on its way to drop supplies to SAS troops. Severe ground fighting was still going on in Normandy and the Stirling was hit fatally about midnight by a shell or fragments from an 88 mm anti-tank gun. The barrel could be elevated and one round from the artillery unit probably accounted for the Stirling. A single hit, or a close explosion, would have been enough.

The Stirling plunged down in a field just outside the tiny village of Notre-Dame-de-Livaye, west of Lisieux. The village lies in the heart of the rich Normandy hedgerow country, fifteen miles from the sea.

According to village mayor Paul David, on whose fields the Stirling crashed, the aircraft exploded violently into flames on impact, burning and smouldering for four days. The RAF's Missing Research and Enquiry Service, the unit that investigated crash sites to try to account for missing airmen and aircraft, made its first visit to Notre-Dame-de-Livaye on 2 October 1944, and others followed.

As late as September 1945 officers of No. 3 Mobile Section (France) were still trying to piece together what had happened to the nine men on Stirling LJ920. They concluded all had died instantly when the plane hit the ground. But there was a grisly aftermath. The MRES said the Germans found human body parts 'all over the place'. Only one body was almost complete. The Germans told David they had been 'able to account for eight and a half bodies and they got rid of the remains by throwing them into the blazing aircraft.' Such action was considered a war crime. Forced labourers working for the artillery unit named the German culprits but it seems no action was taken. The MRES recovered the identity discs of the English flight engineer and no graves were ever found. Eventually a few bones were discovered and buried in a collective grave at Tilly-sur-Seulles War Cemetery. Individual headstones honour the lost men.

The chilling 'regret-to-advise' missing-on-air-operations telegrams began to go out on 5 August to the families of LJ920's crew once it became clear the plane was not coming back – one to Beatrice Robinson in Leicester, another to Robinson's parents in Wellington, another to Trainor's wife in Rotorua, one to the mother of rear gunner Peter Sturges in Muradup, a tiny country settlement in southern Western Australia, another to Wingham, Ontario, to the parents of Ramsay Habkirk, the Canadian second bomb aimer. And others to the families of the rest of the crew who lived in various parts of Britain.

All round the world they lived in hope their husbands or sons would somehow be alive, perhaps POWs, perhaps on the run in enemy territory. They had little idea of what their men were doing, what 'operations' involved. They would have had letters from 620 Squadron's CO saying how sorry he was and not to give up hope.

There wasn't much else he could say. He couldn't tell them the only thing they wanted to know – whether their men were alive. He didn't know.

The waiting dragged on. Hope diminished when there was no word from the Red Cross of the crew in POW camps. As late as 20 May 1945, when most POWs were back in Britain, Pearl Robinson wrote from Wellington to Ivy Sturges in Australia, saying that because no bodies were found 'we think the crew all baled out and were probably taken prisoners. We're hoping to have news within the next few weeks.' She offered Mrs Sturges a photo of her son and his bride with the crew: 'We are looking forward to meeting our daughter-in-law Beatrice as she seems a lovely natured girl and writes to us twice a week. She has had word from our N.Z. government saying she can come out … [but] … will wait for definite news of Edward before she decides anything.' (She did move to New Zealand, stayed and remarried).

The news that Trainor was missing on air operations was a hammer blow to his parents who were still mourning the loss of his younger brother Tahae (25), dead of wounds in Italy on 24 May, a little over two months earlier while serving with 28 (Maori) Battalion. He died from loss of blood after his legs were shattered by shrapnel from an exploding artillery round at Cassino. His sister Kay MacDougall was only a young teen when her brothers were killed but remembers what a blow it was for her parents. Only a year earlier the family thrilled to the news that Tahae, a sergeant, had won the Military Medal for gallantry during the New Zealand assault on Takrouna in Tunisia. He and the nine remaining men of his platoon charged machine guns covering two 75 mm guns. 28 Battalion's official history says: 'He led his party straight at the pocket, silencing the guns and taking twenty-seven Germans prisoner.' Trainor rests in the war cemetery at Cassino.

Tahae Trainor was single but his brother Ike had wed Iris Takirua Boynton not long before he enlisted on 7 March 1942. There were no children. A graduate of Lincoln Agricultural College, Ike was managing a farm in Rotorua when he joined the RNZAF.

Ike Trainor sailed for Canada in July 1942 and reached England in January 1943. Six months later he and Robinson met and crewed up on Wellingtons at 11 OTU Westcott before learning to fly Stirlings and the posting to 620 Squadron.

Rear gunner Ron Reader jumped from his blazing 298 Squadron Halifax over Normandy in the early hours of D-Day. Flak hit the aircraft after it released its glider on target just north of Caen. Skipper Charles Anderson, RCAF, ordered the crew out and everyone survived, falling in British lines. Reader was unhurt but probably stunned at finding himself on the ground – even if uninjured, jumping was an unnerving experience. The New Zealander was back in England in a few days.

After survivors' leave for the rest of June Reader, back on ops, flew two SOE drops to France in July and another two on 1 and 2 August. He was lucky to survive his next. His Halifax took off just before midnight 5 August on Diplomat 9 in support of SAS troops on the ground, bound for a DZ near Dijon. The plane was one of a mixed group of thirty-eight Halis and Stirlings dropping men and supplies.

Fifty miles short of Dijon the aircraft was intercepted by an ME 110 night fighter and shot down. The aircraft was too low for the crew to jump and Anderson took the burning Halifax down, managing to keep the nose up to make a good crash-landing, according to Oliver Clutton-Brock in his book *Massacre over the Marne*. The plane came down about 2 a.m. on 6 August a couple of miles northeast of the village of Essoyes.

The crash killed Anderson. The others escaped with various hurts, some minor, some serious. The crash tore off the gun turret and it's thought Reader, who woke up in hospital, suffered pelvic injuries as it careered along the ground. Crew who scrambled clear of the wreck made off but Reader (24) was found by Germans and taken to hospital. His captivity was short. Four days later the American 3rd Army, driving east, overran the area. When he was well enough Reader was moved west and reached England on 18 September for further treatment in an RAF hospital. His war over, by 18 February 1945 he was home in New Zealand.

298 Squadron CO Derek Duder had to write twice to Reader's next of kin, his sister in Auckland. After Normandy he said, '… Unfortunately the aircraft never returned …' and on 7 August he had to do it again. 'Your brother, P/O R. F. Reader has again been reported missing …' No doubt Duder was relieved when Reader finished flying.

New Zealanders Henare Uru and Jack Braddock, pilot and navigator, lie with the rest of their crew in the wall-enclosed communal cemetery of the the Britanny village of Plougoumelen, killed the night of 5–6 August 1944. They are the only war casualties in this small graveyard lying close to the shoreline of Quiberon Bay.

A victim of flak, Uru's Stirling fell in flames from 1500 feet, crashing on one of several joined-up stone-frame farmhouses on the outskirts of the village. The six-man crew and three people in one family died in the huge explosive fire following impact. None of them had the slightest chance of survival. Residents of the other dwellings escaped with their lives but their homes lay in smouldering ruins amid the stink of aviation fuel. Burned parts of the plane lay scattered in close-by fields. The crew's bodies were burned beyond recognition and only one identity disc was found, that of Australian Len Tunson, from Preston, Victoria.

In the circumstances the people of Plougoumelen could have been forgiven for resentment toward the RAF men who came without warning at night, visiting death and destruction on a sleeping village. Instead, the crew members are remembered as heroes. More than 1000 people from Plougoumelen and the surrounding countryside watched as the fliers' remains were lowered into a collective grave in the cemetery, headstones erected postwar by the Commonwealth Graves Commission. The graves are tended and flowers still placed regularly. The road leading to the centre of the village passing the burned-out dwellings was renamed Rue du Cing Aout 1944 (5 August 1944 Street) to honour the dead airmen.

Uru's 299 Squadron, 38 Group aircraft took off from Keevil, Wiltshire, an hour before midnight, packed with supplies for a French Resistance group at Baden, just a couple of miles from Plougoumelen. The operation carried the code name IAN 7. The aircraft was crewed by a Commonwealth team – the New Zealanders, two Canadians, an Australian and a Briton, the latter, as usual, the flight engineer. The area where the Stirling was hit by flak was not one where Uru and his team might have expected such gunfire – a quiet rural area with no big war industries. But 20 mm flak guns, probably coastal defences, caught the Stirling at 1500 feet as it crossed Bono, just over a mile from the Baden drop target, according to eyewitnesses. The crew wouldn't have had any warning. Suddenly the plane would have been a flying bonfire – no one had time to jump. A school teacher called Le Rouzic recalled seeing and hearing the Stirling getting lower, its engines now and again revving.

> Soon I saw a flame at the base of the tail. The plane kept coming down and I thought it was going to crash on the school. No, it passed over, skimming the roof. Then I heard an explosion and saw a bright light … [He and his wife hurried down the street to a second school] … I thought that perhaps the plane contained bombs and we [took] refuge behind the cemetery wall …
>
> Eventually I returned to the village in front of the church. The flames illuminated the clock tower … In front of the Sommer house [people] were putting a ladder to get on the roof to hose it to prevent the straw and hay of the granary from catching fire. Behind, a horse refused to leave the burning stable and a pig, a little burned, was squealing as it escaped. The tyres of the plane were burning with the landing gear with a magnesium light. The aluminium was melting and the burning fuel was running into the gutter. We thought of the [Le Rays] trapped in their house. We went to have a look from the back but it was impossible … When day broke, we could get nearer to see the extent of the catastrophe.

Jean-Marie Le Ray, his wife Marie Francoise and daughter Mathurine perished as their home took the full brunt of the crash.

Henare Whakatau Uru (23) was known to his family and friends as K – nothing else. Jack Dawber, a close friend as they grew up in Christchurch, and later a navigator on 500 Squadron in the

Mediterranean, says Uru was small because of childhood illness. The youngster was known by everyone as 'Cupid', later 'Kewpie' and finally K. Uru was the second son and third child of a family of four. K had an elder brother, another John, the father of Bill whose sons Storm and Jade have rowed successfully at Olympic and world championship regattas. K was working on a farm at Oxford when war broke out and among the earliest to enlist in the air force, joining on 20 September 1939. Two years later he was chosen for pilot training, and eventually joined 299 Squadron. He was on his ninth operation the night he was killed.

Uru's navigator Jack Braddock (26) was a Hutt Valley man. His mother was a Whiteman and her father cut and milled trees in valleys running off both sides of Upper Hutt. Whitemans Valley, now a leafy suburb, bears the family name. The young Braddock went to Hutt Valley Memorial Tech. When he enlisted in November 1941 he was shovelling coal with the railways. He went into the air force for pilot training but his training was terminated and in April 1942 he sailed to Canada for navigation courses. When he graduated he was posted to Pennfield Ridge, where he crewed up with Uru and flew on Venturas. The two of them sailed on the same ship to England in May 1943 and followed the same path to 299 Squadron and, eventually, to their deaths in France. Neither man was married but Uru was engaged to a woman in Oxford when he was killed.

William Pembroke Bell was big – six feet and solid in the way of Hawke's Bay sheep farmers. Blue eyes, fair hair. A strapping frame for a start, hardened by the outdoor life. He was known to everyone as Bill but inevitably the air force bestowed the nickname 'Dinger'. It had a good ring to it. Arnold King met him when they learned to fly in mid-1942 on Course 29 in the South Island. Bell was eleven years older than King but they became good friends. In a late-life memoir, Wellington-born King remembered Bell as 'a large, rugby-playing bloke, as strong in physique as in self-reliance. He showed amusement often with a high-pitched giggle. And he relentlessly rolled his own.'

It's not quite clear why Bell joined up, at almost 30, from a protected job. Perhaps it had something to do with the death in England of his pilot brother Peter, five years younger. The Blenheim on which Peter flew as second pilot on an OTU night-training flight in August 1941 was shot down, crashing near Ely, Cambridgeshire. All three on the plane died. The Bell boys were cousins of AE (Arthur) Clouston, the famous New Zealand aviator and wartime pilot.

King and Bell didn't travel on the same ship as most of their course. The new pilot officers sailed on the liner *Mauretania* as she left Wellington on Christmas Eve 1942 with a draft of 177 aircrew for training in Canada. 'I rejoiced to see him,' King wrote of Bell, apprehensive after learning he was going to be more or less responsible for the draft under the direction of Ray Somerville, a flying officer bound for a desk job with the RNZAF in Ottawa. 'Our leader outlined the daily routine – one of us would lead the boys at PT, the other would provide a lecture. There was a sort of growling noise: "Leave the poor blighters alone," said Bill. "They'll get pushed around enough in Canada." And that was the end of that subject.'

Before the ship left, the draft was lined up on the promenade deck and Minister of Defence Fred Jones appeared. 'He and the people of New Zealand were proud of us – blah blah. He then wrung every hand and pushed toward the gangway but not before another growling noise and a voice measuring many decibels above stage whisper at my elbow said, "that two-faced conchie", who must have been stone deaf not to have heard but didn't twitch a muscle. Labour Party politicians were not top o' the charts with the farming community.' For the record, Jones wasn't a conscientious World War I objector.

Befitting their officer status, lowly as it was, King and Bell enjoyed enormous staterooms and a French menu as the ship steamed for San Francisco. They rode the train to Vancouver and across Canada to Halifax to join the *Andes*. In England they trained together before postings, King to 218 Squadron, Bell to 620, both 3 Group Stirling squadrons.

218 transferred from 2 Group in 1940 and remained with 3 Group until war's end. 620 had an entirely different life, not formed in 3 group until June 1943 and then switched to 38 Group, the glider-towing and transport outfit, the following November. 620 crews welcomed the end of operations over Germany, which had cost the squadron seventeen Stirlings. Bell flew a search and rescue op and two mining trips before he did his first and only bombing op with 3 Group – to Mannheim, the night of 18–19 November. Enemy fire claimed twenty-three bombers, one from 620. Bell made it home unscathed. The next night the squadron finished its time with Bomber Command, participating in a failed raid on Leverkusen. The attack also marked the end of the Stirling's role as a Main Force bomber. It was too vulnerable – it couldn't reach the operating altitude of the Halifax and Lancaster and the design of its bomb bay restricted its bomb-carrying capacity.

Bell and other 620 pilots flew their Mark III Stirlings from 218's Chedburgh field to muddy, unfinished RAF Leicester East and on

25 November began the training flights that would lead to SOE Operations, and six months later to Normandy. On 19 December squadron CO Derek Lee towed a glider off the field for the first time and early in the 1944 New Year 620 was joined by the first elements of the re-formed 190 Squadron, which was to fly the new Mark IV Stirling. 620's bomber Mark III Stirlings were adapted for their new role – the mid-upper turret (and its gunner) disappeared, while towing gear and other refinements were added. The Mark IVs came off the production lines without nose and mid-upper turrets, a large hole with doors in the aircraft's rear floor through which paratroops and supplies were dropped, and fitted glider-towing equipment.

Bell pulled his first glider off the runway on 16 January, under supervision of another pilot officer. In early February Bell was one of several pilots who took their planes and crews to RAF Hurn, for the squadron's first special duties SOE flights – dropping supplies to Resistance groups in France. The small detachment stayed at Hurn for a couple of weeks and in that time Bell was thoroughly blooded, flying ops the nights of 5–6, 8–9 and 11–12 February over France. He had no problem but SOE drops were dangerous. One of the handful of 620 Stirlings at Burn was shot down, crew dead, and another, badly damaged, crash-landed on return.

The heavy training schedule continued, hardly interrupted by the two squadrons moving to Fairford on 18 March: glider cross countries, container dropping, parachute dropping, group exercises. And then D-Day was upon them. Bell carried 18 paratroopers to the drop zone near Caen, an hour or so into 6 June. He was out again on the night of 7–8 June, one of two aircraft carrying advance elements of 1 SAS, one of the five regiments making up the SAS Brigade. 1 SAS was establishing an Operation Bulbasket base in the wooded hills of the Vienne region in the deep south of France. For Bell it was a long six-hour return flight. Dennis Williams in *Stirlings in Action with the Airborne Forces* says one of the aircraft couldn't get a reception signal but Bell did. He 'reached the DZ late but observed three white lights, plus a fourth flashing the recognition letter B. As the Stirling flew over the DZ at 600 feet, an officer and eight men jumped with their kitbags and were quickly followed by nine containers packed with supplies and equipment including a Eureka homing beacon.'

Bell flew another five container-dropping ops in June and July and then on the night of 9–10 August made his name and won an immediate DFC. Four 620 Stirlings set off with French paratroopers of 3 (French) SAS for a DZ in the Saone-et-Loire area, about 200 miles southeast of Paris. Three of them couldn't get a reception signal and took the French troops back to England. Bell got nowhere near the DZ, his plane ending up in the sea somewhere off Cherbourg. Bell wrote almost nothing in his log except the bare essentials but this night warranted a few comments: 'Operations – 8 paratroops, 1 dispatcher, 16 containers. Ditched on outward journey. Picked up by ASR launch 2556 and taken to Cherbourg.'

LJ866 was normally Bell's Stirling but this night he skippered EF256, a plane he'd flown before. Flak winged the plane and the inland Normandy battleground of St Lo has been suggested as the source of the gunfire, perhaps from trigger-happy Americans. Another account, by a French writer, has the flak coming from German batteries, further west near St Malo. No one knows. What is certain is that the crippled EF256 went down in the sea, Bell doing a masterful job of getting the big Stirling, a machine notoriously difficult to ditch, safely on the water in the dark.

Flight engineer Arthur Northfield, knocked cold and severely concussed, wrote an account years later for the *Stirling Times*. It is unreliable in some details but he was clear on what happened when flak found them:

> … we were hit at 5000 feet, first in the port inboard engine, losing the propeller and rupturing the inboard petrol tank, allowing petrol to flood into the cabin. We were ankle deep and not smiling [two other engines failed]. Bill shouted, 'Hang on, we are ditching.' Then another shell burst in the rear of the plane wounding Stan [Dutton], our gunner, and one of the French paratroops. Bill was finding it difficult to control the aircraft [and] asked Ace (Philip Anstruther, the Australian bomb aimer) to give him a hand and the two of them managed to [get the plane into] a level glide. Meanwhile, I was undoing the astrodome and the top hatches and getting the ladders ready for when we hit the sea.

Northfield, standing and off the intercom, missed hearing Bell say 'prepare for contact'. The impact threw him onto the cross spar and knocked him out. 'I hit my head and don't remember a lot afterwards.'

Bell's wireless operator, Dennis Bridges, coolly sent off a Mayday and a precise position report. The ASR, positioned in Cherbourg with three high-speed launches, responded instantly. They found the men in their dinghies an hour out of Cherbourg and were back an hour later. HSL 2556 brought in all six of the crew, six of the eight French and their British dispatcher. One Frenchman was killed in the aircraft and a second drowned. Colin Hanson, in *By Such Deeds*, wrote that Bell dived into the water to rescue one man who couldn't swim. The rescued thirteen were treated overnight in an American hospital, awarded and embarrassed by purple hearts, US wound decorations, and back in England on survivors' leave within two days. Bell's mother received a message on 12 August reporting her son missing, followed by another just two days later. 'Pleased to advise he is now reported safe and returning to his unit.' She had already lost one son and must have wept over both telegrams.

Bell's immediate DFC, gazetted in late October, noted he had accomplished the ditching with great skill. 'In trying circumstances this officer displayed courage and leadership of a high order.' Bell flew at Arnhem and on the Rhine crossing operation in March 1945 and did several long, dangerous flights to Norway late in the war.

In recent years French divers working with enthusiasts researching wartime aviation in the area have discovered several aircraft wrecks on the sea floor off Normandy's coastline in the general area where EF256 might have gone down. They have located one upside-down Stirling with wings and engines still attached but seventy years underwater have stripped away identifying squadron codes and serial numbers. So far divers haven't been able to figure whether the plane had a mid-upper turret. If it doesn't, it's almost certainly a Stirling used for SOE/SAS flights – such planes had only a rear turret. Researcher Mickael Simon says the project is hampered by the fact the team hasn't been able to find any trace of messages from RAF or ASR records to pinpoint the exact position the plane ditched. The wreck being investigated lies at a depth of about 50 metres, near Cape La Hague, a little west of Cherbourg and a mile offshore.

CHAPTER 6

On the run in Occupied Europe

Fighter pilot Jim Mortimer got a lot more than he bargained for the afternoon in October 1943 when he flew his Spitfire across the Channel with 485 (NZ) Squadron to meet and protect a homebound squadron of Boston light bombers: eleven months on the ground in France. He spent all that time dodging Germans, shuttled by the Resistance from safe house to safe house, sheltered all the time by the French; enduring a series of highs when he thought he was on his way back to England, lows when he found he wasn't. Eventually, three months after the Normandy landings, Mortimer was freed by the Americans.

Mortimer, born in Auckland in 1916, volunteered for aircrew as soon as war broke out but had to wait until April 1941 to join up. He left for Canada and pilot training in July that year, among a group of 103 that included such future fighter pilot luminaries as Keith Taylor-Cannon, Vaughan Fittall and Warren Schrader. With his wings and in England, Mortimer flew Spitfires with 122 Squadron, then transferred to Malta, flying a Spitfire to the embattled island from the carrier HMS *Furious* in mid-August 1942. He flew two tours there with 126 Squadron and was credited with a couple of German aircraft. On 25 October, on patrol with fellow New Zealander Nigel 'Tiger' Park, a nephew of Air Vice-Marshal Sir Keith Park, then Air Officer Commanding in Malta, his friend's aircraft was riddled in combat. Appalled, Mortimer watched Park's starboard wing fold up. The stricken fighter, in a deadly spin, plunged into the sea. Park, who'd been in Malta a month longer than Mortimer, had been awarded the Distinguished Flying Medal and was commissioned just before his death. A standout pilot, he was already a double 'ace' with ten enemy aircraft destroyed during his short time on the island.

Back in England in February 1943, Mortimer 'rested' for the usual six months, training bomber crews to evade fighter attackers. He was posted to 485 and within three weeks was in the sea fighting for his life. He was disgruntled that day, long before he ended up in the water. On the morning of 3 October he'd left Biggin Hill at dawn, flown to Manston on the South Coast and then across the Channel to escort Marauders, which had been deep into France on a bombing raid. Safely home he was told he was finished for the day. But his relief failed to arrive and his refuelled, rearmed fighter was without a pilot as the squadron prepared to fly again. 'I was obliged to rejoin and take part again. Much to my disgust,' he wrote in a family memoir.

This time the squadron was to meet Bostons, also homebound. German fighters swirled around the bombers, attacking heavily. 485's Spitfires joined the melee and Mortimer engaged an FW 190 at high level, the scrap ending with Mortimer downing the German at ground level. Now low on fuel and ammunition, the New Zealander turned for the coast but was spotted by another 190. The two clashed head on. Mortimer later claimed the 190 as a second victim but it was a pyrrhic victory as bullets thudded into his own engine. 'Oil spewed everywhere, my windscreen became useless and each time I tried putting my head out of the cockpit [to see where I was] I received a face full of oil.' Engine failing, Mortimer managed to reach the coast but couldn't make height to bale out and had no option but to ditch, always difficult in engine-heavy Spitfires, which usually flipped hitting the water. Somehow Mortimer managed, struggling to the surface as his fighter hit the shallow bottom of the Somme Estuary and eventually clambered into his dinghy, collapsing into unconsciousness. When he came to he could see the White Cliffs of Dover but France was closer, three to five miles away. His watch had stopped at 3 p.m. Mortimer passed out again. Night had fallen when he revived and the tide had carried him south into the small fishing port of Le Treport, twenty miles northeast of Dieppe. His little dinghy carried him through open lock gates; German guards on either side didn't see him. The tide bore the dinghy well past the town up the Bresle River. As the tide peaked and began to fall Mortimer didn't fancy his chances of surviving another trip through the lock. 'I had now to leave my dinghy and make a one-man invasion of France.' And try not to get caught.

So began Mortimer's big adventure. He clung to branches of trees similar to mangroves as the tide fell, then plodded up muddy channels to firm ground. He was miserable, wet and cold, his uniform saturated with oil and coloured with yellow marker dye, his face caked in dried blood from hitting his cockpit gunsight when he ditched. For several days he stumbled away from the coast, receiving help from the French he met – dry clothes, some food, his first taste of French wine, directions east. From a hiding place on his fifth day he watched groups of Catholic brothers walking a forest trail. Eventually he approached two of them. One spoke English. He said they'd return after nightfall and take him back to their school, which proved to be out of the ordinary.

> Was led through the woods and was amazed as I entered a story-book chateau that was their school. Now came the best part. They told me I would be safe as they had no dealings with the Germans at all and would I like a shower. Certainly enjoyed that shower as I was encrusted with salt, grime and blood all over. Afterward I was helped up flights of very steep steps to a bedroom high in a turret and was given food and drink. Thankfully turned into a bed to appreciate a decent night's sleep.

The chateau was in the village of Sailly Flibeaucourt, north of the Somme River. Mortimer stayed with the brothers some weeks, recovering, and only once left his hiding place – at the request of the brothers, to visit a forest some miles away that had been bombed. The area contained nothing of importance but the New Zealander was able to tell the brothers the area had probably been bombed because of Resistance suspicion it harboured troops and armour.

Mortimer had his first contact with the Resistance while he was at the chateau and finally he was moved and put in an escape line that had been used in late 1943 by fellow New Zealander and 485 CO Johnny Checketts. He hoped for a speedy return to England but was hurriedly moved elsewhere when the line was compromised. Hiding place followed hiding place – ten in all. He spent Christmas

1943 in Saint Quentin, giving the children of the people with whom he stayed English lessons and visited the local cinema.

In his memoir Mortimer says he was set to escape by air several times but arrangements collapsed. One planned pick-up by Lysander in May 1944 failed when the aircraft was shot down and the house where Mortimer had been sheltered was stormed by Germans, its occupants shot. He was quickly moved elsewhere. After D-Day, Mortimer says the Resistance assumed the war would be over in a couple of days and gathered Allied evaders together, despite pleas that this was dangerous. Once it became clear the war wasn't going to be over quickly the men were separated and Mortimer was taken to the home of a village butcher, where he stayed for ten weeks. 'We had simply to wait until we ourselves were liberated.' Which is what happened on 2 September when the Americans overran his hiding area. Mortimer was back in England on 8 September after two days in Paris, eleven months after being shot down, and was on a ship on the way home to New Zealand when the war in Europe ended. His DFC, awarded in June 1946, praised Mortimer's conduct in France: 'He displayed great resolution and unfailing courage in the face of great odds'.

Joe Helean arrived on 486 (NZ) Squadron in late October 1943. Four days before Christmas he dropped the bombs slung under his Typhoon's wings on a Somme V-1 site. Diving to attack, his engine stuttered and failed as he pulled away. Too low to bale out, the outcome was a crash-landing five miles west of Abbeville, the German fighter base outside the town of the same name. He emerged from his cockpit knowing German troops had seen him coming down. Dazed, he staggered away, no time to destroy the plane. After reaching a patch of woods, he walked along the Somme until he spotted a Frenchman on the the other side waving to him to keep down. The man crossed the river on a nearby bridge and came to his aid. Helean was taken to the man's house and put in touch with the Resistance. After a long bike ride and a car trip he was deposited further east in the tiny three-room home of an elderly couple in Varennes, a small village of about 600. And there he stayed from Christmas Eve until 2 August 1944.

Helean said in his later interrogation report that during this time he was able to move around the countryside fairly easily because the forces of the FFI (French Forces of the Interior), the formal name for Resistance forces, were well organised and closely protected evaders. Helean even helped the FFI on sabotage trips. Attempts were made to get him back to England but something always went wrong. Eventually his hosts' house bulged with relatives and, at the end, several other air force evaders. He was moved to another dwelling and was there when liberators arrived in Varennes a month later. Five days later he was back in England.

New Zealander Sid Gay and his all-British crew were on their 28th op the night of 10–11 April 1944 when German anti-aircraft fire put an end to it all over France. Flying low on a run to drop supplies to a Resistance group, light flak hit their 90 Squadron Stirling. With the plane on fire and no chance of baling out, Gay had no option but a crash-landing.

Luck rode with them as the big plane hit the ground, crashing through trees in a wooded area. Astonishingly everyone got out of the blazing wreck in one piece. Gay (30), from Napier, and three others raced off from the scene and for ten days, often hungry, wet and tired, they eluded German patrols searching for them. Surprisingly, they were never put in touch with the Resistance. Heading for Spain, they got as far as Vichy France, now occupied by the Germans, where they believed they might have a better chance of getting help. Instead collaborators gave them up to local police who turned them over to the Germans. They had given it their best shot.

While he was a POW in Sagan, Gay wrote an account of their crash-landing and adventure on the ground in a Red Cross diary. Their last flight began from 90's base at RAF Tuddenham, Suffolk. The airfield, three miles from RAF Mildenhall, was completed in the autumn of 1943 and 90 Squadron moved there in the October. Because the squadron was still flying Stirlings, it was roped in when demand for aircraft for SOE/SAS operations outpaced requirements.

Loaded with supplies for a Resistance group in central France near Bourges, 125 miles south of Paris, Gay took off at 10.43 p.m. on 10 April. He and his crew had an uneventful flight until Gien, a small town on the Loire. In 1940 bombs had razed much of Gien as the Germans tried to destroy its bridge.

Gay and his navigator probably felt they were safe flying overhead at 200 feet at 3 a.m – what German gunner would be awake and at his post at that hour of the day? But someone was. The big Stirling must have filled the gunner's sights as he let fly, hitting his target. The Stirling crash-landed about one and a half miles southwest of Gien, near the village of Lion-en-Sullias on the south bank of the Loire. Gay wrote:

> The aircraft was in very bad shape. Both starboard engines were feathered and on fire, most of the wing was on fire and the bomb

bays were blazing merrily. I had hoped to put out the fires with the Graviner [an engine fire extinguisher system] but it could not cope. I did not have the height to dive and put out the flames but the most cheering sound on the way down was Tom Foreman. The rear gunner was still blazing away at the flak position … I was not strapped in and came to under the 2nd pilot's seat with the cockpit full of stifling fumes in spite of Reg [Prior], the navigator, having opened both cockpit windows. We tried to get back to 'Sleepy' [Taylor], the mid-upper gunner, from whom we heard nothing after being hit, but we could not get through the smoke and fumes, and the starboard fuel tanks started to explode so we had to get out. I crawled through the escape hatch above my seat, followed by Reg, Smokey [wireless operator Smokey Latchford], Denny [bomb aimer Dennis Storer] and Johnny [flight engineer Johnny Allen]. We threw away our chute harnesses and Mae Wests and made off through the woods. Johnny missed us and afterwards we discovered [he] met up with Tom and Sleepy [and became POWs]. Before we had gone very far Denny kept saying, 'I have lost my ear', but he still had it though it had nearly been torn off. We then heard Tom and Johnny calling and answered them but we missed each other in the woods and could not hang around too long. Our object was to get as far away as we could from the aircraft and cover as much ground as possible before daylight. [They had gone about a mile when the Stirling blew up with an enormous blast, sparking a blaze that lit the sky for half an hour. As daylight approached the men went to earth in a tiny wood and tried to sleep.] Around 8am we had a cigarette and took stock of our situation. There were four of us in good health, uninjured in enemy-held territory where we expected the natives to be more or less friendly … If we could … avoid capture for three days our chances of getting assistance and getting to Spain were good … If we couldn't get assistance, as long as we could beg or steal food we would be there in about 60 days.

New Zealander Les Brown and Englishman George Griffin, down in southwest France the same night, were put into the hands of the Resistance almost immediately, then shuffled from group to group. But the Gay party had no such fortune. And without it, a 60-day march to the Spanish frontier seemed wildly optimistic. They knocked on a good number of farmhouse doors, were well treated and sometimes fed. But four men were conspicuous. Nowhere did they strike a family who seemed to be in touch with the Resistance. Perhaps it was just bad luck, or perhaps the Resistance was thin on the ground in their area. They were often wet and cold, drenched by heavy spring rains, hungry, sometimes very thirsty. Usually they slept on the ground in small forested areas, gathering layers of leaves to lie on. Wrote Gay of one such bed-down:

> My turn to sleep in the middle tonight. After last night we discovered the two in the middle were moderately warm while the two on the outside froze. We woke up frozen at 8am and had our Horlicks tablets for breakfast. [Their best experience came at a large farmhouse. They wanted to sleep in the barn but the farmer insisted on beds in the house, beds with thick mattresses and big eiderdown quilts.] They also proceeded to prepare what to me was the best meal I ever had. They broke fourteen or sixteen eggs into a large frying pan and made a very large omelette which we ate with plenty of bread and clean white lard. This was followed by a large bowl of apples. After surviving on bread and whatever we could scrounge, we rather made pigs of ourselves.

They kept walking, crossing small rivers and canals, visiting farms, seeking food. One young man they met in the yard of a farmhouse trailed after them, telling them the woman they'd spoken to was a collaborator. He then took them deep into a wood and showed them a small stone building where they could shelter. Desperate for a smoke, they asked him for cigarettes. He had none but said he could get them on the black market. Gay and his crew had plenty of escape-kit money and handed over a fistful. They didn't think they'd see the youngster again but he reappeared as they were bedding down for the night. Their money had bought four loaves of bread, a large piece of cheese, three small cheeses, a slab of boiled bacon, a pot of jam – and cigarettes. Their saviour, offended, refused more money. 'After he left us we had a good tuck in and smoked half a cigarette.' Denny's 21st birthday didn't turn out too badly after all. And they had enough food for the next day.

> We woke about 5am, frozen, and set off on our way just before dawn. We were all very tired and footsore about 11 a.m. so we holed up in a big wood after travelling about seven miles, gathering wood as we walked. We lit a fire and dried our socks and boots, been wet through for about three days. We lay there until 2.30 p.m. and we ate our remaining food and got our boots quite dry.

So it continued, until the afternoon of the tenth day on the run, when they squatted in a deserted house down a lane in a small village, their clothes sodden with incessant rain. Someone had seen them and the mayor of the village, accompanied by other men, came knocking on the door. He brought food, as did a few women. But just before they prepared to move off 'four Gendarmes with rifles and revolvers dashed in and it was all up. All our trouble was to no purpose. We were prisoners.' They were captured about twenty miles south of Bourges and had covered more than seventy miles south toward Spain.

Three days later they were in the infamous Fresnes Prison outside Paris before being taken across Germany to spend three weeks in a Gestapo jail in Wiesbaden – accused of being spies. Then Dulag Luft, at Oberursel near Frankfurt, for more solitary confinement and bouts of endless interrogations before a day or two at the nearby satellite camp of Wetzlar. And a hot shower, the first for six weeks, and Red Cross parcels with two packets of Camels. Finally to Sagan. Gay wrote that after meeting up there with Denny, who'd sorted out a spot for him in his hut, he 'turned in and had a wizard sleep'. The Allied invasion of Europe was just five days away.

New Zealand pilot Les Brown shouted to be heard over the noise of the roaring petrol-fuelled flames and the plane's exploding ammunition. 'I'm off into the forest. Who's coming with me?' Rear gunner George Griffin answered his call and they hared off, disappearing among the trees. The other three survivors of the crash, more shaken and battered, chose to head for help at the farmhouse whose lights they could see a few hundred yards away. So began Brown's four-month saga dodging and fighting the Germans in southwest France in mid-1944. Eventually he scaled the Pyrenees and got back to England and a well-deserved Military Medal, a rare decoration for an airman.

It all started at Fairford, Gloucestershire, home to 190 and 620 Squadrons, on 11 April when rookie pilot Brown flew his Stirling to Tarrant Rushton in Dorset to load supplies to deliver to

Resistance forces. Kenneth Merrick in *Flights of the Forgotten* notes pre-invasion pressures continued to mount in April, reflected in the increasing number of support aircraft drawn into the special duties programme. 38 Group participated on a much larger scale and Bomber Command's 3 Group again committed 90 Squadron and its Stirlings. Merrick says the US had begun similar operations on 5 April when their two squadrons, known as the Carpetbaggers, sent seventeen Liberators to France.

In improving weather, 38 Group dispatched a record fifty-five aircraft the night of 11–12 April to drop men and supplies to Resistance groups in occupied Europe, mostly in France. Fifteen Stirlings from the two Fairford squadrons took part. Thirty-eight of the aircraft found their target drop zones, flashing torches on the ground indicating it was OK to unload. Just two of the group's aircraft were lost that night – both piloted by New Zealanders doing their first op. Brown survived, becoming a hero to the French, but Peter Croudis perished with his entire crew. He had trouble taking off, his Stirling twice swinging badly to starboard as it rolled down Tarrant Rushton's runway. Croudis wrestled the plane off the ground and it climbed away to starboard. A few minutes later it nosed over and spun in, exploding on farmland a bare eight miles from the airfield. Croudis (24) was a West Coaster from Greymouth. His navigator was fellow New Zealander Doug Sampson, also 24, from Ngaruawahia. They'd crewed up together to fly Venturas at Pennfield Ridge a year earlier and stayed together until their deaths.

Brown, 26, a school teacher, was a flight sergeant, his crew all also sergeants aged between 21 and 23 – with one notable exception. George Griffin was 'old' at 35 and commissioned, a pilot officer. The Londoner was married with two children. He volunteered when the war began and trained as a wireless operator. Grounded by a perforated eardrum and posted to the RAF Regiment, he underwent weapons training. Later, as RAF casualties soared, Griffin was re-accepted for aircrew as a gunner.

The Brown Stirling, on Operation Wheelwright, flew low across the English Channel, climbed high to avoid coastal flak then sank again, often down to 500 feet as the bomb aimer lying in the nose of the aircraft helped the navigator, map reading to the drop zone under bright moonlight. They were headed for an area southeast of Bordeaux, on the edge of the vast pine forests of southwest France. They avoided Bordeaux and its flak-heavy defences, then followed the Garonne, the major southwestern waterway. The river was easy to see in the moonlight and the crew had no trouble spotting the big bend at Langon. They were 50-odd miles short of their target DZ at Lagrange when alert German gunners on the ground heard them and opened up. Their fire was accurate, scoring hits on the port wing, and soon both engines on that side were on fire.

The plane flew on for a few minutes while Brown looked for a place to crash-land. There was no question of jumping at such a low height. Griffin had been firing at the guns that hit them, tracer showing where they were, and barely had time to scramble forward and hunker down behind the main spar as Brown ordered his crew to crash positions. Brown picked what appeared to be an open field but turned out to be a patch of forest. It was almost midnight when the Stirling smashed through the tops of pines and crashed to earth, grinding along the ground to end up against a huge oak tree. With engines flaming and plenty of fuel left in the wing tanks, fire erupted. The crew scrambled frantically to safety through escape hatches but navigator Benny Barnett never made it. The three who chose the farmhouse for help were welcomed but other people living nearby called the Germans and the trio were soon captured and taken to hospital for treatment.

The plane had come down southeast of Bordeaux in a tiny village called Anzex. Brown and Griffin, slightly burned but otherwise uninjured, raced off on dark forest paths. Farms in cleared areas dotted the countryside and the men were sheltered by brave French families who assisted Allied airmen at grave risk to themselves. Early on they were taken in by Jean Darrouman who lived in an isolated farmhouse four or five miles from the crash site with his wife, their six children and his parents. The man built the fliers a hideout deep in the forest, where they stayed for a fortnight. He got them medical help and contacted the Resistance. According to family lore, one of the children realised Granny was cooking more than the family was eating and when she spotted her carrying food into the forest, figured the old lady was consuming more than her share.

From the Darrouman farm the two airmen were shuttled from one Resistance group to another in forested areas, which made eluding German army patrols, the Gestapo and the hated Vichy French militia – the Milice – easier. The German occupation of Vichy France in November 1942 bolstered Resistance numbers as young men fled into the forests to avoid Nazi roundups for forced labour in Germany. Numbers grew dramatically as the invasion neared and the RAF responded with drops of weapons and military supplies and SAS paratroopers, French and English, to give professional guidance and help. A sprinkling of anti-Fascist Spaniards fleeing the Franco regime bolstered the movement.

The huge Resistance area, bordered by Bordeaux, Toulouse and the Pyrenees, was where the Wheelwright network run by

Englishman George Starr operated. Starr, code name Hilaire, was infiltrated into the Gascony region in November 1942, posing as a Belgian mining engineer. He was a mining engineer and, ironically, after the war helped rebuild Germany's coal-mining industry. The BBC has called him one of the SOE's most successful wartime agents, his network harassing the Germans in the run-up to D-Day. 'In the spring of 1944, [his] Armagnac Group swung into action, blowing up railway lines, cutting telephone wires, sabotaging fuel dumps and disrupting communications.' The BBC adds the network's main campaign came after D-Day itself, when the 2nd SS Panzer division (Das Reich) tried to move from the Toulouse area to Normandy. 'In a series of daring attacks, Starr's Resistance fighters forced the division to fight their way north, so they eventually arrived disorganised and far too late to attack the Allied invasion beaches.'

John Griffin, who wrote an account of his father's time in France, says Griffin and Brown first met Starr in early May. The Englishman told them he had standing instructions from London to return evading aircrew to England immediately via the Pyrenees and Spain but because D-Day was so close he wanted them to give raw young recruits weapons training. Once the Allies waded ashore there were other and more pressing tasks. On the night of 7 June, the day after the Normandy landings, Starr dispatched a group of men in a small car to sabotage a railway line. Brown and Griffin were to ride shotgun but the vehicle was so crowded Griffin found himself squeezed onto the car's floor. They ran into a roadblock. John Griffin says the Maquis (Resistance) thought it was men from their own side. Shouting greetings, they leapt from the car to be met by shots – Milice manned the road block. 'Brown, never slow to react, ran for his life, escaping unscathed.' Griffin, trapped, became a POW.

Brown never wrote or talked to his family about his time on the ground in France. A rare account of his exploits with the Maquis is in Anne-Marie Walters' 1946 book *Moondrop to Gascony*. Walters, a WAAF fluent in French, was recruited into the SOE and parachuted into France in early 1944 to act as Starr's courier. She led a charmed life for more than six months, travelling all over the region for Hilaire.

Walters met Brown, code name Mike, for the first time on D-Day at Starr's headquarters in the tiny village of Castelnau-sur-l'Auvignon, four miles northeast of Condom, a town of about 7000 and centre of the armagnac brandy-producing area.

Brown was introduced by Starr: 'A New Zealand pilot who has just joined us. He was shot down a month or two ago and has been moving from maquis to maquis. Now he will stay with us for a while.' Walters, code name Colette, wrote that Brown was six feet or more [actually 6 feet 2 inches] with 'large blue eyes in a thin bird-like face. He stuttered a little because he was shy and stepped out of [Starr's] car like an overgrown spider.'

Castelnau-sur-l'Auvignon, perched on a high point and thus not easily surprised, was an ideal spot from which to launch guerrilla attacks and Brown took a full part in sabotage. He earned great plaudits for his role in defending Castelnau on 21 June when it was attacked, taken and destroyed by German troops. When it was clear the village was to be besieged, women and children were evacuated, leaving the Maquis to defend the hilltop. Brown and his Bren gun were to cause the Germans no end of trouble. In the confused situation as the men prepared their defence against the 189th Division, a reserve outfit, not a front-line unit, Brown spoke to Walters. 'Why do Frenchmen get so excited? I don't understand anything that's happening. I'm going to the command post.' The Germans are said to have pitted about 700 troops against 150 Maquisards at Castelnau, suffering four dead and upwards of twenty wounded. French historian Guy Labedan says the Resistance had four Maquisards and seven Spaniards killed. A couple of civilians also died. The Germans set fire to the village as payback and blew up the larger buildings. Postwar Castelnau was awarded the War Cross, the only village in the region so honoured, and today the road through the hamlet is called Avenue 21 June 1944.

After the battle, one fighter told Walters about Brown's heroics. 'You should have seen him fighting. There he was, right in the front line, firing single shots with his Bren gun … Single shots! I ask you! One, then another, bang, bang! And every time you'd see one of the Boche in the [grape] vines drop to the ground, or little puffs of dust rising just next to him … Ah, what a man!'

Walters added:

Mike, l'Anglais (the Maquisards never remembered his patient explanation of how he was not an Englishman but a New Zealander), became the legendary figure of the Castelnau fight. Everybody spoke of his calmness and his accurate shooting, while a lot of the boys wasted ammunition, excitedly firing long bursts from their automatic firearms. Later on the men would go and ask Mike's advice on all sorts of things. 'First, I can't understand what they say,' he would tell me, throwing his arms to the sky; 'I don't know a damned thing about guns and grenades. I try to tell them I'm a pilot, not an army instructor. But they don't understand me either – what a picnic! Ah, what wouldn't I give for a glass of beer in a quiet pub.'

Walters was ordered back to England in late July to carry secret papers, and Brown and five other Allied evaders were told to go too. The little party climbed to safety over the Pyrenees, the mountainous dividing line between France and Spain, then travelled through Spain to Gibraltar and home to England. On 14 April 1944 a telegraph boy had delivered the dreaded 'missing on air operations' message to Brown's parents in the South Island. The telegram carried the usual 'don't give up hope yet' rider. On 5 June another telegram announced, 'Your son is safe but in enemy territory.' On 12 September the parents received the one they wanted: 'Safe in England'.

The citation accompanying Brown's Military Medal, announced in the King's Birthday honours of June 1945, as well as noting Castelnau, also disclosed he'd taken part in a later battle at Estang. 'He manned a Bren gun and operated at the most dangerous points of the line. He showed an outstanding example of cool courage and daring.'

Brown was flying again in late November at 81 OTU on Whitleys and then returned to 190 Squadron in March 1945 in time to take part in the Rhine crossing, towing a glider.

Navigator Jim Insull guided his 622 Squadron Lancaster, carrying a heavy load of high explosives, to the railway yards at Trappes, just outside Paris, the night of 31 May–1 June 1944. Back safely at 4.30 a.m. he found two crews missing. One of them carried Briton Flight Lieutenant Pete Berry, a rear gunner, Insull's room mate at RAF Mildenhall. That afternoon he helped Adjustment Committee officials sort out and list Berry's gear and pack his bags. The RAF moved quickly once a man was missing. Insull wrote in his diary:

Our room looks very bare without all the photos of his actress girlfriends pinned round the walls, without parts of guns piled in different corners, and without heaps of clothing and odds and ends strewn about. But I expect I shall be better off for sox and handkerchiefs – the only things of mine that would fit Pete. Alex [Insull's skipper] has moved in to take Pete's place. He says he does not mind sleeping in a dead man's bed. 'Even before the body or the bed is cold.' But Pete is only 'missing'. There is still a chance.

There was. On 2 October Insull wrote:

Pete B, my old room mate is safe! He walked into my bedroom last evening … He just said, 'What cher, cock!', as if he had never been away. I said, 'What cher, Pete, what kept you?' 'Engine trouble', he replied. But later he told me what happened.

Twenty minutes before they were due on target a German fighter hit them and set two engines on fire. The skipper told them to jump. Bill Chorley's *Bomber Command Losses* says Berry's Lancaster came under sustained attack from a Ju 88 and exploded, throwing Berry from his turret. He was the only survivor.

Berry landed in a small wood, buried his chute, took a southerly bearing from the small compass in his escape kit then jog-trotted for more than five hours. He parked himself in a thick hedge and next morning hailed an old French farmer on a horse pulling a cart. The man returned at nightfall with food and old clothes and Berry was soon in the hands of the Resistance. Eventually he was delivered to a wooded area and camp holding more than 100 British and American airmen. The men's hopes of rescue grew after the invasion and one night the entire camp was led to American lines and handed over. Berry was back in London and safety in a few days.

Like many others, bomber pilot Ron Clark went down on his first trip before he had a chance to play his part in the war. But he survived and was on the run in Belgium for three months before the Gestapo pounced.

Clark, an Aucklander, was three weeks short of his 23rd birthday on 27–28 May 1944 and making his debut as second pilot prior to flying with his own crew, when his 75 (NZ) Squadron Lancaster was shot down. The target: Aachen, at the tri-nation border with Holland and Belgium. The aircraft, skippered by Christchurch man Frank Scott, carried a 12,000-pound load to add to Aachen's misery but never got there. Clark watched what was going on with intense interest that night and years later wrote about what happened:

> The plane reached 20,000 feet over the enemy [occupied Holland] coast and after 15 to 20 mins target indicators were seen approximately 70 miles distant on the starboard side. At the same time the mid-upper gunner reported enemy fighter flares 10,000 feet below us on the starboard side; also a fighter [with] navigation lights. The German fighter turned off his lights and made for the plane. It was a perfect night, half-moon shining on haze. Three minutes later the fighter got underneath our plane and gave a two-second burst. That burst began a fire in the fuselage which could not be extinguished. [The fighter] then gave us another burst. The skipper gave the order to bale out and I was second out of the plane.

For Your Tomorrow says the Lancaster broke up in the air after being shot down, the wreckage falling west and north of Gilze, a town six miles from the Dutch city of Tilburg. Scott (28), a drapery traveller in civvy life, and his 21-year-old bomb aimer Stephen Cook from Gore died with the RAF wireless operator. Clark, navigator Les Hill (31) from Christchurch, who was wounded in the attack, the RAF flight engineer and both gunners survived. Scott and Cook had both done twenty-seven ops. Two 75 Lancasters were shot down that night. The other plane, skippered by Spencer 'Spanner' Fauvel (21) six days earlier, went down over Belgium. Fauvel, from Wellington, was on his thirty-first op. He and the rest of his crew, three New Zealanders among them, perished.

Clark says he passed out through oxygen deprivation as he swung beneath his parachute at high altitude and when he came to was hanging in a tree six feet above the ground.

> After releasing myself and dropping to the ground I discovered that I was wounded in my right leg and my face was badly scratched [and bloodied] by the branches of the tree. After a short rest I headed due west by pocket compass but came across barbed wire entanglements. For half an hour whichever way I travelled I bumped into wire. I soon discovered I had landed in a German camp.
>
> At 4 a.m. I managed to get out of the wire enclosure and discovered I was travelling due north so I turned in a NW direction across fields. I took cover in a wheat field and stayed there about two hours.

Three days later, thirsty, hungry and very sore, Clark met a cyclist who took him to his home and showed him on a map that he was near Breda. The New Zealander was fed, had his wounds dressed, given a pair of shoes and then headed for the Belgian border, still walking. On 1 June, two or three miles into Belgium, he was almost picked up by a German patrol but avoided the enemy by hiding in a roadside drainpipe. Found by a teenager, he was taken to the boy's home where he stayed five days. His saviours alerted the Resistance and he was shifted to Antwerp. From safe house to safe house – once in a luxury apartment – although some weren't exactly safe. Several times he left barely ahead of the Germans.

Clark stayed seven weeks in one building containing an electrical shop and living quarters that were subject to constant scrutiny and Gestapo checks. Each time a patrol threatened he was rushed to a straw-lined hole dug in the large chicken coop in the back yard, a tight-fitting lid clamped down and earth and hen poop brushed over. The Germans tramped through the yard but never suspected the coop. On one visit they discovered the people caring for him listening to the BBC. Because the couple were agitated and under suspicion, rather than put them at further risk Clark decamped, contacted a Resistance member and was found sanctuary for three weeks in a Catholic hospital staffed by nuns also hiding wanted Belgians. Germans appeared weekly but the nuns shuffled Clark and the others about in a maze of corridors, rooms and buildings, always one step ahead of the searchers.

Finally Clark was moved for one night to another safe house and told that the following day he'd be passed on to a guide who'd take him across the border into France to an escape line. The go-between, a nervous little old man, took him to an Antwerp park and introduced his 'guide'. From there to an apartment building, into a room and questions. Gestapo. The Germans knew a lot about him – where he'd crossed the border and stayed and more. Someone had informed, the escape line penetrated. The Germans marched him out of the building to a car and drove to Gestapo HQ. More questions, then Antwerp Prison. It was 23 August and he'd been loose for almost three months. On 4 September Clark, other airmen and Belgian prisoners were hustled out of the prison, on their way to a POW camp, two and a half hours before British troops hoisted the Union Jack over the city.

New Zealand navigator Bill Cook's month-long 'adventure' on the ground at Arnhem began at 12.20 p.m. on 21 September 1944 when Stirling LJ946 took off from Fairford with Englishman Jack Carey at the controls. It should have been back about four and a half hours later but the squadron's ORB records 'missing' against LJ946. It's still missing, seventy years later. No one knows what happened. Everyone – the six-man crew and the two army dispatchers – baled out and got down safely. But the plane? One of the enduring Arnhem mysteries. Last seen flying away, empty of men. On fire.

Few aerial operations of the war have been so dissected as the RAF's week-long flights in support of the doomed British attempt to capture the bridge at Arnhem – 'the bridge too far'. Researchers have tramped every inch of the area around Arnhem looking for remains of aircraft, investigating crash sites, talking to aircrew veterans, and to the Dutch who saw and remembered the crashes and crash-landings. But of LJ946 – a total blank. No sign of it has ever been found. *The Royal Air Force at Arnhem* says, 'It's not known where the plane crashed, possibly somewhere in the Betuwe area [west-southwest of Arnhem between the two rivers, the Lower Rhine and the Waal].' *Green On* says that according to Carey the aircraft was on fire and flew on in a southwesterly direction. 'However, it is quite certain no unidentified Stirling crashed in the area southwest of Arnhem.' Those which did have all been identified. *Green On*'s author Arie-Jan van Hees speculates that the Stirling blew up in the air or crashed in the Waal, which might explain the puzzle.

Carey, Nelson-born Cook (23) and the rest of the crew were posted to 620 Squadron from 75 (NZ) Squadron on 4 February 1944, as were another 75 crew without a skipper. Next day Des Dawe (25), from Christchurch, his fellow New Zealander and bomb aimer Lor Peterson (29) and the rest of his crew were also off to 620. Another crew whose navigator Gordon Fairhall was also a Christchurch man went to 196 Squadron. A month later Squadron Leader David Gibb, 75's B-Flight commander, was on his way to 190 Squadron. 38 Group, flying Stirlings and due to drop paras and tow gliders at Normandy, needed planes and crews and 75 Squadron, waiting for Lancasters to replace its Stirlings, was one source.

620 Squadron lost only two of the eleven aircraft it sent to Arnhem on the 21st against 190's seven of ten and none was molested by fighters. The 620 planes must have been on a slightly different track, missed by the FW190s and Me 109s, and over the target at a slightly different time. The two aircraft shot down were victims of flak and two others landed at emergency fields in England to offload seriously wounded crew.

Carey, last to lift off and delayed by ground control red-light problems, never caught up. He cut corners and made all possible speed but was still two minutes behind at Eindhoven. Later, he told British intelligence interrogators:

Two Typhoons covered me until we encountered the first flak which they engaged, leaving us alone. I saw the DZ ahead and tried to go in alone. [Met] very heavy flak and therefore had to keep weaving. Dropped supplies and then tried to turn for home. I decided to drop to tree level instead of climbing to cloud which was about 3000 feet. I had nearly completed my turn when we received a direct hit amidships. The flight engineer reported we were on fire and the aircraft immediately filled with smoke. I tried to make height and ordered the crew out … I think they baled out between 800 feet and 1200 feet. The floor of the aircraft had been completely blown out immediately aft the rear centre span and was burning fiercely.

Carey engaged the automatic pilot and jumped himself. Germans on the ground took pot shots as he drifted down but he landed safely on the north bank of the Rhine. Three Dutch appeared almost instantly. They hid Carey's chute and Mae West and rushed him to cover. Jerry patrols came looking for him but his helpers convinced them he'd had landed on the opposite bank. The Dutch sheltered him for two days and he was joined by three crewmen from the other 620 Stirling shot down on the 21st. They were taken across the Rhine on the 23rd, linked up with British forces and whisked back to England, believed to be the first evaders from the battle area north of the Rhine to reach home.

Cook was in German-occupied territory west of Arnhem for four weeks before escaping back across the Rhine. He was the only New Zealander among the group of 148 men who crossed the river that night to the Allied lines in Operation Pegasus 1, a joint mission planned and executed by the British and Dutch Resistance. Those who got away, almost all paratroopers except some RAF aircrew like Cook, had been concealed by brave Dutch in their homes and farms after the Arnhem debacle.

Cook landed in a tree in the Wageningen area, five or six miles west of where the paras were bottled up in the shrinking Oosterbeek perimeter. People living in this thickly populated district watched the overhead dramas and raced to aid downed RAF crew. Cook had barely got down from the tree before a big Dutch teenager arrived on the scene, gesticulating 'follow me'. The youngster rolled up Cook's chute, took him deeper into the woods, almost shoved him into a pre-prepared hole and ordered 'stay here'. The Resistance came for him as night fell and took him to a safe house, the first of two where he was cloistered over the next month. In the first, a farmhouse, he shared an upstairs room with two others, Englishman Fred Padley and a Scot, Robert Law, both from 156 Parachute Battalion. They also escaped in the Pegasus 1 party. Cook had his worst moments in that room. One night German soldiers from a nearby camp hammered on the dwelling's main entrance. Loud voices followed and the airmen could tell people in the house had been ordered outside. Then shots. Cook and his mates froze, ready to flee, fearful for their lives and those of their hosts. Suddenly the crisis was over. The Germans had demanded a pig and when they got it, killed and carried it off.

The threat of sudden death facing all the Dutch who offered havens to British airmen and paras during and after Arnhem was emphasised in a letter in July 1945. Written by a member of the second family to care for him it began, 'At this moment the Germans are away and we are free.' Do you [remember] the time ... you must stay in the room the whole day and that you must sleep in the hay, you might not come out of our house, for the Germans might not know that you was near us, for if they knew this they killed you and us and the farm went up in fire. But it has all gone very well and I thank God for it all the days.'

Pegasus 1 involved the collection of paras and a handful of airmen from hiding places over a wide area, and their transport to a rendezvous in a heavily forested area not far from the Lower Rhine. There the men replaced civilian clothes with military uniforms so they would be treated as combatants if captured. The uniforms and weapons, also handed out, had been smuggled in and harboured by the Dutch. Resistance guides led the men to the edge of the woods about 11 p.m. and from there they worked their way to the river bank through a 300-yard gap between German defence posts, crawling the last 200 yards across an open meadow.

Torch signals flashed across the 100 yards of the cold, swiftly flowing Rhine and rubber boats pushed off from the Allied side, paddled by British sappers. Out of the black night came the muffled words, 'Are you people by any chance looking for some boats?' And the answer, from the evaders' leader, Major Digby Tatham Warter: 'Well, actually, we are rather.'

In the final count Pegasus 1 delivered 138 Commonwealth soldiers and airmen and ten Dutch to safety. Pegasus II, a month later, aimed at rescuing a similar number, ended in disaster. The Germans intercepted the party and only seven men made it across the river. A number of their Dutch helpers and guides were captured and executed.

English researcher John Howes' Pegasus 1 escape list shows Padley and Law in the group with Cook, and so were two other members of the Carey crew, the flight engineer and bomb aimer. Cook didn't spot them nor they him. Not surprising – in the blackness and in a large party where men were silent.

VICTORY

The South Canterbury threesome were on their twelfth op when they came to grief over Denmark on 26 April 1945, the war almost over. Pilot Harry Christian (26) lived in Timaru, navigator Merv Roberts (29) was an agricultural contractor from Pleasant Point and bomb aimer Paddy Hay (22) farmed nearby at Rosewill. They'd never met each other until they arrived at 81 OTU, Sleap, in Shropshire, where they flew old Whitleys and crewed up, adding an English wireless operator and a Canadian gunner. Next stop adjacent Tilstock, where they picked up a flight engineer, another Roberts, met the Stirling and began towing gliders and dropping paras.

In August 1944 they were posted to 644 Squadron and while Christian was converting to the Halifax, Roberts did a couple of trips with other crews, one to the Falaise area of France on 17 August to drop sixteen paratroopers and another three days later to the south of France to drop containers to the Resistance. On the second he flew with a group whose bomb aimer abandoned his spot in the nose for the comfort of the second pilot's seat because the rain sluicing down as they flew was 'pissing' into his position. And according to Roberts, 'complained non-stop in his Oxford accent'. Roberts grabbed the opportunity to do some work. Helping the navigator as his eyes, he soon had them going in the right direction. Then the pilot turned back. Roberts didn't speak his mind but worried about the reception group on the ground who were never going to see a Halifax or get their supplies that night.

'Now the great day!' Roberts wrote in an account of his wartime days in *Drop Zone*. 'My first operation with my own crew.' They flew the night of 25–26 September, a week after the start of Arnhem, completing an almost six-hours run to and from Holland, an SOE drop code-named Draughts 1. They dropped fourteen containers and one package to the Dutchmen waiting below. This was followed by a couple of bomb runs to little-known German targets, other SOE flights including several long trips to Norway – one of eleven hours – interrupted by their participation in the daylight Operation Varsity, the Rhine crossing on 24 March. After delivering containers on one Norwegian op the Halifax flew home via Oslo to drop leaflets. '[They] took an hour to reach the ground as the wind was 30 mph the release point was 30 miles upwind from the city. Just more complications for the navigator,' said Roberts.

The South Canterbury team made three trips to Norway after Varsity and Christian asked at the briefing for the last if they could have a different target next time. 'Yes, you can have Denmark.' The briefing officer warned it wouldn't be a piece of cake. 'How right he was!' Roberts wrote.

They made their Danish landfall at Ringkobing on the western side of the main peninsula, then flew cross country to their target, an island just a bit further on from Langeland. Flak trailed them all the way back to Ringkobing. Roberts: 'We heard later the flak guns were manned by Hungarians and the Germans paid them 5000 marks for every plane they shot down. There were a lot of bounty hunters out that night.'

The Halifax had just reached the sea when the Hungarians found them. Flying almost at sea level and fatally damaged, Christian reacted instantly, putting the tail down to hit first so the nose wouldn't dig in, and ditched. Roberts was in his cubbyhole working when it happened:

> Next ... [the tail] was in the water and Mac [MacDougall, the gunner] was telling us, 'It's raining back here.' The water was flying over his turret – out of a cloudless sky with bright moonlight. I guess we went from 200 mph to zero in about 10 seconds. Paddy and I were under water when we stood up ... Paddy kicked a hole through the Perspex nose and we both escaped ... All the crew were out and uninjured. We still had most of the fuselage and the wings were more or less intact. The engines were torn off and I could see part of one sticking out of the water 100 yards back [the water was extremely shallow]. The rubber dinghy was there beside the wing, inflated and ready to board.

As they paddled for shore about a mile away, Danes in a row boat appeared and took them aboard. But their rescuers wanted ammunition so they returned to the wreck lying in shallow coastal water. Christian swam into it and emerged draped in several thousand rounds. The Danes dumped their loot in the sea close to shore to be retrieved later.

Ashore the six men split into pairs and and took off in different directions. Six men walking together would beg arrest. Roberts and Hay walked until dawn, then found cover in two rows of young pines. They holed up all that day and started walking again at nightfall. At the end of the next day, tired and hungry, they chose a small isolated farmhouse without a telephone line. They needed help. Roberts knocked. A man opened the door. 'There was a long silence while we looked at each other. Finally I said, "Royal Air Force." His face lit up and he grabbed me by the arm to lead me inside. ... Instinctively I trusted this man.'

The farmer cleaned up a cut on Roberts' head and got his wife out of bed to cook a meal. That night the evaders slept the sleep of the dead in a warm haystack. They stayed three or four days, photos were taken and the farmer's contacts with the Resistance delivered identity cards, Roberts becoming a farmer, Hay a traveller. With the Resistance taking care of them, they ended up in a swank country estate owned by a businessman in Copenhagen. Out for a stroll in his grounds one night they heard shots and, panicked, raced back to the house. The firing was in celebration. The war was over.

Roberts and Hay were the star attraction at a victory do in a nearby town, then the Resistance whisked them off to the capital where they linked up with Christian. Feted by the Danes, the three of them had a whale of a time for a week, until they were spotted by an army officer. 'Hello, boys, what are you doing here?' Next morning they were on a cramped Dakota back to England, Tarrant Rushton and reality.

CHAPTER 7

Air Sea Rescue

The irony of it all. New Zealand pilot 'Kiwi' Saunders spent a lot of time on the water in a Walrus and a Sea Otter, the little amphibians flown by his ASR squadron, but couldn't swim a stroke. 'I never learned to swim. Too bloody cold down in Owaka,' he says. Owaka, a tiny South Otago settlement at the northern end of the Catlins Forest Park coastal road, was his birthplace on 26 September 1916. He grew up on a dairy farm, had his first flight in 1923. 'The plane took one adult or two kids as passengers. As I was the biggest kid I got in first and my mate … sat on my lap and all I saw was the back of his neck … In spite of that I must have been impressed for over the next dozen or so years I took every opportunity to go for a flight.'

Four months before the war started Saunders joined the Otago Aero Club and began flying lessons but hadn't soloed by September 1939 when all private flying halted abruptly. He applied to join the RNZAF, was accepted for pilot training – and then the usual wait. By October 1940 he was in, whizzed through training at Taieri and Wigram and left New Zealand on 21 April the following year for England and his first squadron posting to 132 at Peterhead on Scotland's northeast coast. A short time there and on to 616 (South Yorkshire) Squadron, a fighter unit at Westhampnett near Chichester, West Sussex, now the site of Goodwood airfield.

There a hiccup determined his war career. At that time of his life he stuttered. 'A mental thing; only when I was face to face with someone. Never in the air when I was alone.' But his flight commander, Flight Lieutenant Johnnie Johnson, later a wing leader and the highest scoring RAF pilot of the war, was having none of it. 'You're no use to me with that stutter so bugger off' is basically what he said. 'You can't blame him but he got it wrong,' says Saunders. He was posted after just ten days at 616, to join the Lysander ASR Flight at Friston on the cliff tops at Beachy Head on the South Coast on 12 October 1941. There no one cared about a minor stutter on the ground, a stutter never heard on any of his RT transmissions. He had found his war niche.

An RAF ASR service was non-existent in the early stages of the war, at the cost of many lives, and it wasn't until July 1940 that New Zealand Air Vice-Marshal Keith Park took a hand, ordering Lysanders to spot downed aircraft and their aircrew and call high-speed launches (HSLs) to the rescue. Another New Zealander, Russell 'Digger' Aitken, took it a step further. Based near Portsmouth, he scrounged a Walrus and experimented. In a brief period, Aitken and his crew picked up thirty-five men from both sides, alive and dead. His work led to the establishment of the ASR service in February 1942, an arm of the RAF that ultimately became a sophisticated rescue organisation which by war's end had saved countless aircrew. 'It was a great comfort to fliers to know that if they went into the drink they had a reasonable chance of being picked up; a morale booster,' says Saunders.

The New Zealander's flight moved to Shoreham where, with other flights scattered along the South Coast and at Martlesham Heath on the Suffolk coast, it became 277 Squadron on 22 December 1941. When 277 formed it was using Lysanders to spot and Walruses to pick up. Gradually the Lysanders were replaced with faster Defiants and then Spitfires; the Walrus by its successor, the Sea Otter. The Walrus first flew in 1933, a bi-plane with a pusher engine mounted above the fuselage between the wings designed by RJ Mitchell of Spitfire fame. The Sea Otter had an improved hull, a tractor engine set into the top wing, better performance and could carry heavier loads off the water. It was the last bi-plane to enter RAF aircraft ranks. Saunders was entirely happy with all the aircraft he operated at Shoreham. He only ever crashed one, a Spitfire, and escaped without a scratch. 'I was guilty of doing a fancy side-slip approach and it went straight into the ground. Not many pilots walk away from a written-off Spitfire with only their pride hurt.' There are no red endorsements in Saunders' log book thanks to a very understanding boss. 'The only punishment I got was the CO saying, "Very careless of you, Kiwi, don't do it again."'

Everyone called him Kiwi at Shoreham. An Australian noted his arrival: 'another bloody Kiwi'. The name stuck. During his three years at Shoreham he was involved in the rescue of almost forty men – as a spotter calling rescuers in or as an amphibian pilot holding the plane steady, occasionally in tumultuous seas, while his crewmen dragged in sodden, half-dead survivors. Sometimes they were dead.

277 always picked up the dead, German or Allied – a matter of principle. Once in a while the seemingly dead were alive. When they rescued Mosquito navigator Jim Haugh, a Wellington man, out of a glassy Channel 25 miles south of Beachy Head on Anzac Day 1944, they were certain he was a goner. The crew discovered he was still breathing, though deeply unconscious. The Mosquito pilot, Lorenzo 'Snow' Fittock (24), another New Zealander, was nowhere to be seen. They alerted Friston, lifted off and flew straight to the field, where an ambulance was waiting.

Haugh (21), who survived the ordeal with bruising, a shattered eardrum and pneumonia, had teamed up in Canada with Fittock and was flying with him on 464 (RAAF) Squadron the day they came to grief. They had attacked a V-1 site with bombs and then crossed the French coast on return. Fittock dropped the plane down to sea level – and disaster. The Mosquito hit the sea and ploughed in. A later court of inquiry report ruled the pilot had made an error of judgment, something the court termed a 'hazard of war'. All pilots were warned of the deceptive appearance of a smooth sea.

Haugh wrote a harrowing account of that day for Norman Franks' *Another Kind of Courage*. He described the Mosquito sinking like a stone and his frantic efforts to escape. Eventually he shot to the surface like 'a cork out of a bottle' and climbed into the inflated dinghy released from the aircraft. Fittock had also escaped from the sinking plane but Haugh couldn't get the big man into the little craft. Fittock's toggle on his Mae West bottle punctured the dinghy, leaving both men floundering in the freezing water. Haugh, exhausted and cold, couldn't get into his own one-man dinghy, the little inflatable attached to aircrew parachutes. 'I put my head and shoulders in the dinghy and wound my hands in the side ropes. I then lost consciousness.' He was rescued in the nick of time. Fittock, a plasterer living in Napier when he enlisted in October 1941, is remembered at Runnymede.

Saunders spotted or rescued British, American, Canadian, Dutch and German aircrew. They were from Spitfires and Lancasters, American Fortresses, Liberators and Marauders, the four Dutchmen on a Mitchell light bomber, and German aircraft. Haugh was the only New Zealander Saunders picked up. The Americans gave him the Air Medal for his 15 April 1943 rescue of Lt Col Chesney G Peterson, forced down in the Channel about 10 miles from the enemy coast.

The DFC, awarded to Saunders in July 1944 for his 'great courage and determination' in many rescues, made special mention of his saving of Canadian Mac Hume, a 403 (RCAF) Squadron pilot flying a Spitfire, 15 miles off Cayeux, on the French coast north of Dieppe, on 3 May 1944. This astonishing rescue in the face of heavy breaking seas, which ultimately destroyed Saunders' Sea Otter, stood out in his memory seventy years later:

> There'd been a mayday and the two Spits were off and away doing three times my speed so I trundled along behind them. Hume was in the water in just a Mae West when I finally got there. The searching Spits had found him and dropped dinghies but the wind was too strong and they missed him but they had also dropped four smoke floats and this helped me judge the wind strength and direction. The sea was very rough and I knew there was not a hope in hell of getting off again but the poor guy was there, alive, and we had to go down. He was in just his life jacket and had been in the water for about an hour so he must have been pretty healthy although after we got him aboard he told us he had got to the stage where he had stopped

shivering and didn't feel the cold. That was a bad sign [hypothermia setting in]. The silly bugger. When he got into his Spit he attached his dinghy to the chute rather than to his life jacket. When he hit the water the chute didn't collapse and took him for quite a rough ride before he got rid of it and his dinghy as well. It was a crucial mistake.

Saunders accomplished the difficult landing but one of the floats was damaged and the Otter was shipping water. Then the RT failed and the interior lights went out. The bright navigation lights on the wings still blinked, as day faded into night. The rescuers had been just in time. After they hauled Hume in one of the crew pumped furiously to keep the water level down as Saunders headed north, motoring slowly through the big seas, progress painfully slow.

> We taxied the plane from about 10 p.m. to 2 a.m. or 3 a.m., about 30 miles. At one stage the sea started to drop a wee bit, and through a break in the cloud I saw something circling above us, a Mossie or something that had its landing lights on. Within an hour an HSL came and picked us up. As it pulled alongside someone shouted to us to 'put the fucking nav lights out'. They couldn't see us properly. So I put the fucking lights out. The old story about the captain being the last man off the ship didn't work in our case because every man getting out had to stand on my seat to do so and I had no option but to go first. I did remember to switch off the engine though because the prop was whirling just behind our exit point.

The men on the HSL looked after everyone with rum, hot drinks and warm clothes and returned them safely into Dover sometime after 4 a.m. The airmen were back in Shoreham by mid-morning.

VICTORY

*

John Curtis was 21 on 13 June 1944, as the V1s began to fall. There were a few beers with fellow pilots, one of them close friend Rad Lewis, a New Zealander also training at Finmere. Curtis, born in Te Aroha, 13 June 1923, had the urge to fly early. When he was eleven, he wagged school and walked four miles to watch an aeroplane. A bunch of keen local aviation enthusiasts had formed a club and the Auckland Aero Club sent down a DH-6 once a week.

> I skipped school and walked the four miles because I'd never seen an aeroplane except once or twice a year when one flew high overhead. I got to the gate of this paddock and a car pulls up beside me and it's my Dad. He managed a garage in town and he'd skipped work too. He asked me what I was doing and then said, 'Do you want a flight?' I went up and so it started. That sowed the seed.

The war began as Curtis finished high school. Too young to join the air force, he worked at temporary jobs until he received the call-up, sailing from New Zealand in February1943 on the *Matsonia*. Rad Lewis was on the same ship. They'd met at Taieri for their initial flight training. Rad's family was still grieving for his older brother Bob, killed while serving in the Middle East in June 1942. Bob joined the RAF a week before war broke out and became a WOp/AG, posted to the Middle East to 203 Squadron on Blenheims. He was awarded a DFM for helping his crew destroy a number of Iraqi aircraft on the ground in the Anglo-Iraq conflict in April-May 1941 but lost his life in an accidental explosion in Egypt on 22 June 1942.

Curtis and Lewis did their flight training in Brandon, Manitoba, graduating as sergeants the same day, then flew Venturas at 34 OTU, Pennfield Ridge. They expected to join 487 (NZ) Squadron, then equipped with the same American-built aircraft, but the Ventura was a poor performer. 487 watched without regret as the last one left in late September 1943, replaced by Mosquitoes. When Curtis and Lewis reached England, Curtis had a posting to a Mosquito conversion unit but he was sent to Finmere for type conversion on Mitchells, with Lewis.

Late in June Curtis and Lewis, who had two New Zealanders in his crew, were posted to 180 Squadron at Dunsfold, Surrey, the home of 2TAF's 139 Wing with its three Mitchell units, 98, 180 and 320 (Dutch) Squadrons. The RAF's fourth Mitchell squadron, 226, was at Hartford Bridge. Curtis did his opening op in mid-July, the first of forty-nine – to Chartres, to bomb a fuel dump. The American-designed and built B-25 Mitchell light bombers were powered by two 1700 hp Wright Cyclone engines. They carried 4000-pound loads – eight x 500 or four x 1000.

The Mitchell squadrons, sometimes accompanied by Spitfires, mainly flew by day – Curtis did only three night ops – attacking fuel dumps, barracks, bridges, railway marshalling yards, troop and tank concentrations and enemy strongpoints. They dropped their bombs at about 12,000 to 14,000 feet. 'There was no low-level stuff for us. We were above light flak's effective range but vulnerable to the 88s and there were plenty of them having a go at us.' Curtis remembers flying to Caen when Montgomery was attacking. 'The Germans ran their Tiger tanks up on ramps, elevated their big guns and used them for anti-aircraft fire.' He carried his bombs home that day, despite running over the target twice. 'There was so much smoke and dust kicked up by shelling and bombing we just couldn't see. Canadian troops were close to the target mark and we couldn't risk hitting them. We returned the next morning and plastered the German positions in clear conditions.'

A daylight attack on a fuel dump in a forest near Lyon deep in France on 9 August 1944 proved to be his toughest trip. Heavy flak downed two of the three planes in the 'Vic' in which Curtis was flying. One crew got down safely to become POWs but two men on the other plane died, including British pilot Robert Wood. 'We were lucky because we had much damage but we weren't hit in a vital spot and we didn't catch fire.' Curtis remembers Robert Wood with great respect for his bravery, which went unrecognised:

> We were all hit badly by flak. There was quite a dollop of it. Then fuel began pouring out of Wood's aircraft and the next minute there was a sheet of flame. Navigator Harry John went to pick up his chute and found it was burnt. The cockpit was well and truly alight by then. Wood pulled his own chute out from just behind his seat and told John, 'put that on and go.' Wood signed his own death warrant. He was left without a chute and was killed in the crash. He gave his life and I think he deserved a medal. A brave act.

Though John suffered burns he landed safely and avoided capture. One of two WOp/AGs died, the other parachuted to become a POW. It was a bad day for the wing. Two 320 Mitchells were also damaged, one ditching in the Channel, the other force-landing in England with a dead WOp.

Curtis and Lewis, in different flights, were well on in their tours when Lewis lost his life on 25 August. Both were on a raid to

Clermont to bomb a fuel dump. Curtis didn't know at the time but Lewis turned back on the outward leg when an engine failed. Curtis discovered his friend missing when he landed at Dunsfold but didn't find out what happened until the next day:

> He ditched the aircraft successfully, about 12 miles south of Beachy Head on a major flight path but it was 90 minutes before rescue craft reached the scene and by then only one man was alive, navigator George Hodder, a Londoner who'd lost members of his family in the Blitz. It emerged that Rad gashed his head in the ditching and streamed blood but was fully conscious and chirpy when he got out of the aircraft. But the cold water took its toll and he was dead when picked up. Loss of blood, shock and hypothermia were blamed.

Lewis' two New Zealand crewmen, WOp/AG Ken Curtis (21), from Nelson, and gunner Harry Walters (26), from Auckland, died with him. Walters is remembered at Runnymede. The bodies of Lewis and Curtis lie side by side in Brookwood Military cemetery in Surrey.

180 moved to Melsbroek, Belgium – today Brussels International Airport – on 18 October and Curtis did another five ops before he was tour expired, seeing out the war as a staff pilot at a Group Support Unit in Norfolk.

CHAPTER 8

Falaise

While it seemed everyone in the RAF was flying Typhoons and inflicting enormous death and destruction on the Germans trapped in Normandy's Falaise pocket in August 1944, New Zealander Alan Barley trundled in to do his bit in a slow old Dakota. The Aucklander had joined 46 Group's 233 Squadron in early March after a long stint on Lancasters with 44 Squadron to fly Daks dropping paras and hauling gliders for the invasion. He emerged from D-Day unscathed and when the Allies opened up the first airfields in the beachhead area he and others began flying in supplies and taking out the wounded.

At 10 p.m. on 21 August, all 233 crews at RAF Blakehill Farm, Wiltshire, were called to the briefing room on the double. Allied divisions were clamping shut the Falaise gap, through which elements of the German 7th Army had been escaping, to temporary sanctuary behind the Seine. Canadians and Poles bearing south, against stubborn German resistance from the small town of Falaise, birthplace of William the Conqueror, would meet Americans driving north from Argentan and so close off the neck of the pocket.

'The Poles were running out of anti-tank ammunition, the position was most serious and we were to help them,' Barley wrote in a family memoir. 233's job was to parachute ammunition in wicker panniers but by the time the shells had been delivered to the airfield it was too late for a night drop and the chosen crews were airborne at 5 a.m. Because the weather was too bad for formation flying, the Dakotas flew singly.

'We made landfall on the Normandy Peninsula … just as dawn was breaking … it was pouring heavens bad with patchy low cloud right on the deck while the actual cloud base was about 500 feet,' Barley wrote. They found their drop point and at very low altitude saw small fires everywhere: '… it seemed the British Army was cooking breakfast … we could identify the Canadian troops by their darker uniforms … occasionally a stream of Bren tracer was directed towards us and we decided this was the army's way of welcoming us.' Barley made two runs over the DZ to check and then the dispatchers rolled out the panniers. 'I like to think our load of ammunition at least assisted those Poles in … obliterating the Germans.' Altogether Barley flew ninety ops on 233 for an overall wartime tally of 140.

Falaise was the deciding battle of the Normandy campaign. After that the Allies, on the land and from the air, pursued the shocked and battered German remnants across the Seine, not stopping until they reached the fringes of the German-Franco border. Paris fell on 23 August, the Americans allowing the French the honour of leading the march into the capital. The capture of Caen, the pivotal eastern point, took Montgomery until 20 July but the German panzer divisions, the bulk of the Nazi armour, were fatally weakened by weeks of fighting, artillery bombardment and constant aerial attack. There was little left to combat the Americans when they broke out of their bridgehead in Operation Cobra and roared north toward Cherbourg and west into Britanny, Patton's troops spearheading the drive. German tank divisions were drawn west from Caen for Hitler's plan to attack Mortain, south of St Lo, and push on to Avaranches on the west coast of the Cotentin Peninsula to drive a wedge between the American divisions racing to Britanny and those heading for the French interior.

In vain Hitler's generals in the field resisted his decision. The Germans made initial advances but American troops halted the assault and the RAF's Typhoon wings did their deadly work. The Allies saw their chance. The Americans looped around behind the Germans from the west and south while the British came in from the north. By the time the Germans recognised the threat, the encirclement was almost in place. Too late the Germans realised they'd been trapped but didn't start to pull out until 17 August, when it became a panicked rush. The 1st Polish Division – the unit to which Barley had dropped ammunition – and the Canadians tried desperately to reach the Americans to finally seal the pocket. On 21 August the gap was closed. Thousands of Germans escaped in those last few chaotic days, but thousands more were killed or captured. Effectively the 7th Army ceased to exist – Germany's worst defeat since Stalingrad. The British, free of Caen, began their advance through France into Belgium and southern Holland.

The Typhoon wings had their best days of the war at Mortain and Falaise. Patrolling the battlefield, they swooped to attack tanks with their rockets and soft-skinned traffic with cannon fire. They devastated German columns, hitting their first and last tanks to halt everything, before starting on the middle. In their panic to flee, many Germans quit their tanks and other armoured vehicles, running for ditches and cover. The Typhoons' psychological hold was complete. They were the Stukas of 1940 magnified a hundredfold.

One of the many New Zealanders flying Typhoons was South Otago man Erle Brough. Born near Owaka, on the northern edge of the Catlins, in 1918, Brough was awarded his wings in August 1941 and trained on Spitfires before a posting to 132 Squadron in the Orkneys. A month later he was launched from the carrier HMS *Eagle*, flying his Spitfire the 745 miles to Malta. He didn't make a good start. Landing, one wing clipped sandbags and an irate CO called him 'a bloody traitor,' adding, 'It's planes we want here. Pilots mean nothing.' Brough, who had no combat experience, learnt quickly. When he left for England five months later, he had two German aircraft to his credit and 70 operational hours in his log.

On rest, he was commissioned. After instructing on Hurricanes he had his first flight on a Typhoon on 21 April 1943, then a posting to 182 (Typhoon) Squadron in August 1943. After eight days he was flying operationally. More practice, more ops and at the end of January 'above average' ratings. As preparation for D-Day stepped up he was in the thick of it, rocketing bridges, radar stations, gun emplacements across the Channel and flying anti-flak for other squadrons. Promotion followed – flying officer in March, flight lieutenant in May and temporary command of the squadron in July when the CO, a South African Air Force (SAAF) major was hit by flak, baled out and taken prisoner. On D-Day he led the squadron on an armed recce over the beachhead. 'Strafed transport, but very hard to find as no transport on the roads,' he wrote in his log. 'One tank on fire.' A 'flamer'. 'Smokers' were just that – no flames, just smoke. Through August Brough was heavily involved at Falaise and the surrounding region. He flew twenty-six sorties, three on the 11th. On the day of the Germans' Mortain attack, 7 August, while on an armed recce over the Vire-Mortain sector 182 was subject to 'very intense medium flak' attacking tanks. He was 'severely' hit in the tail plane but 'returned to base OK'. Brough's log entries give a taste of what it was like over Falaise:

> 17th – Armed recce [northeast] Trun area. 4 tanks and 12 MT left burning. 4 tanks smokers. Light flak.
>
> 18th – (3 sorties). Attack on transport [east] of Vimoutiers. 19 MT (flamers), 10 MT, 1 tank (smokers), 15 MT damaged. Attack on MT [east] of Vimoutiers. 10 MT (flamers), 1 MT (smoker) 2 MT (damaged), 2 m/cs destroyed. Attack on MT [east] of Vimoutiers – 5 MT (flamers), 5 MT damaged. F/Lt Hay killed.
>
> 19th (2 sorties) – Armed recce Orbec area. 5 MT (flamers). Several more damaged. Armed recce Vimoutiers area. 3 tanks. 3 MT (flamers). Med flak. Lt Jennings [SAAF] killed.
>
> 25th [when 2TAF was attacking retreating Germans trying to cross the Seine] – Attack on barges Seine River. Attacked 2 barges. 1 destroyed. Heavy flak. 3 a/c hit.

Brough's log extract notes the deaths of two squadron pilots – more appear on other pages. Young men loved flying Typhoons but paid a huge price. The memorial in a village near Caen lists 151, all killed in the three months of the Normandy campaign. Six are New Zealanders. Before war's end another fourteen New Zealand Typhoon pilots died, taking the final toll to twenty. Other fighters flown by New Zealanders after D-Day lost their share of pilots – sixteen in Spitfires, thirteen in Tempests and six in Mustangs – but the chance of death was highest on Typhoons.

Brough continued to live a charmed life and in September 1944 he was promoted to squadron leader in command of 137 Squadron on the same 124 Wing as 182. On 23 September he was awarded a DFC for his outstanding ability as a flight commander on 182 and his performance over Falaise leading attacks on German armour. He is credited with four tanks and nine armoured vehicles. The next day he downed an FW 190 over Kleve-Emmerich. He commanded 137 until a week before Christmas, when he was on his way home. On the wharf in Wellington his future brother-in-law waited for him. No sign. Turned out he was below decks, finishing off a game of poker with Freddie 'Popeye' Lucas, the outstanding 75 (NZ) Squadron pilot.

For Your Tomorrow records the death of Auckland pilot Alick Mewa at Falaise, believed to be the first member of the New Zealand Indian community to be commissioned in the RNZAF. Mewa (25) commanded the crew of a 98 Squadron Mitchell that left its base at Dunsfold, Surrey, just before midnight on 18 August. He was to drop flares in support of Mosquito operations in the Falaise area but was lost without trace and is commemorated at Runnymede.

Ian Waddy's luck ran out on 25 August 1944. As the wide-ranging deadly Typhoon squadrons chased desperate Germans trying to flee across the Seine, flak shot him down. On an armed reconnaissance leading 164 Squadron, the unit he had commanded for six days, his Typhoon was hit over Rouen. He crash-landed in a barley field and began running. The area was thick with Germans and they pounced, two of them on a motorcycle and side car. Waddy was put on a train, escaped briefly, only to be recaptured by an elderly German policeman. The luck which had deserted him in the air returned – in spades. SS troops, their divisions battered by the Typhoons, wanted to execute Waddy. The policeman saved the New Zealander's life, haranguing the SS. 'He's my prisoner, not yours, so bugger off.' Waddy began the long journey to a POW camp.

Waddy was fortunate. A number of Allied airmen were executed by SS troops after capture, and those taken by the Germans in an area which had just been attacked from the air were at great risk. On 16 August New Zealand Spitfire pilot Dennis Burman (23), from Invercargill, was executed. Flying on a sweep from Tangmere with 74 Squadron, he was shot down while attacking tanks on a train between Arras and Waziers. *For Your Tomorrow* says that though wounded and surrendering immediately, he was shot on the spot by an SS officer.

The day before Burman's killing, Aucklander Bob Harden (22) perhaps suffered the same fate. After his 132 Squadron Spitfire was hit by flak over the Falaise battlefield, he was last seen very low, his aircraft streaming glycol. When the area was cleared of Germans his fighter's remains were found in a field but extensive searches then and later failed to find any trace of the pilot, who is commemorated at Runnymede.

On 21 February 1945, Dunedin Typhoon pilot Hector Young, a newcomer to 245 Squadron, flying from Volkel, Holland, and on his sixteenth op, was winged by flak over Germany. He forced landed a few miles from Vreden, north of the Ruhr. Hitler Youth flak battery gunners captured him but he was shot in the back 'while trying to escape'. *For Your Tomorrow* says the exact circumstances of his shooting are unknown, but in 1948 a War Crimes trial convicted a former German army quartermaster of the killing and jailed him for twenty years.

Did something similar happen to 486's CO Keith Taylor-Cannon? Widely known as 'Hyphen', Omakau-born Taylor-Cannon was 23 at the time of his death. Leading a formation of Tempests, his plane was hit by flak as he attacked ground transport at Domitz on the east bank of the Elbe southeast of Hamburg on 13 April 1945. *For Your Tomorrow* says his aircraft took a direct 88 mm shell almost over the Domitz bridge. The pilot was seen to bale out and touch down. Later, a British POW held nearby reported seeing a wounded Taylor-Cannon taken away. He was never seen again and is commemorated at Runnymede. Paul Sortehaug's *The Wild Winds*, 486's history, says it was rumoured Taylor-Cannon landed close to the column he was attacking and 'brutal retaliation was probably meted out'. He says another report had him succumbing from wounds while being taken for medical treatment. Post-war investigations couldn't find a grave or discover his fate. Christopher Shores says in *2nd Tactical Air Force* the New Zealander is thought to have been killed after reaching the ground. Taylor-Cannon, a foundation member of 486 Squadron, was on his 406th op. He died on a Black Friday, the fourth anniversary of his enlistment. The squadron was deeply affected by the death of the hugely popular CO, coming closely after the loss of previous commander Arthur 'Spike' Umbers. Like Taylor-Cannon, Umbers had been in charge of 486 for just a short time before he was killed. He died attacking barges on the Dortmund-Ems Canal on 14 February. Hit by rocket flak his plane rolled over, hit the ground and exploded. Umbers (25) was Dunedin born and raised.

German flak proved effective again on 25 August, when 164 Squadron lost Waddy and two other squadron pilots, one of them New Zealander George Trafford (23), from Gisborne. Eight Typhoons took off from Martragny, southeast of Bayeux, just before 7 p.m. Only five returned. Trafford, a married man, went down at Fresquiennes, just north of Rouen, and is buried there. He'd been with 164 for more than two years and flown Spitfires and Hurricanes before converting to Typhoons. The third pilot lost was an Englishman – all three victims of accurate, heavy flak.

Waddy, a sheep and cattle farmer from Seddon, sailed for England in late April 1941. He was one of a draft of ninety-two pilots, half of whom would be killed. The survivors included twelve who became POWs. Among Waddy's ship-board companions were survivors Woe Wilson, a lifelong friend and fellow pilot on 486 (NZ) Squadron, top bomber skipper Gordon Cochrane, noted Air Sea Rescue pilot Keith Saunders, and Wally Runciman, who flew bombers and then Mosquitoes. Waddy, a 486 foundation member, climbed the ranks and in September 1943 was appointed to command the squadron. He held the post until January 1944 when 486 began converting to Tempests. He was the third CO of 486 after Londoner Bob Roberts and New Zealander Des Scott. After six months instructing, Waddy was posted to command 164 on 19 August 1944, just short of his 30th birthday.

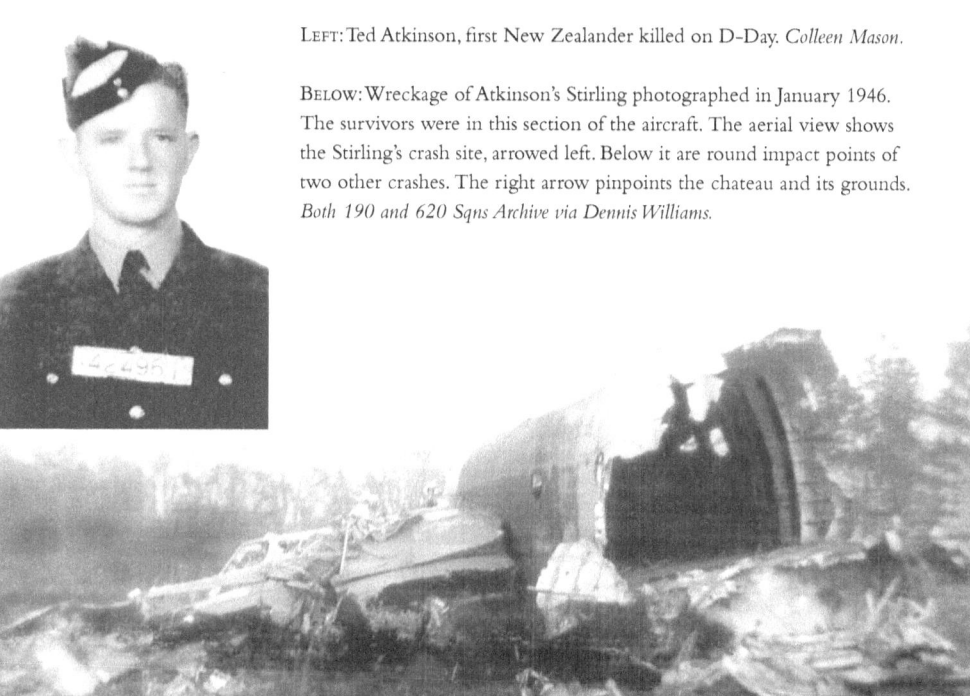

LEFT: Ted Atkinson, first New Zealander killed on D-Day. *Colleen Mason.*

BELOW: Wreckage of Atkinson's Stirling photographed in January 1946. The survivors were in this section of the aircraft. The aerial view shows the Stirling's crash site, arrowed left. Below it are round impact points of two other crashes. The right arrow pinpoints the chateau and its grounds. *Both 190 and 620 Sqns Archive via Dennis Williams.*

Among New Zealand aircrew who flew on D-Day. CLOCKWISE FROM TOP LEFT: Pilot Bob Spurdle, pilot Basil Bretherton, air gunner Des Reevely, pilot Les Baveystock. *Anne Powell and John Spurdle, Ray Bretherton, Alastair Reevely, Jill Speir respectively.*

BELOW: Map for fighter pilots on D-Day. *Wendy Gibson.*

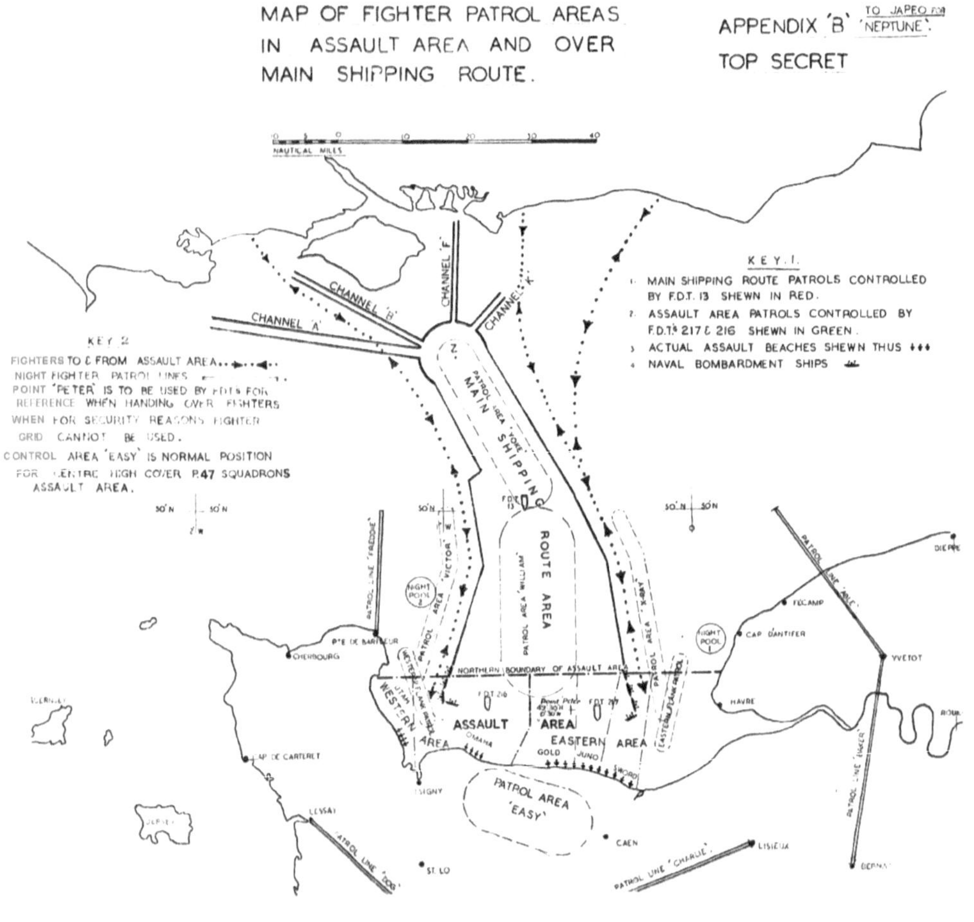

June						
"	1	MaGister		SELF	F/O Ewing	GRAVESEND + RETURN
"	1	Mosquito		"	SGT McLaren	N.F.T.
"	2	"		"	"	Bombing
"	5	"		"	"	N.F.T.
"	5	Mosquito	L	SELF	SGT McLaren	Ops. EVREUX. ST. ANDRE. IN Support of D. Day operation. 1. ME. 410 DESTROYED. 1st ENEMY AIRCRAFT DESTROYED ON D.-Day.
"	6	Mosquito	L	SELF	SGT McLaren	N.F.T.
"	6	Mosquito	L	SELF	SGT McLaren	Ops. METZ. ST DIZIER.
"	7	"	L	"	"	N.F.T.
"	7	"	L	"	"	Ops. Returned Bad Weather
"	9	"	L	"	"	N.F.T.
"	10	"	L	"	"	N.F.T.
"	10	Mosquito	L	SELF	SGT McLaren	Ops. COULOMIERS 1 JU188 DES
"	13	"	L	"	"	N.F.T.
"	13	Mosquito	L	SELF	SGT McLaren	Ops. Special patrol for No Ball
"	14	"	L	"	"	N.F.T.
"	14	Mosquito	L	SELF	SGT. McLaren	Ops. VITRY. CAMBRAI.
"	17	Mosquito	L	SELF	SGT McLaren	Ops. ANTI-ROCKET - BOMB SORTIE
"	18	"	P	"	"	N.F.T.
"	21	"	W	"	"	N.F.T.
"	21	"	W	SELF	SGT. McLaren	Ops. CHIEVRE - CAMBRAI.

GRAND TOTAL [Cols. (1) to (10)].
1018 Hrs. 20 Mins.

TOTALS CARRIED FORWARD

ABOVE: Roy Le Long's logbook page for the first three weeks of June records his flight on 5–6 June when he shot down the first enemy aircraft on D-Day. The page also shows his success on the night of 10–11 June. *Noel Le Long.*

BELOW: Pilot Noel Sutherland peers from the cockpit. His 190 Squadron Stirling shows prominent nose art. The plane was called *It's Easy Cobber*, the artwork adorned with flying kiwi and kangaroo. The symbols at right indicate 21 completed ops – container drops (parachutes), Special Air Service para drops (daggers), glider towing (aeroplane) and one bombing trip (bomb). The photograph was taken near the end of Sutherland's tour. *Noel Sutherland.*

ABOVE: Ian Lock crashed-landed his out-of-fuel 218 Squadron Stirling in rainswept darkness on the edge of RAF St Eval, Cornwall, on 17 December 1943. Amazingly the entire crew survived, minor injuries to just three of them. *Barbara Lock.*

ABOVE: All smiles and time for a cuppa and a smoke at the post-raid briefing on return from a more successful trip. Lock at centre. As the squadron converted from Stirlings, Lock and his crew got to fly this nice new Lancaster. *Barbara Lock.*

RIGHT: Michael Dillon, a mid-upper gunner, died when his 103 Squadron Lancaster piloted by fellow New Zealander John Armstrong was shot down attacking a rail junction in northwest France the night of 10–11 April 1944. Armstrong was also killed. *Jane Dillon.*

ABOVE AND BELOW: Neil Couchman lost his life attacking French railway yards at Tergnier the night of 10–11 April. He and all his crew perished. This is the remains of their plane. *Couchman Family.*

BELOW: Railway yards at Revigny, northeast France, after the last of three attacks in a week in July 1944. The cost to the RAF was fearsome – forty-one Lancasters and 231 aircrew deaths. The bombing did little substantial damage despite the apparent devastation. *Bernard Parisse via Oliver Clutton-Brock.*

OVERLEAF: Collateral damage at Revigny. The bomb that blasted the enormous crater in the middle photograph also destroyed the nut and bolt factory in the background. Other bombs wrecked French dwellings. *Bernard Parisse via Oliver Clutton-Brock.*

Stuttgart, late July 1944. Three quick raids on this southwest German city cost the RAF seventy-two aircraft and 377 aircrew – fourteen of them New Zealanders.

ABOVE FROM LEFT: New Zealand pilot James Archibald, sole survivor from one Lancaster. *Pat Kearney.* English navigator John Kearney was among the dead on New Zealander George Joblin's aircraft. *Pat Kearney.* Joblin. *Joblin Family.*

RIGHT: English bomb aimer Charles Beeson, the only survivor from Joblin's crew. *Helen Wilson.*

BELOW: Shattered and burned trees in a French forest where major parts of the wreckage of Archibald's Lancaster fell. Some wreckage visible among trees at right. *Aircrew Remembered.*

Les Baveystock sinks *U-955* early on 7 June, the first enemy submarine destroyed after D-Day.

LEFT: Powerful flares dropped from Baveystock's 201 Squadron Sunderland illuminate the blasts from the exploding depth charges that sealed the U-boat's destruction. *Jill Speir.*

BELOW: A 201 Sunderland, just after takeoff, starts its long patrol. *Jill Speir.*

RIGHT: The long and short of it. The big man is William Hender; his small, slim companion is Ian Riddell. New Zealand mates photographed after graduating as sergeant observers (navigators) in Canada. Hender flew more than sixty ops with 279 Squadron, an Air Sea Rescue unit. Riddell was on Les Baveystock's Sunderland when the famous *U-107* was destroyed, Baveystock's second success. *Penny Mill.*

BELOW: The Baveystock crew that sank the submarine in a daylight attack in August 1944. Riddell is second from left, middle row, and Baveystock is on the right-hand end of that row. *Jill Speir.*

BOTTOM: A vast mass of escaping foam and oil marks the spot where *U-107* went down. *Jill Speir.*

Going, going, almost gone. Huge explosions sink *U-675* in Norwegian coastal waters two weeks before D-Day. This remarkable sequence of photographs was taken from a Sunderland piloted by Australian Peter Frizell with New Zealander Jack MacDonald as the second pilot. MacDonald and his New Zealand crew were at a Coastal Command Operational Training Unit in Scotland. Frizell was their skipper and instructor. *U-675* was one of only two U-boats sunk by OTU crews during the war. *Frizell Family*.

Wellingtonian Des Carter played a major role in the sinking of *U-317* on 26 June 1944. Manning the heavy machine gun in the nose of an 86 Squadron Liberator, he cleared the submarine's gun platforms of men, allowing his aircraft a free run at the target. He was rewarded with an immediate DFM. 'Excellent gunnery,' the navy said.

TOP: The Liberator closes in on the U-boat. Photograph from the aircraft. *Dr Phillip Carter.*
BELOW LEFT: Des Carter. *Dr Phillip Carter.*
BELOW RIGHT: Sketch from the navy's attack assessment report. *UK National Archives.*

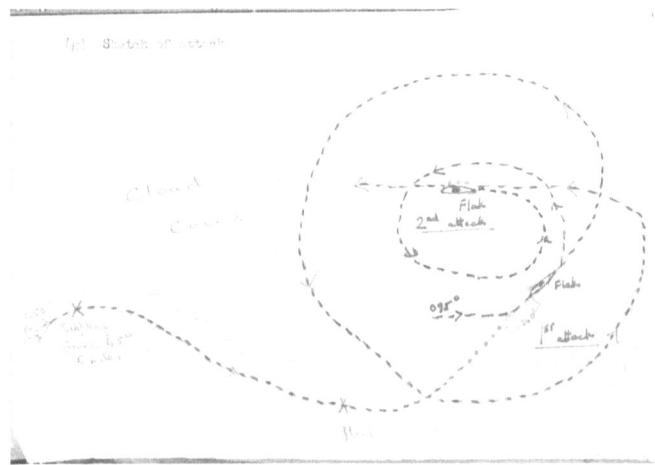

ABOVE: Lysanders, the little planes that played important roles as spotters in Air Sea Rescue ops, and in picking up and delivering agents in secret operations in occupied Europe. Left: Wartime photograph. *Kiwi Saunders*. Right: Preserved and still flying, this Lysander is pictured at an air show in Hamilton, Ontario, in the summer of 2013. *Les Mellor*.

RIGHT: Sitting under the wing of their Stirling on a container used for dropping supplies to Resistance forces, left to right: Eric Elgar (England) and New Zealanders Colin Rouse and Reggie Vincent. Skipper Noel Sutherland stands behind. *Noel Sutherland*.

BELOW: Comrades in arms. Fifty years after Arnhem Sutherland and his crew – minus Elgar – met for a reunion in Motueka on Anzac Day 1994. Left to right: Dave 'Bertie' Bertram (Australia), Ian 'Nix' Nixon (Australia), Sutherland, Rouse and Vincent. Sutherland, 93, is now the only survivor. *Noel Sutherland*.

RIGHT: Ted Robinson and wife Beatrice emerge from a Leicester church 15 April 1944 after their marriage ceremony. Robinson and all his crew were killed four months later.

BELOW: The bride and bridegroom with the rest of Robinson's crew. Bomb aimer, fellow New Zealander and best man Ike Trainor is at his skipper's right. Robinson holds the crew's mascot, Laddie, a West Highland terrier. Beatrice Robinson emigrated to New Zealand postwar and remarried.
Both Beatrice Shearer.

Pilot Henare Uru and his crew died the night of 5–6 August 1944 when their Stirling flying to France to drop supplies to the Resistance was shot down over the Brittany coastal village of Plougoumelen.

ABOVE LEFT: Jack Braddock, Uru's navigator. *Braddock Family*. Right: Henare Uru. *Christine Clark-Hill*.
BELOW LEFT: The remains of the dwelling on which the plane crashed. Right: The crew's village graves with temporary cross. *Both Braddock Family*.

Top Left: Bill Bell's younger brother Peter, shot down and killed by an enemy intruder over England in 1941. Alongside is his sister Hazel. *Tailyour Family.*

Top Right: Bill Bell won a DFC for the safe ditching of his flak-riddled Stirling in the sea near Cherbourg in August 1944. He and all his crew and most of the French paratroopers he had aboard were picked up by an Air Sea Rescue launch. In this photograph Bell, a sheep stud owner postwar, poses with one of his champions at a Central Hawkes Bay show. He died suddenly in 1966. *Tailyour Family.*

Above and Left: Almost seventy years after the ditching event French divers working with aviation researchers found the wreck of what may be the remains of Bell's aircraft. One photograph shows a twisted propeller, another a wing gasoline tank and a third the hazy interior of a fuselage section. *The three photos Olivier Brichet.*

485 (NZ) Squadron Spitfire pilot Jim Mortimer was on the run in France for almost a year. His first hosts were monks in a chateau. Later various families gave him sanctuary and he was liberated in September 1944 by Americans.

LEFT: 'Pilot Officer Mortimer is reported missing' – return-to-sender mail.

BELOW: Monks took Mortimer with them to ask about this bomb crater in a forest. Mortimer blended in well with the local population. Here he is (third from left) with family and friends of a village butcher. *All photos Mortimer Family.*

South Island pilot Les Brown distinguished himself during his four months on the loose in southwest France. His Stirling was shot down in April 1944 but he crash-landed successfully and joined a Resistance group. He used his Bren with great effect in a gun battle against Germans in the hilltop village of Castelnau-sur-l'Auvignon on 21 June 1944. He eventually escaped across the Pyrenees and home to England to be awarded a Military Medal.

ABOVE: Brown, 6ft 2in, towers above members of his new crew after evading. *190 and 620 Sqns Archive via Dennis Williams.*

LEFT: The imposing memorial at Castelnau to the victims of the June clash. *Author's collection.*

RIGHT: 620 Squadron Sqn navigator Bill Cook escaped back to British lines across the Lower Rhine a month after his Stirling was shot down over Arnhem on 21 September 1944. He was found and harboured by the Dutch. *Adair Eady*.

MIDDLE: Sixty years later Cook returned to Arnhem, walked the forest track that led him to the Rhine and visited a flower-strewn memorial. *Adair Eady*.

BOTTOM: South Canterbury crew mates. Left to right: Merv Roberts, Paddy Hay and Harry Christian, shot down over the Danish coast a week before war's end, evaded. Here, they take it easy in England. *Christine and Geoff Roberts*.

ABOVE: Kiwi Saunders after his first solo flight at Taieri in 1940 (*Saunders*) and at ninety-seven in Queensland, November 2013. *Ike Wolhuter*.

RIGHT: Saunders sits at left on the nose of an amphibian Walrus, a 277 Squadron Air Sea Rescue plane. *Saunders*.

BELOW: A full view of a Walrus, an aircraft designed by RJ Mitchell of Spitfire fame. Saunders is not among the aircrew clustered on the plane. *Saunders*.

Pilot Gerry Whincop's Mosquito was shot down over France but he evaded successfully. His navigator and fellow New Zealander Trevor Mullinder was captured.

ABOVE LEFT: Whincop at the controls. RIGHT: Whincop and his new navigator after reaching England. Note the four cannon in the nose of their Mosquito. *Both Paul Whincop.*

BELOW: English navigator John 'Mac' McLaren (left) and New Zealand pilot Roy Le Long became a highly successful Mosquito team claiming seven planes in combat and the same number on the ground. Among their many victims was the first German aircraft shot down on D-Day. *Noel Le Long.*

ABOVE: Whangarei Mosquito pilot Stan McCabe at far left back row on his way to England on the Trojan Star in late 1942 (the woman is a South African novelist). Four of these young men were killed. McCabe shot down two enemy aircraft during his tour with 488 (NZ) Squadron. *McCabe Family.*

MIDDLE: Owaka pilot Erle Brough flew 235 ops with four squadrons and commanded 137 (Typhoon) Squadron in late 1944. One of the Typhoons he flew was this one, rockets slung under the wings. *Both Brough Family.*

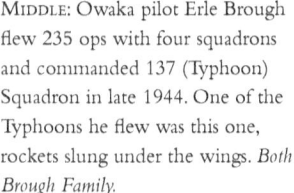

RIGHT: Pilot Ian Waddy (left) with Des Scott, commander of 486 (NZ) Squadron, and Scott's dog. Waddy had just taken command of 164 Squadron when he was shot down by flak over Normandy and captured. He was lucky not to be murdered by SS troops. *David Waddy.*

OPPOSITE PAGE – TOP: Halifaxes and gliders lined up to go at Tarrant Rushton, Dorset. *Alastair Reevely.*

MIDDLE: Halifax lifts off with a Horsa in tow. *Derek Archibald.*

BOTTOM: Gliders down successfully at Arnhem on the first day of Operation Market, 17 September 1944. *Alastair Reevely.*

THIS PAGE – ABOVE: 620 Squadron Stirlings in formation on their way home from Arnhem. *190 and 620 Sqns Archive via Dennis Williams.*

LEFT: New Zealand rear gunner Reggie Vincent stands by his Stirling's rudder, damaged by flak over Arnhem on 20 September. *Noel Sutherland.*

BELOW: Wing Commander Donald Lee's 620 Squadron Stirling burns after a successful crash-landing short of Arnhem on 23 September. *190 and 620 Sqns Archive via Dennis Williams.*

New Zealand Arnhem survivors.
LEFT: Larry Siegert's crew on a Gloucestershire farm before Arnhem. They'd been out shooting rabbits. Note the gun in the hand of one crewman. Siegert, future head of the RNZAF, is at centre back. Siegert's wireless operator, fellow New Zealander Jim Thomson, squats in front. *Bruce Thomson.*

MIDDLE LEFT: Navigator Bill Longhurst gets treatment for his wounded right arm in an RAF Hospital. *Duncan Longhurst.*

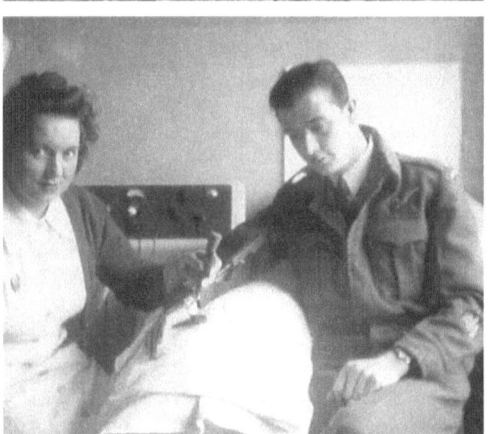

ABOVE RIGHT: Trevor Harris and his crew, Harris at centre in front. Navigator Harry Reek holds his newborn son, named Trevor after his skipper. *Maria Harris.*

BELOW: Pilot Alan Barley (left) poses with mates in front of the open doors of a Dakota. *Barley Family.*

New Zealand dead at Arnhem.
ABOVE, LEFT TO RIGHT: Brian Bebarfald, Barry Brierley, Donald Mathewson. *Ron Bebarfald, Tony Brierley, Peter Rothwell respectively.*

RIGHT: Bebarfald's crew. Bebarfald crouches. Fellow New Zealander Mick Yarwood at left. *Ron Bebarfald.*

BELOW: The graves of Yarwood and Bebarfald are in left foreground at Jonkerbos War Cemetery near Nijmegen, The Netherlands. More than 1600 Commonwealth dead lie here. *Ron Bebarfald.*

ABOVE: Three workhorses of Coastal Command's anti-submarine force.
TOP: Liberator. CENTRE: Catalina. BOTTOM: Hudsons. *Air Force Museum.*

Top - Left: Rescue. A U-boat found this sub-hunting crew adrift in the Atlantic in 1941 and took them aboard – as POWs. New Zealanders John Grocott and Pat Millar were among the rescued. *Arthur Arculus.*
Right: Severe deck damage to U-505 attacked east of Trinidad by a Hudson in 1942. New Zealander Pat Nelson died in the attack. *Author's collection.*

Centre - Left: Tony Spooner's 53 Sqn crew, among them three New Zealanders at left front row. Left to right: Hugh Mills, Fred Bailey and Ian Thomson. *Roseanna Wohnsiedler.* Earlier, Ian Heays, a fourth New Zealander serving on the crew was killed in combat.
Right: Thomson (left) and Mills salute their comrade at his interment. *Lorraine Cook.*

Below - Left: What anti-sub hunters searched for – U-boats. This one's on the surface in the Mediterranean. Southlander Harold Poole found it. *Tony Poole.*
Right: Poole as a sergeant pilot. *Tony Poole.*

ABOVE: Southlander Wattie Stirling's crew on a 10,000-pound bomb at RAF Witchford. Stirling at centre, Scot Jock Adamson on his left. *Jock Adamson.*

BELOW: Stirling's captains' map of the route to and from Dresden (arrowed) the night of the controversial 13–14 February 1945 raid on the eastern German city. *Tup Stirling.*

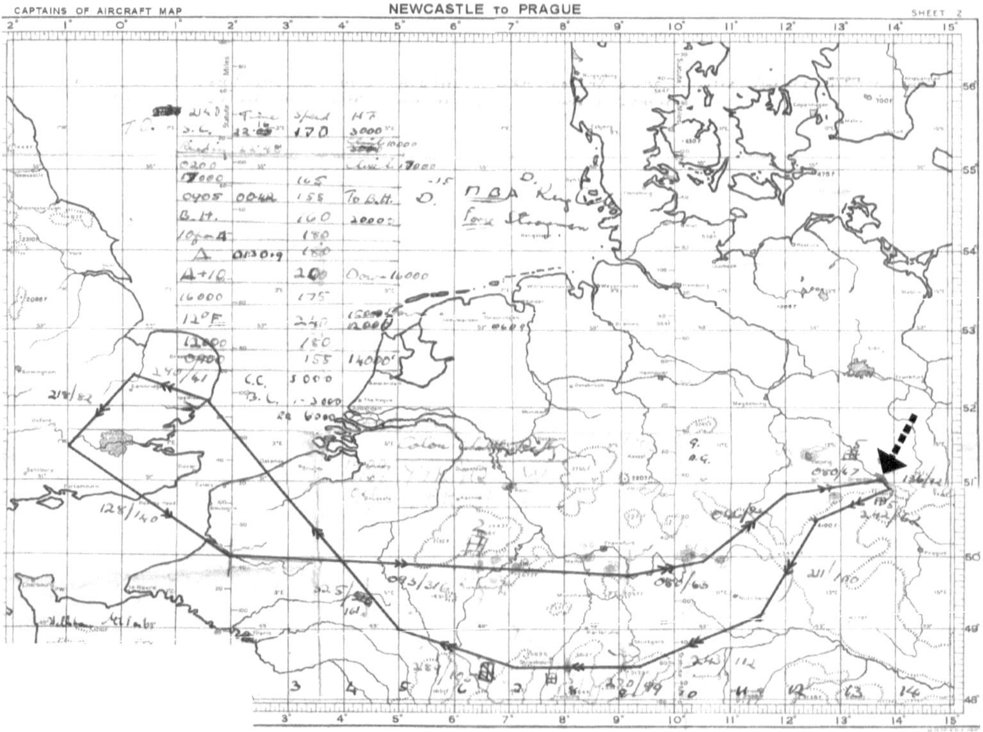

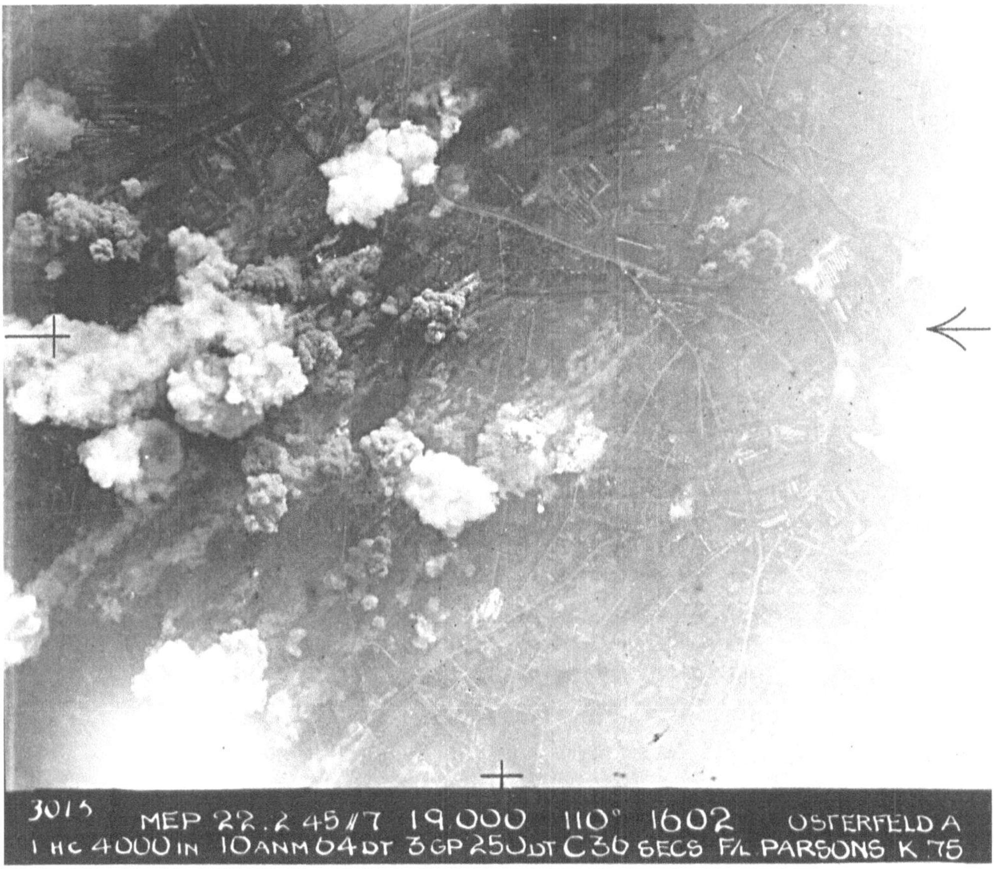

ABOVE: Bombs explode at the Osterfeld benzol refinery in the Ruhr on the afternoon of 22 February 1945. This was the raid when Ray Tait's aircraft was hit badly. The photo was taken from another 75 Sqn Lancaster. *Ray Tait.*

BELOW: Ex POWs await a flight home in this 620 Sqn Stirling at Brussels 20 April 1945. *190 and 620 Sqns Archive via Dennis Williams.*

War over, the troopship *Mooltan* steams into Wellington Harbour 22 December 1945 packed with returning servicemen, among them pilot Ken Orman. His father took this photo from the family home in the eastern suburbs hills. *Ken Orman.*

BELOW: Des Reevely, home safely with his wife Primrose. *Alastair Reevely.*

ABOVE: So many didn't come back. James Gutzewitz (24) from Roxburgh, lies in Reichswald Forest War Cemetery. He was killed the night of 2–3 February 1945 attacking an oil refinery at the end of his tour, among the last of 1850 New Zealanders who lost their lives flying with Bomber Command, 350 of them in the last year of the war. *Gutzewitz Family.*

CHAPTER 9

Arnhem – Montgomery's folly

In the history of British military disasters, Arnhem in September 1944 takes some beating. The undoubted valour of the men on the ground and in the air was marked by five Victoria Crosses and a host of other decorations. Field Marshal Bernard Montgomery's grand vision saw airborne troops capturing vital bridges in southeast Holland allowing his 21st Army Group to sweep into the Ruhr and across the plains of northern Germany, bringing a swift end to the war. It backfired badly – at the cost of many lives.

Montgomery's sluggish moves to chase the Germans out of the Scheldt Estuary allowed them to regroup, saving thousands of troops. Meanwhile Montgomery sat on his hands, plotting the capture of the vital bridge at Arnhem. Success would have permitted a decisive early thrust into Germany but it all went wrong, Montgomery's record forever stained.

While the Americans roared east after the breakout from Normandy the British turned north, sweeping German remnants ahead of them as they raced into Belgium, liberating Brussels and Antwerp. Instead of keeping his divisions hard on the heels of the retreating and demoralised Germans, Montgomery tarried. Time was all the Germans needed. Their officers rallied the troops and stemmed the rout. Reinforcements desperately scraped together stiffened their lines. The Dutch watched in dismay as the advance faltered on their southern border, in some places well short of it. When Montgomery finally ordered the clearance of the Scheldt Estuary, the Germans took some winkling out. The unlucky Canadians were given the job of taking the water-logged estuary, eating up weeks and countless lives. The lack of access to Antwerp, with the Germans controlling the Scheldt, meant the Allies' sole major point for supplies was the harbour at Cherbourg in France, far to the west. American tanks ground to a stop, out of fuel, and Bomber Command flew jerry cans of petrol to Belgium in their bomb bays and fuselage for the British.

Montgomery's bid for acclaim didn't impress General Dwight Eisenhower. The supreme commander didn't like the plan and neither did his staff. But Montgomery argued and cajoled and Eisenhower eventually assented. Operation Market-Garden was on – Market for the air component, Garden for the ground action. The great adventure had simple objectives – capture bridges over rivers and canals over a 90-mile stretch of southwest Holland, allowing Lieutenant General Brian Horrocks' British XXX Corps of three divisions to roll up the land corridor to Arnhem, giving the British a bridgehead over the Rhine. The American 101st Airborne was to capture bridges and land between Eindhoven and Veghel while its counterpart, the 82nd Airborne, would seize bridges at Grave over the Maas and the Waal Rivers crossing at Nijmegen. Further northeast the RAF would carry Britain's 1st Airborne Division and the Polish Brigade to Arnhem to take the bridge over the Nederrijn (the Lower Rhine). Pushing on from Arnhem, the Allies could skirt the northern end of the enemy's West Wall defences, based on the World War I Siegfried Line, and flood into Germany.

The Americans, carried into battle by their own aircraft, seized their objectives slowly and painfully, but the British forces failed to capture their bridge – the famous bridge too far. On 17 September, the first day of action, leading elements of 1st Airborne captured the northern end of the bridge but the Germans held on to the southern approaches and eventually retook the British end. The Germans, so good on defence and counter-attack, blocked the British paras' attempts to reinforce the group at the bridge and gradually forced them back into the shrinking Oosterbeek perimeter. XXX Corps, tasked with reaching Arnhem to relieve the paras, found the job impossible. They reached just beyond Nijmegen, ten or so miles from Arnhem, where they found the road north open and unobstructed – and halted for the night. By the time the ponderous advance got going the Germans were in position and stopped them. In their defence, Horrocks' troops had problems all the way, largely because they couldn't leave the highway to out-flank the defenders. The road on which they were advancing was surrounded on both sides by marshy land, unable to take trucks and tanks and frequently blocked by knocked-out vehicles. For Horrocks, Arnhem was a target too far. Remnants of 1st Airborne squeezed into the diminishing Oosterbeek circle, then withdrew across the Rhine on the night of 25–26 September, bloodied and beaten.

About 10,300 troops were airlifted to Arnhem mainly by gliders, towed by Stirlings and Dakotas and flown by soldiers serving in the Glider Pilot Regiment. They had volunteered for training as pilots and fought as ground troops after landing. When it was all over the British left behind 1400 dead and 1600 wounded. More than 2500 escaped back to Allied territory. About 6000 men became POWs. The Poles also suffered heavily. The RAF lost 370 aircrew, five New Zealanders among them. Eighty became POWs or were logged as missing.

Arnhem was an awful defeat. It would be spring – six months away – before the Allies burst into Germany. Montgomery gambled and lost. It may have been different had he listened to Major Brian Urquhart, chief intelligence officer of Britain's Airborne Corps. Urquhart thought the British paras were being dropped too far from the bridge. More important, he had intelligence reports, backed by word from the Dutch Resistance, that elements of the 9th and 10th SS Panzer divisions, mauled in France, but still hugely dangerous, were refitting in the Arnhem area. He warned Montgomery but was ignored. In 1996 Urquhart told an interviewer he was also 'worried about the state of mind of the senior officers in my outfit, who were all extremely gung-ho and talking about Christmas in Berlin.' Montgomery and others brushed aside Urquhart's objections, irritated by his 'defeatist attitude' and packed him off on sick leave. 'Everyone thought I was hysterical, nervous and so on, and I finally got sent away.'

Debate continues about the Arnhem operation. Many argue the landings at Oosterbeek, five miles west of Arnhem, were too far from the bridge. Perhaps, but it didn't make much difference in the long run. The Germans were just too good. They marshalled rag-tag forces rapidly and aggressively and prevented reinforcements reaching the bridge. The 5000 or so men who remained of the 9th and 10th Panzers after Normandy were battle-hardened veterans and their remaining tanks and guns were too much for paratroops armed only with personal weapons, machine guns and the odd anti-tank weapon. The Germans rushed in extra men, and also skilfully held up XXX Corps' advance toward Arnhem. Flak batteries – 20 mm, 37 mm and the awesome 88s – poured into Arnhem and proved deadly against the RAF delivering supplies.

The RAF's 38 and 46 Groups suffered grievous losses as they tried valiantly to keep the troops supplied with ammunition, food and medical supplies. Poor planning and inter-service rivalry haunted the Market phase of the operation. It's hard to believe but ground-to-air communications were non-existent. Ground radios didn't work – technical issues. Army contact with England was poor. Fighter support for the Stirlings and Halifaxes of 38 Group and the Dakotas of 46 Group was organised in England and flown by British and American squadrons based in England. 2nd Tactical Air Force, flying from nearby airfields in Belgium and France, was hardly involved. 2TAF was told firmly to keep away while supply-dropping was under way. On bad-weather days in England the fighters remained grounded. On 21 September when Luftwaffe fighters battered the supply aircraft, Allied fighters were nowhere to be seen. Because of poor communications, the RAF and its air supply crews had little idea of the situation. They paid a heavy price for a shoddy ground operation.

In the skies over Arnhem, Market went well for the first two days. Then it all turned to custard. Mid-morning on Sunday, 17

September 1944 in the opening act of the week-long battle, twelve Stirlings from 190 and 620 Squadrons, six from each, took off from their base at Fairford in Gloucestershire. They were on a 'pathfinder' mission to drop paratroopers to secure and mark LZs and DZs for gliders and paras five to eight miles west of Arnhem. Two of the pilots chosen for this key flight were New Zealanders, both flying officers, Brian Bebarfald (23), and Larry Siegert (21).

Their fates highlighted the stark fortunes of war. Bebarfald was killed four days later, as he struggled to keep his aircraft aloft long enough for some of his crew to bale out. Siegert narrowly survived Arnhem, with a DFC to show for it, flew transport aircraft from Britain for two years postwar, participated in the 1949 Berlin airlift, ferried the young Queen Elizabeth around New Zealand skies during the 1953–54 Royal Tour, and in due course became an air vice-marshal and New Zealand's Chief of Air Staff. Bebarfald, whose life had hardly begun in 1944, was one of five New Zealand airmen killed at Arnhem.

Stirlings, Halifaxes and Albemarles of 38 Group and Dakota transports of 46 Group followed not far behind the pathfinders on the 17th, towing gliders packed with paras and their equipment and weapons. On that first day 358 aircraft hauling gliders were dispatched, carrying troops of the 1st Airborne Division. The operation passed off without a hitch. No aircraft were lost and only a relative handful of gliders failed to make their intended LZs, broken tow ropes often a problem. Ground fire damaged six aircraft but flak was basically non-existent.

Day two went almost as well, the rest of the division being ferried in on gliders with two 38 Group Stirling squadrons, 295 and 570, para dropping supplies. One of the 570 Stirlings was destroyed by flak, killing the entire crew, and another two from the same squadron crash-landed, one army dispatcher dying. One Dakota made an emergency landing in Holland, another's pilot was killed by flak, the second pilot flying it home. All these aircraft were hit by flak. No enemy aircraft were encountered.

Bebarfald, off the Fairford runway three minutes before midday heading to Arnhem for the second time, didn't get very far. The tow rope broke and both the Stirling and its Horsa glider landed safely at Woodbridge, the giant emergency field on the Suffolk coast. New tow rope attached, Bebarfald hauled his glider back to base.

Deadly flak began to scythe the skies above Arnhem on 19 September, as the Germans rushed in batteries of the feared 88 mm guns from the Ruhr Valley, plus more and more of the lighter calibre 20 mm and 37 mm pieces. Upwards of twenty aircraft crashed or made crash- and emergency-landings, the majority of damage caused by curtains of ground fire over the Oosterbeek area just west of Arnhem, where the paras were concentrated. Unwieldy gliders and low-flying, slow-moving tug aircraft made easy targets for gunners. German infantry and machine-gunners turned their weapons skyward, unleashing fire on the aerial fleets. During the week of Market many aircrew were wounded and killed by small-arms fire, including a number of Royal Army Service Corps dispatchers, who were carried on all aircraft to manhandle heavy panniers – wicker baskets much like giant picnic baskets – of supplies out of Dakotas and the large exit holes cut in the rear floors of the 38 group aircraft. Many planes returned to England with hundreds of bullet holes, some looking like giant sieves.

Bad weather postponed the planned landing of the Polish Parachute Brigade on the 19th but their Jeeps, six-pounder guns and other equipment were flown to Holland. Eight of the thirty-five tug-glider combinations in the air were units that had failed to make the trip the day before, Bebarfald among them. The New Zealander probably couldn't believe his bad luck – the tow rope parted again in the rough conditions, this time over the Channel, and his glider ditched in the sea off Ostend. It's believed the two glider pilots died but three other men on the glider were picked up. The near all-wood Horsas floated well and the rescue services had boats waiting. A second glider ditched that day and others went down over land. Thirteen big Stirlings were lost. A despondent Bebarfald and his crew were given the next day off.

Five Victoria Crosses were awarded after Arnhem – four for valour on the ground and one in the air. Flight Lieutenant David Lord, DFC, an English 271 Squadron Dakota pilot, died winning his on 19 September. Three minutes from the drop zone flak twice hit the plane, setting the starboard engine afire. On learning the flak bursts hadn't hurt any of the crew or dispatchers, Lord dropped the plane down to 900 feet from 1500 feet and continued his run, though he would have been justified in staying higher or even abandoning the aircraft. Although the furiously burning engine endangered the wing, Lord kept the Dakota straight and level on the run-in, braving heavy ground fire. The dispatchers pushed the supplies out but as the plane turned away Lord was told two containers remained. He immediately rejoined the stream and made a second run. Delivery task complete, Lord urged his crew to jump at a now critically low 500 feet. Moments later the burned-out wing collapsed and the plane crashed in flames on one of Arnhem's original LZs. Navigator Harold King, sole survivor, was thrown out while helping other crew don parachutes. When he returned from POW camp King told the story of his captain's bravery and Lord's posthumous VC was gazetted on 13 November 1945. Lord's act epitomised that of many aircrew at Arnhem. They flew gallantly against heavy odds to get supplies to the men trapped on the ground. Three of the other four Arnhem VCs were also awarded posthumously.

An anonymous glider pilot who went in on the first day and then fought as a paratrooper over the following week before escaping across the Rhine wrote about it in a 1945 booklet called *Arnhem Lift*. He talked of the courage of the Stirling crews who dropped urgently needed food and ammunition.

> The cold-blooded pluck and heroism of the pilots was quite incredible. They came in in their lumbering four-engined machines at fifteen hundred feet, searching for our positions. The ack-ack was such as I have only heard during the worst raids on London, but concentrated on one small area. The German gunners were firing at point-blank range, and the supply planes were more or less sitting targets. The rattle of machine guns from the scores of planes, the heavy ack-ack batteries all around us, the sky filled with flashes and puffs of exploding shells, burning planes diving towards the ground and the hundreds and hundreds of red, white, yellow and blue supply parachutes [the colours ID'd the contents of containers – one colour for medical supplies, another for weapons and ammunition and so on] dropping in this very small area, looked more like an overcrowded and crazy illustration to a child's book … how those pilots could have gone into [this inferno] with their eyes open is beyond my imagination.

The lack of radio communications, the outcome of botched planning, became serious. Arnhem headquarters' contact with England was poor and there was no radio contact between aircraft and the ground, where ammunition, food and medical supplies were desperately needed. By midweek about eighty percent of material dropped from aircraft braving storms of shot and shell was falling on German positions. The airmen seemed to know what was happening – they could see enemy helmets in the area where their drops were falling, areas previously occupied by British troops. But they didn't get new coordinates to drop into British positions and continued to unload, more or less in hope. It's not as if ground-to-air and vice versa communication was unknown at the time. It was old hat. Ground controllers and spotters routinely directed pinpoint attacks on military targets on the front lines in Normandy by 2TAF, giving pilots map coordinates and other directions. They routinely called in Typhoons to destroy strongpoints, gun batteries, tanks – whatever they wanted destroyed. It was known as the cab-rank system – the Typhoons circled overhead waiting for instructions from the ground.

Aerial support for 38 and 46 Group aircraft was planned in England, if you could call it planning, and the fighter support – British and American – operated from bases in England. 2TAF, now entrenched on French and nearby Belgian bases, was hardly consulted. It wasn't their show. They were told, very firmly, to keep away from the Arnhem area when the RAF transports and gliders were overhead going about their business. Sheer madness. When Spitfires, Mustangs and Thunderbolts didn't fly because their fields in England were shrouded in fog or drizzle, there was nothing shielding 38 and 46 aircraft. Sometimes the defensive umbrella arrived over Arnhem, found no transports on hand and buzzed off home, shrugging that the transports apparently weren't flying. The lack of cooperation on rendezvous times was mind-boggling. All the time 2TAF's fighters and the brilliant rocket- and bomb-carrying Typhoons sat on the ground at their much closer fields. When aircraft lugging vital supplies to Arnhem were being shot down right, left and centre by ground fire, not a flak-busting Typhoon was to be seen.

All these planning snafus had been fixed by time the RAF mounted its airborne landings over the main Rhine in March 1945 – no consolation to the families of men needlessly killed over Arnhem.

On Wednesday, 20 September the first New Zealander died at Arnhem. Pilot Neil Couper, an Oamaru farmer's son three weeks away from his 22nd birthday, was killed when his 295 Squadron Stirling was hit by flak, caught fire and exploded, crashing near the town of Druten on the south bank of the Waal. The aircraft, one of sixteen taking off from Harwell just before midday, was part of a fleet of sixty-four dropping supplies in the first of two re-supply waves. Another 100 flew to Arnhem later in the afternoon. Couper's crew and the two army dispatchers aboard jumped safely before the blazing plane exploded. Years later his wireless operator, Australian Ken Nolan, wrote a moving account of what happened for an Arnhem veterans' club. A nicely balanced crew flew to Arnhem that autumn afternoon – Couper, his navigator Jack Corcoran, a fellow New Zealander from Dunedin, Nolan, two Englishmen and Dubliner Paddy Bowers, the rear gunner. Nolan:

> As we approached Arnhem we ran into intense and accurate 88 mm fire from gun emplacements, vehicles and flak barges on the rivers. It

sounded like being inside a tin shed and being bombarded with small stones and gravel. Large holes appeared in the side of the aircraft. By the time we approached the dropping zone the aircraft had suffered considerable damage and was full of blackish, acrid smoke and cordite fumes. We released the containers in the bomb bays … and the dispatchers pushed the large baskets of supplies out to the troops below. We were at about 500 feet and received several direct hits which set the aircraft on fire.

Couper, who now ordered the crew out, must have climbed – 500 feet was far too low for safe jumping. Nolan said there was no response from Bowers and the dispatchers at the back of the plane to Couper's cry so he scrambled down the fuselage to them:

The dispatchers had pulled their plugs out of the intercom as they moved around so I shouted at them, clipped on their parachutes and opened the rear door for them. When I reached [Bowers] I could see his turret had been hit, his intercom cut and his leg jammed. I managed to turn the turret until the doors faced outward and undid his flying boot. He left his boot behind as he baled out backwards. I then headed back to the pilot. By now the engines and fuel tanks were on fire and the cabin full of smoke. When I reached Couper, he was standing up at the controls and beating his chest, indicating that he did not have his parachute. I searched for it desperately, eventually locating it under the navigator's table. I clipped on his chute and then mine and he gave me the thumbs up. With my arms raised, I dropped my legs through the front hatch to bale out. Then, almost immediately, the aircraft exploded. There was an awesome noise and searing heat and then silence.

Blown clear and hanging beneath his chute, Nolan plunged into the Waal, inflated his life jacket and swam for the bank. As he neared it, shots fired at him from the opposite side pinged into the water and he ducked under. Eventually he clambered out and huddled in a ditch before Dutch patriots found him and hustled him to safety. The next day, reunited with Corcoran, Bowers and the English flight engineer, he discovered the Germans had nabbed the English bomb aimer and dispatchers. Nolan, Corcoran and the others made contact with British troops in the area and soon were on the road to Belgium, looking for air transport. At 6 p.m. on the 22nd the four scruffy unshaven men walked into the operations room at Harwell, without their skipper.

Couper lies in the Puiflijk Roman Catholic Church burial yard, a mile or so from Druten, alongside the graves of three British soldiers killed in the area, their four graves tended faithfully by the villagers. They are specially honoured every 4 May, The Netherlands' war remembrance day.

Noel Sutherland experienced the full fury of German ground fire on the 20th, his last flight to Arnhem. He and his crew had flown on the first and second days of Market, towing gliders when what flak there was proved light and ineffective. They'd tugged a Horsa with a Jeep and trailer the first day and followed up the next day with a Jeep, a six-pounder (57 mm) anti-tank gun, and three paras. They were slow, uneventful, 5½-hour trips. The 20th was different. Sutherland remembers:

> We went in, slowed, and dropped down to 600 feet. And suddenly, this storm of light stuff, rifle fire and machine guns. I didn't mind

that but amid it all there was 20 mm stuff and I didn't like the sound of that. The small stuff we could take but the 20 mm was different. We dropped our containers and panniers and were ready to climb out of it but I could see if we climbed we were opening ourselves up to a lot more munitions from the ground. So I stuffed the nose down to ground level.

The crews had been told not to fly at low level but they did in an effort to stay alive. Sutherland didn't know it at the time but he had a large hole in the rudder, some control cables were cut – the flight engineer collected everyone's boot laces and tied the severed lines together – and ailerons weren't working properly. With sloppy controls he had a struggle to get one wing over a church spire. 'We just cleared it, there wasn't much in it. Then we were out of it, climbed up and off home. We tuned into the BBC and had a nice programme all the way back.'

The crew emerged virtually unscathed but Dave 'Bertie' Bertram, map reading in the bomb aimer's position to help navigate, got what Sutherland called 'a ping in his behind'. Bertram wouldn't go to the hospital – 'they had girl nurses and he wasn't having any of that.' The Stirling fared worse. It had a great chunk out of the rudder and ground crew found more than 150 holes, mainly from small arms fire. Sutherland's New Zealand navigator Colin Rouse was quoted by NZPA from London as saying the Stirling carried sixteen tears caused by shells. Ground staff set to on repairs but E-Easy was a mess and wasn't flyable the next day. But at least E-Easy was home. 190 Squadron lost three of the seventeen aircraft it had dispatched. Crews and planes were becoming scarce. 620 Squadron sent the same number and lost two.

Sutherland went into Arnhem as a flight sergeant and came out with a commission and a DFC, the citation specifically noting his performance on the 20th with a severely damaged aircraft. 'By superb skill and determination he then flew the aircraft to England and landed successfully.' Sutherland went on to complete twenty-eight ops with the same crew, most being SOE flights to Holland, Norway and Denmark. He also towed a Horsa glider to Germany on the Rhine crossing.

20 September was tough but it was a milk-run compared with the next day. German fighters had been conspicuously absent in Market's early days but Me 109s and FW 190s appeared in force over Arnhem on the 21st as the later-arriving Dakotas and Stirlings began their supply drops. The fighters made a meal of unprotected RAF transports – shooting-gallery stuff. One German pilot struck down four Dakotas in five minutes. The flak was still awful – worse, if that were possible. Years later English flight engineer Les Hillyard remembered the flak that afternoon – 'absolutely terrible'. He was quoted in *Green On* by Arie-Jan van Hees: 'We could see it about 10 miles from the dropping zone like a big black cloud.' He and the gunner were the only survivors when their 190 Squadron Stirling was knocked down by German batteries. A wireless operator on another 190 Stirling that crash-landed was also quoted in *Green On* as saying, 'On the approach it was very evident that the reception was going to be hot – the sky was patchy and dark with flak bursts; smoking aircraft could be seen falling out of the sky, and enemy fighters, Me 109s and FW 190s, were much in evidence.'

21 September, a Thursday, was the RAF's worst day at Arnhem. For 190 Squadron it couldn't have more terrible. Ten of its Stirlings

took off from Fairford carrying supplies for the beleaguered 1st Airborne, hanging on at Arnhem in the face of German superiority in numbers and weapons. Four and a half hours later just three of the ten came home. Five crashed, three of them downed by fighters, two by flak. The other two crash-landed, beaten down by a combination of fighters and flak. Twenty-three crew died in the downed planes including four New Zealanders – Brian Bebarfald and his navigator, Malcolm Yarwood (34), from Gisborne, killed on Stirling LJ881, navigator Don Mathewson (36), from Central Otago, and pilot Barry Brierley (21), from Wellington, who flew with Wing Commander Graeme Harrison's crew and died with him.

620 Squadron, 190's partner squadron at Fairford, suffered nothing like the same casualties but lost two of the eleven aircraft it sent. Just one of the twelve crew died – a Canadian gunner thrown from the aircraft when his rear turret was wrecked by flak. The entire crew of the other Stirling baled successfully, including navigator Bill Cook (23), from Nelson, who was sheltered by Dutch patriots and eventually escaped back across the Rhine (see Chapter 6).

Highly respected Allen Wheeler, Fairford's station commander, was dismayed by the 21 September losses and the deaths of many of the men he knew personally. He was quoted in *Green On*: 'The losses were very heavy indeed throughout the group, Fairford included … During the few days we kept supplying and reinforcing the 1st Airborne Division near Arnhem we lost one quarter of Fairford's operational Stirlings.'

The Stirling and Dakota squadrons of 38 and 46 Groups sent 117 aircraft to Arnhem on the 21st. Thirty didn't make it home and another crashed on the Norfolk coast. Twenty-three crashed or crash-landed, shot down by fighters or shredded by gunfire; the rest, badly damaged, made emergency landings in Holland and Belgium. Many others arrived back at their bases with heavy damage.

The transports, watched anxiously for their supplies by airborne troops fighting on the ground in a shrinking perimeter outside Arnhem, flew over the battlefield in four waves. The first two had the protection of fighters operating from English bases but the third and fourth waves were left to go it alone, the fighters grounded by deteriorating weather over southern England. The weather was OK over Holland but 2TAF's forces, close at hand, didn't fly. *Green On* notes that 2TAF was still under orders to keep their ground attack and fighter-to-fighter forces away from Arnhem while re-supply was in progress. *Green On* adds that 2TAF 'was by this time the only formation sufficiently well informed [about] the tactical situation to deal adequately with the German opposition. Nevertheless, First Allied Airborne Army planning centre was still unwilling to part with any of its authority. It required yet another day's tragedy to bring about a change.'

The loss of so many lives and aircraft was unforgivable. 2TAF Spitfires, Tempests and Mustangs would have seen off the Germans – a squadron or two of Typhoons would have quietened the flak. The 'it's our patch' attitude of the planners in England was monstrous. Defenceless Dakotas without guns and self-sealing fuel tanks, and Stirlings with only rear turrets, were left to fend for themselves.

Brian Bebarfald's Stirling was the first or second 190 aircraft to go down, hit by flak and then savaged by Me 109s short of Arnhem. Australian rear gunner George Morris, one of the two survivors from the crew, is quoted in *Green On*:

We were badly holed by flak over Elst and shortly afterwards we were attacked by enemy aircraft. I managed to hit one Me 109 and saw it catch fire … Our port inner was set on fire and the tail badly damaged and we received the order to bale out … When I was in the air I saw the aircraft fall to pieces on the way down and crash nose in.

Canadian wireless operator Les Munro and one of the army dispatchers also jumped and all three got back to England with the help of the Dutch Resistance. The Stirling smashed to earth in a field at Andelst on the north bank of the Waal. Bebarfald, his fellow New Zealander and navigator Mick Yarwood and the others who died with him were buried at nearby Herveld but later reinterred in the Jonkerbos War Cemetery at Nijmegen.

Bebarfald, known to everyone as Beb, grew up in Wanganui. The family trace paternal roots to Poland and a history of beaver-hunting, tailoring and hat-making before immigration to England in the early 1800s and an Anglicised name. Beb's younger brother Ron says Beb was quite short (he always used a cushion on his pilot's seat) but made up for it with body-building exercises. 'His great love was radio and the *Lamphouse Annual* and he was slick with morse – 30 words per minute long before he went into the air force.' Bebarfald had become infected with the adventure of flying after seeing Kingsford-Smith and wanted to be a pilot. A good education at Wanganui Tech and then Scots College in Wellington enabled him to fulfil his dream and he was accepted for pilot training, enlisting in September 1941. The usual but always daunting routine followed. Two months' elementary flight training, solo flights and more demonstrated he had what it took. Then off to Canada where he earned his wings in April 1942, followed by six months as a staff pilot on a training field – a job given to some of the best graduating pilots.

Bebarfald was posted to Pennfield Ridge, where dozens of New Zealanders crewed up and flew four-man, twin-engined Venturas. It was here he met Malcolm 'Mick' Yarwood. Yarwood, born in Broken Hill, New South Wales, came here with his parents at an early age. He went to Waipukurau District High School and was working as a clerk in Gisborne when he enlisted. Bebarfald and Yarwood flew together for the first time on 13 January 1943, with Canadian Les Munro working the radio and a Scot called Hughes on the guns. They embarked for England in April 1943 and after adding a bomb aimer cum map reader and a flight engineer joined 190 in March 1944. By Arnhem, the crew was one of the more experienced on the squadron – having flown fourteen SOE ops to France. For some reason Hughes was grounded before Normandy and replaced by Australian George Morris. Late on the night of 5 June theirs were among the hundreds of planes flying to France to drop paras near Caen, the start of D-Day. Their last flight to Arnhem was their twentieth.

Munro and Morris both wrote to Bebarfald's parents in early 1945, by which stage both were home – in Vancouver and Sydney. Their accounts indicate the mayhem and desperation inside the aircraft caused first by flak, then fighters. Munro was trapped near the rear of the plane and couldn't get forward (over DZs wireless operators usually helped the army dispatchers with the cargo) but could see Yarwood and the engineer lying on the floor, either dead or wounded:

> Brian and the bomb aimer were still talking about the shortest way to get out of the district. Brian may have been hit by shrapnel but I

cannot say for sure. A few seconds after we had escaped the gunfire we were set upon by six enemy fighters which scored hits on us no matter what evasive action Brian took. There were too many against us ... the fire was getting worse and we were very low by this time. The next thing I heard, and the last, was Brian's calm command to abandon the aircraft. The gunner and I baled out 600 feet above the ground and were very fortunate our chutes opened in time. The plane crashed before we hit the ground and I was only in the air seven seconds from the time I left the plane until I was on the ground.

Munro added Bebarfald was a superb pilot and his death hit hard. 'Since the loss of Brian and the rest of the crew I haven't much of an inclination to fly ... Brian was the finest pilot I ever knew and I shall be eternally grateful to him.'

Morris' shorter account said Bebarfald reported over the intercom he had been hit but still had control of the plane:

Fighters were now attacking us; our port wing was on fire and our plane was in a bad shape ... Our aircraft was breaking up in the air and at 600 feet Brian gave the order to abandon ship. I acknowledged and baled out.

He called Bebarfald a skilful and thoughtful skipper. *Green On* says the Bebarfald Stirling was the first from Fairford to be shot down but Morris indicates this wasn't the case. He says their wing commander Graeme Harrison's aircraft 'came round us in flames and blew up on the ground' before their own plane was attacked by fighters. Harrison's Stirling had dropped its supplies and was making a sweeping turn to climb out when it was hit by fighters and crashed. Two of the crew managed to bale out but were too low and died. The other seven men aboard, two of them dispatchers, were also killed. It went down on farmland at Zetten, not far from Andelst.

Barry Brierley is listed as Harrison's second pilot on 21 September which is quite true, but why he was flying as number two is unusual. The practice of using second pilots, widespread early in the war, was abandoned by Bomber Command in 1942 and Stirlings operating with 38 Group flew with only one pilot unless special circumstances put a man in the second seat. Brierley tripped over a wire and broke his left wrist in mid-June. In a letter home to his wife Vi on 17 June, Don Mathewson wrote, 'Hard luck. Barry went to jump over a wire, slipped and fell. Bone broken in two places. Just unlucky that he could not jump about six inches higher but these things happen.' Brierley's arm was encased in plaster and he was off pilot duties. Strength was needed to fly the big four-engined heavies and even when the plaster was removed it would take several weeks for his arm to regain full strength. The breaks should have healed quickly but the bone ends were slow to knit and plaster was still on the day he died. It's been said Brierley was frustrated at being out of action and agitated to fly as a passenger. He did so once with his own crew and Harrison as pilot – to France on a long successful SOE drop on 9–10 September. Anxious to go again – especially to see Arnhem – he flew on 21 September with fatal results.

Before smashing his arm, Brierley, Mathewson and the rest of the crew had flown together on ops just three times, including D-Day evening when they delivered paras to Normandy. After that Mathewson and the others built up their ops totals flying with other pilots. By the time he died at Arnhem, Mathewson had completed nineteen. He did nine trips with Briton Johnny Hay, whom he knew well from Pennfield Ridge, two with New Zealand squadron leader David Gibb and several with Harrison, including Arnhem's opening day when Harrison's glider carried Major General Roy Urquhart, commander of the 1st Airborne.

Mathewson, a farmer from Kokonga in Central Otago, was 34 when he enlisted in February 1942. He sailed for Canada in the *Uruguay* two months later, with fifty-two other would-be navigators. Twenty-five would be killed. Yarwood, with whom he would become close, was on the same ship and after graduation they went to Pennfield Ridge, where they got to know their pilots. Brierley had gone to Wellington College and drove a delivery van. Another of Mathewson's navigator friends, Geoff Norriss (37), a self-employed bricklayer from Nelson when he joined up, died on 23 January 1943, when his Canadian pilot crashed their Ventura.

With Brierley and two army dispatchers aboard, Harrison's Stirling carried nine men. None survived, although the wireless operator and flight engineer apparently jumped before the plane smashed into the ground. The crew were buried in a churchyard at Zetten but re-interred postwar in Arnhem Oosterbeek War Cemetery, Brierley's body easily identified by the plaster cast on his arm.

Hay, the man with whom Brierley's crew had often flown, was forced down on the 21st by fighters east of Tilburg according to 190's ORB, miles off the planned homeward-bound course. What happened and exactly where the crash occurred has never been established. The crew, some wounded, were taken prisoner.

One of the saddest 190 losses that day was the Stirling skippered by Briton Sandy Anderson, which was shot down by German fighters and crashed in the Maas. Just two of the crew and one dispatcher survived, paddling ashore in the plane's dinghy. The rest drowned. The bomb aimer, a man called Orange, was one of those who lived. He is quoted in *Green On* as saying they'd been told they'd have heavy American fighter support over Arnhem. 'The last words of our rear gunner were, "There is our escort. Christ – they're Jerries!"'

The pilot of one of the three 190 Stirlings that came home told Wheeler he'd got on OK because a section of Typhoons had kept just above and behind on the way in to the DZ. *Green On* quotes Wheeler:

> I told him no Typhoons had taken off that day. I did not need to remind him of the superficial similarity between a Typhoon and the German FW 190 ... the large engine of the FW 190 might well have prevented the German pilots from seeing the Stirling just below. Fortunately the rear gunner in the Stirling made the same mistake and did not shoot at the fighters ... [and] ... the position of the fighters almost certainly prevented the ground defences from firing at that particular Stirling.

Larry Siegert, like Noel Sutherland, won his DFC at Arnhem on the 21st – and an enhanced reputation – by the skin of his teeth. His Stirling, vulnerable to the intense flak streaming up as it lumbered in at low level on its run in to drop supplies, was hit and damaged several times. As Siegert put power on the engines, turning the big plane away to climb for home, German fighters waiting outside the flak zone bore in, the last thing Siegert expected. The squadron had been briefed that RAF fighters would be there to protect them, so when he saw four planes coming at him he was happy. Siegert told an RNZAF magazine interviewer in September 1994, the fiftieth anniversary of Arnhem, he thought to himself, Good, the fighter escort has caught up with us ...,' until he caught sight of the aircrafts' markings and realised what they were. Deadly FW 190s. 'My heart headed through the floor of the Stirling.'

Siegert was made of stern stuff. As two of the fighters peeled off to attack, he realised he and his crew had one chance. He put the nose of the Stirling down and headed for the ground. Soon he was just 50 feet off the deck, thundering over trees, buildings, fields to prevent the Germans getting under him, twisting this way and that to the commands of rear gunner John Welton, an Englishman, as the fighters came in. For eight fraught minutes they battled for their lives. The German attacks and their fire caused more damage, wounding New Zealand wireless operator Jim Thomson and the two army dispatchers. Then Welton caught one fighter, pouring return fire into him. He claimed to have shot it down, to have seen it dive into the ground. The other fighter pulled away and suddenly it was all over.

Despite damage, nothing vital had been hit and the Stirling's engines beat strongly as it fled for England. Siegert's DFC citation said that despite the series of fighter attacks his 'superb handling of his aircraft [enabled him] to ward off the enemy and make a safe return to base'. The Stirling touched down at Fairford at 4.35 p.m. – 4 hours 27 minutes after takeoff. Waiting ambulances whisked Thomson off for treatment of leg and head wounds before transfer to RAF Hospital Wroughton in Wiltshire – wounds serious enough to finish his war. Thomson flew thirteen ops with Siegert including Normandy, and one with fellow New Zealander David Gibb, his flight commander. On his first op, an SOE trip to France on 20 July 1944 dropping containers, Thomson noted in his log, 'Injured in eye and leg over target.' Flak splinters must have caught him but the wounds couldn't have been serious because he was flying over France dropping supplies to the Resistance three weeks later.

Siegert and Thomson flew to Arnhem three times before their eventful 21st battle with fighters – on the 17th (carrying pathfinder paras), the 18th and 19th. Of the day German fighter fire terminated his war, Thomson wrote, 'Operations – Holland – Supplies to British 1st Airborne Army. 10 FW 190s encountered at target area. Later, two 190s made attack lasting 8 minutes. Gunner destroyed one. Aircraft badly damaged. Self and two dispatchers wounded.'

Siegert later caused fellow 190 pilot George Chesterton unintended grief. Chesterton had watched, appalled, as losses mounted. In the long summer of 1944 and through Normandy and its aftermath 190 lost only three aircraft, two of them flown by the New Zealanders Peter Croudis and Danny Kilgour. Arnhem changed all that. In his war memoir, written more than sixty years after the event, Chesterton said that approaching the dropping zone at a height of 600 feet and a speed of 150 knots, through lines of quick-firing guns, was a stomach-turning experience. 'I … still remember, to my shame, as Roderick Matheson's aircraft plummeted to the ground in a ball of fire, saying out loud, "Thank God it's not us!" Nightmares of this lived with me for years.' He wrote that the Germans reacted to the airborne landings with 'savage efficiency'.

Detailed to fly again on the 23rd, Chesterton said: 'I didn't see how I could possibly survive another venture into that cauldron.' He did but was diverted to another airfield. Chesterton was so sure he wouldn't survive he wrote to his parents telling them how much he loved them and thanking them for everything they had done. He entrusted his 'last letter' to Siegert with instructions to mail it if he didn't come back. When he didn't show on the 23rd the New Zealander posted the letter. The English flier apparently didn't contact Fairford to let the station know he was down safely at another field and when he did get back was horrified to learn the letter had gone. He dashed to the phone to call his father. The letter had been delivered but the elderly man hadn't told his wife their son was missing. He was waiting for official word.

Siegert, Percy to his air force friends, was born in Fairlie on 14 March 1923. He started a law degree at Victoria University but never finished, instead enlisting in March 1942. Thirty-seven years after he joined the colours, a lowly airman pilot under training, he retired with a chestful of well-earned decorations and the rank of Air Vice-Marshal Cyril Laurence Siegert, Chief of Air Staff – top post in the RNZAF. He flew with 190 until June 1945, thirty-three ops to his credit.

After the first two days of Market, the Blakehill Farm Dakota squadrons 233 and 437 RCAF returned to their transport duties, but were called in on the 21st as the ground situation became serious. New Zealander Rex Daniell, a veteran Dakota captain and now a flight commander squadron leader on 233 under Wing Commander Bill Coles, had towed a glider to Arnhem on 17 September. Daniell, leading a V of three on the 21st, flew in thick cloud to Holland, talking to fellow pilots by RT to maintain vertical separation. The weather cleared over Belgium and Daniell could see. The squadron formed up over Eindhoven and began the run into the DZ. Daniell in his book *What Did You Do in the War, Poppa Rekka?*:

> We had been briefed to expect a fighter escort on this last leg but no one turned up. As we sighted the city we noticed some four-engined

Stirlings just completing their supply drop under heavy fire. As we came nearer the sky was black with flak-bursts … Two Stirlings coming away from the area suddenly blew up within seconds of each other and the picture looked far from rosy. For the first time ever I thought to myself this was one operation I might not survive but there was no alternative but to go through with it.

Daniell was right to be perturbed. The four Dakota squadrons suffered just as badly from the depredations of the German flak and fighters on the 21st as the Stirlings. 233 Squadron lost four and 437 five. The Down Ampney Dakota squadrons, 48 and 271, lost six and four, respectively. One German fighter downed four Dakotas in four minutes. The squadrons suffered heavy losses – almost thirty aircrew were killed and many dispatchers lost.

One of the lost 48 Squadron aircraft was hit by a load dropped from a Dakota. A wing folded up and the plane crashed. Daniell narrowly avoided the same fate, standing his plane on one wing to avoid a pannier swinging from a chute as he signalled his four army dispatchers to start dropping. 'They did a fine job and I could feel the panniers rumbling down the tram tracks in a matter of seconds.' (The heavy cane panniers were trundled out of the plane on tracks attached to the fuselage floor. Static lines jerked their parachutes open once they left the plane.) 'As soon as they had gone it was a case of full throttle and climb like a home-sick angel,' Daniell wrote. 'There was so much metal in the sky it could be heard pattering down on the wings.' The New Zealander, an old hand wise in ways of survival, looked for and found a cloud where he hid long enough 'for the Allied fighters to join the fracas and send the Focke Wulfs on their way'. But not before a great deal of damage had been done to the Dakotas. 233 CO Coles' aircraft was damaged by flak and he had to put down at an Allied field at Brussels to get attention for his badly wounded wireless operator (the group captain station commander flew as second pilot to Coles that day – and probably wished he hadn't). One of Coles' dispatchers died when he was thrown from the plane. He must have gone out with a pannier because Daniell saw him clinging to it, dangling from the plane and desperately trying to open its canopy.

Daniell, awarded an AFC at New Year 1944 for his transport and casualty-evacuation flying in North Africa, won a DFC in June 1945, the citation noting Arnhem and the later airborne Rhine crossing. Queen Wilhelmina bestowed a Dutch Flying Cross on the New Zealander in late 1946, when she announced awards for RAF airmen who flew at Arnhem (the only New Zealand, so honoured).

Flying out of Arnhem Aucklander Alan Barley (31) was able to escape enemy fighters and reach friendly clouds – and stay there, safe, until reaching Belgium. Barley was a flight lieutenant pilot on 233 with Rex Daniell, towing a glider to Arnhem on the 17th and taking part in the support landing. He knew the Germans would be waiting for them on the 21st and impressed on the two dispatchers the necessity of doing their job quickly and to 'sit on their tin hats and keep their fingers crossed'. For himself, he piled the American flak suit issued to all crew on his seat and sat 'hopefully' on it. In a family memoir he wrote:

> We started our run in to Arnhem at about 400 feet. What a sight. Arnhem appeared to be sizzling, smoke, gun flashes and signal cartridges everywhere and right over the DZ a formation of Dakotas

was churning through the smoke of the ack ack. They had lots of light tracer going and also a continuous pattern of 88 mm shells bursting ... a bit high ... the whole area was a mass of drifting smoke with the glow of fires showing through here and there. As we came up to the DZ things became a bit tense and as soon as the leader signalled we started dropping on the dot. Fortunately there were no hitches and as soon as the wireless operator reported 'all gone' I started a steep climbing turn on full power intent on getting away as soon as possible. On our way out ... we were somewhat shaken to see a Stirling slowly going down in flames with the crew baling out ... On the ground two more Stirlings were burning themselves out ... pity the poor airborne division with whom we had lived [during training] for the past few months. Having cleared the immediate vicinity of Arnhem we all relaxed somewhat, removed our parachute harnesses and broke open coffee flasks and packets of sandwiches. A bush picnic was never as good as this. I had just lit a cigarette after putting 'George' in when I was shaken by a yell of 'fighters' from my navigator. Boy oh by, I had 'George' out and the aircraft in a steep turn in nothing flat. Looking back I was able to see at least four Dakotas either in flames in the air or burning on the ground. The nearest was only about 800 yards behind us and I could see his attacker finishing his 'peel off' ... immediately I opened to full power and fine pitch and was flat out for the nearest cloud, slightly above and ahead. I weaved the whole way and had all hands on the lookout and standing by to abandon the aircraft if it became necessary. Our luck held and we were able to reach cloud unmolested. [Back at base Barley found the squadron had suffered heavy losses and most of the returning aircraft had been riddled by flak.] We all agreed there didn't seem much future for the airborne division ... it was obvious from the fighting on the ground at Arnhem that they couldn't do anything very decisive with 6 pounders and Piat [anti-armour] guns against tanks. None of us could see much future in the business for ourselves either although we went there again the next day. However, the whole business had a lot of lessons in it and procedure was radically altered for the glider landings in the Rhine crossing.

After the disasters of the 21st, poor weather gave the airmen of 38 and 46 Groups a day off on the 22nd. But they were flying again the next day. The 1st Airborne, inside a strangling German ring, desperately needed food and ammunition. The RAF responded, despite the heavy losses of the past few days and ferocious flak. The pilots and crews knew most of the supplies fell into enemy hands but were prepared to do their best for the troops on the ground. It was the last re-supply operation from England. On the 24th and 25th, a small group of 575 Squadron Dakotas, transferred to Brussels, flew in food and medical supplies. No planes were lost in those two days but one was hit by friendly fire as it returned. On the night of the 25th 1st Airborne Division remnants escaped over the Rhine, leaving behind several thousand dead, wounded and captured comrades.

On the last big re-supply mission on the 23rd, 38 and 46 Groups dispatched 122 Stirlings and Dakotas, half of which arrived home damaged by flak. Five aircraft crashed – two Dakotas and three Stirlings from Harwell's 570 Squadron. A good number of other aircraft made crash-landings, belly landings, forced landings, call it what you will. There wasn't much difference as crippled aircraft put down. At least there were no fighter attacks – the RAF was at the rendezvous and warded off any Jerries. Fairford's 190 and 620 Squadrons, hard-hit in previous days, were short of planes and crews.

190 could only put up seven aircraft and 620 eleven. 190 got away scot free and CO, Wing Commander Donald Lee's Stirling was 620's only casualty, hit by flak and crash-landing. Everyone got out safely.

The dramas of the day involved several New Zealanders, two of them pilots. Bill Sparks crash-landed his Stirling while Barry Stableford took one look at the blood gushing from his Dakota skipper, took over the controls and landed the damaged plane back in England. Bill Longhurst, navigator on another Stirling, was seriously wounded by flak. His pilot and wireless operator were also injured but the pilot managed to make a safe emergency landing.

Bill Sparks, Riwaka-born in 1920 and the son of a tobacco grower, was a sole-charge teacher at Pangatotara in the Motueka Valley when he got the word to report for pilot training. He'd waited a while since volunteering, doing the correspondence course for would-be air crew. His mother had lost a brother in France and he had no desire to serve in the army. Sparks sailed on Christmas Eve 1942 to complete his training in Canada. Coincidentally, Opotiki man Jack Herring, who would become his wireless operator, was on the same ship.

After Sparks earned his wings the RCAF tried to make him an instructor but he arranged for a just-married Canadian to do the job. He went to Charlottetown, Prince Edward Island, on a navigation course, then back to Vancouver Island and Patricia Bay. 'They tried to make me a torpedo pilot, flying Hampdens, but I was no good at that, thank God,' Sparks said in an interview in 2011. In England at RAF Tilstock, Shropshire, home to 1665 Heavy Conversion Unit, he and his crew waited for a squadron posting. And waited and waited … 'We were ready by Normandy … but they didn't need us until Arnhem.' Finally they got the call, joining 196 Squadron at Keevil, Wiltshire, on the 21st, briefed to fly the following day. But the weather ruled out flying and it was the 23rd when Sparks and his men took to the air, nervously, on their maiden operational flight at the tail end of the long stream of aircraft. 'We were last off on the squadron, tail-end Charlie. But it was a quite uneventful trip until we got to the target.' Sparks felt reassured and lucky, because of the experience of two members of his crew. Gunner Don Leech held a DFM from his days on Hampdens while bomb aimer Ralph Wilson had done a tour on Lancasters. He told Sparks later the flak at Arnhem was worse than in the Ruhr – then the benchmark. In the end the tyro Sparks saved them all.

> As soon as the cargo had gone I dived to the right as instructed. If I'd gone left we'd have had no trouble. You think about it afterwards but it was just follow the leader. As I turned right we got hit. I don't know how many shells but one hit the starboard inner, another the starboard side of the fuselage in line with the cockpit. The flight engineer pushed the feathering button but she wouldn't feather. Then I got a call on the intercom to say Jack had been wounded – a bullet in one leg and another in an arm, near his shoulder. He'd been hit by rifle or machine-gun fire while standing by the open cargo hatch at the rear of the plane. [Next, the gunner was on the intercom:] 'Couple of fighters coming up, skip.'
>
> 'Can you do anything about them, Don?'
>
> 'No, I'm out of ammo.' [He'd been firing non-stop and the heat had bent one of the barrels. A few seconds later the fighters arrived. Big stars on wings and fuselage. American Thunderbolts.] They sat alongside us; they could see we were in trouble. She was leaking oil or something. So we flew back [toward the Allied lines], two

planes alongside. As we crossed the Rhine some silly clot had a go at us from a barge. The fighters peeled off to deal with that, then turned back up and stayed with us. When we got to Eindhoven I said we had to go down. We were too low to bale out. As well as the windmilling inner, out of oil and getting white hot, the starboard outer was also damaged. The electrics were gone. The inner powered everything. I picked out a nice big sugar beet field just south of Eindhoven [at Leende] but there were no flaps to slow her down. She just floated over that field. We dropped the wheels but they wouldn't lock down, just swung there. We went into the next field between two haystacks and landed. It was a belly landing but you could call it a crash-landing.

The undercarriage smashed up into the wings and the windmilling prop dropped off but they were down and no fire. They'd gone a couple of hundreds yards from touchdown to a grinding stop, gouging a deep trail across the field. The two army dispatchers, out the back door in a flash, beat the rest of the crew to safety. Sparks was bloodied from flak splinters in his right arm and face but hardly knew he'd been hit until afterwards. 'When I got to hospital they tossed out my flying jacket. Too much blood.' Unbelievably, a British army ambulance was parked behind one of the haystacks and Herring was bundled into it. The medics wanted Sparks too, but he wasn't ready to go – they had to get their papers out and destroy the IFF equipment. And he had to confront a farmer, angered by the mess in his beet field. The Dutchman calmed down when the crew showed him where to siphon petrol from the wing tanks.

Sparks didn't know it but he also had concussion – and a half-inch square of metal in him that clunked into a dish half a century later when a doctor cut out what he thought was a cyst. Sparks and Herring spent two weeks in hospital in Brussels, jabbed full of the new penicillin wonder drug before being flown back to England.

Sparks flew for the rest of the war – dropping SOE supplies in Holland and later Norway. He also took part in the Rhine crossing and carried petrol into Germany (110 four-gallon cans) to fuel British fighter planes, then back to Brussels to fly freed POWs home. With hundreds of other New Zealand airmen he was home on the *Andes* at Labour weekend 1945.

The Blakehill Farm Dakota squadrons in Wiltshire provided thirty-two aircraft the afternoon of 23 September – seventeen from 233 and fifteen from 437 RCAF (Husky). Theirs was the greatest contribution by number of any 46 Group base on this last mass re-supply flight. All but one came home – a 437 lost with its crew and dispatchers. One of the lucky ones was FZ681, flown back to England by a New Zealander after his skipper was badly knocked about by flak.

Barry Stableford (25) from Palmerston North, another New Zealander on 233 Squadron, grabbed the controls when Knivett Cranefield, a young Canadian, had his right leg shredded just short of the target. In an account written for *The Royal Air Force at Arnhem*, Cranefield said the aircraft was hit several times, the first blow sounding like peanuts rattling the length of the fuselage. Then another jolt made the controls difficult to handle. His wireless operator shouted, 'Skipper, the starboard wing's on fire.' It looked that way but it was yellow lining fabric flapping in the breeze. The Dakota flew on, unsteadily, Cranefield's nerves not helped by seeing an aircraft on his port side hit fatally, almost certainly the unlucky 437 Squadron Dakota.

[It] went down in flames. I saw it cartwheel over as it hit the ground. I was shaking with fear and dripping with perspiration. We were almost over the dropping zone when suddenly I felt a searing, agonising pain ... my right leg ... was split open from about six inches above my ankle to about five inches above my knee. Momentarily I saw white bone through my ripped battle dress trousers and then the blood was gushing.

Second pilot Stableford, who hadn't yet completed his conversion on Dakotas, took over, telling wireless operator Mike Hastings to get the first-aid kit. The box was locked but Hastings smashed it open with the aircraft axe. With no tourniquet, they used the flex from cockpit hand microphones. Cranefield declined morphine, concerned he might be needed at the end of the return flight.

The four army dispatchers rolled the cargo out of the aircraft and Stableford turned the damaged Dakota for home. To Cranefield the homebound leg seemed interminable. Stableford had both throttles wide open, the engine temperature needles in the red. But they made it and Stableford made a perfect landing. 'He did a splendid landing with the crippled aircraft,' Cranefield said. The Canadian was awarded a DFC but there was nothing for Stableford.

The 23 September supply drop to Arnhem ended the war for Wellington commercial artist Bill Longhurst, navigator on a flak-damaged 299 Squadron Stirling. 'Multiple gun-shot wounds', a New Zealand medical examination report said in April 1946, eight months after he arrived home.

Longhurst's plane, flown by a Canadian pilot officer called Rowell in an all-Canadian crew apart from the New Zealander and the British flight engineer, was briefed to drop its supply load at 1000 feet. Over the DZ flak and machine-gun fire hit the plane and wounded Rowell, Longhurst and the wireless operator. *Green On* says the pilot was forced to make a crash-landing at a village called Slijk-Ewijk, just north of the Waal. The wounded men were hospitalised by Allied troops in the area. *The Royal Air Force at Arnhem* says the plane landed in the southern part of the Allied sector. 299's ORB says observers claimed it made a successful crash-landing six miles south of the DZ and that the crew waved to aircraft going home signalling all were OK.

Longhurst's log tells what really happened. 'Landed at Ghent [Belgium],' he wrote. And a message to Wellington from RNZAF HQ in London on 16 October said Rowell 'decided to land as soon as possible and obtain medical assistance, so Ghent was chosen and a safe landing made there.' The two Arnhem books and 299's ORB say the Stirling's serial number was LJ893 but an RNZAF report gives it correctly as LJ915. Arie-Jan van Hees, author of *Green On*, having seen the log page and the RNZAF report, graciously conceded he was wrong.

Longhurst, the most seriously wounded, was hospitalised in Ghent. His family holds letters from two admirers, one of whom expressed 'shock' to find him gone when she arrived to visit. 'I could cry like a baby,' Denyse wrote. 'I have been thinking so much of you my little Bill … [he was slim but six feet] we loved to give you the best of our heart to help you to be again a nice strong boy.' Denyse didn't sign her letter with her surname and her identity is unknown, but it's likely she was one of his nurses. Longhurst was flown to England at the end of September and admitted to RAF hospital Church Valley in Wales, where he was treated for ulnar nerve paralysis and recuperated until well into the New Year. He was home in August 1945.

The New Zealander had started out to be a pilot, but after a narrow escape in training remustered as a navigator. Longhurst was flying a Tiger Moth from Harewood late afternoon in January 1942 and while practising sideslipping at 800 feet in an unauthorised area lost control. He was unable to recover in the available height and plunged onto the beach at the mouth of the Waimakariri. The aircraft was written off. Astonishingly, he survived and recovered from serious injuries to sail for Canada and navigation training at the end of May. He ended up at 299 at Stoney Cross, Hampshire, and then Keevil, Wiltshire. By the start of Market he had flown thirteen ops, including Normandy, flying to Arnhem with his crew on the 17th, 19th and 20th before the final flight on the 23rd.

Trevor Harris was lucky from the start. He survived a frightening horse and cart accident without injury on the way to school. As a teenager he flipped a car at high speed – not a scratch. Luck ran in the family. Harris' father survived Gallipoli and the horrors of the Western Front in World War I. His son's streak of good fortune continued throughout World War II. Though he flew at Normandy, Arnhem, the Rhine crossing and a clutch of dangerous SOE operations, he and his crew – and their planes – emerged virtually unscathed. One rifle bullet drove through the fuselage over Normandy and occasional minor flak splinters rattled on the aircraft. Other than that, nothing. Harris was precisely 16½ the day war was declared, far too young to go to war. He enlisted in January 1942 when he was still only 18. Thirteen months later, Harris was in England with his wings and a commission. After extended training he found himself on 299 Squadron in February 1944, with a crew including Yorkshireman Harry Reek, a policeman in civvy life. Reek was a superb navigator and he and Harris became lifelong friends. Reek called his first-born son Trevor after his pilot and the crew were godfathers. Reek wrote a memoir about his war, in which he described Harris as mature, with an old head on his young shoulders. 'He was an extremely capable pilot and an excellent skip. In flight he and I had to work very closely together and we never had any problems.'

Reek thought the six men who flew their Stirling made a 'wonderful' crew. 'On the ground we drank ourselves silly most of the time, but in the air we each performed with distinction, realising we depended on one another for our ultimate survival.' They had a Welsh bomb aimer/map reader, a Cockney flight engineer who'd been a Covent Garden fruit and vegetable trader, and a couple of Canadians – the wireless operator and gunner. Like many of the 38 Group crews they'd done a minimal number of ops before Normandy – three in their case. On two they'd not been able to receive reception signals from the Resistance forces to which they were dropping. They carried twenty paras, four containers and a collapsible bike to Caen late on the night of 5 June and towed a glider to the same destination late the next day. Between Normandy and Arnhem they flew six SOE ops. Amid the work and training flights Reek remembered a hectic, carefree existence because life in the air was often short.

> Mess parties were really wild – drink and song, drink and song! Pint upon pint with gin and orange chasers. We would stand in a large circle and sing the Royal Flying Corps song with its rousing, 'Here's to the dead already – and here's to the next man to die,' chorus.

Harris never wrote about his time with 299 or, more particularly, about Arnhem but a record of his three trips to the battle zone on 18, 19 and 23 September 1944 is preserved in the squadron's ORB. It carries a precis from each captain's post-op debrief. Harris:

18 [the second day of Operation Market] – Successful glider release on LZ 'Z' by map reading. Load – 3 troops, 1 Jeep, 1 trailer and 2 M/cycles. Vis hazy. Good trip.

19 – Successful glider release at LZ 'L'. Load carried 3 troops and 2 Jeeps. Glider pilot very good especially in cloud. Glider seen to land safely. VIS poor. H/F [heavy flak] seen at 51.08N-04.55E and spasmodically up to LZ. No damage. Good trip. [299 Sqn's CO, Wing Commander Peter Davis, was shot down and killed this day. He was on a re-supply operation, not glider delivery.]

23 – Successfully dropped 24 containers and 4 panniers on DZ. Avoiding action necessary to avoid containers falling from a/c ahead dropping too high. Good weather. Very good trip. [Other 299 pilots also complained about high dropping by the squadron ahead of them and some pilots also noted good fighter protection.]

Arnhem over, 299 and other 38 Group squadrons returned to training and their role of dropping supplies to Resistance units. But with France and Belgium and southern parts of Holland liberated, requirements for aircraft were fewer and Harris and other captains flew infrequently. Poor autumn weather and the onset of a fearful winter with heavy snow were also factors. The squadron had moved from Keevil, Wiltshire, to Wethersfield, in Essex near Braintree, on 9 October, moving once more on 25 January, to Shepherd's Grove just outside the small Suffolk village of Stanton.

Both East Anglian bases were open to cruel weather sweeping across the flat countryside from the North Sea but 299's moves, along with similar transfers by other 38 Group and 46 Group squadrons, made a shorter flight path across the North Sea over Holland to Germany for the Rhine Crossing.

In the six months between Arnhem and the Rhine on 24 March 1945, Harris flew one short tactical bombing trip, and four SOE operations, the last two in February and March to Norway, which assumed greater importance in the final months of the war. The long, cold winter-spring SOE trips across the North Sea to Norway were difficult and dangerous. (New Zealand fighter pilot Brian Woodman hated the crossing, even in high summer: 'Sea! Never again. Lived a lifetime every minute of this trip – 300 miles of it.') Harris gave thanks once more to Reek on 20 February when the man's pinpoint navigation brought their Stirling down through cloud to emerge in a valley surrounded by tall mountains. 'A great navigator; the best in the squadron,' Harris told his son years afterwards. Harris and his crew found their reception party that night; half of the ninety-four aircraft from 38 group flying to Norway didn't.

299's move from Keevil to Wethersfield turned out to be a life-changer for Harris. It was a short trip from Wethersfield to Chelmsford, where one night Harris poked his nose into a hall. He spotted a young woman on the dance floor. In a succession of excuse-me dances, he excused himself into her arms four times. It was the beginning of a romance which led to the altar of Chelmsford Cathedral on 1 January 1945 and lasted sixty-four years, until Harris' death. His bride, Maria Parravani, had three brothers in the British Army. Harris's best man was his Canadian rear gunner, Al Horner. The wedding cake was made with ingredients mailed from New

Zealand and iced by a woman the bride had nursed, who had lost a fighter pilot son. Harris was warned by the women of his new family not to let his crew eat all the cake. Some had to be left for relatives.

Harris, home safely from the Rhine crossing, his twenty-second and last op, was soon on a ship to New Zealand with the prospect of months before his wife could join him. Hordes of servicemen and wives were awaiting berths. In early August 1945, just as the war in the East was ending, Mrs Harris had a phone call. Could she take a priority passage on the *Rimutaka* from Liverpool within seven days? She was soon installed in a first-class single cabin on her way Down Under. She never learned who had pulled strings, but suspects her husband's friendship with the manager of the National Bank's London office paid off.

CHAPTER 10

Flying Mosquitoes and other aircraft

Aucklander Roy Le Long built himself quite a record as a Mosquito pilot. He and his imperturbable navigator, John 'Mac' McLaren, an Englishman who once peeled an orange as his skipper chased an enemy aircraft in a life-and-death struggle, are credited with destroying seven planes in aerial combat plus the same number on the ground or on the water and a good number of probables, shareds and damageds. He shot down the first German plane to fall on D-Day, creating RAF history (see chapters 1 and 2).

He got another, a Ju 188, a successor to the famed 88, over Coulommiers airfield, 35 miles east of Paris, just five nights later on 10–11 June as his 605 Squadron flew in support of Bomber Command's raids near Paris. The Mosquito twosome spotted the enemy plane as it flew toward them on a left-hand circuit of the base, confirmed visually it was a 188, closed, and at 2.38 a.m. on the 11th 'a short burst … was fired, strikes being seen on the port motor.' Flames flared briefly before dying away so Le Long went in even closer, opening up at 100 yards, 800 feet above the ground. Now more fire as strikes covered the whole of the fuselage and engines.

Le Long's combat report: 'The a/c soon began to disintegrate and burst into flames, losing height rapidly. The flames were so brilliant that the whole countryside around was clearly visible and the aircraft crashed with a terrific explosion 3 miles [southeast] of Coulommiers airfield and continued to burn.' On the way out to the coast they poured cannon fire into a freight train, seeing large explosions from three wagons but unable to determine if they'd hit the locomotive. Violent evasion was necessary as they crossed the coast homebound, two flak ships off Dieppe throwing up an intense light barrage until they were out of range. Undamaged, the Mossie landed at Manston.

Le Long's score continued to mount in the months following but nothing matched the afternoon of 2 October on a Ranger patrol, a long-range penetration into enemy territory. They flew from Manston and after a fuel top-up at RAF Coltishall east across the North Sea, over the Flensburg Peninsula and Kiel, on into the Baltic Sea. Then further east to the maze of German islands, lagoons and bays, heading for Great Jasmunder Bay. At 2.08 p.m. in the southernmost corner of the bay they found a tempting target – thirteen Dornier 24s, three-engined maritime patrol, reconnaissance and ASR float planes. They couldn't believe their eyes.

'They lay in lines of three abreast and line astern,' Le Long wrote in his combat report. With no defensive fire to hinder them, the airmen had the time of their lives. Eight times they attacked at low level, expending every cannon shell they had. At close range they couldn't miss and in a few minutes the anchorage was alight with blazing and sinking Dorniers. At times the Mosquito flew 'through heavy smoke and at one [stage] through heavy turbulence caused by a Do 24 exploding on the water'. The destructive attack lasted just seven minutes. That night Le Long claimed six destroyed, one probable and four damaged. Eighty miles away they could still see thick black smoke behind them.

The day's excitement wasn't over. Heading for Manston they sighted a Blohm and Voss 138, another sea plane, flying in the Baltic a little north of Cape Arkona. They closed to 150 yards and a game rear gunner fired at them. Le Long turned his machine guns on the plane; the firing stopped. He sprayed more bullets, watching strikes on the wings and near the engines. But it was cannon fire he needed. He broke off as heavy shore batteries opened fire. The 138 turned southeast trailing black smoke. And still the afternoon wasn't finished.

Two minutes after crossing into Flensburg, south of Denmark's border, a single light gun's shell thumped into the port engine. Flames erupted. Le Long feathered the prop and hit the Graviner button. Gradually the fire died, but not before more flak had a go at them. Finally safe over the North Sea they relaxed. The Mosquito landed at Manston at 5.30 p.m. Quite an afternoon.

Le Long's war service was rewarded with a DFC and bar.

Stan McCabe had a tough Depression-era upbringing. He was born in 1921 in Ohaupo. The family was poor and moved from job to job, eventually to the Whangarei area after their home burned down. McCabe went to high school – where he did well, leaving after two years. McCabe remembered in a family memoir: 'Dad was unemployed, we were on relief meat and groceries and kids at school were pinching one another's lunches.' He worked as a telegram boy, then as a postman. When war was declared, he had no doubt – the air force. He couldn't afford a £1 flight but he helped push the *Southern Cross* clear when it bogged down in Whangarei's Kensington Park mud, and filled scrapbooks with 1930s air race clippings. He studied hard at night school and by correspondence to better his education, joined the Territorials, improved his Post Office Morse code by listening to 2YA's Morse casts on Sundays at 9.30 p.m. – and applied to join the RNZAF. At his air force interview he was assessed for navigation. McCabe talked himself out of that and was reclassified for pilot training. He caught the train from Auckland for Levin's Initial Training Wing two weeks after the Japanese bombed Pearl Harbor. He soloed on his 21st birthday, 18 April 1942. Before that he had never driven so much as a motor bike, let alone a car. He left New Zealand with the coveted wings and his dad's advice: 'Stay away from wild women.'

By September 1943 Flight Sergeant Owen James McCabe had joined 488 (NZ) Squadron, a night-fighter unit at Bradwell Bay, Essex, flying Mosquitoes with navigator Terry Riley, who told him he'd been a burglar in Bournemouth. They got on famously. Two nights on, two off and ten days' leave every six weeks flying night defence of the London area. In mid-January 1944 McCabe was interviewed for a commission by Air Vice-Marshal Hugh Saunders, the chief of 11 Group Fighter Command/ADGB, who as a group captain had been Chief of Air Staff in New Zealand 1939–41. 'He told me I could order my officer's uniform. So I was to be an officer and a gentleman.' A month earlier he met Phyllis Pilcher, a WAAF telephonist in the Bradwell Bay control tower, who became his wife.

By D-Day 488 was on the offensive from RAF Zeals in southwest Wiltshire and on 6 June McCabe was off at dusk for one of the squadron's first night-fighter patrols over the landing beaches. 'As I turned toward Normandy I was kicking myself for forgetting to send off my work assignment for the town planning course I was studying with the War Correspondence School.'

On the night of 22 June McCabe shot down his first German plane – a Ju 188. 'Blue streaks' of machine-gun fire came at him from the rear gun, 'which made me duck down despite the 1-1/2 inch bullet proof windscreen [then] poured on heavy 20 mm cannon which devastated [him]. Circled around checking no one was behind me. Can't remember any reception when I got back but was quietly stunned by having a successful first combat!' Two months later, now flying from Colerne, also in Wiltshire, he had another success, another Ju 88. 'It was another dusk patrol over Normandy and our radar was all "mushed" by the metal strips the target was tossing out. But looking to the western sunset over the Atlantic, I saw him as a moving dot in the Western sky [closed] behind him and shot him down.' McCabe was in a borrowed Canadian Mosquito and when he fired his guns he lost some propeller control and the starboard prop started 'winding up'. He felt it was likely to pull him down into the Channel so shut the engine down and asked for a Normandy base for landing. He was given B5, Camilly northwest of Caen five miles from the coast, and made a difficult approach through thick cloud. He said his stand-in navigator was petrified. 'Soon saw some landing lights … and began my [single engine] approach through the airfield artillery fire with a powder smell in the cockpit. With my wheels down just had to land and did so very fast and ran off the end of the airstrip.' Quitting the plane he saw men waving torches, walking up his tyre tracks, and shouting, 'Don't get out, you're in a minefield!'

'Got into my tracks and made it to the tent, supper and a good breakfast next morning.'

The Cockney airfield commander and the repair sergeant seemed to like their New Zealand visitor and he received special engine service ahead of more senior officers. Then he flew home, 'my married navigator greatly relieved to have survived his first successful combat and emergency night landing in the Normandy beachhead on his final operational flight.'

George Jameson tallied eleven enemy planes while serving with 125 Squadron on Beaufighters and 488 (NZ) Squadron flying Mosquitoes, his successes the most by any New Zealand night-fighter pilot – two with 125, the rest with 488. But he will be forever remembered for the remarkable single sortie he flew the night of 30 July 1944. He and British navigator Norman Crookes took off for France from RAF Colerne, Wiltshire, at 2.35 a.m. and by the time they landed they'd destroyed four German planes. Jameson, a North Canterbury farmer's son, was 22 at the time.

Patrolling over Normandy he was given 'trade' by ground controllers at 5 a.m. Jameson's combat report tells what happened. No. 1 was a Ju 88. Crookes' night glasses confirmed Jameson's visual sighting against the dawn background. The 88 must have been aware of the Mosquito, and dropped its bombs. According to Jameson: 'I closed in and gave the enemy two short bursts from dead astern … the enemy aircraft went down through the clouds vertically and well alight and about 20 seconds later hit the ground with a terrific explosion 5 to 6 miles south of Caen at 5.05 a.m.'

No. 2 – another Ju 88 in the same area, almost immediately after the first. He was skimming the cloud tops and Jameson gave chase. But then another 88 zoomed up through the clouds a mile away and Jameson locked on to him. The German appeared to have seen him and turned hard port diving for a thick cloud layer. To no avail. 'I followed on the turn and closed in to 350–400 yards and opened fire. Strikes … caused a large fire in the starboard engine. The enemy, well alight, disappeared vertically through cloud.' Satisfied this combat had ended in a kill, Jameson went looking for more.

No. 3 – another Ju 88 near Lisieux. The chase started at 4000 feet, the German leading him a merry chase to tree-top levels while taking violent evasive action. The Mosquito was more than a match. 'I closed in to 250 yards and gave it a short burst [and saw] strikes. The E/A pulled up almost vertically and turned to port with debris falling and sparks issuing from it. The enemy stalled then nose dived into a four-acre field and exploded.'

No. 4. – this time a Do 217. Jameson had turned back toward Caen and at 2.55 a.m. picked up two aircraft on radar. He went for the nearer and at 4000 yards made visual contact with the Dornier. The German must have seen him and dived into cloud, taking intensive evasive action. Jameson followed by radar. 'I closed to 300 yards and fired a short burst. Strikes were seen on the fuselage which began to burn furiously … The E/A dived into the ground in flames and exploded.'

Jameson's short bursts were just that. An excellent shot, he fired just ninety shells from each of his four cannon to destroy the four planes. His outstanding results, one of the best night-fighter single-patrol outcomes of the war, earned him an immediate DSO to go with his DFC awarded after his tour on Beaufighters. Crookes was rewarded with a DFC.

Not all night-bombing Mosquito crews in 487 (NZ) Squadron had a charmed life. Pilot Gerry Whincop and navigators Bill Judson and Trevor Mullinder were shot down on night ops in their Mosquitoes over France. Whincop and Judson, down safely, evaded with the help of French patriots. Mullinder, less fortunate, was nabbed by the Germans.

Whincop, flying with Mullinder, was downed by a German fighter on the night of 12 June 1944, six days after the Invasion, while attacking enemy positions behind the Normandy battle lines. Both baled out successfully over the village of Bourgtheroulde, 40 miles southeast of Le Havre but lost contact. Taihape-born Mullinder (25) was on the run for two or three days. He was sheltered in a barn by a farmer but a German soldier walked into the building to have a pee and discovered him. The game was up and Mullinder spent the rest of the war in POW camp.

His pilot was luckier. Whincop, a Wellingtonian just turned 22, sprained his ankle landing but was helped for several days by a French farming family, until the Germans arrived. Somehow he escaped and made off. Helped again, he was taken on 21 June to another house where he stayed two months until Canadian troops overran the area.

In 1946 the French awarded Whincop the Croix de Guerre and in 1995, Whincop was there when Mrs Beatrix de Masiu, the matriarch of the family which hid him in their attic, was honoured in a London ceremony with membership of the Queen's Service Order for her bravery.

Judson had done thirty-three ops with 487 before he and his British pilot Bob Coombes came to grief the night of 6 August 1944. Prior to the Normandy landings they flew daylight intruder sorties – 'all at very low level, just over the top of horses ploughing in the fields' – but after D-Day began night operations over France. He wrote about 6 August and the aftermath for his family:

> My last op was a rail patrol La Rochelle [on the French Atlantic coast] to Nantes [further north on the Loire River]. We were the last aircraft in and had to patrol with the moon behind us to finish before the Typhoons started at daybreak. Flying at 50 feet over marshalling yards at La Rochelle we received a direct hit at 3.30 a.m. Felt absolutely no fear. After a few minutes Bob managed to climb to 750 feet but there were no hydraulics so we could not open the bomb doors [to] drop the bomb so we set course for the Canadian zone north of Nantes. The port engine was faulty so I was told to put on my parachute and jettison the door. Then I found my watch on the aircraft floor … blown off my wrist. Lots of blood and gore around.

Judson's immediate DFC said he was badly hit and seriously wounded. 'Half conscious and blinded with blood from injuries to his head and right eye, he navigated his aircraft back towards American lines until his pilot could no longer retain control.' Coombes got down safely and also evaded.

'I was told to jump and my chute opened just before hitting the ground,' Judson said. 'I landed in a field of winter crops about 4 a.m.' Late in the afternoon he approached a house, his right arm swollen and sore. The woman in the dwelling cleaned up his head and arm with alcohol and hid him in a shed for two days. Then he walked on across the countryside for three nights using the polar star to guide himself and sleeping by day under hedgerows. While eating a meal provided by a man he accosted on the fourth day, an FFI leader called Clement Potier turned up. He drove Judson by car to a farm on the outskirts of Touvois, a small Britanny town, then through the town by cycle to Potier's home, where he stayed for a month. Eventually Judson was driven to American lines, taken to Cherbourg and shipped to England and an American hospital in Portsmouth, undergoing immediate surgery to remove shrapnel from his head and right eye. He was then transferred to an RAF hospital for more treatment. Eventually he lost his eye. His war was over.

The death of Wing Commander Steve Watts, DSO, DFC, mid, commanding officer of 692 Squadron of the Light Night Striking Force (LNSF) was covered in *Night after Night*. He had finished ops, and was waiting for a ship to take him home. He had told his fiancée in Morrinsville they would be married the moment he returned and she had already bought her wedding dress.

On the night of 10–11 July 1944 he flew to Berlin on a raid with thirty-four other Mosquitoes. The LNSF did this on a regular basis. Watts (28) had flown to the German capital sixteen times previously. He never returned from his seventeenth – lost without trace. It seemed the mystery would never be solved. But now, seventy years later, Dutch and German wartime aviation enthusiasts delving into Luftwaffe records have determined exactly what happened to Watts and his navigator, fellow New Zealander Arch Matheson (29), who left a wife in Featherston.

Watts' Mosquito was shot into the North Sea by a German night fighter scrambled from Venlo, a major Nazi field in occupied southeast Holland. It was the only RAF aircraft lost that night. Significantly, only one German night fighter made a claim that night – for a Mosquito.

He was shot down by Major Hans Karlewski, flying a Heinkel 219 off Terschelling, one of the Dutch Frisian Islands, at a height of 15,400 feet at 3.18 a.m. on the 11th. The Venlo fighters failed to intercept any of the Mosquitoes after they made landfall over northern Holland a few minutes after midnight, bound for Berlin. The records say the Venlo controller had his aircraft back in the air later, hoping to catch the Mosquitoes on their way home. Watts was the unlucky one, and Karlewski's victory was confirmed by Germany's air ministry. His He 219 was given the position of the New Zealander's plane in the Ijsselmeer (Zuider Zee) area and he must have followed it out to Terschelling and then moved in for the kill. No combat report exists.

The 219, called the Uru (Eagle-Owl), was the best night fighter Germany produced but only a handful were ever built because Heinkel was out of favour. Fewer than 300 of the twin-engined fighters rolled off the firm's assembly lines. Just as well for Bomber Command. Technically advanced, the 219s were the only planes – before jets – able to match the Mosquitoes. They bristled with cannon, including upward-firing Schrage Musik guns, and carried the latest radar.

Karlewski, who survived the war with six kills, five at night, probably locked onto the New Zealanders' aircraft and followed it out to sea to shoot it down. Watts and Matheson would have been hit without warning. The New Zealanders are remembered on Runnymede's panels.

*

Alan Barley and his crew returned to 44 Squadron in late April 1943 for a second tour covering most of the Battle of the Ruhr, a long series of raids to cities such as Cologne, Essen, Duisberg and Wuppertal, attacks that cost the RAF 1000 bombers in five months and did massive damage to Germany's industrial heartland.

Early on that second tour, homebound from Essen the night of 27–28 May, they were halfway across the North Sea when the flight engineer looked down. The intercom crackled. 'Skip,' he shouted, 'there's a bloody Jerry right underneath us.' Barley had a quick look and was dumbfounded. An Me 110 was about 10 feet below them:

> I could quite clearly see the pilot and gunner looking up at us ... I can still see his luminous instrument panel ... Obviously he intended crossing the coast with us, making use of our IFF. He would then shoot us down and be free to go intruding in the heart of bomber country with good pickings served up to him on a platter ... This character had hit on a good plan and looked good enough to get away with it.

The enemy plane hadn't been spotted as it zoomed up under them. Locked together as a single blip on radar screens, the Lancaster flew on as the crew debated what to do.

'I was fairly good in a Lanc at this stage and I did everything possible to get him out of the blind spot [so the gunners could get a crack at him] – steep turns, diving and climbing corkscrews, pulling off power and lowering flaps and undercarriage etc.'

Nothing worked. The Me 110 stuck like glue. The wireless op called up Group with brief details, position and their intentions. Everyone donned parachutes. By now, flying parallel to the English coastline and straight and level to keep the fighter tucked up close, 'I suddenly shoved the stick hard forward'. That did the trick. One of the gunners saw the fighter flick over into a dive and he was gone. 'As we crossed the coast [we] got a radar check that we were alone. We were lucky to get away with it.'

They tangled with another Me 110 for ten minutes over the Dutch coast on the way home from another raid. 'He was pretty good but not keen enough,' Barley wrote. On 3–4 July they went to Cologne 'and darned near stayed there'. They were hit by bombs from above over the target. 'Front turret and fuselage bashed in and two unexploded incendiaries stuck in the port inner petrol tank.' On 15–16 August heading for Milan they were picked up by two Ju 88s at Chartres. 'Played with them for over 20 mins then port outer caught fire, wouldn't feather. Starboard outer overheated badly and starboard inner started to blow coolant.' Despite all this they made the target, dropped their load and turned for Spain in case they had to force-land or ditch. 'Got the port outer feathered so made for North Africa. Landed Blida [Algeria]. Lousy trip.'

Barley made his first and only trip to Berlin on the last op of his second tour, taking off 31 August 1943 on the third of the four August-September raids to Berlin, the opening act of the bitter and costly winter attacks on the German capital. 'Berlin tonight,' Barley wrote in his diary. It wasn't a great trip for many of the fleet and 44 Squadron lost one Lancaster. Twenty Halifaxes, seventeen Stirlings and another nine Lancasters of the attacking force were also shot down. Stirling squadrons lost 16 percent of their number. Among the heavy sufferers – 75 (NZ) Squadron with four downed and a fifth crash-landing in Norfolk after a night-fighter attack over the

North Sea. Barley's second-tour twenty ops took his total to fifty. He was finished with Bomber Command.

Rest tour over he did an instructors' course then taught young men to fly Wellingtons in Northern Ireland. Barley, who had joined the RAF prewar, transferred to the RNZAF on 1 January 1944 and joined RAF Transport Command and 233 Squadron in March, flying Dakotas and training with gliders and paratroops in preparation for D-Day. He flew at Normandy and Arnhem and the March 1945 Rhine crossing. In between he crossed the Channel delivering ammunition, supplies and mail for the British forces in northwest Europe and evacuating casualties on return flights to England. His was the fourth Dakota to land at B2 (Bazenville) in the Normandy invasion area.

The two Dutch girls were the last thing Don Tunnicliffe remembered before he was hit. As his 489 (NZ) Squadron Beaufighter, guns empty, fled from the fire streaming up from the ships and Den Helder's port defences on 25 September 1944, he roared down the city's main street almost at ground level. That's when he saw the girls. They were leaning out a second-storey window cheering the RAF and frantically waving material which looked like tea towels. And then …

> I was still travelling at nearly full throttle and heading for the sea and home when my short spell of utopia was abruptly broken by a dull thud and a kick like a horse down my left side, back, left arm, left leg and right knee. With a shock I realised that my luck had run out and I had copped a packet. I took in rather dazedly the gaping round hole of about 5 inches through the fuselage on the port side at roughly waist level … I started to black out.

He revived momentarily and, shaking his head to clear his vision, heard navigator-wireless operator Byron 'Aitch' Haywood yelling in his earphones. Haywood was standing behind him. Tunnicliffe told Haywood he couldn't see properly, kept blacking out and they'd probably have to ditch. Dimly he could see sand dunes flashing by. He passed out again but a flying habit saved them. He always trimmed his Beau to fly slightly nose up, and when he came to again they were at 1000 feet. He wrote in his autobiography *From Bunnies to Beaufighters*: 'This little quirk saved our lives, I'm sure of that.' The plane had climbed while he was out. In a few minutes, headed for England, he told Haywood to return to his office.

> I felt like an old old man but with repeated shaking of my head and gritting of my teeth, my head cleared and I told Aitch that I could see, that the aircraft was handling normally and that we would try to reach Langham [their home base on the Norfolk coast 15 miles northwest of Norwich].

Tunnicliffe's blackouts eased. They were belting along at three-quarter throttle so it was going to be a quick trip – thirty-five minutes. Tunnicliffe kept reassuring Haywood they'd make it. His big worry was landing. His left leg and arm were numb and felt like lead when he tried to hold the control column and lift it to move the throttles. He couldn't. Tunnicliffe called up the Langham control tower, told them what had happened and was told to land on the main runway. He worked the controls like a 'one-armed paperhanger,' levelled off and touched down safely.

Tunnicliffe was whisked off to the base hospital, morphine dulling the pain. Doctors took two hours to clean up the shrapnel wounds and patch him up. Every few seconds he heard the sound of extracted metal clanking into a pan beside him. Bits continued to work their way out of his body for years.

Born in Invercargill in 1922, he was always known as Tunney. He enlisted in February 1942, and on the platform at Wellington waiting for the train to the Initial Training Wing at Levin, Tunnicliffe was introduced to Mark Langley from Dunedin, who would become a lifelong friend.

In November 1943, Tunnicliffe and Langley reached 489 (NZ) Squadron at Leuchars on Scotland's west coast, south of Dundee. He fell in love with the two-man Beau. 'It handled beautifully without using brute strength, a joy to fly.' 489 was matched with Australia's 455 Squadron, flying as the Anzac Wing out over the North Sea to the long, difficult coastline of Norway with a mix of torpedo-carrying and cannon-armed Beaus. They hunted merchant ships loaded with precious cargoes for Germany's war industry, tankers, colliers and naval units. The ships usually steamed south by night, anchoring at daybreak in Norway's forbidding steep-sided fjords, tucked in against the rock walls. They were accompanied by flak ships armed with an enormous array of guns, which put up fierce and deadly resistance. Shore-based flak added to the German fire power. The risks were high and so were the casualties. Thirty-three New Zealanders lost their lives on 489.

On calm nights they flew to Norway 10 to fifteen feet above the water, often not picked up by German radar. The propellers reached four and a half feet below the fuselage, giving a reasonable margin of safety if flying was accurate. Fortunately the Beaus' radio altimeters were accurate to within two feet. They needed to be.

In April 1944 the Anzac Wing moved south to Langham as preparations for D-Day quickened, part of the wing's role to combat the fast, heavily armed German E-boats ducking in an out of the Dutch, Belgian and French coasts to make lightning attacks.

Langham was commanded by the now Group Captain AE (Arthur) Clouston. Tunnicliffe remembered him fondly. 'He was straight as a die, sincere, knowledgeable and humane. He couldn't be bothered with the typical RAF bull such as parades and saluting [and] he certainly knew how to join in with crews under strain letting off steam, by throwing a rip-snorter party.' Clouston's trick when a big do reached its climax – piano smashing with a fireman's axe. He held the Langham record – about ten seconds.

In May Tunnicliffe flew seven missions and participated in one strike, on the 14th, to Borkum, one of the German Frisian Islands, targeting four merchant ships with sixteen escorts. The planes faced intense flak. 'My torpedo scored a hit so I suppose I could claim a share of one.' Flak damaged his port engine but he feathered the prop and made it back. But he mourned the loss of another friend, Ivan Pettitt, 21, Dunedin, and his navigator who dived to their deaths in the sea. Three months later, Pettitt's older brother died in a mid-air training collision at Wigram.

Five days later another two Beaus and their crew were lost, one of them yet another close friend, pilot Alan Wright (23), also of Dunedin. The aircraft, silhouetted against a twilight sky, flew into a curtain of fire from E-boats – and a Sperrbrecher – and was blown to pieces. Sperrbrechers were converted merchant ships, bristling with oerlikons (20 mm cannon), machine guns and rocket wire projectiles. Tunnicliffe's mate Langley, lucky to survive, was grievously wounded and won the CGM, one of just four awarded to New Zealand aircrew in World War II.

> Mark dived down to have a go at the Sperrbrecher but [its] awesome firepower almost finished him. One engine was badly damaged and he was wounded in the throat, left leg and left arm … On the return journey he couldn't talk to his navigator due to his throat wounds. Ernie Parrish … went up to the cockpit to stand behind Mark in case he could assist. Mark scrawled SOS in blood on the cupola with his finger and Ernie got through to base via the radio. [Despite grievous wounds Langley landed safely.] … I inspected the plane next morning and how the damaged engine kept going was a miracle. A third of the cylinders were literally blown to pieces and fragments lay inside. The air cooler was blown right off and shrapnel holes were evident all over the fuselage and wings.

The loss of crew was regular and the deaths hit hard. On 8 August during a dual wing attack on a convoy off Norway where the shore guns could reach the planes, a heavy shell burst between the two Beaus just in front of Tunnicliffe. The explosion blew a wing off one and the tail off another. 'Both fluttered down like two stricken moths, to crash into the sea about 50 yards apart.' After the attack, Tunnicliffe curved away to fly alongside another Beau. The aircraft steamed fire from one engine but there was nothing the New Zealander could do. The pilot parachuted and was picked up by the Germans, the navigator died, sucked out the open canopy before he had clipped on his chute.

Post-invasion 489 ranged far and wide – Norway, Heligoland, the Frisian Islands and down to Calais, Dieppe and Ostend. Tunnicliffe felt perpetually tired. 'Perhaps it was also the strain of losing close friends.' Spirits lifted on 6 September when the wing sank all four merchant ships in a convoy. All six aircraft carrying torpedoes scored hits. As he turned away and strafed his target end to end he took a flak hit that ruined his hydraulics and was forced to make a belly landing at Langham.

Tunnicliffe's lucky escape over Den Helder on 25 September was the second time that month he'd been to the Dutch port. On the 12th he participated in a four-squadron Beaufighter strike led by fellow New Zealander Bill Tacon, CO of 143 squadron, part of another wing at North Coates on the Lincolnshire coast. He was flying close by when Tacon's plane erupted into a ball of fire. Tacon used his parachute and survived, becoming a POW. His navigator was killed.

Forty Beaus, a mix of torpedo and rocket carriers, were assembled at Langham for the second operation to Den Helder after the RAF learned a large convoy was about to make a dash for it. The strike was led by Squadron Leader Derek Hammond. 'Hammy was a no-nonsense man at briefings and when the target of each force had been outlined, he summed up the general feeling with these succinct words: "We'll go in, rip shit or bust."'

489 CO Wing Commander Les Robertson led the Torbeaus, the torpedo-carrying Beaus, and Hammond, then a flight commander, the cannon attack with 455 Squadron to hit the shipping with rockets and cannon. The Beaus approached Den Helder from the back door, crossing between Texel and Vlieland, two of the Frisians, and then turning to starboard over the Zuider Zee to come in from the land side.

> We went screaming down from a thousand feet to hit the main part of this heavily defended area. The heavy stuff was like gigantic

puffballs floating about but had to be flown through. Underneath, down to ground level, the visible tracer lanced all over the air space and it seemed a miracle would be needed to penetrate to our targets. There were so many red-spitting barrels of guns all along the wharves and up on gun towers that it was only possible to squirt several targets to keep their heads down but there were innumerable others, all piercing the sky with 20 mm, 40 mm heavier stuff and the unseen machine gun bullets. Ships tied up to the docks were also chiming in and I emptied my cannons in one long burst along the ships and docks.

And that's when Tunnicliffe saw the girls waving from the window, and was hit as he bolted for the safety of the open sea. He spent several weeks in hospital before he could walk again and was awarded an immediate DFC, the citation saying he displayed 'courage and fortitude of a very high order'.

Another New Zealand friend joined Tunnicliffe in hospital. Pilot Doug Mann (25), from Greymouth, had hit the mast of a target ship on the night of 3–4 October off the Dutch coast, shearing off part of one wing. He just had time to jettison his torpedo before ditching. He and his navigator clambered into their dinghy and endured eights days bobbing about in rough seas before they were spotted by a fighter and rescued, famished, wet, frozen and near death. Tunnicliffe says they fought constant wind, rain and hail, had to bail constantly and had six Horlicks tablets between them. They had two days in an English coastal hospital before transfer to Langham and arrival in Tunnicliffe's ward. 'Raw backsides, legs and arms … and faces and necks chafed like red meat. They weighed only about 6 stone.'

When Tunnicliffe was ready to fly operations again he'd been away from 489 for seven weeks and the squadron was now at RAF Dallachy, 120 miles north of Edinburgh on the southeast coast of Moray Firth. After refresher training at Turnberry Tunnicliffe flew seven more ops. His last, on 16 March 1945, was flown in atrocious weather to Norway. The next day New Zealand CO Hammond told him his tour was at an end. Tunnicliffe, now the longest-serving pilot on the squadron, protested the war wasn't over but Hammond said he was going to make damned sure Tunnicliffe survived. And he did.

CHAPTER 11

The Rhine Crossing – 24 March 1945

Compared with Arnhem, the Rhine crossing on 24 March 1945 – a great single-day airborne operation – was a doddle. One hundred and ninety-four Stirlings and 120 Halifaxes from the ten squadrons of 38 Group, and 120 Dakotas from the six transport squadrons of 46 Group, a total of 434, participated. Most towed Horsas but forty-eight of the Halifaxes hauled the bigger Hamilcars into battle. A handful carried American-designed Locust light tanks. Just four of 38's aircraft were lost, victims of flak. Thirty-odd suffered damage. 46's Dakota losses were light.

Operation Varsity was a joint British-American action involving glider and paratroop landings on the east bank of the Rhine in the Emmerich-Wesel area to support British and American divisions that began crossing the river by boat on the night of 23–24 March.

Britain's 6th Airborne started landing from gliders about 10 a.m. – the American 17th Airborne from its gliders at the same time. Paratroopers flown in by the Americans had dropped earlier to secure the LZs. The airborne troops were to capture key villages and small towns and other points, so the advancing army troops wouldn't be delayed by enemy resistance.

Few problems emerged on the day and the armies linked up with airborne units to create a bridgehead. From there the Allied divisions began their march to the Elbe and the end of the war. From the west bank of the Rhine, British Prime Minister Churchill and military chiefs Eisenhower and Montgomery watched the skies, dark with hundreds of planes, gliders and the huge canopy of covering fighters and fighter bombers.

It was a stark contrast with the Arnhem disaster. Flak? Trifling. The Luftwaffe didn't show and the weather cooperated brilliantly, with excellent visibility except for dust clouds on some LZs – the brown haze raised by the sustained artillery barrages from the west bank. This time ground-to-air radio functioned. RAF observers carried in on the gliders, New Zealander Bob Spurdle among them, were soon on the go, giving the air force target coordinates for attacks. The entire 6th Airborne Division was landed in one lift, not in two. The lessons of Arnhem had been well learned, though at great cost.

Other New Zealanders flew in Operation Varsity, among them 190 Squadron's Noel Sutherland and Larry Siegert, both decorated for their exploits at Arnhem. Trevor Harris flew a 299 Squadron Stirling, a tour-finishing flight. Some of these New Zealand pilots had fellow countrymen in their crews. Bill Sparks' wireless operator, New Zealander Jack Herring, wounded at Arnhem but now recovered, was with him for the flight.

Sparks remembered a briefing for the trip and pilots being ordered to get their gliders to the DZ or else. He recalled the groan that went up when pilots were told to bring their tow ropes home. At a later briefing the order was cancelled and aircrew were given the OK to let them go over the Rhine. 'Pilots cheered.' In an article he wrote for the *British Airborne Forces (NZ)* magazine he said, 'We flew in pairs at about 1200 feet across Belgium and France until we reached our turning point. Then it was north towards the Rhine.' He watched the Americans in their Dakotas coming up from France, towing their Wacos. 'Flying faster, we kept on passing the Dakota stream until we were ahead of them just before the Rhine.' Sparks had no problems and their glider, called matchboxes by tug crews, released on schedule. 'We had been in contact with the pilot for the whole trip, telling him the turning points and when the LZ was coming up. We wished them well, they released and we dived away to port.' Low over the Rhine a few minutes later the Stirling dropped its long, heavy tow rope into the water. Sparks landed his aircraft 5 hours 20 minutes after takeoff. The crews were ready for a re-supply operation the following day but it was not needed. A few days after the flight, Sparks received a postcard from the pilot of the glider he'd towed into action:

> Dear Skipper – You'll be glad to learn that glider 310 which you recently abandoned at 4000 feet over Germany came to no serious harm. Sgt Wilson and myself are back at Fairford, sound in wind and limb. The passengers were unscathed when last we saw them and the Jeep and trailer went intact into action. The Horsa left a port wing in an apple tree and the starboard wing wrapped lovingly around a telegraph pole. Hope that [your] crew returned undamaged. All the best from Staff Sgt Holwell.

The only New Zealand casualty on the Rhine Crossing day was 21-year-old Dick Egley, a 137 Squadron pilot, killed while attacking German flak positions. 137 was one of four Typhoon units in 124 Wing, based at Helmond, just inside Holland. Egley, a Wellington College old boy barely out of school, enlisted in March 1942 while working in the Air Department. He joined 137, his first and only squadron, on 1 March 1944 and went with it when it moved from Manston to the Continent in August. Egley had flown almost 100 ops when he was killed. He and the squadron had just returned from an armament course at Warmwell, Dorset, when he took off from Helmond about 10.30 a.m. on the 24th. The Typhoons were attacking flak posts to suppress enemy fire directed at the airborne armada of Allied planes involved in Operation Varsity. The New Zealander was one of the unlucky ones, hit near the small town of Brunen, four miles east of Hamminkeln and baled out a short distance away over Dingden. His parachute opened and fellow pilots overhead reported he appeared to land safely. However, he was found dead near the scene of the crash and buried in Dingden. Postwar he was reinterred in the Reichswald Forest War Cemetery where several thousand Commonwealth aircrew lie. After his death he was awarded a DFC, backdated to 12 March.

124's Wing Commander Flying was the redoubtable Christopher 'Kit' North-Lewis, formerly an army man who transferred to the RAF. He commanded 181 Squadron, one of the wing's units, before promotion to wing commander. He was a flak casualty of 24 March but survived his crash-landing and returned to Helmond.

Superb New Zealand pilot Johnny Gibson's war ended on the 24th, another of the lucky ones. Flying an 80 Squadron Tempest from Volkel, in Holland, he was hit by flak near Goch, just across the German border. Gibson managed to get his damaged aircraft back to Allied territory in Holland, landing 6 miles southeast of Helmond, but broke a shoulder as he force-landed. Evacuated to an English hospital, he didn't fly operationally again.

Gibson, a Short Service Commission pilot in 1938, was thrown into action on 501 Squadron in France in 1940, claiming three successes on Hurricanes, an aircraft he hadn't flown before, and emerged with a DFC. Gibson added another eight during the Battle of Britain, again with 501, to become the leading New Zealand pilot on Hurricanes. Later he commanded the RNZAF's 15 Squadron in the Solomons before returning to England in late 1944 and converting to Tempests. He was flying as a supernumerary squadron leader on 24 March to refresh his operational experience. His service in the RNZAF was rewarded with a DSO, gazetted just a week before his last flight.

Bob Spurdle had seen it all and done it all. The larger-than-life New Zealander flew in the Battle of Britain, survived the sweeps and Rhubarbs over the Channel into France, was catapulted from vessels in the Atlantic to hunt enemy aircraft shadowing convoys and then flew with the RNZAF in the Pacific. He returned to England in time for D-Day and command of 80 (Tempest) Squadron. Battle weary, he had taken off ops on 4 January 1945 by Jamie Jameson, a fellow New Zealander, who knew exhaustion when he saw it. Jameson, one of a handful of survivors from the disastrous sinking of the carrier *Glorious* off Norway in 1940, a Battle of Britain veteran and now commander of 122 Wing's five Tempest squadrons – 3, 56, 80, 274 and 486 (NZ) – told him: 'Sorry, Spud ... you've done more than your fair share.' He had flown an astonishing five tours and

564 ops. Posted to a desk, Spurdle volunteered for a 'special job'. He soon discovered that meant a ground stint with the airborne forces in Germany directing rocket- and cannon-firing Typhoons to targets following the Rhine Crossing and flying in a glider. According to his blunt book *The Blue Arena*, he was given a Red Beret which he wore with 'intense pride' – and drew up a fresh will. His four-man team would fly in with a Jeep carrying generators and powerful ground-to-air RT sets. The lessons from Arnhem, where American radios and operators on the ground couldn't contact aircraft above, had been learned. This time Montgomery insisted on all-RAF crew and radio equipment.

Spurdle flew to the Rhine in a Horsa glider towed by a 38 Group Stirling. 'The glider crew got in, cheerful as crickets,' he wrote in his book. 'Thank God! RAF types, a flight lieutenant and a sergeant pilot. [Arnhem had cost the lives of so many Glider Pilot Regiment pilots who stayed to fight as infantry after landing that the RAF needed to supply many of the pilots for the Rhine crossing.] Our Jeep and trailer squatted in the darkness like fat brown toads.'

Spurdle was interviewed later by a journalist in London and his graphic account appeared in Wellington's *Evening Post* on 16 June.

> When we had crossed the Rhine … I left the cockpit, where I had been peering out over the shoulders of the pilot and co-pilot, and went back where I could see nothing. I was scared stiff. I have never been so scared in my life before. While flying up to the Rhine we had seen the tail unit fall away from a glider in front of us, spewing out its crew and their Jeep. They had no parachutes. We had seen a Stirling, weaving slow spirals and streaming black smoke, go down to its death crash. We had seen Dakotas, hit by flak, burning furiously,

diving helplessly out of control. I didn't want to see any more, and so I went back and stared at the Jeep, the inside of the glider, the floor boards – anything to try to forget, even momentarily, how scared I was. It was quiet at first, after the tow-rope had been released; but soon we heard the sounds of battle below us. And it wasn't very encouraging. As we got lower the explosions seemed to blend into one big roar, and soon they were being punctuated with cracks and smacks from the glider itself. We were touching down at 90 miles an hour, and the pilots were deliberately hitting a tree there, a post here, to check our speed. Suddenly the nose-wheel burst through the floor beneath my feet, and as we jerked over the last few yards our Jeep and trailer, chained up inside the glider, bucketed backwards and forwards in answer to every collision. It seemed almost alive, straining at its chains to smash us. Then we stopped. There was a blanketing din outside, punctuated with the staccato rattle of machine guns. We were down all right, but now we had to keep alive, and get the Jeep out of the glider and find our position. In addition to the pilots, there were three men with me. The hardest part of the entire day was to get out of that glider. Inside it was relatively peaceful, and the shell of the fuselage, hiding the battle, seemed as safe as a castle. We poked our noses out. We were on the edge of a wood. Bound to be Germans there, we thought, and so we dashed out, a few yards away from the glider, and fell flat in the grass and lay there. We wanted to get acclimatised. We could see American parachutists, hanging from the trees by their parachutes, dead. One was lying, quite still, in a puddle. Gilders were sailing down, and flak posts were spouting shells at them; many caught fire, some blew up. Mortar bombs seemed to be coming from all directions. We could not hear them coming because of the din. There was just a flat 'whack'; then a burst of grey-brown smoke. It was a burning hot day. Misty haze, mingled with smoke from the fires at Wesel, hung low over the ground. We saw men appearing and disappearing in it. Feeling better, we returned to the glider and stripped to our shirts, tried to get the Jeep free. It was worrying work. Shell splinters and bullets occasionally burst through the flimsy fuselage, startling us, each one bringing a renewed spurt of fear. Soon we got both the Jeep and trailer clear … We were feeling much better now, not scared, and it even seemed amusing to notice a number of different fights going on all around us about 400 yards away. Here and there our chaps were walking about doing various jobs, quite unconcerned, while not far away German machine-gunners were blazing away at other troops attacking them. A bulldozer, glider delivered, trundled up from somewhere. We got the driver to make two big scoops for us, and then we drove the Jeep and the trailer in, and felt more comfortable for being partly hidden, although by now we were not ducking and flinching instinctively every time we heard an explosion. Soon we were in radio contact with a forward RAF control post. We looked at our watches. An hour and a half had passed since our glider had crash-landed. We could see Typhoons milling about overhead, but it was too soon yet to give them targets. The fighting was too mixed up, too confused. Gradually the din began to die down. Bangs, pops, and rattles quietened, and as the day wore on batches of German prisoners began to arrive. We selected the toughest-looking SS troops and made them dig slit trenches for us. Some of them seemed to think they were digging their own graves. They looked white and scared [and] most relieved when they found we were not going to shoot them. The next two days passed quickly. Our communications were going to plan and we found the boys plenty of targets. Sometimes

I talked to pilots in my old squadron. Once they shot down two Messerschmitt 109s in a battle fight over our heads. We spent five days with the Jeep altogether. There was plenty to do during the days; at nights, in the full moonlight, we had occasional visits from Junkers 88. Then we were recalled, back to our group headquarters [in Eindhoven], and there we were invited to lunch by Air Vice-Marshal Sir Harry Broadhurst, the Air Officer Commanding, who seemed quite satisfied with the way everything had turned out.

Broadhurst OKed Spurdle's return to the battleground to continue ground-to-air control, calling down the Typhoons and other aircraft to attack targets the army wanted destroyed. He joined 11th Armoured Division and rode a tank as the unit roared across Germany to the Elbe, where it linked up with the Red Army. Finis. The war was almost over and he had emerged unscathed.

CHAPTER 12

Friendly fire

Six weeks before war's end 486 Squadron lost one of its most popular and long-serving pilots. William Arthur 'Wacky' Kalka drowned in the Maas River on 25 March 1945, after baling out of his crippled Tempest. A 21-year-old Aucklander, just promoted to flying officer after being commissioned the previous August, he joined 486 in December 1943 and had flown 186 ops by the time he died. He had survived one earlier bale-out, shot down by the Americans in the infamous friendly fire incident of 13 January, which accounted for three 486 Tempests.

The squadron was asked for support in the St Vith area for elements of the US 1st Army facing an attack in the last stages of the Germans' Ardennes offensive. 486 put up eight aircraft and in poor weather with a low cloud base, the Tempests were at 700 feet approaching the area. Despite their black and white striped wings a hail of ground fire met them and in a moment three fighters were on their way down.

Two others were badly damaged, only three escaping unscathed. CO Spike Umbers and Lloyd 'Happy' Appleton crash-landed within American lines while Kalka took to his parachute. American troops loosed off pot shots at him as he floated down but their aim wasn't as good; he wasn't hit.

Paul Sortehaug in *The Wild Winds* says Appleton suffered severe neck and face injuries and was missing for eight days until discovered in an American hospital and transferred to British care. The crash and injuries ended his war and he was invalided home. Sortehaug quotes Ralph Evans, one of the other pilots, as saying that when the flak started to crisscross from all directions, 'I looked across at the pilot next to me, who was Happy Appleton, just in time to see his coupe top fly off and his plane start to drop down. There was a wall of golden tracer straight ahead of me which automatically made me pull straight up through the cloud.'

Sortehaug says that after Umbers emerged uninjured from his crashed Tempest he 'stormed' into an American command post, causing such a disturbance he was physically ejected from the scene by MPs. 'There is some likelihood that pistols were even drawn during the heated confrontation that took place.'

He adds: 'The episode did not go down well with the squadron at all, and was made even worse when no apology was received for the blunder. Nobody expected the Yank gunners to individually recognise all aircraft types, but at the height the Tempests were flying, their slow speed, and given that each aircraft sported black and white banding, there really was little excuse for such ineptitude.'

Kalka's luck ran out on 25 March. Flak jammed the Tempest's ailerons while he and another pilot hemmed in a small recce aircraft for the other pilot to shoot it down. Sortehaug: 'Wacky got home [to his base at Volkel] alright but was told by ops to proceed north and bale out. In doing so he must have hit his own tailplane and been injured, because he drifted directly into the middle of the Maas.'

Apparently unconscious under his parachute, which he had managed to open, Kalka landed in the icy river and drowned despite the brave efforts of a young Dutchwoman to save him. Riet Jansen jumped into the river fully clothed. *For Your Tomorrow* says she reached Kalka but couldn't untangle him from the parachute shrouds. Unable to pull him ashore, she had to let him go. The New Zealander floated away. His body, found later, lies in Uden War Cemetery in Holland. Jansen's bike was stolen from the river bank while she was in the water but was replaced soon after by New Zealanders grateful for her efforts.

So-called 'friendly' fire was very unfriendly and a good number of pilots were shot down in unfortunate circumstances. Countless stories are told of US fighters attacking their RAF opposites. To be fair it happened the other way round too, though not as often. The navy was notorious for firing at anything that came within their sights. Their gunners blazed away at both friend and foe, giving no heed to the black and white invasion stripes painted on RAF aircraft from Normandy onwards. The Royal Navy destroyer HMS *Onslow* killed 224 Squadron second pilot, New Zealander Bill Andrews, 23, the night of 11–12 August 1944 over the Bay of Biscay. The warship's fire, 25 miles off the French coast, exploded the aircraft while it was on anti-submarine patrol and all aboard perished, bodies never found. This wasn't the same Bill Andrews who flew with Mick Ensor on the same squadron, although both came from Christchurch.

Earlier the same month over France American fire may have winged Hawke's Bay man Bill Bell's Stirling, causing him to ditch on an SAS flight. Without doubt US batteries at Namur, southeast of Brussels, shot down two homebound Lancasters from a raid on the Vohwinkel railway yards in the Ruhr the night of 1–2 January 1945. Only one of the fifteen crew survived. Among the dead was 115 Squadron pilot New Zealander Joe Sterling (23) of Matakohe, Northland. He flew that night as second pilot, on his seventh op. The same night 75 Squadron CO Ray Newton, a veteran bomber pilot, and his crew lost their lives on the Vohwinkel raid, possibly the victim of friendly fire. Their plane crashed near Maastricht.

Night after Night notes that trigger-happy Americans manning anti-aircraft batteries claimed considerable numbers of RAF bombers in the last months of the conflict, although it wasn't only Americans at fault. British land-based ack-ack accounted for a good number of their own bombers. Bill Chorley records that a coastal battery in Essex shot down an RCAF Halifax on the night of 5–6 March 1945, killing all eight crewmen. The same night New Zealand wireless operator Alan Twaddle survived, blown free with flash burns, when his 199 Squadron special duties Stirling was exploded by American shells with proximity fuses, while flying radio counter-measures duties in France just south of Luxembourg.

Chris Shores' 2nd Tactical Air Force records that during a tactical reconnaissance flight the afternoon of 14 January 1945, a pair of RAF 268 Squadron Mustangs were attacked by Spitfires east of Arnhem. One of the 401 Squadron Spitfires claimed an Me 109 shot down. But the 'kill' claim was disallowed by 2TAF, which said in all probability the unfortunate Spitfire pilot had downed the Mustang – which crashed and killed its pilot.

One friendly fire incident involved New Zealand 485 Squadron Spitfire pilot Allan Stead, 23 at the time, who shot down a 3

Naval Fighter Wing Seafire Mk III on 10 June 1944, killing the pilot. Gerard Morris in *Spitfire – The New Zealand Story* tells what happened and notes the squadron ORB says: 'F/O AB Stead was persistently attacked by a Spitfire V which he eventually shot down.'

Stead, an experienced fighter pilot on his second tour, was leading one of three sections patrolling the beachhead when the Seafire (the navy version of the Spitfire) made a pass at him. The New Zealander turned steeply to display the distinctive elliptical wings of his plane and invasion stripes. That didn't deter the navy pilot who came in again, firing this time. Stead evaded, then targeted his tormentor and shot it down. Morris quotes two of the other 485 pilots as hearing Stead over the RT asking what he should do. Back came the answer: 'Shoot him down.' Morris says Johnnie Houlton in *Spitfire Strikes* wrote the voice was that of their wing leader Ray Harries, while Norby King in *Green Kiwi versus German Eagle* said, 'Chalky White, I reckon.' King adds: 'It was a navy Seafire – never been on ops before – and some admiral is jumping up and down. Al is all cut up too.'

Nothing came of the subsequent court martial and Stead resumed operations with 485 in late July. Along with another 485 pilot, he was killed on 6 January 1945. A train they were attacking blew up, debris damaging their planes. Stead, too low to jump, died trying to crash-land in Allied lines. A third squadron pilot was killed the following month. The three losses were the last suffered by 485 and the first since the previous October.

CHAPTER 13

Wrecking Germany's petroleum industry

Bomber pilots Ken Orman and Ray Tait's logs show the emphasis Bomber Command placed on attacking Germany's petroleum industry in the last year of the war. Heavy raids hammered the oil refineries and synthetic plants and hastened the end. Had it begun earlier, the campaign might have had an even more devastating effect.

Both New Zealanders began their tours in October 1944 and their logs note a preponderance of petroleum industry targets. Orman flew fourteen of his thirty-six ops to such targets and Tait seventeen of his thirty-five. The rest were split – railway yards, specific factories, ops in support of ground troops and attack on towns and cities – area bombing.

Oil campaign statistics in Richard Davis' book *Bombing the European Axis Powers* reveal that between 12 June 1944 and 25 April 1945, two weeks before Germany's surrender, the RAF carried out 219 oil raids – 22,225 sorties, dropping 101,157 tons of bombs. The attacks cost 354 aircraft, less than two per raid. Loss figures were minuscule compared with earlier area-bombing raids. True, but tell that to the relatives of the men who died – the lost planes carried more than 2500 aircrew. There were survivors – but crashes took a heavy toll. Flak was dense at most oil sites as the Germans strove to protect these vital plants. Fighters, though a declining factor, made kills.

From 12 June 1944 until war's end about seventy-five New Zealand Bomber Command aircrew died raiding oil targets, including about ten men from 100 Group aircraft flying with electronic countermeasures equipment in support of these operations.

Many oil raids were completed without loss, but six went into double figures, the three worst occurring in June and July 1944. Thirty-two of 300 aircraft were lost the night of 16–17 June (10.7 percent), thirty-seven of 118 went down (a horrifying 31.3 percent) five nights later and the Germans accounted for twenty of 146 on 20–21 July (13.7 percent).

The first of the three, an attack on the Holten synthetic-oil plant at Sterkade near Bocholt, just over the Dutch border into Germany, caused little damage as thick cloud obscured the markers and bombing was scattered. Bomber Command Diaries (BCD) says the bombers' route passed near a German night-fighter base and their planes took a heavy toll. Although 3 Group didn't go on this raid four New Zealanders lost their lives, two of them without trace from a 199 Squadron Stirling flying radio counter-measures support. Pilot Thomas Dale (25) and his navigator, Stratford-born Ron Whittleston (28), are remembered at Runnymede. Dale's brother James, a 75 Squadron navigator, was killed over Germany just two months later raiding motor works at Russelsheim. The disastrous attack on the Union Rheinische synthetic plant at Wesseling just south of Cologne the night of 21–22 June cost another three New Zealand lives plus a fourth lost on the twin raid on the Buer plant at Gelsenkirchen, in the Ruhr. BCD reports that cloud covered the target and the bombers caused only slight damage.

The RAF's 20–21 July assault on the Meerbeck plant at Homberg in the Ruhr rated a major success, causing severe damage. When 840 tons of explosives rained down, BCD says German documents show production at the plant, nearly 6000 tons a day, fluctuated between 120 and 970 tons a day after British and American raids. Homberg proved a nemesis target for 75 (NZ) Squadron. Twenty-six Lancasters lifted off from Mepal, seven didn't come home. That night the squadron suffered its worst single-raid losses of the entire war. Night fighters scythed through the force attacking Homberg and twenty bombers fell. Of the forty-nine men aboard the New Zealand planes, forty-one died, sixteen of them New Zealanders. In addition a 514 Squadron Lancaster was shot down near the target and the seven men making up its rookie crew died, four of them New Zealanders.

The three airfields making up RAF Waterbeach lost thirteen Lancasters, the seven from Mepal, two from 115 at Witchford and four from 514 at Waterbeach itself. Years later New Zealand David Mercier, navigator on a 75 plane that did get home, remembered:

> What a shambles. Don't know whether they knew we were coming but the night fighters were waiting for us as we crossed the coast [into Holland]. Kites were going down all the way in … to the Ruhr and back out again. Happy Valley? [aircrew's name for the Ruhr

Valley] … it was some of the heaviest and most accurate flak I've seen. 3 Group really took a beating.

Homberg wasn't finished with 75 – the squadron went back three times, all daylight trips, and on 20 November lost another three aircraft. Only one man among the three crews was a New Zealander, who survived to become a POW. Another 514 Squadron Lancaster was lost with all its crew, four of them New Zealanders.

Many petroleum installations were hit time after time and though they sometimes escaped major damage, accumulated destruction left them smoking ruins. Production was virtually non-existent. The Krupp Treibstoff plant at Wanne-Eickel in the Ruhr was attacked on twelve occasions, three of them during six days in February 1945. In the first raid on the night of 2–3, two New Zealand pilots were lost, both flying Yorkshire-based 4 Group Halifaxes – William Arnold (23), a pre-war shepherd at Ruatoria, was on 51 Squadron at Snaith, and James Gutzewitz (24), from Roxburgh, who flew with 78 Squadron at Breighton.

Arnold's aircraft was brought down south of the Ruhr, crashing near Dormagen, New Zealand navigator Doug Balfour the sole survivor. The son of a Seddon-area farmer, Balfour abandoned the doomed Halifax safely and landed in snow on a property owned by a German farming family. They fed and cared for him for several days, wrapping an injured leg in his parachute cloth. Troops began searching the area for downed aircrew and fearing death if they were discovered to have helped an airman, the family sent Balfour on his way – with a block of cheese. It wasn't long before he was captured.

Three survived from the Gutzewitz Halifax, two of them New Zealanders – Leo Stuart, the navigator, and Leo O'Brien, the bomb aimer, both 31 and both commissioned in early November 1944. With the flight engineer, they parachuted down to become POWs. The bodies of Gutzewitz and two of his crew were recovered from their wrecked aircraft. The remains of the RAF wireless operator were never found and his name is on Runnymede's panels.

According to one report the bomber went down less than a mile from a small village on the east bank of the Rhine, near Wessel. A man and his wife who lived 100 yards from the crash scene told RAF investigators postwar the burning plane approached from the east, so low they feared it would set their house on fire, making a flat landing. Wreckage was spread over a wide area.

When Stuart, an Auckland school teacher, reached home in September 1945 he wrote immediately to the Gutzewitz family. His letter said he had spent a lot of his time in England between returning from POW camp and sailing for home trying to discover 'something more definite about Jim's fate,' without success. And because he didn't have her address, he couldn't find the 'little nurse' of whom Jim had spoken highly. He said his German captors had told him during interrogation that 'all the boys must have been killed instantly' and would be buried with military honours. 'I know this note to you can only be a further heartbreak … and yet it may help to serve as some sort of solace.'

Stuart praised his friend and captain. 'I learnt to have great confidence in him. He was a fine skipper, an excellent pilot, who did his job conscientiously and safely [and took no risks] … That this great misfortune should have [happened] when we were so close to the end of our tour was the greatest tragedy.' He said they had only one more trip left to complete a 'successful and brilliant tour'. Gutzewitz was on his thirtieth op that night, one more than his crew, saying he'd fly a

31st so they could complete their required thirty together. Stuart said destiny appeared to play a hand over the Krupp plant. 'The ground batteries seemed to have selected our particular craft as their one target for the night for they followed us with their flak for eight minutes after we'd bombed until they finally caught us.' Stuart gave no account of the damage they suffered but said, 'Jim gave us the order to bale out but so quickly did things happen that only the bomb aimer [O'Brien], the engineer and myself got away. How we managed it still amazes me for we had only split seconds in which to act.'

Some young men had a job to get into RNZAF in the early years, when the air force was swamped with volunteers. One was Ken Orman of Wellington, who turned 17 a month before war broke out. He finished at Rongotai College in 1939, and joined the Public Works Department, first as a clerk then as a draughting cadet. In June 1941 his application to join the air force as aircrew was accepted. Then he waited. Nothing happened. In early 1942 the army began conscripting 18-year-olds and Orman was called in the first ballot. He had five weeks at Waiouru then was sent to Linton to train as a gunner in 2 Field Regiment. A week later he was confronted by the adjutant, with papers showing he'd applied for aircrew. And the the air force wanted him.

'Why did you volunteer for the air force?' the man asked.

'Because it's better than the army.'

The officer looked at him disdainfully: 'Pack your things then and bugger off.'

Orman spent four and a half months in army uniform with an air force cap as a member of the Aerodrome Defence Force night-guarding aircraft at Whenuapai, as he continued work on the

RNZAF's pre-entry course. On 15 October 1942 Orman reached the Initial Training Wing at Rotorua. He was in. Two weeks short of two years later he flew his first op, bombing the Krupps works in Essen. Getting to fly a Lancaster on ops was a long time coming and, like many young pilots who began their tour late in the war, Orman was scared the war would end before he got involved in the real stuff. On D-Day, as he watched fleets of aircraft towing gliders bound for France, he thought the war was almost over.

Orman had a loudmouthed Texan bully, a man called 'Butch', teach him on his wings course in Calgary from April 1943 and had a chance to ditch him on the grounds of 'incompatibility' in the first two weeks. Two of the four Canadians assigned to Butch quit but Orman and fellow New Zealander, Jimmy Wood (27), a Blenheim carpenter, accepted the challenge and stuck with him. 'Jimmy was easy going, laughed a lot and played the mouth-organ,' Orman remembered in a family memoir he wrote five years after the war 'when my memory of it was still strong'.

Wood wasn't a natural pilot and failed his wings test then remustered as a bomb aimer. He was posted to 75 (NZ) Squadron on 15 March 1945 and killed just six days later, on his second op. A bomb knocked off the nose of Wood's Lancaster, taking him with it. Orman says he heard later his friend's chute was still in its rack in the wreckage. 75 got itself into a tragic tangle that day, losing three Lancasters. The lead planes on a daylight to Munster overshot and turned back to bomb on the wrong course. A hail of flak and bombs falling from above met them, the bombs destroying two of the aircraft, including Wood's. The losses were 75's last of the war – the only ones on the raid. Twelve of the twenty-one crewmen died, six of them New Zealanders.

Orman topped his wings navigation test, one of two pilots commissioned. He sailed from Halifax, a 'miserable place', and was pleased to get onto the *Queen Elizabeth*. She was packed with between 18,000 and 20,000 servicemen – twelve officers to a two-berth cabin.

Arrival in England in September 1943 meant more than a year of flying and interminable courses. Crewing up on Wellingtons was followed by conversion to Stirlings, a Lancaster Finishing School (LFS) and eventually a posting to 186 Squadron at Tuddenham, Suffolk, on 12 October 1944. At his OTU he slotted in with three other New Zealanders and two Scots gunners, settling down to get to know them. The flight engineer, almost always a Brit, would be added later. Orman was about to start flying when his new crew was whisked away. 'A certain Kiwi wing commander hadn't deigned to sort out his own crew [and took mine]. My fate was to be transferred to an earlier crew already carrying out flying duties.'

His new lot were 'headless'. They'd lost their Australian skipper who couldn't cope and had been sent home LMF (lack of moral fibre). His crew were dejected, scared and unhappy as they'd been subjected to some pretty bad flying and captaincy.

> When another colonial pilot, myself, appeared to take his place they weren't overly impressed. At the stage when I flew the Wellington for my first solo, only the wireless operator and rear gunner accompanied me; the rest stood by to see how I would cope. After brief discussion it was agreed that I was coping and we flew as a crew without an instructor for the first time.

At Stradishall, Suffolk, Orman and his crew found they were about to be posted to 214 Squadron on Fortresses in Norfolk. No one liked the idea and it took some smart talking to the CO, emphasising they'd trained on H2S [radar] which the Forts didn't have, 'to swing the argument our way'. Ironically 86 aircraft didn't have radar either.

At LFS Feltwell, 75's old airfield, their conversion to Lancasters took just three days. Orman loved the Lancaster. 'It was a beautiful aircraft to fly, the pilot had a magnificent position, comfortable and tremendous all-round vision.' On their last night, flying a Lanc III for the first time, Orman admitted boobing the startup because the engine-firing sequence was different from the Lanc he'd been flying. When he landed at midnight the school's chief, New Zealander Wing Commander Roy Max, former 75 Squadron CO, was waiting. He wore a raincoat and field cap so his rank wasn't showing. He asked about the delayed takeoff. Orman admitted his mistake but Max only chuckled and said 'it happens to all of us'. Max then wanted to know if they'd like to go to 75 Squadron. 'I was about to say "yes" when our Aussie wireless operator, Reg [Simon] walked by and heard the question. In typical Aussie manner he said, "We're not going there, skipper. 75 is a 'chop' squadron. [Bill Chorley's *Bomber Command Losses* says 75 suffered the second highest casualties of any squadron in Bomber Command. However, Chorley also noted that 75 flew the most sorties.]"' Orman introduced Max to Simon who said, 'Oh, I've put my bloody foot in it.' With only one New Zealander in the crew their chances of being posted to a New Zealand squadron were slight but that episode extinguished any hope.

Max's parting words when they went to 186: 'By the way, keep that rabble of yours under control.' But the 'rabble' turned out to be a top crew, eventually leading 3 Group G-H precision-bombing raids on German targets. It was a well-balanced team – Orman, flight engineer Len Sewell (London), bomb aimer Barney Earrey (Ipswich), navigator Rolly Ward (Northampton), WOp Simon (New South Wales), mid-upper Geordie Bennett (Durham) and rear gunner Geordie Bear (Newcastle). Bear was the baby of the crew at 18; at 31 Sewell was the oldest. Simon (29) was the only married man.

Together they did a single tour of thirty-eight ops, accompanied a few times by a mid-under gunner firing through a circle cut in the floor of the fuselage where the planned H2S radar was to go – but didn't. 186 was re-formed at Tuddenham on 5 October 1944, after a couple of earlier lives, from C flight of 190 Squadron, and the two squadrons flew from there until 186 transferred to Stradishall in mid-December 1944. The Orman crew did its initial trip to Essen the night of 23–24 October, just five days after 186 operated for the first time.

Orman kept careful records. One noted each bomb load and he figures his aircraft, mostly Q-Queenie, dropped 121 tons of bombs, plus loads he didn't detail on four occasions. Just short of half the bomb loads were the 4000-pound 'cookies', whose enormous blast effect was devastating, and along with the incendiaries they dropped in tandem, did their fiery work in building wrecks. Orman summarised their targets – fourteen on oil refineries, eight on railway yards, four on troops and transport, five on factories and five on towns. Twice they were recalled without bombing. The only time they didn't go to Germany was Boxing Day 1944, when they hit the Belgian town of St Vith after raids on the 21st and 23rd to the German town of Trier just over the border from Luxembourg. Both were vital crossroads for the German breakthrough into Belgium through the Ardennes. St Vith, a town of 10,000, was largely destroyed by ground battles and bombing by the USAAF and the RAF. Of the RAF's 300-aircraft attack on St Vith, Orman wrote:

> The powers-that-be deemed their destruction would hinder the advance and no doubt kill a few troops. The fact that civilians, some of whom were our allies, would also suffer didn't come into the equation. The explosive effect of our cookies on the snow-covered ground was awe-inspiring.

That first raid to Essen (1050 bombers, the greatest number dispatched so far in the war) was eventful for an unblooded crew. The Gee set, a navigation aid, packed up as soon as they were airborne; they couldn't see the French coast to get a fix and changed wind direction meant they arrived over the cloud-shrouded target five minutes early – alone.

> We must have had the undivided attention of the flak and I managed to stall the aircraft [and lose 2000 feet]. This seemed to bluff the German gunners for a while … presently the rear gunner reported red target markers going down astern so now we knew where we were. We did a wide circuit to the right and bombed about 20 minutes later than we should have but we had done it … After the first ten minutes of the raid we failed to see another aircraft until we arrived back at base … Although we had mentally prepared ourselves for this trip over a long period I must say I was pretty apprehensive. Was this typical of the thirty trips [the normal length of a tour] we were embarking on? A pat on the back and 'well done' from the CO was a help but the unease persisted. A day later we returned to Essen in a daylight attack and a lot of my fears and doubts were dispelled. I

could see now the bomber force strung out over several miles and at different heights, I could see the flak bursts, our Gee worked and I could understand why at night you might never see another aircraft.

On his long tour Orman and his men flew ten times at night, the rest in daylight. The decline of the Luftwaffe from the summer of 1994, the result of many factors, meant the RAF could safely resume the daylights it had abandoned much earlier in the war. Long-range Allied fighters now accompanied the British bombers and Luftwaffe day fighters posed less and less of a danger as 1944 waned – their airfields blitzed, their shortages of aviation gas worsened and the quality of their fighters and fighter pilots no match for the Allies. RAF bomber casualties, at their highest in late 1943 and early 1944, declined sharply.

But flak was ever present, giving Orman a nasty surprise on a daylight op to Dortmund on 15 November. By this time the RAF's daylight tactics in 3 Group, of which 186 was a part, were groups of four in a diamond shape led by a G-H-equipped Lancaster. Each diamond flew in line astern and the planes stretched back a couple of miles. When each leader reached the target he dropped his bombs and the other three followed suit. Approaching the target one by one, as they reached the same final turn point the aircraft hauled around 90 degrees on a set bearing to the drop point, a five-minute bombing run.

On this particular day Orman's diamond leader made the turn early, falling out of the line. 'I can only assume his navigator had decided everybody else was wrong and he was right,' Orman commented. The four Lancs had to follow their leader and were now exposed and about to be singled out by German radar and heavy flak. The shells weren't long coming, bursting slightly ahead but spot on for height. Weaving was forbidden because the G-H bombing run had to be flown accurately. Almost immediately the No. 3 on the left of the diamond was hit and smashed into No. 4 at the rear. Both 115 Squadron Lancasters went down, all sixteen men aboard perishing. Orman warned the crew of their plight and moved away from the leader. At that moment a lump of flak slashed through the rear gunner's turret. Had the gunner not had his head down between the gun's breechblocks for protection he might have lost it. (A 90 Squadron crew on its last op lost their navigator this way – the man's head was taken clean off. The skipper aborted the raid and returned to base. Orman saw ground crew hosing out the Lanc after it landed and the shattered crew were sent on leave.) Now it was his turn.

> I had adopted the precaution of pulling my heavy goggles over my dark glasses during the bombing run. It was as well I had … as a one-inch jagged piece of flak ploughed through the windscreen and thumped me in the face. My head was thrown back against the steel amour plating forming the backing to my seat. What with the oxygen mask and goggles the resulting wound was not as bad as I first imagined.

A few minutes later the bombs went down and Queenie broke away. 'My face felt numb and a deep cut alongside my nose was splashing blood down my Mae West and generally making a mess.' The flight engineer stemmed the blood with a bandage wad but black eyes and a swollen face soon developed. Orman had difficulty talking to the engineer and a concerned crew heard the fractured conversation over the intercom. Orman told them not to worry, it was only a scratch. He was stitched up at Tuddenham and eight days later was back on ops. He and the crew finished their tour on 4 April 1945 with a 7 hours 50 minutes raid on the Leuna oil works at Merseburg, near Leipzig.

The piece of shrapnel was on the cockpit floor. Orman has it still, along with the scar. And the DFC, the citation noting he'd executed a successful raid despite the face wound. In July 1945 a bar to his DFC was announced to recognise his many sorties and his 'steadfastness, courage and determination'.

Ray Tait was only 15 and still at school when war broke out. He was accepted at 18, when he enlisted for pilot training in October 1942, with a strong academic record. After a spell at Waipapakauri's Aerodrome Defence Unit, he was on his way for pilot training at Taieri. 'They knew I was good at maths, had my University Entrance and was studying part time for a B.Com at Auckland University. I was told the air force was short of navigators and it would be better for the war effort if I changed trades.' So he did and in August 1943 was on his way to Canada.

He was in England the following March, bound for the 'New Zealand' OTU at Westcott, Buckinghamshire, where hordes of young New Zealanders crewed up and trained to fly bombers. On the train he met a fellow countryman. Tait remembers pilot Marty Kilpatrick from Inglewood as 'a bit scruffy, old at 25 but a relaxed sort of bloke'. They liked the look of each other and agreed to fly as a team. At Westcott they added a Scot and four Poms to make up their Stirling crew. They stayed together throughout their coming tour. From 11 OTU they went on to finish their training at Chedburgh, Suffolk, then converted to Lancasters at Stradishall. Their posting to 75 (NZ) Squadron followed. The Kilpatrick crew did their first op on 28 October 1944, a daylight raid on railway yards at Cologne.

It was a rude awakening. On the run in, the bomb aimer complained the target was obscured by black smoke. He couldn't see properly. 'It's flak, you silly bastard,' someone said in withering tones over the intercom. It was – bursting shells with their black explosions. The Lancaster was badly hit, flak riddling the fuselage, luckily without fatal results and the Merlins still purred. The German fighter force wasn't what it had been and friendly fighters, Spitfires and the longer-range Mustangs, accompanied them. But flak was lethal and there was plenty of it.

75, in 3 Group, converted to Lancasters in March–April 1944 and by October the entire group's Stirlings had gone. It was now an all-Lanc fleet. Martin Middlebrook in *The Bomber Command War Diaries* says 3 Group had borne the brunt of Bomber Command's early war years with the Wellington but then suffered and 'languished in near idleness' with the Stirlings. He adds many of 3's Lancasters would be fitted with G-H, the blind-bombing device enabling the group's aircraft to bomb accurately in any weather provided cloud tops didn't reach the Lancasters' operational height. '3 group was then permitted to operate on its own on most occasions.'

Middlebrook also noted a directive to both the RAF and the US Eighth Air Force on 25 August 1944 placed the highest priority on bombing 'the petroleum industry with special emphasis on petrol including storage'. Germany's rail and waterways transport network, tank and motor vehicle production were joint second priority. The bombers could attack cities (area bombing) 'when weather and tactical conditions are unsuitable for operations against specific primary objectives'.

Bomber Command chief Arthur Harris unleashed the RAF against petroleum targets in a major operation that lasted until war's end. The directive should have been in operation earlier, even given the need for the campaign against French and Belgian railways, V1 rocket sites and the support of ground troops in Normandy. The concentrated raids on refineries, particularly by the Americans, wrecked Germany's ability to produce aviation gas and other fuels. The enemy's production and stockpiles declined precipitously in late 1944 and continued to fall in 1945, with an immense and devastating effect on the Luftwaffe's operational flying, training and German industry.

3 Group played a key role in the oil bombing and within the group 75 Squadron made a major contribution. Between the start of the Kilpatrick crew's tour in late October and its end five months later, petroleum targets figured prominently – with seventeen attacks on refineries.

G-H was installed in a number of 75 Squadron's Lancs, and Kilpatrick's aircraft was equipped about midway through their tour, when they had become an experienced and a senior crew. They became one of the squadron's lead aircraft and when their bomb doors opened and the load went down, it signalled to following crews that they were on target and time to follow suit. 'The bomb aimer set us up but I had the G-H set in my office and when the pulses on it merged I pressed the tit to drop the bombs,' says Tait.

The Kilpatrick crew's worst moments occurred on a daylight oil attack on the Osterfeld benzol plant at Oberhausen, in the heart of the Ruhr Valley. Eighty-five Lancs from 3 Group bombed a refinery at nearby Gelsenkirchen (one was lost over the target) and eighty-two attacked Osterfeld. The Kilpatrick aircraft was lucky to get home. Tait remembers:

75 had twenty-one Lancasters up that day [one aborted] and we were one of the leaders. Because we led and had to keep a steady line we couldn't deviate or take evasive action to avoid the heavy flak. Two minutes out from the drop point the German guns found us. The radio alongside me was blown to pieces, my table was splattered by bits of flak and other pieces hit my parachute harness. The port inner was shattered and then the starboard outer was hit and set on fire. The Graviner system [pouring out CO_2] put the fire out but we had two propellers feathered. Marty was a pretty confident and non-excitable captain and he finished the run-in and we dropped the bombs. No one was hurt but there was a great deal of damage.

Flak hit their aircraft often because of their lead role out in front but the hits over Osterfeld was by far the most serious. The Lancaster took its battering at 20,000 feet and on only two engines it gradually lost height. A Mustang spotted the plane was in trouble and nudged up alongside to escort it home. By the time the Lancaster had cleared German and French airspace and reached the Channel over the Belgian coast the altimeter read 5000 feet and the plane had lost considerable speed, its engines labouring. As it approached 75's base at Mepal it was at 1000 feet. Kilpatrick did a high landing and lost height by a neat side-slip which astonished watchers and scattered them in fear of a crash. Says Tait: 'It was a nice landing.'

Kilpatrick, awarded an immediate DFC, was called a 'resolute pilot' in the citation which added he set a splendid example of skill and coolness. Tait was awarded an end-of-tour DFC.

Dresden will be forever remembered as the city in eastern Germany destroyed by the RAF the night of 13–14 February 1945. The

Russians, now within Germany's frontiers, were closing in, the city was packed with troops and refugees fleeing the fighting. Martin Middlebrook says in *The Bomber Command War Diaries* that Berlin, Dresden, Chemnitz and Leipzig were considered vital communications and supply centres for the eastern front. Stalin wanted raids to support their advance. Contrary to what many latter-day critics believe, Dresden had military and industrial targets, including important plants manufacturing optical equipment vital to the war effort. The Air Ministry, encouraged by Churchill, chose Dresden as the first target in Operation Thunderclap, followed in short order by Chemnitz. Deep in the east, they were a long way from British airfields and hadn't been hit before.

The RAF was directed to attack Dresden. Bomber Command didn't make the decision – it was doing what it was trained for and unjustly copped the condemnation which followed, then and postwar. Bomber crews were the heroes of the dark days of the war when they pretty much carried the war to Germany alone, but no one wanted to know them when the war ended. People had short memories in the safety of peace.

Bomber Command attacked Dresden in strength: two raids three hours apart. Middlebrook tallies a total strike force of 796 Lancasters and nine Mosquitoes, which dropped 1478 tons of high explosive and 1182 tons of incendiary bombs. The first comprised aircraft from 5 Group, the second an all-Lancaster attack by aircraft of 1, 3, 6 and 8 Groups. He says a band of cloud in the target area affected the opening assault which was 'only moderately successful' but by the time the second fleet of aeroplanes appeared over the city the weather had cleared and the Lancasters unloaded 'with great accuracy'. The majority of the bombs hit the centre of the city.

With conditions ripe, a firestorm of vast proportions developed, the city's inhabitants died in their thousands and much of the central area collapsed into utter destruction. Germany claimed a death toll of 200,000 but the most recent figure, the outcome of patient, detailed research of official German figures compiled by city authorities at the time, counted 20,000 dead. This was far fewer than the Hamburg firestorm raids of July 1943 and only a fraction of the total in the United States' attack on Tokyo 9–10 March 1945, the single most destructive raid of the war. A firestorm devastated 16 square miles with deaths of between 80,000 and 100,000.

The main criticism of the 13–14 February attacks and the USAAF's follow-up raids the next day and on the 15th and 2 March was the 'unwarranted' destruction of a great cultural city with wonderful buildings and a priceless art heritage. To his discredit, Churchill distanced himself from the raid in the face of mounting public concern at home and in the United States. Shamefully, he ignored Bomber Command and its 55,000 dead, among them 1850 New Zealanders, in his victory speech and Britain did not award bomber aircrew a campaign medal. It took until June 2012 before a Bomber Command memorial was dedicated in London and not until 2013 that the Government, under public pressure, announced the award of a Bomber Command clasp. Even that didn't satisfy many former aircrew, who continue to demand a medal.

Dresden contributed to its own destruction. The city, smug in its belief that it wouldn't be attacked because of its iconic cultural status, had removed its flak guns for use against Soviet ground forces. Night-fighter aircraft were almost non-existent. By this stage of the war most German cities had built large and effective air-raid shelters, holding thousands. Dresden was shelterless and unlike other German cities under aerial attack, hadn't evacuated its women and children to safer rural areas. However, Dresden's local Nazi leader had built himself an elaborate shelter. Those who still clamour about Dresden conveniently overlook these facts and the savage deaths of countless millions Germany inflicted on Soviets and Poles – as well as the horrors of the Holocaust.

Tony Lindsay (23), from Whangarei, flew to Dresden as navigator on the 635 Squadron pathfinder Lancaster that acted as Master Bomber for the second raid. Wing Command Peter de Wesselow orbited the target for 21 minutes, directing the bombers to the correct target indicators. Not one for many words, Lindsay wrote, 'Enormous fires.' They were enormous – smoke and flames reaching hundreds of feet into the air. For most crews the trip to Dresden was uneventful, with no opposition. Just four of the big force of Lancasters were lost to enemy action, one in southern Germany on the return flight. Another was abandoned over Holland after an engine fire and two others collided and crashed soon after takeoff.

Ken Orman was on his twenty-seventh op the night he flew to Dresden. He recalls being told at the pre-flight briefing the attack was in aid of the approaching Russians. As his Lancaster passed over the city about 2 a.m. he could see the frontline gunfire. He adds: 'There were immense fires from the first raid when we arrived and the Master Bomber was explicit where he wanted our incendiaries; those areas not burning.' There was no opposition in the form of flak, searchlights or fighters. In other words, an absurdly easy run for crews who'd faced stiff defences over other parts of Germany.

Pilot Bill Petersen, from Auckland, also saw the Dresden fires though he wasn't on the raid. His new Mark VI Halifax, the latest model, was among the 368 aircraft attacking a synthetic-oil plant at Bohlen, just south of Leipzig and about 60 miles from Dresden. Almost seventy years on, he remembers the red glow reaching skyward. 'We could see them alright. We had a full view.' Earlier he had seen the bomber stream headed for Dresden. Petersen arrived at 102 Squadron, based in Pocklington, Yorkshire, in early 1945 and by the time the war ended had flown twenty ops. He had a routine trip to Bohlen, unlike his second op the night of 2–3 February 1945 to an oil target, the Krupp Treibstoff plant at Wanne-Eickel in the Ruhr. Petersen was on the run in to drop his bombs when his Halifax missed a collision with another aircraft by a whisker.

> I glanced up to my left and saw this other plane coming at us. He was only about 50 yards away; he was corkscrewing down. I went down and he went up; we missed by inches. The ventral gunner [some Halifaxes had a hole in the floor through which a third gunner with 0.5 calibre guns operated to defeat upward-firing cannons on German night fighters] screamed out, "that was bloody close". I said, "How close?" and he replied, "All I could see was one very big engine and a bit of wing. It filled my view."

Scot Jock Adamson, 20, was the mid-upper gunner on Southlander Wattie Stirling's crew on 115 Squadron, a 3 Group unit. Adamson recalls Stirling as 'a good skipper and fine pilot'. The crew were nearing the end of their tour when they flew to Dresden. Adamson has never forgotten the fires. 'We were told at briefing not to look down; it could impair your night vision and you could miss a night fighter coming at you. Still, it was impossible not to see the huge fires. It was so bright I could have read a newspaper. We dropped our load and just got out of it and away home.' He knows the RAF killed a lot of people that night but has little sympathy for the German victims. He'd seen the bomb damage in Britain. 'We gave it back to them and a bit more.' That view was shared by most of the men in Bomber Command. The Germans deserved all they got and the aircrew were simply doing what they trained for.

Adamson was born in Balmangan, Kirkcudbrightshire, in October 1924. He met Stirling, a Southland farmer from Waikaia in the Gore district, at 11 OTU, Westcott, in June 1944 and agreed to fly with him. The skipper ran into Max White, another Southlander he knew, who joined the crew as the wireless operator. The rest were Britons. Then the posting to 115 Squadron. They learnt the grim realities of the air war on their second op, a daylight to Cologne on 27 November 1944, the first with Stirling in command. A sprog crew, they followed another 115 Lancaster on the bombing run and watched in horror as flak scored a direct hit and exploded the plane. Nine men (the plane carried two extra gunners) gone in an instant. The Stirling crew proved lucky after that early fright. Flak hit and damaged their port inner, one fuel tank and the starboard tyre in its housing on one trip but that was the only major alarm. Adamson never fired his guns in anger.

Back from Dresden at 6 a.m. on 14 February they found themselves on the battle list again for that night – to Chemnitz. Another long flight. 'No problems,' says Adamson. 'That's what we were there for.' Dresden took nine hours, Chemnitz 8 hours 40 minutes. In February alone they did twelve ops, up almost every second night. Adamson imemigrated to Southland postwar and still lives there.

Casualties were more severe at Chemnitz on the night of 14–15 February – another twin raid from which fifteen aircraft failed to return, one of them piloted by Dunedin-born George Davies (21).

His 75 Squadron Lancaster was just half an hour into Germany, north of Karlsruhe, when a fire developed in one of the wings – probably from a fractured oil line. Unable to feather the propeller or put out the fire, he jettisoned the bombs and ordered everyone out. He and the crew including fellow New Zealander, navigator Claude Greenough (24), parachuted safely but were all captured. On 2 March he and Greenough and the other members of the crew were on their way by rail to the big Stalag camp at Nuremberg with other RAF and USAAF aircrew POWs when their train was attacked by Allied fighters. Raking fire tore into one of the box cars carrying prisoners and Davies' bomb aimer Henry Chalmers died with about twenty-five others. Davies and Greenough emerged unscathed from another boxcar.

Another New Zealander also abandoned his aircraft for similar reasons. James Gapes (27), a married pilot on 158 Squadron at Lissett, Yorkshire, took off for Chemnitz but didn't get far. Outbound both port engines on his Halifax, a veteran of 69 ops, began to misfire, then the starboard outer failed according to Bill Chorley in *Bomber Command Losses*. The crew abandoned the aircraft over friendly territory near the France-Belgium border and all seven landed safely. They were soon together and returned to England via Paris.

The second and last Thunderclap raid on Chemnitz on 5–6 March cost even more bombers than the first – twenty-two aircraft plus another nine, which crashed after takeoff in icy conditions. The attack cost the lives of four New Zealanders, all killed on different aircraft.

CHAPTER 14

The last weeks

486 Squadron lost its second squadron leader within two months on 13 April 1945, a Black Friday, when Keith 'Hyphen' Taylor-Cannon died while attacking enemy vehicles in his Typhoon. It was indeed a black day and the squadron was still mourning the next day when another pilot was killed, the last it lost before peace. Owen Mitchell (23), Nelson born and an engineering student at Canterbury University when he enlisted, was a newcomer to 486 and on his fourteenth op when he was the loser in a one-on-one low-level duel with Willi Reschke. The German was flying a Ta 152, an updated, long-nosed version of the FW 190, rated by some as the best fighter in service at the time. The aircraft, often mistaken for an Me 109, had a tight turning circle and superior climb rate, but appeared in limited numbers in the last weeks of the war.

Four 486 Tempests on an armed reconnaissance southeast of Lubeck split up into pairs, one off strafing while two Ta 152s bounced the second – that of Aucklander Sid Short and Mitchell. Short and his German fought a draw, each apparently pleased. Reschke took on Mitchell and won when the young New Zealander crashed, outmanoeuvred and hit. The German wrote a widely published account of their deadly clash.

We knew the Tempest to be a very fast fighter ... but here, in a fight which was never to climb above 50 metres, speed would not play a big part. The machines' ability to turn would be all important. Both pilots realised it would be a fight to the finish and used every flying trick and tactical ploy possible to try to gain the upper hand. At this altitude neither could afford to make the slightest mistake. And for the first time since flying the Ta 152 I began to appreciate exactly what this aircraft could do. Pulling ever tighter turns I got closer and closer to the Tempest never once feeling I was even approaching the limit of the Ta's capabilities. And in order to keep out of my sights, the Tempest pilot was being forced to take increasingly dangerous evasive action. When he flicked over on to the opposite wing I knew his last attempt to turn inside me had failed. The first burst of fire ... caught the Tempest in the tail and rear fuselage. The aircraft shuddered noticeably and, probably as an instinctive reaction [he] immediately yoked into a starboard turn, giving me an even greater advantage. Now there was no escape ... I pressed my gun buttons a second time but after a few rounds my weapons fell silent and despite all my efforts to clear them refused to fire another shot. But unfortunately the Tempest pilot didn't realise my predicament as he'd already taken hits. Instead he continued desperately to twist and turn and I positioned myself so that I was always within his field of vision. Eventually – inevitably – he stalled. The Tempest's left wing dropped and he crashed into the woods below us.

Another Ta 152 had gone down just a few minutes earlier, its pilot killed, only 500 yards from where the New Zealander crashed. Reschke claims the fighter dived into the ground but not as the result of enemy action. The two were buried at Neustadt-Glewe side by side with full military honours, Reschke present. Postwar Mitchell was reinterred in Berlin.

Woe Wilson was another New Zealander who crash-landed his Tempest – just a few days before Ginger Eagleson did the same. Like Eagleson, he was in and out of consciousness before he reached earth, severely hurt. Unlike Eagleson, he got his plane back to the British lines.

Wilson, 18 when he enlisted a year after war was declared, in October 1942 joined 486 (NZ) Squadron at North Weald on Typhoons. Two years later, after a long tour with 486, he returned to New Zealand, an option open to aircrew who been overseas for three years and if operational requirements permitted. His father was seriously ill and he wanted to see him. Almost through his leave he was called to Wellington to see what he wanted to do next. What he wanted was to return to Europe. 'I was getting word from the other side that they were desperate for trained Typhoon and Tempest pilots [Wilson had flown both on 486]. The Germans were knocking them down faster than the RAF could train them. I wanted to go back to that. I must have been mad.'

'We're no longer sending anyone to England, sorry,' Air Department officials told him. Understandably – it was now January 1945 and the end of the war was fast approaching. But the department didn't realise Wilson had friends in very high places. After all, he'd worked as a clerk in the department prewar and some of those friends 'had now attained considerable rank', such as the Senior Air Staff Officer at RNZAF HQ London. He got together with Wilson's former CO, the now Group Captain Des Scott, who had an 'I-want-to-go-back' letter from another 486 flier, Robert (Bluey) Dall, also back in New Zealand. A signal from London directed 'that Flt Lt Dall and Flg Off Wilson … be returned to UK by swiftest possible means.' The message landed on 15 March 1945. 'On 29 March Dall and I were on a train going from Glasgow to London.' They'd been flown back to Britain. Australian-born Dall, who operated Spitfires with 132 Squadron and Typhoons with 486 and 198 Squadrons, joined 33 Squadron in Holland on Tempests after returning to Europe. He survived the war but died in Germany in July 1945 while doing aerobatics.

Wilson was posted to 222 Squadron, colloquially known as the 'Trembling Two', on 18 April, two days before they moved to Germany and the wonderfully named Quackenbruck, an ex Luftwaffe field near Osnabruck and frequent Bomber Command target. On the 24th, flak ended Wilson's short second tour. He wrote about what happened in an article for the New Zealand Fighter Pilots Association. The squadron was briefed to attack a seaplane base at Ratzeburg Lake – now famous for its international rowing regattas – just south of Lubeck. Twelve aircraft took off on the op, emerging through broken cloud to achieve complete surprise and considerable damage to the moored seaplanes.

> In fact, so successful was it that I was mentally urging the CO to round and have another go which he did. He and his section did another

very damaging run and then it was the turn of the section in which I was flying No. 2 to my flight commander, another New Zealander, Bill Mart, with whom I'd worked in Wellington in 1936 [William Mart, 25, DFC, three tours totalling at least 415 ops on four squadrons flying Spitfires, Mustangs and lastly Tempests on 222]. Placing myself at a strategic distance behind Bill, I watched his approach to the target area. Suddenly all the local defences, by now having scrambled into position, opened up on him – everything but the kitchen sink.

Wilson was still chuckling about this as he attacked the target he'd sorted out when the gunners turned their weapons on him and wham. A 37 mm shell smashed into his cockpit about eight inches from his shoulder. Half conscious, 'silly as a chook', he looked down to find the left leg of his trousers ripped open and a long wound across his thigh. It was 'full to the brim with blood'.

The rest of the squadron veered off to port to re-form but Wilson, knocked senseless, went starboard and suddenly he was alone. In a befuddled state he couldn't figure out what course to steer toward: his base or British lines. Then he realised his uncaged (turned on) Gyroscope (an instrument indicating a plane's attitude) had been set to zero at the start of the op. By steering 180 degrees he should be able to get back. Though the powerful engine was still running sweetly he was suffering increasing bouts of blackouts – his blood pressure was dropping steadily, as blood pumped out 'through a number of holes in my hide'. Then he remembered reading that if wounded and losing blood, aircrew should turn the oxygen on to emergency for a bit of extra time. 'So I did, and it did give me about another 10–15 minutes.' Once the oxygen boost ran out, 'the flake-outs returned and I decided it was time to head for Mother Earth.'

I picked out a decent-sized ploughed field far enough from any towns to make it unlikely that its inhabitants had suffered from the 'terrorfliegers' and set about getting myself down there. Memory gets a bit fragmentary about this stage but I do recall that I did a semi-gliding turn of about 270 degrees and that in the course of it I passed out either four or five times – and I wasn't much above a thousand feet to start with. Luckily, I was in one of my bouts of consciousness when we reached ground level, and the landing, wheels up of course, was uneventful. I still didn't know whether I'd reached our territory; nor, by that stage did I care very much. I had though, not far from Soltau, a small town about 50 miles south of Hamburg. Having slithered to a halt, I got out; I didn't feel well. I tried lying down on the wing but that was hard and knobbly, so I sat on the leading edge, feet in the ploughed earth … and felt sorry for myself. After a while … I just buried my head in my hands and felt terrible.

Wilson had a short wait for help. A Jeep-load of Brits were scouting the area for a site for a new headquarters for General Dempsey's 2nd Army. They shortly found it at nearby Luneburg Heath, where Field Marshal Montgomery later accepted the surrender of German forces in northwest Europe. The soldiers had seen the lone Tempest heading for the ground, heard the loud clang of its landing, pulled up and sprinted across the fields. When they got to Wilson, their leader uttered one word: 'Christ.'

'At that stage I decided to rejoin the world, gave him what I suppose was a fairly sickly grin and murmured "hello".'

The 'brown jobs' staunched the blood with field dressings, carried him to the Jeep, bundled him in and sped to a temporary field hospital in the small village of Belsen – alongside the infamous concentration camp. Wilson was the only serviceman in the packed marquee hospital. The rest were camp inmates – and by evening there were a lot fewer than in the morning. He was taken next morning to Celle, an RAF base, then evacuated to Brussels and back to England on VE day for two months of repairs at Wroughton, an RAF hospital.

Owen 'Ginger' Eagleson was good. A long-serving top pilot with 486 (NZ) Squadron flying Tempests, he shot down more V-1 flying bombs over England than any other New Zealander (twenty-one and three shared) and won the DFC, the citation calling him a 'brave and resolute pilot', with a 'strong sense of duty'. But the colourful story of how he was shot down in the last days of the European war, survived, was captured, escaped and evaded, and then took part in the surrender of a Luftwaffe Field Marshal, trumps it all.

He left no record of his wartime exploits but some time before his death in 1994, he talked to Napier's *Daily Telegraph* reporter Roger Moroney about the events of early May 1945. He had been with 486 since November 1943, since just before the squadron switched from Typhoons to Tempests. Jack Stafford was on the same ship to England in January that year and both ended up on 486, serving with distinction.

Eagleson's late-war adventure began from 486's base at Fassberg, 50 miles south of Hamburg, on 2 May. That day he flew three successful patrols, bagging a small seaplane on one and a Fiesler Storch, a three-seater reconnaissance and casualty evacuation aircraft, on the next. On the third, motor transport had a going over. Late in the day he and another pilot, Bill Reid, took off looking for more targets. They found one, a standing train, smoking quietly by a wood northwest of Lubeck. Such trains often posed a threat – flak traps – idling innocently, but bristling with well-camouflaged guns.

Telling his partner to stay back, he flew in to take a closer look, which nearly proved fatal. One brief cannon burst at the train and he realised his mistake. 'I got it well and truly. Everything opened up at me,' he told Moroney. Flak smashed into the Tempest and Eagleson felt blows to the back of his head and his side. Worse, his radiator, holed by the ground fire, began to spew its vital engine-cooling glycol. He turned for home as the motor began to falter, trying to glide while the engine cooled. Then he'd start it again and run it until the temperature needle went off the gauge before gliding some more. 'I flew it a fair way like that but I was in the same sort of shape, losing consciousness, and eventually went down into a paddock. He woke seeing what he thought were two gargoyles sitting in a hedge. 'My head was playing tricks on me. I was looking at grinning German soldiers.'

The Germans were good guys. They hadn't been attacked by Tempests. They dressed his head wound and Eagleson was then driven off, a POW. Another car took him on an all-night trip. Dazed, he didn't remember much about it but clear-headed in the morning, found his vehicle in a monster traffic jam. Just the sort of tempting target he knew prowling Typhoons would be seeking. They were, found it and attacked. Eagleson leapt from the car in the chaos and threw himself into a ditch. The rockets arrived in a shower of smoke, noise and horror. 'I'll never forget the sight of a truck being hit and lifted off the ground and flung over a hedge … the power of those rockets.'

Once the Typhoons had gone he began aiding the injured, wanting to help but aware he was still wearing his air force uniform.

Several soldiers were already looking at him in a 'strange sort of way'. At a nearby field hospital he did a runner, using a compass in a trouser button to make for the British lines but walked straight into more Jerries. POW again. He was taken to an enormous farm building occupied by hundreds of soldiers. The colonel in charge recognised him as the man who'd been tending the wounded after the Typhoons attack and asked if there was anything he could do for him. Bold as brass, Eagleson suggested the officer surrender to him. The colonel laughed but offered a bath and shave. Then dinner with his captor, wife and other officers. The food – potato and cabbage soup – was poor but there was plenty to drink. 'They were excellent hosts and I got pretty full.'

Next morning he escaped again, walking out of the place with some sleepy German soldiers, his uniform not unlike German field garb. Then he hived off and joined a stream of refugees, some of them forced labourers, carrying a Polish baby whenever they met a German patrol. An hour and a half later a British Jeep drove up and Eagleson stepped out of line, opening the ragged coat he'd pinched to show his uniform. The sergeant and two privates were hopelessly lost and delighted to have Eagleson and his map-reading skills. The New Zealander soon had the Brits, part of the 52nd (Lowland) Division, back on course to their unit headquarters. 'I had a hell of a night and next morning sitting outside, two privates arrived to say a message had been received that Field Marshal Erhard Milch wanted to surrender.' As the only air force man in the area, he was invited to go with a party of officers to accept the surrender.

Milch played a key role in the development of the Luftwaffe. He commanded Luftflotte 5 during the Norwegian invasion and was promoted Field Marshal after the defeat of France. When he tried and failed to persuade Hitler to sack Luftwaffe head Herman Goering after the German defeat in the Soviet Union, he was sidelined.

The story of his surrender is fascinating … and controversial. The brigadier heading the British party is said to have either just visited Bergen-Belsen concentration camp or seen the bodies of hundreds of concentration camp inmates littering the seashore near Lubeck on the Baltic coast, floating in from the former liner *Cap Arcona*. She was set afire and sunk on 3 May in Lubeck Bay by Typhoons of 2TAF's 83 Group. She burned and capsized, her hulk drifting ashore. About 5000 perished, with only 350 survivors. One story is that in a fury the brigadier grabbed Milch's baton, broke it over his head and beat the field marshal to the ground. The debate about this incident still continues. Unfortunately, Eagleson didn't go into details about the scene in his interview with Moroney, saying simply: 'He wanted to give me his baton but the Brits wouldn't have that. It was bloody beautiful too.' His last sight of Milch was the man, tears in his eyes, being told he would scrub out a room in a concentration camp. While Eagleson didn't get the prized baton he scored Milch's luxurious Mercedes, complete with cocktail cabinet.

The next morning he drove off in style, Union Jack flapping in the breeze at the side of the bonnet. And who should he meet just a few miles along the autobahn? Fellow squadron member Keith Smith of Masterton, shot down over the Kiel Canal area on 26 April. They cracked a bottle and motored on. Some miles later they picked up a British pilot, also walking 'home'. Eagleson enjoyed the trip back to Fassberg. 'When people saw us driving along they stopped and stood to attention. Inevitably, Eagleson lost the car to authority at Fassberg.

Stitches out, Eagleson went on survivors' leave in London for some days then visited an aunt on the South Coast, who fainted when she saw him. He had listed her as next of kin in England and when told he was missing she had feared the worst. His mother in New Zealand also needed telling he was alive and well, and a cable went off promptly.

South Islander Brian Woodman almost missed the war because of his extended training. It wasn't as if he was a slow learner – that was just how it was as the war wore on. Some New Zealand fighter pilots sailed to England after the start of the Battle of Britain, had a couple of hours on a Miles Master, two or three flights on a Spitfire or Hurricane, were posted to a squadron and pitched into action while the battle still raged. Not surprising that some of them didn't survive. By the time Woodman began training at Taieri on 6 April 1943 it was entirely different. The drastic shortage of pilots of 1940 into 1941 was over. Training was much more thorough, took much longer and produced superbly trained aircrew. It was almost two years before Woodman reached 130 (Spitfire) Squadron in late January 1945. By the time he joined his unit his log book shows he had flown just on 400 hours. By war's end he posted only another 100 hours.

Woodman began his service career in New Zealand. In Canada he flew Harvards at a service flight training school in Ontario followed by six months at an OTU in Quebec on Hurricanes. In January 1944 he did two wheels-up landings because of engine failure and in May, while on a course in Greenwood, Nova Scotia, put his Hurricane down in an emergency landing – engine trouble again. This earned him a log book green endorsement which noted he accomplished the landing while the cockpit was full of smoke and his forward view obliterated by oil [on his windscreen]. 'This pilot is to be highly commended on his skill and coolness under difficulties.'

He reached England in late June 1944 and in August was posted to RAF Eshott, north of Newcastle, where he converted to Spitfires, then to 83 Group Support Unit, which maintained reserves of pilots and aircraft for immediate dispatch to 83's squadrons. He was ready for combat and had just made the war – he must have wondered if he'd ever see action. He was posted to 130 in January 1945, making his first operational flight on bomber escort duties on the 24th that month. His unit was officially 130 (Punjab) Squadron formed in June 1941 after the Indian state of Punjab donated a squadron of Spitfires. It was disbanded in February 1944 but two months later, to maintain the tradition of a Punjab squadron, 186 Squadron was renumbered 130.

The squadron moved to Belgium from England in September 1944, based at Deurne on the outskirts of Antwerp. Like most other fighter squadrons on the Continent after the Invasion, 130 moved frequently, after Deurne – to Grave (Holland), back to Belgium at Diest and Ophoven and then to Eindhoven and Twente (Holland). After the late-March airborne crossing of the Rhine as British ground forces swept across the plains of northern Germany, Holland became too distant and as the advance quickened fighter and fighter-bomber squadrons followed the armies through conquered territory. 130 went first to Celle on 17 April, northeast of Hanover, and then to Fassberg, 40 miles south of Hamburg, the day before VE-Day. At war's end, 130 was swiftly recalled and was back home at North Weald on 10 May. Woodman complained in his diary that they flew back to England in 'clapped out IX's [Spitfire nines]. They can't do this to us!' As a final indignity Woodman had to put down at Boxhill, south of London, a US Army Air Corp field, with a duff engine. 'A grim show. Give us back our XIVs.' There was a reason for the quick recall. In late May the squadron flew to Dyce in Scotland, and the next month went on to Kristiansand, Norway to help with the re-establishment of the Norwegian air force.

Woodman played a full part in the final months of the war on 130, claiming five German aircraft and one shared. He shot down FW 190s on 28 March and 25 April. On 30 April he destroyed a Siebel 204, a small, twin-engined transport aircraft and trainer. The next day he claimed a Heinkel 111 and the day after a Buckner 131, a two-seat bi-plane trainer, sharing in the destruction of a second. The Heinkel 111, famous as the smooth, glazed-nosed bomber of the Battle of Britain and London's Blitz, by 1944 and 1945 was outdated and relegated to transport duties. Both he and fellow 130 pilot, Yorkshireman Geoff Lord, with whom he shared the Bu 131, were awarded a DFC. The New Zealander called his Spitfires 'Shirley' after his fiancée in New Zealand and painted her name on the nose. By the time he finished flying in Europe he was up to Shirley V.

In the last chaotic days of the war, as the advancing British and Russian armies squeezed the enemy into an ever-diminishing sector in northeast Germany, thousands of Luftwaffe aircraft, flying from fewer and fewer airfields, offered myriad targets in the air and on the ground. Occasionally fighter pilots came up against Germans with vast experience in Russia and paid the price. But the majority of enemy pilots were poorly trained, inexperienced in combat and proved easy meat. Ground fire was a much greater danger and even in the last days flak downed British planes, Typhoons again proving the most vulnerable as they flew low to attack airfields and other targets. Christopher Shores in 2nd Tactical Air Force notes, for example, that on 30 March flak shot down five Typhoons, two

Spitfires and a Tempest, four pilots losing their lives. Another four Typhoon and two Spitfire pilots died on 23 April.

Then it was finished and Brian Woodman wrote in his log on 9 May 1945, in large underlined letters: 'War in Europe Over'. On the next line, 'No Huns, No Flak, No Nothing.'

APPENDIX

The battle against the U-boats

The 1939–45 battle against German U-boats, played out on the world stage but concentrated mainly in the North and Middle Atlantic, the Arctic, Mediterranean and the Caribbean-US east coast, was brutal and unforgiving on men, their vessels and aircraft. The struggle lasted from day one until the end of hostilities.

Figures vary, but the U-boat fleet lost close to 800 submarines. Almost 28,000 German sailors lost their lives on U-boats, three in every four who served in the submarines. Paul Kemp in *U-Boats Destroyed* adds that 'no other military or naval force suffered casualties on such a scale as did the U-bootWaffe'. More than 32,000 names of submariners lost at sea in both world wars are etched on brass plates at the sombre U-boat crew memorial in Laboe, Kiel.

Britain's Coastal Command is said to have lost more than 700 aircraft and several thousand aircrew as it hunted submarines. Again, figures differ. Losses by American, Canadian and other Allied nations swell the tallies. Allied naval units, particularly those on the North Atlantic convoy routes between North American and Britain, sustained heavy casualties in men and ships. Britain's Merchant Navy lost 32,000 sailors (including 130 New Zealanders) on the freighters, tankers and other ships sunk in convoy or sailing alone. Thousands more were rescued by convoy escorts and brave merchant navy captains who dangerously slowed or stopped their ships to haul in comrades. Little known are the small, specially fitted rescue ships with medical teams, which trailed convoys to rescue torpedoed survivors. Such ships picked up 4200 survivors: 2300 from the Commonwealth, 1000 Americans, the rest other nationalities, among them four U-boat survivors.

Newspapers of the time and countless films and books post-war painted the Battle of the Atlantic as a pivotal event in World War II, a contest which almost severed Britain's lifeline to North America, denying Britain and her fighting forces food, petrol and oil and other vital supplies. American Clay Blair in his gripping two-volume history *Hitler's U-Boat War* argues that this is pure fiction on the part of newspaper editors, authors and film-makers sucked in by wartime propaganda and hysteria. He says that contrary to the accepted mythology, 'U-boats never even came close at any time to cutting the vital North Atlantic lifeline to the British Isles.' He presents compelling evidence. Quoting official British and American sources he says that from September 1942 to May 1945, the period covered in his second volume, the Allies sailed 953 convoys east and west on the North and Middle Atlantic runs. 'These convoys were composed of 43,526 merchant ships. Of these, 272 were sunk by U-boats.' He adds that 99.4 percent of all Allied merchant ships sailing in convoy in this period reached their destinations intact.

Blair also highlights the fallacies surrounding the fabled Arctic convoys. The courage of the crews manning the freighters and their escorts in the appalling conditions they faced is unquestioned, and rightly lauded. But losses of ships were far lower than in the public's imagination. Blair records that from 1941 to 1945 the Allies sailed forty convoys totalling 811 merchant ships to Northern Russia. Thirty-three aborted. Of the rest, 720 vessels arrived safely. Fifty-eight were sunk – eight percent. The Arctic U-boat force accounted for only twenty of the fifty-eight. The return convoys tallied 715 merchant ships. Just twenty-nine were lost – four percent. U-boats sank twenty-one of them. In destroying forty-one merchantmen the U-boat force lost forty-three submarines.

Blair also rubbishes the popular idea that the Murmansk convoys saved the Soviet Union from 'certain defeat'. His figures show the Arctic route delivered 22.7 percent of the 'vast tonnage' of vehicles and weapons delivered to the Russians. Most of it went via the Persian Gulf or across the Sea of Japan to Vladivostok.

Even in 1942, when the U-boats wreaked appalling havoc in Caribbean waters and on the United States east coast – and to a lesser extent the North Atlantic – Britain's lifeline was never in danger. By the spring of 1943 the U-boat fleet was under pressure, in irreversible decline as losses mounted spectacularly. Merchant seamen, navy sailors and Allied aircrew continued to die but the war against the submarines was won.

Once the United States entered the war in December 1941, and its giant economy attained full stride, its prodigious output of ships, aircraft and other war material, allied with Britain's, dwarfed Germany's. American shipyards rolled thousands of navy and merchant vessels down their slipways, the new shipping far outranking losses to the U-boats. And Germany never matched the Allies' developing superiority in weapons and technology.

When the war began, Coastal Command was the RAF's Cinderella, its handful of squadrons equipped with unsuitable or outdated aircraft, apart from the four-engined Sunderland – no radar or rudimentary navigation aids. It took time but by war's end the command had a powerful anti-sub and anti-ship strike force, relentlessly hunting down and sinking U-boats and German shipping. No Allied aircraft in World War II was designed specifically as a sub-hunter although the US-built Liberator came closest. Technology came to the aid of the Allies in the latter part of the conflict, when Liberators, Halifaxes, Fortresses, Sunderlands and Wellingtons flew with radar so advanced and powerful, much of it due to British scientific and technical genius, it could pick up the head of a snorkel, inches above the ocean surface. Allied technical advances, far ahead of Germany's, simply overwhelmed the enemy.

Only nine U-boats were sunk in 1939 and not many more in the following two years and German U-boat chiefs scoffed at the ability of aircraft to sink submarines. Aircraft, unaided by naval units, sank only a handful of U-boats in the opening years of the war but by late 1942 and into 1943 Allied aircraft – and there were many more of them – gradually gained the upper hand. They closed the mid-Atlantic gap where U-boats had been safe from aerial attack. Long-range Liberators, aided by radar and much improved weapons systems, put great pressure on U-boats hunting convoys and began to destroy them in rising numbers. An enormous increase in convoy escorts and independently operating hunter-killer groups, equipped with an array of U-boat detection equipment, gave the Allies supremacy. U-boat kills in 1943 rose from 1942's eighty-six to 243, outpacing German production. In May 1943 forty-three U-boats were destroyed. Though the U-boats continued to sink ships and shoot down aircraft, their effectiveness declined. The submarine force lost another 249 boats in 1944 and 120 in the last five months of the war to all causes. As the war progressed aircraft sank more and more U-boats unaided. By May 1945 planes alone had destroyed almost 250 submarines. They combined with ships to sink another thirty-seven.

Author's note: In the following section readers will find accounts of New Zealanders' attacks and successes against U-boats before D-Day. Though they do not fall into this book's time frame they are here because they illuminate the anti-submarine war on a personal level. Their stories, Mick Ensor's apart, have never been told before. Ensor was a major player in the war against the Nazi submarines but other New Zealanders served with great distinction in the struggle. Seventy years on the men involved are largely unknown or forgotten. Their bravery deserves to be remembered.

Remarkably, six men on a 612 Squadron Whitley that ditched on an anti-submarine patrol far out into the Atlantic west of Scotland in late August 1941 owed their lives to the enemy. Two of the crew were New Zealanders, navigator Pat Millar (30), Masterton, and the rear gunner, Aucklander John Grocott (41).

The Whitley ditched 300 miles from land after one of its two engines seized and it could not maintain height. The plane transmitted a position report before landing safely but the crew's survival prospects looked bleak. As the light faded the men saw a small ship and fired a flare. The small ship turned out, to their astonishment, to be a German submarine. In a few minutes *U-206* cruised alongside and rescued them all. They were questioned by the skipper Herbert Opitz and taken below, POWs.

'We had little rest because of the cramped conditions but considering the fact that we must have been a considerable nuisance to them our treatment was very good,' Millar is quoted as saying in Volume I of the official history *New Zealanders with the Royal Air Force*. He said the U-boat sighted nothing during the rest of its patrol but before reaching its St Nazaire base on the French coast on 10 September crash-dived several times to avoid aircraft attack. *U-206*, again under Opitz's command, was lost with all hands on 30 November 1941 in the Bay of Biscay.

Grocott was unusually old for aircrew. Auckland aviation researcher Arthur Arculus has discovered he made his own way to England in 1939 and enlisted, understating his age by seven years.

On 10 November 1942 *U-505* was cruising on the surface east of Trinidad when an RAF Hudson, unseen by the Germans, roared out of the clouds, dropping depth charges. One scored a direct hit, exploding on contact and wreaking immense damage. The blast also caught the low-flying plane, piloted by Australian Ron Sillcock, flinging it into the sea nearby. All five on the plane perished, including New Zealand navigator Patrick Nelson, only 21 but already on his forty-second op. He was the first New Zealander to die attacking submarines from the air in World War II.

Nelson was working in a Wanganui bank when he enlisted in March 1941. He sailed for Canada two months later to learn a navigator's trade, reached England in December and after further training joined 53 Squadron in late April 1942. Three months later Nelson went with the squadron to Trinidad and Tobago for anti-submarine work, the crews flying their aircraft to their new base via Iceland, Greenland, Newfoundland and the United States. The US needed help to combat the the U-boats wreaking havoc along their eastern seaboard and in the Caribbean. The squadron later returned to England in December 1942.

A sailor on *U-505* has been quoted as saying the damage 'looked as if a bulldozer had run over the deck – twisted steel, crumpled sheet metal, broken and twisted pipelines ... the 37 mm [gun] blown overboard'. Despite ruptured fuel tanks leaving a trail of oil, the embattled *U-505* somehow evaded further detection, worked on repairs, and later off-loaded two seriously injured crew to a U-boat tanker for medical treatment. Young skipper Peter Zschech nursed his craft back to Lorient on the French Atlantic coast on 12 December. At the time no one knew what happened to Hudson V9253-L, the mystery of its loss unsolved until German U-boat records were opened postwar. Nelson and the other British crewmen are remembered on the Ottawa Memorial to the 800 airmen lost in the Western Hemisphere with no known graves. The fifth man on the Hudson was an American serviceman along for the ride.

Repairs to *U-505* took a full six months and even then problems plagued her subsequent patrols. On one outing from Lorient in July 1943 she was lucky to escape destruction, three British destroyers chasing and depth-charging her before she managed to escape. Zschech continued to command but sank into depression when *U-505* became a laughing stock, continually aborting patrols. He committed suicide on 24 October 1943, shooting himself in the head while in the control room as the U-boat was heavily depth-charged between Portugal and the Azores. The boat's number two took *U-505* home. Zschech was the only German submarine commander to kill himself this way during the war.

U-505's final patrol starting 16 March 1944 lasted eighty-one days and ended in a final insult in the Atlantic – capture. Under Harald Lange, the submarine had a singularly unproductive time patrolling off West Africa. Aided by Enigma and intercepted radio signals, an American escort carrier (called Jeeps or baby flat tops by the Americans, they carried a limited number of aircraft used for patrols and attacks) and hunter-killer ships were waiting for *U-505* on her way home. They found her on the morning of 4 June, off Dakar. Depth-charged and damaged, the sub shot to the surface. The crew poured on deck, jumping into the sea or trying to surrender. The American ships stopped firing and hastened boarding parties across. In their rush to quit the boat the Germans had not tried to scuttle her or destroy papers and the Americans found a rich haul. The submarine was towed to Bermuda and used for secret trials and training until war's end. Today she is on display in Chicago.

He was born 5 January 1922, the son of Canterbury sheep-farming parents and christened Maechel Anthony Ensor, later known in Coastal Command as Mick. He enlisted when he was 18½ on 28 July 1940, earned his wings here and sailed in late February 1941. His ship, the *Awatea*, carried fifty-eight fully trained pilots bound for England. Thirty-four would die in the service of their country and of the surviving twenty-four, ten would become POWs. The *Awatea* docked in Vancouver.

The pilots were eventually dropped off their cross-Canada train at Debert airbase near New Glasgow, Nova Scotia, 100 miles from Halifax, to join a convoy for the Atlantic crossing. When it sailed, Ensor, his *Awatea* cabin mate Frank Reece, and Reg Baker, both from Dunedin, remained behind because they tested positive in a scarlet fever scare, then sailed a week behind the main body. Baker, who was to lose his life as a wing commander in the final stages of the war, was even later getting away.

Vincent Orange, who in 1994 wrote Ensor's biography *Ensor's Endeavour*, says Ensor was lucky to test positive. The group that went ahead was posted to Bomber Command and many, including Ensor's cousin and close friend Roddy McCracken, were dead by Christmas 1941. Ensor and Reece were assigned to Coastal Command and Orange wrote that in Ensor's case the decision 'probably saved his life and gave him the opportunity to excel'.

Ensor and Reece were posted in late July 1941 to 500 (County of Kent) Squadron at Bircham Newton, a grass-strip field near The Wash coast of Norfolk and just forty air miles from the Norfolk village where Ensor's grandfather lived, before sailing to New Zealand the previous century. He flew his first op on 15 August and did another eight on Blenheims before the squadron converted to Hudsons three months later. Ensor's first op was checking marker buoys, some of them fitted as havens for ditched aircrew survivors and sailors on the east coast convoy route. He told his parents in a letter:

> Three of us went out, one turned back through bad weather, the other (my room mate by the way) was shot down and, like asses, we finished our job while flying through shocking rain at fifty feet over

the sea a few miles off the Dutch coast. It took us four and a half hours but we got back quite OK.

500 Squadron had four tasks – searching the sea for downed aircrew, standing by at nights for ops against German E-boats (fast torpedo boats) attacking convoys, strikes against enemy shipping, and attacks on German airfields in Holland. These jobs weren't much different from those given to Bomber Command's Blenheims – and just as dangerous. Both commands' Blenheim squadrons were inadequate against German day and night fighters, suffering appalling losses. Ensor would say the Blenheim 'was not a machine to go to war in; not in winter, not across water and least of all not against Germans.'

Ensor's first op shows his determination to succeed and complete the job, whatever the odds, his natural flying talent, knowledge of his aircraft – and luck. His determination was displayed again the night of 17–18 September when a squadron detachment was based for three weeks at Harrowfield, a new base at Yelverton, just outside Plymouth, whose runway cores were made of rubble from the heavily bombed city. Six crews were to fly from Harrowfield to St Eval on the Cornish coast for a night strike on St Nazaire. Only two took off, the other four reporting they were U/S (unserviceable). Ensor was one of the two. The other aircraft didn't find the target but the New Zealander did. Ensor in a letter home:

> It was only by good luck as it was a very black night and we just flew round where we thought it was until they started shooting at us. We knew we must be pretty close by then and by a bit of luck the moon started to come up and we could see the docks way below us. My

navigator dropped his bombs very well and I think we must have done quite a lot of damage although it us not for us to say.

In another letter to his parents on 3 October Ensor said: 'It gives me great pleasure to drop a few bombs on some of Mr Hitler's toys now and again, but each of us feel that the little we do is insignificant when compared with the tremendous efforts of Bomber Command.' If only he'd known. Bomber Command's raids at this time of the war were just as insignificant as Coastal Command's, highly inaccurate and nuisance value only. It would be another 18 months before Bomber Command began to really savage Germany with concentrated attacks.

Orange says another pilot wrote of Ensor's St Nazaire performance in his diary: 'A bloody good show.' The same man said several night raids were attempted on Biscay ports. 'We did our best at a task for which we'd had no training and at which we were totally inexperienced. [That] made our losses ever sadder.' One such loss was Reece, on the night of 29–30 September after he failed to return from the Bay of Biscay. The squadron had no word of him for months and assumed the worst. Reece had crash-landed his damaged Blenheim on the north coast of Brittany, and was on the run with his crew in France for six weeks until picked up by the Germans in Nantes. By year's end 1941 at least four New Zealanders had been lost from 500 since the squadron moved to Bircham Newton in the April: Reece and three who were killed – a pilot and a navigator on ops and a pilot in a training crash.

By late 1941, Ensor had flown nine ops in Blenheims for a total of 33 hours 10 minutes, when the squadron converted to Hudsons, a major improvement. The new plane had a Boulton-Paul turret toward the rear of the aircraft atop the fuselage, so a second WOp/AG, Cyril Prior, joined the current team of Ensor, navigator Bertie Paige, a Canadian, and WOp/AG Horace Roe, a Suffolk farmer's son. Prior arrived with basic training in the use of the radar installed in the plane. While this primitive radar was no help in finding the enemy, it was a sign of things to come. In the next few years British scientists would make great progress in the development of radar.

The conversion to the new aircraft was matched by a new squadron CO, and flight commanders – New Zealander Ian Patterson and Englishman John Ensor, no relation to Mick. Patterson commanded Mick's flight, with both newcomers experienced on Hudsons.

Ensor's second op on a Hudson, on the freezing night of 29–30 January 1942, started out as a search for a dinghy but led to a decoration and an against-the-odds survival. In foul weather and piercing cold, Ensor was to go east over the North Sea to Heligoland, turn north, fly almost to Norway and then head for home. Orange said approaching Heligoland about 4 a.m., Ensor spotted three small ships and attacked at mast height. The crew reported a bomb hit on one of them. 'While taking violent evasive action to avoid fire from the vessels, there came a sudden grinding crash and the aircraft bounded up a good many feet.' Ensor said at the time the Hudson had struck a rock and so did the DFC citation. There was no rock. The Hudson had clipped the sea and somehow bounced back into the air. And Ensor kept it there.

Ensor's battle to bring the damaged aircraft home began. The starboard propeller blades were bent right back, one petrol tank holed, lights failed, air speed indicator gone. The wireless, radar and turret were out. Ensor shut down the protesting starboard engine but couldn't feather the propeller, which made it even more difficult to fly and maintain height. He nursed the craft up to 1000 feet and turned for England. When flak streamed up at them over a town they figured was in Holland, Ensor realised the compass was also wildly astray. He dropped the Hudson to almost ground level, hedge hopping to avoid the flak. Paige, in the nose, called out when to avoid obstructions. Orange says it took about half an hour to get back over water. As petrol burned off and the load lightened, Ensor was able to ease back on the labouring engine. 'It took two and a half hours to get back to England on one engine.'

Almost home, the Hudson struck a blinding snowstorm, which gave the crew horrors about icing. But the storm passed, and then snow-covered Norfolk. Ensor had to land the petrol-short Hudson. Helped by Very lights fired from the plane to illuminate the ground, he picked a likely spot, belly-landing on a field he soon learned was still pitted with anti-invasion poles and crossed by tension power lines – and just five miles from where his grandfather once lived. The gas tanks held just ten gallons. Ensor arrived home to acclaim for a notable feat and an immediate DFC, the citation noting 'great courage, skill and tenacity'. He had just turned 20.

500 Squadron moved to Stornoway in the Hebrides in late March 1942 and down to St Eval five months later. In November 500 flew to Gibraltar. By then Ensor had a bar to his DFC, the citation noting 'many sorties' since the first DFC and said 'by his keenness and personal example he has set a magnificent example to his squadron'. He'd done another forty ops while at Stornoway and St Eval, far out into the Atlantic, way to the north and deep into the Bay of Biscay. And attacked three submarines. None of the submarines, all found on the surface north of the Hebrides, were sunk or indeed reported damage. The explosives in depth charges then at the time were not

powerful enough to do more than rattle the teeth of submariners. But by late 1942 anti-submarine weapons carried the much more powerful British-developed Torpex – and submarine sinkings by aircraft began to rise sharply.

Ensor's 27 April U-boat attack, the first by a 500 squadron crew flying from Stornoway, was also the squadron's first sighting. Coastal Command called Ensor down to describe hunting U-boats to Sir Philip Joubert de la Ferte, then the command's chief. Ensor was being noticed and his triple attacks gave him valuable know-how.

Their Hudsons painted white for Mediterranean skies, the squadron flew to Gibraltar on 5 and 6 November to support the Allied North African landings and a week later shifted to Tafaraoui, near Oran in Algeria. On the 12th, flying home from a submarine sweep, Ensor spotted a liner aground and blazing at Bougie, east of Algiers – the *Awatea*. The Mediterranean seemed alive with U-boats and a day later Ensor attacked *U-458*. He dropped depth charges and attacked with machine-gun fire. She was down at the bows when last seen but escaped and struggled back to base. However, three days later on his sixty-sixth op, *U-259* was a clear-cut sinking to Ensor's credit but the premature explosion of one of his depth charges did for his Hudson and cost the lives of two of his crew.

New Zealander Ian Patterson first met Terry Bulloch, the most successful airborne U-boat destroyer of World War II – with four to his credit – in 1940, on a ship sailing down the Clyde bound for Canada a week before Christmas. They'd been assigned to what was then known as the Trans-Atlantic Ferry Pool, soon to become RAF Ferry Command, the group that would fly thousands of wartime aircraft to Britain from the United States and Canada. Belfast-born

Bulloch and Patterson volunteered from Coastal Command for pool duties at the end of taxing tours, Bulloch via 220 and 206 Squadrons at Bircham Newton in Norfolk, Patterson from 269 Squadron at Wick, Scotland. Bulloch heard pilots were wanted for hush-hush work and Patterson spotted a signal from the Air Ministry seeking aircrew to fly a B-17, the Boeing Fortress, from the United States to England.

The two men and others in the party eventually reached a US Army Air Corps base in California, where they learned to fly the Fortress. Tony Spooner, in his biography of Bulloch, says he was assigned Patterson as his co-pilot – 'a capable young New Zealander with a toothbrush moustache'.

Patterson, born in Auckland in August 1917, sailed on the *Tainui* for England in February 1939, a fully trained pilot for the RAF on a Short Service Commission (SSC). War was looming. Within two weeks of arriving in Britain, Patterson was on 269 Squadron at Abbotsinch, Glasgow, being introduced to Ansons. Two others from the draft of eighteen young New Zealanders on the *Tainui* accompanied Patterson to 269 – Angus Macdonald (24), an Auckland teacher, and Peter Trolove (24), who was working for Ernest Adams in Dunedin when he enlisted. Both would soon be dead – Macdonald before year's end, Trolove in mid-1940, both lost on air operations. Trolove was one of three brothers killed serving in the air force. Patterson was one of just six of the *Tainui* draft who survived the war.

Patterson moved with 269 from Abbotsinch to Montrose on the coast north of Dundee a few days before the war started, and then in October 1939 to Wick on Scotland's far northeastern coast, next stop the Shetlands. There 269 stayed for 18 months and in April 1940 the squadron exchanged its old, reliable Ansons – Faithful Annies, as they came to be known – for Hudsons. The squadron flew general reconnaissance patrols as far as Norway, convoy protection, anti-submarine, patrols, shipping strikes and air sea rescue searches. Three times he was among squadron aircraft that attacked the powerful battle cruiser *Scharnhorst*. They never had a chance against the curtain of fire erupting from the big ship and her escorts. Their puny bomb loads were hopelessly inadequate. Patterson watched friends being shot down, fortunate not to be one of the dead.

By the time Patterson joined the ferry pool he was an experienced flying officer and had finished a long tour. In mid-March 1941 Bulloch and Patterson picked up their Fortress, built at Boeing's Seattle factory, and flew it in stages to Dorval, Montreal. From there to Gander, Newfoundland. As night fell on 13 April Fortress AN534 took off from Gander for Britain, the first of thousands of the four-engined bombers to cross the Atlantic in wartime. Flying at 30,000 feet, the Fortress covered the 2100 miles in a record time of eight hours forty minutes – an average speed of 245 mph. The big plane touched down on an airfield just south of Prestwick, Scotland. Prestwick, thirty-odd miles from Glasgow and soon to be the arrival point for the Atlantic shuttle, was being enlarged and its runways were unusable when the Fortress arrived. In the early stages of the ferry service pilots went by ship to North America but this slow process was soon changed, crews being flown to North America to pick up their aircraft.

Patterson barely had time to catch his breath before he was back at sea, headed again for Canada, this time to pick up a Hudson. On 6 May his ship steamed out of the Bristol Channel in convoy and turned north. He reached Montreal on 23 May but bureaucratic delays meant he didn't make the Atlantic flight, captaining his new Hudson, until late July. The trip across was routine – until the plane reached Scotland. The inexperienced navigator had the aircraft's landfall out by 200 miles in murky weather over a dangerous coastline (one of the Hudsons in the same delivery batch slammed into a hill, killing all aboard). In the end Patterson landed at Prestwick 14 hours 17 minutes after leaving Gander. He had 14 gallons of fuel left.

Trans-Atlantic flights over, Patterson, now a squadron leader, was posted to 500 Squadron. He must have felt at home among fellow New Zealanders – pilots Mick Ensor, Harold Poole, Frank Reece and Huntley Holmes, plus navigators John Kay and Ivan Mitchell.

Mick Ensor spotted the submarine while the Hudson was patrolling at 7000 feet off Algiers, capital of French Algeria, on 15 November, a typical Med day – hot, blue sky, clear, calm sea. 'I'm fairly confident that we won't be spotted by the boat, thanks to our high altitude and white under-surface: sea-birds use height and camouflage and they're better hunters than we are,'' Orange's biography quotes Ensor as writing later.

The sub was fifteen miles away, fully surfaced, leaving a huge white wake. Ensor, three or four minutes away from his prey in a dive at full speed, said he had the hunter's calm certainty he couldn't miss. He didn't. The U-boat didn't see the aircraft approach and made no attempt to dive. The four depth charges, packed with 250 pounds of Torpex explosives, dropped in a row fifty feet apart, timed to explode at a depth of twenty-five feet. If they landed accurately – and close enough – they would blast open the submarine's pressure hull and destroy the boat. The plane would have flown on past before the depth charges exploded. After his earlier submarine attacks, Ensor had a good idea how to land his depth charges in the right place (the plane didn't have a bombsight). His aim was excellent but the second depth charge landed squarely on the submarine and exploded instantly right beneath him. It spelled the end of *U-259* and wrecked the Hudson.

> I press the button and a second or so later ... there's a great whoomph and a feeling of being compressed. To me even now, it seems I was in a slow-motion horror movie. For a moment, I've no outside vision – but my instinct is to pull the nose up.

Ensor noted the damage: elevators and rudders blown off, six feet of each wing bent up, windows shattered. The loss of the elevators and rudders from the tail unit made control almost impossible but Ensor showed superb airmanship, using the engine power and the little movement left in the ailerons – plus his crew.

> Fortunately, I can talk to Horace Roe (in the rear turret) on the intercom. I ask: 'What can you see, Horace?' 'Sub's blown up,' he replies. 'Bits everywhere and I saw a gun in the air.' That at least is marvellous news, I think, and makes our effort worthwhile whatever happens now. Then I ask: 'What's wrong with the tailplane?' and he tells me: 'The elevators and one rudder have gone, other rudder is just hanging on and there's a bloody great hole under my feet!' I tell him to come forward to help me balance the aeroplane, watch my hand signals and organise the other two accordingly.

All three came to the front of the plane and Ensor used them as moving ballast, a human elevator substitute. He managed to get the stricken plane to 3000 feet and head for land but knew they would have to jump because there was no way he could land. The crew moved to various parts of the plane to get their chutes but as they did so Ensor lost his human elevators and the plane sank. With the men back in the cabin Ensor clawed it back to 1500 feet when the port engine quit. Ensor closed the starboard throttle to stop the Hudson going into a dive. It stayed more or less level but was going down rapidly. The crew jumped, Ensor last out:

> Not without difficulty because our combined weight is now all at the rear of the cabin and the Hudson is very nose-up and banking to the left, making the escape-door face up, towards the sky. I can't recall order of departure, though I do remember helping Neville [Atkinson, the navigator who'd replaced Paige the previous February when the Canadian went home]. I have difficulty levering myself over the edge, then fumble for the ripcord and pull it at once. It works, giving me a moment of pure joy, and hanging there I look down in time to see the poor old Hudson in a steep diving turn, just before it plunges into the sea with a mighty splash. In a matter of seconds, I'm in the water myself.

Ensor was rescued a short time later by the sloop HMS *Erne*, which he'd seen from the Hudson, while Roe was picked up by another sloop, which also retrieved the bodies of the Hudson's other crewmen. Atkinson's head hit the fuselage as he baled out and Prior's parachute failed to open.

Orange notes that author Alfred Price in his *Aircraft vs. Submarine* said Ensor gave a 'display of airmanship and cool-headedness that can have few equals in the entire history of flying', and HL Thompson in Volume I of his official history *New Zealanders with the Royal Air Force* described *U-259*'s sinking as 'probably the most spectacular attack of the whole war'. Orange adds that in a letter to another author, Ensor's CO Denis Spotswood said he suspected the depth charges were imperfectly fused and a 'dry hit' caused one to explode on impact. 'His was a remarkable piece of airmanship thereafter.'

Ensor was recalled to England for a debriefing after sinking *U-259* and he and Roe flew a beaten up Hudson home to Portreath. He arrived to acclaim, promotion to squadron leader and news he was getting an immediate DSO and would serve six months as a staff officer at Coastal Command headquarters. The DSO, gazetted 11 February 1943 said Ensor, supported by Roe, 'displayed courage and devotion to duty of a high order'. Roe, awarded the DFM, had jettisoned everything movable to lighten the aircraft and played a leading role in helping to keep the plane on an even keel. Ensor was the first man in Coastal Command to hold the DSO, DFC and bar – and had just turned 21.

Coastal Command chief Joubert personally requested Ensor for the staff at headquarters during his 'rest' period from operations, and Sir John Slessor kept the New Zealander on when he took over in February 1943. In his seven months at Eastbury, just north of London, he became deeply involved in the critical work aimed at improving the command's ability to find and destroy U-boats. But Ensor thirsted to get back on ops, to fly Liberators, his wish finally granted with his posting to a Coastal OTU at Beaulieu in Hampshire where he converted to the big plane. Then on to 224 Squadron at St Eval, joining as flight commander on 26 August 1943. His CO was fellow New Zealander Arthur Clouston, the air-race ace of pre-war days. Orange quotes Ensor as saying, 'I don't think Arthur particularly welcomed me because I had no experience on Liberators.' But Orange adds it didn't take long for such a superb pilot as Clouston to recognise in Ensor a man who knew what he was about in the air, and to be impressed by his work as flight commander.

Ensor began ops on 224 on 3 Sept 1943 with an 11 hours 15 minutes Bay of Biscay anti-sub patrol, the sixty-eighth of his career, a total that would reach 114 by the time Germany surrendered. He was promoted to command the squadron on 1 January 1945, succeeding Terry McComb who had followed Clouston. He was awarded a second DSO late in February 1945 for his second tour work as a flight commander. Ensor's crew first crew at St Eval, a new one in from the Bahamas OTU, never clicked with Ensor as far as he was concerned and several U-boat radar sightings were lost. Ensor, unhappy with their performance, eventually replaced them all. He picked a new crew, which included fellow New Zealanders second pilot Bill Andrews and ex-75 Squadron WOp/AG Butch Pugh. The discarded crew, three New Zealanders among them, was lost late in the war, shot down off Norway.

Ensor was widely credited with sinking *U-579*, his second victory, on 5 May 1945 in the Kattegat between Denmark and Sweden as a host of submarines fled the Baltic for Norway. Twenty-one U-boats, including *U-579*, went down between the 2nd and the 6th. Later research suggests the submarine was not Ensor's victim. Kemp in *U-Boats Destroyed* says the boat was originally assessed as being attacked by Liberator T of 224 Squadron (Ensor's) 'but this attack was made on *U-1008*, which was damaged'. He adds *U-1008* was attacked again next day by an 86 Squadron Liberator and so seriously damaged she was scuttled. Before his death in November 2012 Orange told this author he was confident Ensor had sunk a submarine. However, nothing in Kemp's book fits Ensor for 5 May, his last patrol of the war.

Two days after Ensor won his DSO, Ian Patterson made it two. He sighted *U-331* on the surface off Cape Caxine, just west of the Bay of Algiers, at 9.30 a.m. on 17 November, the beginning of an astonishing day. He attacked with depth charges, causing serious damage. Two other 500 Squadron Hudsons joined in, trying to polish off the U-boat. This was no ordinary German submarine and its skipper no ordinary commander. *U-331*, a type VIIC sub, had been in the Mediterranean a year, operating from Italian bases under the command of Hans-Diedrich Freiherr von Tiesenhausen and was on her ninth patrol when Patterson found her. Eight days earlier Tiesenhausen had sunk the 11,000-ton Torch troopship USS *Leedstown*, anchored off Algiers after landing British troops.

Tiesenhausen and *U-331* had only one other ship to their credit but it was some ship – the battleship HMS *Barham*. Late afternoon on 25 November 1941 Tiesenhausen torpedoed the 1914-built warship at close range off the northwest Egyptian coast. *Barham* rolled over to port in just three or four minutes after the three-torpedo strike – a magazine exploded, tearing the hull apart. When the flames and smoke cleared she was gone. More than 860 seamen died. Tiesenhausen didn't learn of his success for some time. Desperately fleeing *Barham*'s escorting destroyers, he didn't see the battleship go down.

On 11 November Patterson's B-flight was dispatched from Gibraltar to Tafaraoui, a primitive dusty strip outside Oran, Algeria, where a big build-up of Allied air units was taking place. Six days later he took off at 9.30 a.m. flying east up the coast out to sea. Half an hour later he saw *U-331*'s wake, the craft moving west. Patterson felt he had probably been seen despite continuing on, course unaltered, to give the impression he hadn't spotted the submarine. He was right. He had been detected and the U-boat submerged. But Patterson planned carefully and waited. His navigator plotted the sub's position, 15 miles due north of Algiers. In a late-life memoir he wrote:

> We climbed to 10,000 feet. At the end of an hour we turned 180 degrees and throttled back just to hold that altitude. It took an hour to manoeuvre to a station that would be directly up sun of a new position 10 miles further west of where the submarine had submerged ... Right on time, there was the U-boat.

She was up again. Patterson's careful stalking and positioning of his Hudson paid off. He attacked out of the sun, unseen until too late. Patterson made his final run of 1500 yards, attacking at just thirty feet above the sea, hoping the four men on *U-331*'s deck scouring the four quadrants of sky with powerful binoculars were searching for higher danger. They were, and didn't see him until too late. The Hudson closed the last 500 feet in five seconds, no gunfire to greet him, and four depth charges tumbled down.

The rear camera recorded the U-boat under a mountain of water as the first two depth charges detonated. Patterson pulled the Hudson into a wrenching turn to port. 'It was so severe and with such a large amount of G force at about 250 knots that the wings were bent permanently about five degrees to normal ... wrinkles appeared on the top surface of the wings beyond the engine mounts.'

The explosions caused severe damage to the submarine but didn't rupture the inch-thick pressure hull. The Hudson roared up and around, bearing down on the U-boat again, guns chattering to keep the crew away from the deck guns. Soon other 500 Squadron Hudsons which happened to be nearby appeared in answer to radio messages and chimed in, dropping more depth charges, causing more havoc. Then they left, leaving Patterson alone. Tiesenhausen had ordered his gunners to the deck and they poured damaging fire at the Hudson. Patterson kept up the attacks, picking off the gunners. Steering wrecked, engines down, and unable to dive because the forward hatch was blasted open, some of her crew dead and others blown overboard, Tiesenhausen hoisted a white flag.

The chase and action had eaten up so much of Patterson's fuel he made a beeline for Algiers to refuel and rearm. A wireless message sent the escort-destroyer HMS *Wilton* pell-mell for the scene, 12 miles from shore, in an attempt to capture the U-boat intact. Patterson landed, refuelled and rearmed and was soon back in the air despite warnings from ground staff that the under-skin of the wings was badly stretched and the plane would be scrapped after its next landing.

Undaunted, Patterson flew back to his 'prize'. Tiesenhausen had plenty of time to destroy the U-boat's papers and secret equipment, but the crew couldn't leave the boat because her dinghies had been destroyed. American U-boat historian Clay Blair says the white flag was probably raised to deter the killing of survivors. 'Doubtless the loyal, defiant and resourceful Tiesenhausen would have scuttled on arrival of a surface ship.' Patterson didn't believe that. He claimed the German skipper would not have scuttled, because he had so many wounded below decks who couldn't leave the boat.

The matter was decided by the arrival of three Fairey Albacores – biplane torpedo bombers – from the carrier HMS *Formidable*, accompanied by Martlet fighters. *Attacker – the Hudson and Its Flyers*, by Geoffrey Jones, says Patterson had everything under control but was afraid the newcomers would wade in. So it proved. Patterson tried to keep his aircraft between them and the crippled U-boat but couldn't stop a Martlet, the Royal Navy name for the American-built Grumman Wildcat, spraying machine-gun fire over the decks and conning tower of *U-331*, killing and wounding crew members. Tiesenhausen was among the wounded. A livid Patterson, helpless, then watched an Albacore zero in, unleashing a torpedo that slammed into the U-boat, killing many men below and blasting others into the sea. *U-331* went down, just seventeen crew surviving to be picked up, Tiesenhausen among them. The New Zealander was so angry he loosed a stream of machine-gun fire at the Martlet. Luckily he missed but the startled fighter pilot fled.

In the day's final drama Patterson's plane staggered back toward Algiers, trailing petrol from the starboard wing close to the engine. Everyone donned parachutes. A red glow appeared behind the engine bay followed by dense black smoke as the Hudson crossed the coastal hills. Patterson cut the engine, feathered the prop and pushed the fire extinguisher button. Now close to the rain-sodden landing strip, Patterson shut down the port engine, feathered its prop and thumbed the electrical switches and petrol cocks to off. Confident they wouldn't undershoot the strip, he put the aircraft down in a wheels-up landing.

> The tail wheel hit, breaking away with the lower part of the tail section fuselage. Then all hell seemed to explode around us with tremendous sounds of crushing and breaking metal ... the starboard wing detached itself.

The remains of the Hudson slithered to a stop and the crew, unhurt, bolted clear seconds before the wreck exploded in flames. Jones says that Patterson, in London on leave two weeks later, was invited by Admiralty Intelligence officers to meet Tiesenhausen, who had been brought to England. He quotes the New Zealander: 'The German was extremely cold and hostile. He told me straight out that he blamed me for the cold-blooded and brutal destruction of his ship and crew.' Jones adds nothing could convince *U-331*'s skipper otherwise and Patterson hastily terminated the meeting.

The unfortunate sinking of *U-331* had repercussions. Jones adds that on the evidence of the *Wilton*'s captain, the pilots of the Albacore and Martlet were both court-martialled but doesn't give a verdict. Jones says the Albacore man was charged with torpedoing the U-boat while it was flying the white flag. The Mediterranean naval commander Admiral Sir Andrew Cunningham credited the Hudsons with sinking of *U-331*, noting the Albacore had simply finished off a cripple. 500 Squadron received special commendation for its three U-boat sinkings (John Ensor also sank one west of Gibraltar on 13 November).

Tiesenhausen, awarded a Knight's Cross for sinking *Barham*, was held captive in England and then in Canada for several years. Patterson's sinking of *U-331* was rewarded with membership in the Distinguished Service Order.

Harold Poole began his war on 14 March 1940 when he climbed into a Tiger Moth at No. 1 Elementary Flight Training School, Taieri, Dunedin. At war's end he was still at it, by now on a four-engined Liberator, the best anti-submarine aircraft in World War II. On Victory in Europe Day, 8 May 1945, while the rest of Britain whooped it up, Poole and his crew took off again from Ballykelly, Northern Ireland, and flew away on a 6 hours 40 minutes sweep looking for surrendering U-boats off the coast. Maybe feeling left out of the celebrations he wrote in his logbook in his forever-neat handwriting 'V.E. Day'. Poole made three more similar flights, the final one of 11 hours 35 minutes, the last six hours in the night blackness of 26 May. As he switched off the engines on KG980 and took off his gear at Ballykelly in the early morning, his war was over. His log shows 1680 hours 20 minutes, a total few pilots achieved. He flew 122 ops on his first tour with 500 Squadron, one in between in the Bahamas and another twenty-nine with 120 on his second. By the time he reached home in October 1945 he'd been away five years, one month and eight days.

Poole didn't sink a submarine in his long stints on 500 and then 201 Squadron, although he came close several times, making a total of six attacks. Who knows what damage he inflicted, how many of those U-boats had to return to port for repairs and how many he caused to submerge and stay down, their claws temorarily drawn. Poole was probably eligible for repatriation by late 1943 – one of the criteria being three years away from New Zealand. But the war was still far from over and men with his experience were not let go readily. He was of those who were the glue of the RAF, a steady above-average pilot any squadron was glad to have, and the air force needed. He came home a flight lieutenant with a DFC and a citation which said a deal more than most end-of-tour decorations, calling him 'a hard-working, conscientious and courageous pilot'.

Born 6 March 1920 in Invercargill, he was working in an office when he enlisted. The air force was always his first choice. He'd joined the Civil Reserve of Pilots in 1939, soloing at the Southland

Aero Club after 8 hours 30 minutes of dual instruction, literally giving him a flying start at Taieri, where he began all over again. The experience showed and he soloed in four days. Then in May on to Wigram, the finishing school. He graduated with his wings in August, flying two-engined Oxfords – not destined to be a fighter pilot.

Poole sailed for Liverpool on 14 September 1940 with twenty-one other pilots. Ten of the draft would not survive. One of the dead was Ted Hall-Jones, a friend of Poole's, a grandson of Sir William Hall-Jones, in 1906 interim Prime Minister for a few weeks. The young Hall-Jones lost his life in a mid-1941 air accident on 500 Squadron. In England there was more training for Sergeant Poole, first at Squires Gate, Blackpool, where flying was restricted by awful winter weather, then at Coastal Command's No. 3 OTU at Chivenor on Devon's North Coast. Poole arrived there in early March 1941, converting to Ansons – some of his flights under the direction of Hall-Jones, already commissioned.

Hall-Jones was posted to 500 on Blenheims at Detling, Kent, in late April 1941 and Poole followed him a month later. He did his first op as second pilot to Hall-Jones on 15 May, a short air-sea patrol, and then on the 24th captained his aircraft for the first time on ops, a four-hour convoy patrol. At the end of May the squadron moved to Bircham Newton near the sea in west Norfolk on The Wash.

He twice flew convoy patrols with Hall-Jones in early June, the second on the 7th. Four days later his friend was dead. Hall-Jones, by then a flying officer, flew into the ground in misty weather at Holme-next-the Sea, just a few miles from their base. He died instantly, his two crewmen with him, and was buried in St Mary's Church graveyard at Great Bircham. He had done just seven ops.

On 15 July, Poole had his first serious op, a daylight strike on a German convoy off the Dutch coast – and saw enemy fighters though there was no scrap. Most of this type of sortie required cloud cover. Without it the inferior Blenheims were at the mercy of enemy fighters. Where possible they scrambled for the clouds, not staying to mix it with Jerry fighters. No cloud, no ops. Hunting E-boats (torpedo boats) and searches for downed crew added variety. On one air sea rescue patrol Poole showed a touch of humour in his log, writing, 'Buoy oh buoy!'.

In mid-September Poole was part of the detachment that went for three weeks to a new barely finished airfield at Harrowfield near Portsmouth. During their stay, Poole took part in several raids, flying to St Eval in Cornwall and then out to sea. During a five-hour flight to attack Nantes at night, Poole's 'engines cut in the Bay of Biscay. Returned in bad visibility.' Scary stuff but there are no details in his log. The second was an anti-shipping patrol by day in the same bay: 'Nothing sighted.' This was an extraordinarily risky venture for frail Blenheims; bigger aircraft were often jumped by fighters in the Bay of Biscay. Poole also bombed the docks at St Nazaire, a long six-hour night flight, and had a go at Brest.

During November 1941 the squadron began converting to Hudsons, a slow process, with icy-snowy winter weather preventing flying on many days.

In late March the squadron shifted to Stornoway on the eastern side of the gale-swept Isle of Lewis in the Western Isles of Scotland, with nothing but sea between Lewis and the United States. After courses at Leuchars and RAF Cranwell, Poole was now his own boss, captaining his Hudson. He did nine ops, anti-submarine flights, before the squadron was on the move again, to St Eval on 30 August in preparation for a move to the Mediterranean.

Throughout September 500 flew anti-sub ops in the Bay of Biscay and on the 17th Poole had his first tussle with a U-boat. 'Sighted and attacked U-boat,' he wrote. 'U-Boat submerged 30 secs before DCs dropped. Bombed 300 ft ahead of swirl. Nothing definite observed.' No U-boats were sunk that day.

And then the Mediterranean. Poole was in the first day's flight from Portreath, Cornwall, to Gibraltar on 5 November. The second half of the squadron flew the next day. The fireworks were about to start. November 1942 would be a standout month for 500 Squadron with three submarines in five days to its credit, and DSOs for Mick Ensor and Patterson. Poole flew the long haul to the 'Rock' in 8 hours 15 minutes. He was probably dead beat but the next day he did 6 hours 30 minutes' flying ahead of an American convoy that had crossed the Strait of Gibraltar – and attacked two U-boats in the space of two hours. His became the first squadron contacts with enemy subs in the Mediterranean. Someone was on the ball – a week later the *Southland Times* had the story, quoting Poole:

> I was sweeping ahead and spotted a U-boat two miles away. I dropped four depth charges which blew the stern to the surface. I spotted the second and let it have two [anti-submarine] bombs. Unfortunately I could not observe the result.

He pasted the newspaper clipping, sent from home, in his log. There was little rest that month. With the start of the North African landings by British and American troops on 8 November under the flag of Operation Torch, aerial cover and the hunt for U-boats was vital and intensive. Poole did six-hour-plus sweeps again on 7 and 8 November, the first out into the Atlantic. November was frantic for 500 and Poole flew fourteen ops, the majority lasting more than six hours.

For the the next four months he flew all over the Western Mediterranean, ranging east to Sardinia and out to the Atlantic from Blida, where the squadron had moved. He and his fellow Hudson pilots swept the rolling sea looking for Italian submarines and U-boats from Italian ports, and those stealthily squeezing past Gibraltar from the Atlantic. One day he spotted a Ju 88 that turned away and ran, and on another let fly at an Italian Breda 88, a two-man ground-attack fighter aircraft, which 'dived towards the sea and outpaced us. Fired 50 rounds.'

Twice more he attacked U-boats. On 20 December he found one on the surface between Menorca and Sardinia and went for it: 'U/Boat submerged 26 seconds before DCs released. Bombed 300 feet ahead of swirl. No results observed,' he wrote in his log. He saw another on 5 January but it had gone under before he was close enough to attack. On 13 February, searching an area southeast of Majorca, the Hudson sighted a U-boat on the surface six miles away. 'Altered course and attacked when U-B started to dive. Dropped 3 DCs 200 feet ahead 15 secs after submarine submerged. I was navigating.'

For the rest of his time at Blida it was regular anti-sub sweeps and convoy patrols. And certainly drinks in the third week of February, when he was commissioned pilot officer and awarded a DFC in a shower of such decorations for 500 aircrew – John Ensor, Ivan Mitchell and Huntley Holmes among them.

Holmes' was a bar to the DFC he was awarded the previous November, for his destruction of an Italian aircraft and his share of the destruction of *U-595*. On 4 April, a long tour over and probably dog-tired, Poole flew to England with John Ensor. They landed at Gosport, Portsmouth. Flight time 9 hours 5 minutes.

For the rest of 1943 he instructed at Coastal Command OTUs before transferring to Nassau in the Bahamas, to convert to Liberators. He took one up by himself for the first time on the 12th and flew one anti-sub sweep east of Florida before his spell in the tropics ended with an above-average pilot rating. Home in England again he did a couple of courses, one of them to learn about flying with a Leigh Light, the powerful wing-attached light with a dazzling beam that lit up submarines at night, and the intricacies of the latest radar. Then he was posted to 120 Squadron, the command's elite unit at Ballykelly on Lough Foyle in northwest Northern Ireland.

His sixth and last brush with a U-boat occurred three hours out to sea southeast of Ireland on the last day of 1944. His logbook:

> Radar contact made 5-3/4 miles starboard while flying in cloud. Height 1400 feet. Homed to 300 feet. Still in cloud when rear gunner saw schnorkel. Returned to position. Nothing seen. Dropped pattern of [sonar buoys]. Heard U/B propellor beats. Remained in area 9 hrs. Landed Chivenor.

So the U-boat was there all right, but attackable. The Liberator couldn't find the sub and the U-boat may have heard the plane and been running submerged when the buoys picked up its telltale signal. (Sonar buoys, a late development in the war, contained a receiver and transmitter in a slim cylinder with an float attached and were dropped by aircraft into the sea. They deployed on contact with the water, the transmitter remaining on the surface with the float while the cylinder with receiver descended to a fixed depth, attached by line to the float. It listened for underwater sounds, the transmitter relaying them to the aircraft.)

Poole was foiled again but six meetings with U-boats when many Coastal Command crews never saw, let alone attacked, one in the entire war was a remarkable achievement.

Telltale wakes on the sea surface led the crew of New Zealander Wilbert 'Andy' Anderson's 53 Squadron Liberator to the U-boats late in the afternoon of 5 July 1943. For hours they'd been unsuccessfully scouring the Bay of Biscay for a reported submarine. Now they could see no fewer than three, four miles off in V formation, home bound for Lorient.

The aircraft, airborne at daylight from its base at Thorney Island on England's South Coast, logged a radio message at 10.16 a.m. telling it to look for a U-boat sighted an hour earlier, roughly 100 miles off the northwest tip of Spain. Once there Anderson swept the area. Nothing. Eventually, he took the Liberator closer in to land, sweeping toward France along Spain's northern coast. Still nothing. At 4.37 p.m. they could see Cape Villano on the coast north of Bilbao, decided that was far enough and turned back. The navigator and flight engineer, calculating fuel supply and miles to England, figured the Liberator was already beyond its Prudent Limit of Endurance (PLE). So Anderson banked the big aircraft and called for the course home. Eleven minutes later, at 2000 feet in a cloudless sky, they saw the wakes and then the subs, one degree east of the morning's search coordinates. The crew didn't need telling Anderson was going to attack.

The Liberator was flying a Musketry patrol, code name for Coastal Command's current offensive in the Bay of Biscay, the intensified

Allied air and naval effort to sink U-boats sailing to or from bases on the French Atlantic coast – Brest, Lorient, St Nazaire, La Pallice and Bordeaux. Successive operations – Derange, Musketry, Seaslug and Percussion – sank 30 U-boats and damaged another 19 between April and September 1943. 'Johnnie' Walker's famous hunter-killer unit, Royal Navy Support Group 2 of five sloops, was credited with three of them, Allied aircraft the rest. Many more of the outgoing subs were so damaged they had to abort their patrol, returning to port for repairs.

In the early war years, U-boats had been able to cross the Bay of Biscay with relative impunity. By mid-1943 the tide of the submarine battle had swung. Navigating the bay had now become perilous. The Allies' manufacturing arsenal was pouring out planes and ships equipped with advanced weaponry and electronics. Aircraft swamped the area, as did hunter-killer warship groups. Submarines couldn't run their powerful diesel engines below the surface and their battery-powered electric motors for underwater running could only operate for short periods and at slow speeds. U-boats needed to resurface to recharge their batteries, but cruising on the surface, especially in the relatively enclosed bay, risked their destruction. However, it couldn't be avoided. And night was no longer a refuge – powerful centimetric radar sought them out, and when it found them the 'Leigh Light' slung under the starboard wing of sub-hunting aircraft bathed its prey in bright light. Centimetric or microwave-band radar allowed the detection of much smaller objects and the use of much smaller antennas.

Anderson flew the Liberator past the submarines, dropped down to 600 feet and turned left to dive out of the sun. The quarry, *U-170*, *U-535* and *U-536*, new IXC 40s of 517 tons, were 200 yards apart, those on the flanks fawny green, the leader black. Anderson and his men faced intense fire from the enemy boats as the big plane bored in, cannon and machine guns blazing at the Liberator from the gunnery 'bandstands' or platforms. The submarines turned sharply left, thwarting the initial attack. Anderson banked away and climbed into the sun for another go, this time across the beam of the nearest sub. He reported in a post-action report that the flak kept up as he attacked again, much of it inaccurate. The Liberator thundered across the subs at 50 feet but this time the depth charges failed to release, an aircrew's worst fear.

Once again the aircraft circled to port and attacked a third time, the sun cloaking its approach. Several books report that by this time *U-170* and *U-536* had dived, leaving *U-535* on the surface to face the Liberator's third run. Wrong. The Coastal Command 'attack assessment report', compiled after Anderson returned to Thorney Island and answered intelligence officers' questions, says the submarines were all still on the surface but now out of formation as they strove to evade the Liberator. Anderson picked out the U-boat furthest to port, *U-535*. This time, at 50 feet, the depth charges didn't hang up. Eight of them dropped. The rear gunner didn't see the depth charges splash in but as he watched explosions erupted and the bow of *U-535* was hidden in the plume. As the Liberator circled away, the U-boat's stern was seen emerging from the turbulent water of the explosions and the boat itself was turning to starboard.

Cannon fire had seriously damaged the Liberator's wings and tail and one shell blasted a large hole in the fuselage. Enemy fire also slightly wounded a beam gunner. With an injured crewman, a damaged aircraft and limited fuel, Anderson didn't tarry. Just 20 minutes had elapsed from the moment the subs were spotted.

Anderson reported that as they left the scene the U-boats were in line astern, the leading pair making about eight knots. The third submarine was lagging, making at the most six knots. Quite what happened to *U-535* isn't known but she went down with her entire 55-man crew – there were no survivors. The other two U-boats involved in Anderson's attack reached Lorient safely, though one of them was later lost. Anderson made Thorney Island as nightfall approached, a round flight just fifteen minutes short of sixteen hours.

The post-action report praised Anderson. 'Captain of aircraft attacked the three U-boats, [which] obviously intended to fight it out, in a very able manner.' Coastal Command HQ air staff commented: 'A very fine effort … [Anderson] did not hesitate to attack three U-Boats, all of which were firing, and made three successive runs over them in the face of heavy opposition.'

The fate of *U-535* wasn't known publicly until after the war, when U-boat war diaries and other records captured by the British were finally able to be analysed. German Navy commander Grand Admiral Karl Donitz had all navy documents preserved, most of them taken from Berlin in late 1944 to a 17th-century northern Bavarian castle. Donitz maintained the Kreigsmarine had done nothing dishonourable, so there was no reason to destroy its records.

The British may well have known in wartime that *U-535* had sunk – through Enigma decrypts and other sources. When Anderson's DFC was gazetted just before D-Day the citation lauded the New Zealander as a 'determined and able captain of aircraft with a fine record of operational flying', noting he had attacked three submarines in the face of fierce enemy fire. However, no mention was made of any sinkings.

Anderson's bold, aggressive assault in the face of joint flak from three subs on 5 July was not the earliest attack on U-boats by 53 Liberators, but it was among the first and he and his crew scored the squadron's initial success. On occasions other ASW aircraft captains attacked U-boat pairs and triples that sent up a hail of flak from quad 20 mm and 37 mm guns but not all skippers risked such odds. Some decided on caution, calling for reinforcements. Anderson didn't hesitate. He was lucky he wasn't shot down or his aircraft didn't suffer more serious damage. He beat the odds.

On 10 December 1943 on a night patrol of almost twelve hours in the Bay of Biscay he made the squadron's first 'successful' attack on a U-boat using the Leigh Light. He wrote in his log: 'Rear gunner and beam gunner observed bows [of the sub] thrown out of water [but] nothing further seen.' The submarine didn't sink. The Air Staff in the attack assessment praised 'a very well planned and executed attack, which indicates a very good standard of crew drill'.

On 5 March 1944 Anderson notched up his third Bay of Biscay U-boat strike. On a night patrol radar again guided him to a surfaced U-boat and it was action stations once more. Confronted by intense flak, he still made two runs at the sub but didn't sink it. 'Returned base three engines,' his log says. His nonchalant entry camouflaged a nightmarish few minutes, followed by a difficult trip home.

Flak ripped into the Liberator as it dropped DCs in its initial attack but it was much worse the second time around, the German gunners knocking out one engine. Anderson flew away, minus an engine and with flak damage in wings and fuselage. 'The loss of the engine and the damage to the ailerons caused the aircraft to fly with the starboard wing down,' Anderson told a reporter. 'Only by banking hard could we maintain a true course. We made a sort of crab-like journey home.'

Anderson was hospitalised in Northern Ireland suffering from high blood pressure in July 1944, his tour over, and didn't fly operationally again. He returned to New Zealand in December that year.

On 24 July 1943, Aucklander James Whyte administered the *coup de grâce* in one of the most extraordinary U-boat sinkings of World War II. Just three weeks later he was dead. Whyte, 25, and his aircraft, a 547 Squadron Wellington, simply disappeared over the Atlantic while on an anti-sub patrol. The men on HZ351-T were lost without trace – no wireless message, nothing. The most likely scenario is that the Wellington was overwhelmed by prowling enemy fighters, fatally damaged and shot down before getting off an SOS. No bodies were recovered and Whyte and the five men who flew with him are all remembered at Runnymede.

Whyte, like Wilbert Anderson, was a Scot. He was born in Kilbarchan, a village now on the western outskirts of Glasgow, on 6 September 1917. The family arrived in New Zealand when James was a youngster and he grew up in Bayswater on Auckland's North Shore. Whyte took to yachting as a youngster and made a name for himself on the Waitemata Harbour. He was part owner and skipper of champion 14-foot T-Class speedster *Invader* in the late 1930s. In late 1939 the *Auckland Star* noted *Invader* had won ten of her nineteen starts in the 1938–39 season, including the anniversary regatta event by a whopping sixteen minutes. When he enlisted, Whyte had never been in a plane but for some now unknown reason chose the air force over the navy.

When he joined the RNZAF in July 1941, Whyte was working as a clerk for Challenge Phosphate in Auckland and studying for a BCom at night school. He did his basic flying training at Whenuapai then sailed for Canada to complete his wings course. He was commissioned on graduation at Saskatoon. After seven or eight top-up months training in England, Whyte was posted to 547 Squadron flying Wellingtons, then at Chivenor, Cornwall, in November 1942. The squadron moved briefly to Tain, Scotland, before returning to Chivenor in April 1943 and then almost immediately moved again to Davidstow Moor, also in Cornwall. It was from there Whyte made his submarine-sinking and last flights.

The events of 24 July 1943 unfolded when a 172 Squadron Wellington, flying from Chivenor and piloted by Englishman Bill Jennings, spotted on radar what turned out to be *U-459* on the surface off Cape Ortegal, Spain, three days out from Bordeaux. The U-boat was a 1600-ton U-tanker, a class of about ten boats known as 'milk cows'. Equipped only with defensive armament, their job was to provide fuel, torpedoes, other equipment, food and medical aid for crews of U-boats already on patrol. The tankers were vital to the German submarine campaign. If a tanker hooked up with a supply-short U-boat it could keep that boat at sea.

Jennings' attack on *U-459* is one of the dramatic stories of the U-boat war. Despite intense fire from the sub's multi 20 mm cannons, Jennings bored in, his own guns blazing. Flak from the surface either smashed the Wellington's engines or wounded, and perhaps killed, the pilot. Out of control, the aircraft crashed onto the starboard side of the U-boat, demolishing a quad gun and plunging half into the sea. Rear gunner Bert Turner, the only survivor of the six-man crew, somehow found himself in the water, uninjured, and alongside one of the aircraft's dinghies.

The U-boat's deck crew tried to deal with the carnage, tending to casualties and cutting away wreckage of the Wellington. They also found three unexploded depth charges – two on the bridge and one on the afterdeck, according to Clay Blair in *Hitler's U-Boat War*, and the skipper ordered them rolled over the side, apparently unaware they were set to explode at shallow depth. 'One or more of the depth charges exploded beneath the stern of *U-459*, inflicting horrendous damage,' Blair says.

Steering disabled, the boat moved only in circles. As the crew tried to fix the problems Whyte arrived on the scene one minute before 6 p.m. – about three quarters of an hour after Jennings' attack. 547's Operations Record Book tells what happened next:

> Attacked immediately, fire being opened up at 1000 yds and replied to ineffectively by U-boat. 7 x DCs were released … from 50 ft at a speed of 210 mph. [First fell] immediately to starboard of conning tower and remainder to port. Fire was maintained by rear gunner after passing over U-boat. After the explosions stem of U-boat lifted and U-boat rolled to starboard … Crew poured out of the conning tower and jumped into sea before disappearance of U-boat. 20–30 seconds after, a violent explosion was seen in the position, several of the crew being blown into the air. When last seen 20–30 survivors were … joining up their dinghies to form a raft. One and a half miles from the scene of the attack a dinghy with a sole survivor from an aircraft [Turner], a portion of which could be seen nearby. Aircraft dropped supplies [to Turner] but doubtful if these were recovered. Remained 2 hrs 10 mins in vicinity [then]

set course for base. Weather dull and sea calm at position. Down 2246 hrs.

Before he left the scene Whyte radioed the outcome of his attack and gave the position of survivors. The Polish destroyer *Orkan* picked up forty-one Germans and Turner who, says one writer, 'was floating in splendid isolation' a short distance from his enemies. The German skipper died. A short time before his boat settled he saluted his crew, went below and did not re-emerge.

Blair says the Admiralty gave credit for the kill to Jennings and in view of his 'high degree of courage' recommended the award of a posthumous Victoria Cross. It was turned down.

Whyte was on his sixteenth operation when he was lost on 15 August – a bad day for 547, another crew gone as well as Whyte's. Squadron records show:

T/547, Capt F/O Whyte, no signals received. Overdue action taken.

C/547, Capt F/O Stephens, no signals received. Overdue action taken.

Nothing was ever learned about the fate of either crew – twelve men missing, their names eventually displayed at Runnymede. Other aircraft reported close encounters with enemy aircraft that day, and Whyte and Stephens probably ran into enemy fighters. 547 Squadron CO, Wing Commander Ralph McKern had no doubts. He wrote to Whyte's mother immediately, putting the matter plainly:

> I can only assume he has been shot down by German fighters who claim four British aircraft in that particular area. Though a widespread search is being made for survivors, I hesitate to encourage

you to hope too much as, in the absence of a signal saying he was being attacked, it seems likely his crew was surprised and shot down before they realised enemy fighters were present.

Bryan Turnbull, 24 when war broke out, enlisted in January 1940 and eight months later was on his way to England, pilot wings on his tunic. He sailed on the *Tamaroa* from Wellington on 14 September, twenty-two men in his draft, ten of whom would die. Turnbull would survive, as would Harold Poole, soon to be on 500 Squadron.

Turnbull was posted to 206 Squadron on Hudsons, beginning his tour in April 1941, first at Bircham Newton, Norfolk, briefly St Eval in Cornwall and then from Aldergrove in Northern Ireland. Aldergrove was a major RAF base just outside Belfast and from there 206 Hudsons patrolled for U-boats in the Irish Sea and the North and South Channels, separating the United Kingdom from Ireland, and out into the eastern Atlantic.

In mid-1942, as an experienced sergeant pilot he might have expected to go with 206 and its new long-range American B-17 Fortresses to remote Benbecula in the Outer Hebrides, to begin patrols into the North Atlantic. Instead, humiliation. In November 1941 a court martial reduced him to the lowly rank of aircraft hand and took him off flying for six months – for pinching two gallons of petrol. Details are long lost but like most New Zealanders serving with the RAF Turnbull probably owned a flivver, or shared in one, bought for a few quid, and used as crew car from base to town (read pub) and sometimes for longer jaunts. Petrol was severely rationed, but available in vast quantities at RAF airfields – for official purposes. Topping up flivvers was definitely not an official purpose, though the practice was widespread, often with the connivance of ground crew in return for favours. Almost every autobiography by wartime aircrew has stories of iffy schemes to filch petrol to keep the old clangers going. Aviation gasoline souped up performance, so was much in demand.

Airbase authorities, aware of what went on, ordered petrol coloured to make pilfering more difficult and organised crackdowns. It still went on. Sometimes blind eyes were turned and offenders let off with a caution. Turnbull was unlucky – and once he was in officialdom's maw he was a goner. But good pilots were precious and Turnbull was very good, so after he'd served his penance he was posted to 120 Squadron. An elite Coastal Command unit, 120 was the first to have the American Liberator. The posting was probably a mark of confidence in Turnbull's flying ability and he lived up to his reputation.

Many Coastal Command anti-sub aircrew never sighted a U-boat, let alone attacked one. They scoured the grey rolling seas of the North Atlantic, the Bay of Biscay, the Arctic Ocean, the North Sea in foul weather, planes buffeted by wind, rain and snow and freezing temperatures – and never saw a thing. Perhaps the standards of the legendary sub-hunter Terry Bulloch on 120 rubbed off on Turnbull. Bulloch, a law unto himself, saw, attacked and sank more U-boats than anyone else. He destroyed four in nine months in 1942–43 and severely damaged another two. His sinkings tally, three of them while with 120, was unmatched. No one else managed more than two. Bulloch's extraordinary eyesight helped – he could pick up the telltale trail of a sub invisible to others.

Turnbull's DFC citation in January 1944 records him attacking five U-boats. 'A first-class pilot, he has performed his duties of escorting North Atlantic convoys with great success, often in adverse weather during the winter months in Iceland.'

From April 1943 until March 1944 the Libs of 120 Squadron were based at Reykjavik. At 68 degrees north, bleak, frigid in winter, not much better in summer, Iceland wasn't a sought-after post but became a vital cog in the network of air fields from which Allied aircraft gradually closed the mid-Atlantic gap. American and Canadian aircraft guarded convoys in the western Atlantic, aerial patrols from Britain the east. German subs, once free to roam there without air attack, were suddenly confronted with Liberators, with their long range and endurance.

120 Squadron Liberators flew south from Iceland to the mid-Atlantic, picking up convoys, patrolling for hours until relieved by other aircraft. They flew patterns over the shipping below, sweeping ahead of convoys to pick up surfaced U-boats, and well astern, hunting submarines tracking convoys before closing at nightfall to seek targets. The planes maintained radio contact with the naval escorts accompanying the convoys, and the presence of these aerial watchdogs paid off handsomely.

Air attacks and sinkings became frequent and numerous U-boats damaged enough for them to abort their missions and return home. Even forcing a submarine to crash-dive without damage counted as a success, as a submerged boat was likely to lose contact with the convoy, its skipper and crew wary of air strikes. Aircraft worked closely with convoy escorts, calling the ships and directing them to the positions of spotted or just-dived U-boats for depth-charge attacks.

Turnbull made his first attack on a U-boat on 8 February 1943. A slow east-bound convoy with sixty-three ships from New York was a magnet, and a pack gathered. The convoy lost eleven ships, the Germans three submarines – *U-187* and *U-609* to elements of the strong escort force and *U-624* to a Fortress of 220 Squadron. Turnbull's attack on *U-135* was one of three nearly-sunks, the damaged submarine forced back to Lorient. Blair says that working closely as a team, aircraft and the eleven escorts scattered the U-boats and drove them under. Five subs reported battle damage and aborted to France. Five months later, in the Atlantic off Morocco, *U-135* was blown to the surface by naval depth charges, rammed and sunk.

Turnbull damaged another U-boat in the North Atlantic on 8 September, the same day three other submarines shadowing a slow east-bound convoy were caught on the surface and sunk by aircraft. The New Zealander's target was *U-762*, a new type VIIC boat. Blair: 'His attack drove U-762 under and a destroyer came up to carry on. Allied authorities assessed the attacks as failures but [skipper Wolfgang] Hille had incurred two wounded and damage to diesel engines, setbacks that took the boat out of action for several days.'

Under a new commander, *U-762* was one of three U-boats sunk in the Atlantic on the night of 8–9 February 1944 by 'Johnnie' Walker's hunter-killer group. Paul Kemp in *U-Boats Destroyed* quotes Walker as saying it took 252 depth charges and 48 Hedgehog bombs to sink the third U-boat. (This British-designed anti-submarine weapon was fired ahead of an attacking vessel from a battery of mortar-like tubes. Fitted with contact fuses they exploded on contact with their target. An underwater blast thus announced a hit – one of these was usually enough to destroy a U-boat.) 'The strain on the ships' companies during these attacks was enormous thanks to the continual buffeting and shaking from depth charge explosions and the never-ending fear of destruction by an acoustic torpedo.'

Turnbull finally got his 'kill' on 17 October 1943, in the middle of the North Atlantic. He and a Liberator pilot of 59 Squadron shared the sinking but it was Turnbull's depth charges which sealed *U-540*'s fate. German submarine forces had latched on to two westbound convoys, sailing close together – 117 ships and twenty-one escorts. Blair writes of the action: 'In the mistaken belief that the T-5 Zaunkonig homing torpedo [the German acoustic torpedo known to the British and Americans as the Gnat] was a wonder weapon and the new flak arrays were deadly effective, U-boat Control became absolutely determined to massacre these convoys. In keeping with the new anti-aircraft policy, Control issued a "Hitlerian" order: Remain surfaced! Shoot your way to the convoy with flak!'

Blair notes that though U-boats complied, only one managed to sink a ship (one of two lost by the Allies on the Atlantic run in October). 'The swarms of aircraft and surface vessels assigned to the two convoys sank six U-boats on 16 and 17 October, one of the worst [German] naval calamities of the war.'

Turnbull wrote an account of the action in a letter to the RNZAF, thinking it might be of use for training purposes. His aircraft had left Reykjavik in the early morning of 17 October to provide anti-U-boat escort and patrol to trans-Atlantic convoy ONS206, about 700 miles south of Iceland.

> Shortly after dawn the convoy was sighted and the patrol commenced. About mid-day we were relieved by another aircraft, and set course for base. At 1430 hours, after being in the air for 12 hours, the 2nd Pilot sighted a surfaced U-boat on the port bow at about 12 miles range … I was in the astro-dome myself taking a shot on the sun-compass to check our course, the navigator was down in his compartment in the nose working out an ETA at base; the 2nd WOp/AG was keeping a listening watch in the wireless compartment; the

3rd WOp/AG was keeping a watch in the rear turret; the engineer was in the galley preparing a meal and a hot drink; the 1st WOp/AG was having a spell off watch. Fortunately the whole crew had their headphones plugged into the inter-communication system, and we were able to get away to a flying start ...

As I came forward to take over the controls I told the 2nd WOp to send out a sighting report. By the time I was in my seat the 2nd pilot had passed the news to the rest of the crew and the engineer and the 1st WOp were on the flight deck. In answer to my call the engineer opened up the boost on all four engines with one hand and increased the propeller revolutions with the other, while I released the automatic pilot, pushed the nose down and adjusted the control surfaces trimming gear. The navigator worked out our position, checked the bombing switches and came up to the flight deck, putting on his Mae West [as presumably the rest of the crew did in case they were shot down or ditched]. The 1st WOp took over the wireless while the 2nd WOp went aft to stand by the life-saving equipment, smoke-floats, and emergency rations. Before we were within range of the four cannons fixed in the Liberator's nose, a second sighting report had been sent, and base knew our position and that we were carrying out an attack on a fully-surfaced U-boat.

With the needle of the airspeed indicator passing the 300 [mph] and the altimeter showing a steady rate of descent we approached the U-boat until, when three or four miles from it, we saw for the first time another Liberator on the far side of the U-boat. The other aircraft was flying very low, its front gun sending up splashes around the U-boat, the crew of which had apparently not noticed us as we came in with the sun behind us. Since the other aircraft was obviously carrying out a depth charge attack, and would arrive over the U-boat at almost the same time as we should, I kept up our speed and at 800 yards blazed away with the cannons at the conning-tower, passing over the U-boat just ahead of the other aircraft which was cut back for its depth charge attack. Some of the ricochetting shots whisked past us as we crossed the front of the other aircraft but the U-boat's gun crew were out of action by this time. We turned away and climbed to come in again. On our second run in I manoeuvred so as to cross the U-boat from stem to bows at an angle of about 30 degrees to its course. At 3000 yards the U-boat opened up with its quick-firing bow gun and as a puff of brown smoke raced under our starboard wing a nest of pom-poms started to blaze away from the conning tower. Slipping and skidding [tactics to confuse the U-boat gunners] we closed to half a mile, when I settled down for my depth charge attack run, cut the throttles back, and opened up with my cannons; the enemy fire ceased as the shells tore into the conning-tower. I dropped a stick of four depth charges across the U-boat. As quickly as possible we came in for another run. The 2nd WOp had reported the result of the depth charge attack from his point of vantage in the aft compartment and it appeared to me that the U-boat must be fairly badly damaged. However, as we approached again there was machine-gun fire from the enemy and once again my cannons put a stop to it. The crew of the U-boat appeared to be abandoning her. Several men jumped overboard, even though she was still moving through the water. I dropped another stick of four depth charges and the 2nd WOp reported almost immediately that the U-boat had broken in two and sunk.

Blair records that Eric Knowles, pilot of the 59 Squadron Liberator whose depth charges had overshot, radioed Turnbull, 'You got him, good show.' He also says that although Turnbull told the surface escorts he could see about thirty survivors in the water, none was rescued. All fifty-five men aboard the *U-540*, a new IXC 40, perished. The boat, on its first patrol, had left Bergen a few days previously to join the north Atlantic fray. Turnbull and Knowles were credited with the sinking of the submarine.

Tour over and worn out by the strain of hundreds of hours of operational flying over the wild Atlantic, Turnbull returned to New Zealand in early 1944.

Londoner Tony Spooner, an exceptional pilot, flew with a Coastal Command squadron early in the war before making his name in Malta, tracking enemy shipping to help the Royal Navy sink vessels supplying the Axis armies in North Africa. Returning from the Med with a DFC, Spooner took charge of a torpedo training unit in Scotland before joining 53 Squadron as one of its two flight commanders in the late spring of 1943, as the squadron equipped with Liberators. In his autobiography *In Full Flight*, Spooner remembered how he picked up his crew at Thorney Island. He and five other second- or third-tour captains were given just a few minutes to choose their crew from the half dozen just in from training.

'I spied a tall officer co-pilot with twinkling eyes and a humorous handlebar moustache. "What kind of crew have you got?" I enquired. "Largely composed of rather fierce New Zealanders," he replied. This was good enough for me. Aussies and New Zealanders had long been favourites of mine ...' Four of his team were New Zealanders, an unusually large number in one Coastal Command crew. Jeff Wilkinson, soon Spooner's 'reliable, loyal and resourceful' co-pilot, and his crew had come through a solid three-month Coastal Command OTU course at Nassau in the Bahamas and knew what they were about. The New Zealanders, all wireless operator/air gunners, were Ian Heays (23), from Tutira, Hawke's Bay; Fred Bailey (33), from Blenheim; Ian Thomson, (22), from Christchurch; and Hugh Mills (21) from Gisborne.

All trained in Canada before moving to Nassau on one of the courses at the newly established 111 OTU. There Heays, Bailey, Thomson and Mills joined up with Wilkinson and several others to form a crew and fly first Mitchells then Liberators, in training and on U-boat patrols. The ability of the long-range Liberators to patrol for almost eighteen hours called for extra crew – no man could sit behind guns for that length of time and stay vigilant, and lack of vigilance could be fatal. The four WOps/AGs moved around, between the guns, the wireless station and the radar set. Long patrols were also the reason for two pilots. A single pilot could cope with six to eight hours in a Bomber Command aircraft, but not sixteen-hours-plus Coastal Command patrols. Sunderlands often carried three pilots and some had a backup navigator.

When he enlisted in the RNZAF on 4 October 1941, Heays was working as a shepherd in northern Hawke's Bay. In wartime some men are unlucky – and unfortunately Heays was one of them. At two minutes before 6 a.m. on 21 September 1943 Spooner and his crew lifted off from Thorney Island on an anti-submarine patrol into the Bay of Biscay. The crew were on just their third op. Two and a half hours out in the Atlantic, as they emerged from cloud, their Liberator was jumped by five Me 110 long-range fighters. The Germans bore in, machine guns and cannons chattering. The Liberator hit back hard. Heays was at the starboard beam machine gun, sending out a stream of bullets, empty cartridge cases clattering to the floor around him. As he worked his gun a cannon shell from one of the 110s exploded inside the fuselage and deadly fragments hit him in the back. It proved to be fatal. 'We eased his pain with morphine injections and wrapped him in the silk of an opened parachute. It was all we could do,' Spooner wrote in his book. 'Two engines were hit and damaged … the aircraft barely survived … the whole experience was a nightmare.' Thomson was hit by other fragments but not seriously hurt. During the ten-minute battle he set one of the fighters on fire and another was damaged and it's thought the other three pulled out of the duel.

Normal drill after the loss of an airman was for his parents to receive a form letter, often written by the adjutant and signed by the squadron wing commander, usually saying the man was highly regarded, a key member of the unit and how sorry they all were. In this case Spooner himself, in a long, moving letter, told Heays' parents about their son's death after his wounding.

> He was at once attended to by the other members of the crew and as soon as the fight was over at about 8.45 a.m., he was made comfortable on a bed of flying clothing laid on the floor of the aircraft. He was wrapped up in the silk of a parachute and kept warm with further clothing laid on top. He was in considerable pain but was given an injection of morphia within a few minutes; this sent him into a semi-conscious coma and eased his pain. We were at the time a long way from our base but after the enemy had been shaken off we at once set course for the nearest aerodrome in the toe of England [St Eval, Cornwall]. … We had warned the aerodrome … of your son's condition and when we landed shortly before 10 o'clock

we were met on the runway by an ambulance and the Senior Medical Officer of the Station, who personally supervised his transfer from the aircraft and who accompanied him to the … RAF hospital. That morning he was given a blood transfusion and an operation was performed in the afternoon. He had by now been given further injections of morphia and was comfortable and out of pain. However, his serious internal injuries were too great even for his fine, healthy physique and by evening he was sinking. At 11 o'clock the same night, he passed peacefully away. [Your] son showed great courage and never complained in spite of his injuries. I give you all these details to assure you that everything possible was done to save your son. We all will remember him with deep regret, for he was a fine fellow and helped to save our aircraft in a difficult situation.

In early October 1943 on a 224 Squadron anti-submarine patrol in the Bay of Biscay, Mick Ensor sighted a Ju 88 and two other unidentified aircraft. 'He promptly turned west, out into the Atlantic to discourage pursuit,' Vincent Orange wrote in his Ensor biography. 'Well armed though the Liberator might be, no prudent captain would willingly mix it with German fighters. Only after fifteen anxious minutes was Mick convinced that he had lost them. He then warily resumed his search for U-boats.' Flying Liberators in those waters, Ensor remembered:

We knew we'd very likely meet up with Ju 88s but on the whole we were careful – and we had radar: it was only the unlucky or careless fellows who got caught. One chum of mine got caught up with half a dozen of them, but he got into a cloud and said later that he was certain that one wing must have been sticking out because every time he put his nose out, the bloody things were still there. He did get burned a bit, but eventually made it home alright.

Four months earlier New Zealander Morrinsville-born Brian Layne, captain of a 201 Squadron Sunderland, tangled with another Ju 88 while he was escorting a convoy of landing craft en route for North Africa. He wrote of the encounter:

> Met them just after dawn ... about 400 miles west of Brest. All went as normal until just before 9 [a.m.] when suddenly a Ju 88 dived on us out of the cloud. The first I knew of it was the announcement by Sgt Ball in the front turret that we had just 'flown over some splashes [from gunfire] in the water.' [The Ju 88] appeared at such short range that Sgt Campbell in the rear turret had to open fire before he could let me know what went on. The Ju 88 broke away over the top of us, flying round to port to make an attack on the port quarter. Steve gave me a good commentary from the astrodome, so that I was able to turn into the attack, and at the same time make for cloud cover. When he saw us turning into him, the enemy turned away, just after which we entered cloud. Campbell saw him a few minutes later low down on the water, presumably making for home, as he must have been fairly near his extreme range from base. Saw nothing and landed back at 1530.

The twin-engined Junkers 88 in all its many models rivalled the RAF's Mosquito claim to be the most versatile aircraft of World War II. 'The final total of 15,000 JU 88s of all models gives an idea of the significance of this aircraft,' says Chris Chant in his *Aircraft of World War II*.

The Ju 88 and the Messerschmitt 110 formed the backbone of the Luftwaffe's night-fighter defence against Bomber Command. The Ju 88 was an especially formidable opponent in the eastern Atlantic, especially in the Bay of Biscay, where they operated from bases on the French Atlantic coast. They hunted RAF aircraft searching for U-boats and had many successes. All too often planes taking off from English bases and posted 'lost without trace' were likely victims of the Ju 88.

However, one thing which worked in favour of RAF aircraft under attack over the sea was that German aircrew were haunted by the spectre of the sea and feared ending up in the water every bit as much as their opponents. As a result, attacks weren't always pressed home with the same determination German night fighters usually showed against Bomber Command over land. After all, parachuting over land meant a good chance of survival for crew. Parachuting over the sea from a crippled fighter in a pitched battle 200 miles out at sea usually ended in death. Parachutes might have one-man dinghies attached but rescue was unlikely. All too often, plonking into the water in a Mae West with a one-man dinghy was a death sentence.

Arthur Clouston wrote in his autobiography: 'If you were shot down, the chances of being picked up by a surface ship were slight … there was always the sea; the vast rolling Atlantic Ocean against a small, five-foot rubber dinghy.'

Cautious German aircraft evened things out even more. A skipper of a large Coastal Command machine who could handle his plane and was aided by skilled gunners could survive against apparently overwhelming German odds. Knock one attacker down, damage another and maybe, with luck, the rest of them would hare off to seek an easier target, or escort a wounded comrade home.

Clouston fought off a multiple Ju 88 attack in December 1943 with the aid of two of his gunners, one of them a fellow New Zealander. Already a distinguished test pilot, Clouston was posted to command 224 Squadron at Beaulieu, Hampshire, in March 1943, just six months after the squadron had equipped with Liberators. Clouston, who'd not flown Liberators before, did several flights as a passenger to familiarise himself with the new plane. On the last of these radar led the Liberator to a Spanish trawler. Clouston wrote:

> These were strongly built steel ships of between 400 and 500 tons and fished in the bay [Bay of Biscay] and the Atlantic. They roamed widely [and] we learned to hate them. The Germans realised our radar would lead us to the trawlers just as much as to their subs. Formations of eight to ten Ju 88s would fly out from their bases in occupied France and wait for us high up in the sun above the trawlers.

Clouston said 88 singletons would normally keep well out of range, making a nuisance of themselves with harrying attacks 'designed at drawing our claws, at making us jettison our DCs to reduce weight and gain speed and manoeuvre for combat and evasive action.' But the Ju 88s usually hunted in packs of eight or ten – giving the Liberators little chance of fighting it out.

But he did fight it out – and survived the long night of 20–21 December 1943, on an eleven-hour flight from Gibraltar. The previous day Clouston had flown Liberator 'M' across the Bay of Biscay into the Atlantic, overnighting in Gibraltar. On the way home after a 10 p.m. takeoff, the plane ran into a group of five 88s, according to one of his WOp/AGs, Allan Souter (21). Wanganui-born Souter was flying his sixth operation with 224. He had spotted and noted enemy aircraft on three of his previous four ops with 224 but there'd been no firing. He kept a little pocket diary in which he made brief entries supplementing his log. On 7 November he noted, 'On my first op [a 10-hour daylight trip] in the Bay of Biscay sighted one Me 110 and seven Ju 88s. Bags of boost.' In other words, meaning the plane put on power and skedaddled. On his second, four days later, he wrote, 'sighted 2 Ju 88s. Didn't stop to ask questions.' About the flight from Gibraltar just before Christmas 1943, Souter wrote laconically: 'Fought Ju 88s for 50 mins. Got four stoppages in guns but still we fooled 'em with evasive action. Got away with our Lib slightly damaged.'

Clouston talked about the scrap with newspaperman Alan Mitchell after Souter was lost. Mitchell, a New Zealand Press Association correspondent in London, wrote prolifically about New Zealand aircrew and in 1945 published *New Zealanders in the Air War*. He quoted Clouston as saying their aircraft was saved by the coolness and accuracy of his gunners – specifically Flight Sergeant Souter and an English lad. 'When we were 250 miles from Land's End, Souter called me up on the intercom and reported, "An aircraft has just passed us going in the opposite direction, sir. I think it was a Wellington." A few minutes later he said, "There are some aircraft following us astern. There are three on one side and two on the other." A moment or two later he said, "Take evasive action quickly. Get ready. Go."'

A superb pilot, Clouston called on all his skills and performed extreme evasive manoeuvres, helped by the calm instructions of his two gunners who told him what the Germans were doing. Mitchell wrote:

He put the Liberator into climbing turns or turning dives, knowing full well that a pilot dislikes both manoeuvres at night, fearing that his aircraft will either stall through losing speed during the climb, or will go straight into a dive. Thus he forced the Junkers' pilots to pay as much attention to their instruments as to the Liberator they were attacking. Eventually Clouston shook off the Germans and returned to base with only six cannon-shell holes showing in the rudders.

Clouston was generous in his praise for Souter, whom he described as 'cool and brilliant'. The crew had been given seven days' leave after tangling with the 88s and Souter spent his last Christmas in London, with close mate Mick Moosman, also from Wanganui. Moosman was two and a half years older than Souter, and at that stage was stationed at a heavy conversion unit, training on Lancasters. When Souter returned to St Eval he had a bad flu ('am barking like a dog') but continued on operations, a 13 hours 45 minutes trip on 4 January 1944 highlighted by an attack on a submarine, the only one of his flight career. Says his diary: 'Attacked enemy submarine 90 miles off France. Heavy flak coming up. Gave him the works, dropped eight DCs. Made second attack with machine guns.'

Souter, lost on the night of 19–20 March 1944, was on his nineteenth op. Liberator BZ776, skippered by Souter's regular captain, Flt Lt Ray Dunn, took off at 9.25 p.m. and disappeared without trace. A signal sent at 11.30 p.m. went unacknowledged. The ten crew are remembered at Runnymede.

Someone has written on the last page of Souter's log: 'Certified that this N.C.O. is missing from an operational sortie on 19th March 1944.' The log is signed off by Terry McComb, 224 Squadron CO, Clouston's successor.

Ten days later Moosman (23) was also dead, a casualty of the RAF's worst night of the bomber war – the 30–31 March raid on Nuremberg. In all, 105 aircraft were lost and 700 aircrew killed – 200 more men than in the entire Battle of Britain. Moosman's aircraft, in which he was wireless operator, was shot down by a night fighter and the crew of seven perished. Moosman lies in the Commonwealth war cemetery at Durnbach, near Munich.

ACKNOWLEDGEMENTS

A writer of a book like this can do so only with the help and cooperation of many people.

Only a few World War II airmen are still living. Most of them are in their nineties now, a vanishing few, national treasures. It was a real pleasure to meet Noel Sutherland and Trevor Mullinder in Havelock North, Bill Sparks (who has since died) in Christchurch, Ken Orman in Wellington, John Curtis in Taupo, Jock Adamson in Waianawa, Southland, and 'Kiwi' Saunders in Queensland – at ninety-seven, the oldest I interviewed.

With few survivors it was a matter of locating family of former airmen for help and behind almost every story in *Victory* are relatives who provided information, photographs and leads, here and overseas. I am grateful to the many people who contributed. Some went to great lengths to assist. It's impossible to name them all but they have my heartfelt thanks. A few who helped will be as disappointed as I am that their kin are not mentioned here. Wordage restraints meant that it was simply impossible to include everyone I wanted to. I hope they understand.

I'm in the debt of Jack Roberts of Taradale, Napier; not a relative but who went out of his way to get me the story of Sid Gay's adventures on the ground in France just before D-Day. Likewise Mike McPhee of Owaka with his great assistance on details and photographs of Erle Brough and who also helped on the 'Kiwi' Saunders story. Karley Johns and her team couldn't have been more welcoming, helpful and encouraging on my frequent visits to New Zealand Defence Force archives at Trentham and I owe

ACKNOWLEDGEMENTS

them a big thank you. The staff at the National Library and the New Zealand Defence Library, especially Katrina Willoughby and Mary Slatter at the latter, were always helpful. I'm grateful too to Matthew O'Sullivan, Keeper of Photographs at the Air Force Museum, Christchurch, for the pictures of the Liberator, Catalina and Hudsons, and likewise museum research officer Simon Moody for his help.

A word of special thanks to friend and professional genealogist Peter Nutt in Essex, whose expert assistance with a single long-shot lead from a contributor on that marvellous website rafcommands.com led me straight to Helen Wilson, daughter of Charles Beeson, the sole survivor of the Lancaster on which New Zealand pilot George Joblin died raiding Stuttgart. The wonder of it all was that Beeson had written an account for his family of what happened. Bingo. Englishman Pat Kearney, whose father was killed on New Zealander James Archibald's aircraft on the same Stuttgart attack, was incredibly helpful and so was Kelvin Youngs of the England's Aircrew Remembered group on the same subject. And John Pollard in Australia on the Stuttgart raid. Thanks also to researcher Mickael Simon and underwater photographer Olivier Brichet in France for their assistance in Bill Bell's ditching story. After a long search I was fortunate to find Roy Le Long's son Noel in England and I'm indebted to him for most of the information about his father.

I also want to mention help from Paul Sortehaug, Dunedin; Rod Mackenzie, Auckland; Ron Palenski, Dunedin; and Doug Drake, Timaru; as well as Dave Homewood at 'Wings over Cambridge' website, Roger Moroney of *Hawke's Bay Today* for permission to use his interview with Ginger Eagleson, and Auckland aviation researcher

Arthur Arculus. Also the late Vincent Orange, Christchurch, who kindly allowed me to quote freely from his biography of Mick Ensor, and the Spurdle family for their permission to use extracts from Bob Spurdle's book.

Steve Smith, 218 Squadron historian in England, was tremendously helpful and I had much assistance from aviation writers Oliver Clutton-Brock, Colin Cummings, Ken Merrick, Jock Manson and Dennis Williams. Much of my section on the Revigny rail yards bombing was built from Clutton-Brock's book on the subject with his permission and both he and Williams generously sent me photographs for use from their books. Author Robert Stitt on Vancouver Island was most helpful and so was John Howes, who lives within sound of Biggin Hill and who has extensive Arnhem knowledge and provided the list he compiled after much research into Operation Pegasus 1 escapers. On Arnhem I'm indebted to Dutch researchers and authors Arie-Jan van Hees and Luuk Buist, whose respective books *'Green On!'* and *The Royal Air Force at Arnhem* are quoted in the chapter on Arnhem and are essential reference tools on the subject of Operation Market. Fellow Dutchman and friend Co Maarschalkerweerd was as ever helpful. Lee Richards of Archive Research and Document Copying (ARCRE) in London was amazingly quick and helpful in getting material from UK National Archives for me. And thanks, too, to editors Lorain Day and Katie Stackhouse, proofreader Eva Chan and publisher Finlay Macdonald.

Above all I am indebted to two friends: Errol Martyn in Christchurch and Colin Smith who lives near me in Wellington. Hundreds of details from Martyn's three volumes of *For Your Tomorrow* are in *Victory* and without them I would have struggled.

Martyn was also ever helpful with my endless questions, frequently interrupting his own aviation research and writing to provide answers. Colin Smith, a whizz on Photoshop, processed all the photographs in this book, some received in poor shape. He spent long hours working on them and then did the layout when he knew which pictures had to go in. A huge thank you to both men.

My final tribute is to my wife, Eileen, for her patience and encouragement through the long gestation of this book. My admiration and love.

Max Lambert
Wellington
February 2014

BIBLIOGRAPHY

Ambrose, Stephen E; *Pegasus Bridge – June 6, 1944*, Simon and Schuster, New York, 1985
Anon; *Arnhem Lift – Diary of a Glider Pilot*, Pilot Press, London, 1945
Barker, Ralph; *Survival in the Sky*, William Kimber, London, 1976
Baveystock, Leslie; *Wavetops at My Wingtips: Flying with RAF and Coastal Commands in World War II*, Airlife Publishing, Shrewsbury, Wiltshire, 2001
Blair, Clay; *Hitler's U-Boat War –* Vol 1, *The Hunters 1939–1942*; Vol 2, *The Hunted 1942–1945*, Modern Library, New York, editions 2000
Buist, Luuk, Reinders, Philip and Maassen, Geert; *The Royal Air Force at Arnhem – Glider and Re-supply Missions in September 1944*, The Society of Friends of the Airborne Museum Oosterbeek, The Netherlands, 2005
Chant, Chris; *Aircraft of World War II*, Dempsey-Parr, Bristol, 1999
Charlwood, Don; *No Moon Tonight*, Angus & Robertson, Australia, paperback edition, 1979
Chesterton, George; *Also Flew*, Aspect Design, Malvern, Worcestershire, 2008
Chorley, WR; *Royal Air Force Bomber Command Losses of the Second World War*, 6 volumes, Midland Counties Publications, Leicester, 1992–98
Clouston, AE; *The Dangerous Skies*, Cassell, London, 1954
Clutton-Brock, Oliver, *RAF Evaders – The Comprehensive Story of Thousands of Escapers and Their Escape Lines, Western Europe, 1940–45*, Bounty Cooks edition, Bounty Books, London, 2012
Clutton-Brock, Oliver; *Massacre over the Marne – The RAF Bombing Raids on Revigny, July 1944*, Patrick Stephens, Yeovil, Somerset, 1994
Cummings, Colin; *Though without Anger – Losses of Special Duties Aircraft and Assault Gliders 1940 to 1945*, Nimbus Publishing, Yelvertoft, Northamptonshire, 2008
Daniell, Rex Donald; *What Did You Do in the War, Poppa Rekka?*, self published, 2005
Davis, Richard G; *Bombing the European Axis Powers, A Historical Digest of the Combined Bomber Offensive, 1939–1945*, Air University Press, Maxwell AFB, Alabama, 2006
Drake, DE; *Wings over South Canterbury*, self published, Timaru, 1994
Franks, Norman; *Another Kind of Courage: Stories of the UK-based Walrus Air-Sea Rescue Squadrons*, Patrick Stephens, Cambridge, England, 1994
Franks, Norman; *Search, Find and Kill – Coastal Command's U-Boat Successes*, Aston Publications, Bourne End, Buckinghamshire, England, 1990
Hall, Tony (Ed); *D-Day – The Strategy, the Men, the Equipment*, Salamander Books, London, 2001

Hanson, Colin; *By Such Deeds – Honours and Awards in the RNZAF 1923–1999*, Volplane Press, Christchurch, 2001

Hastings, Max; *Overlord – D-Day and the Battle for Normandy 1944*, Michael Joseph, London, 1984

Hastings, Max; *Das Reich – The March of the 2nd SS Panzer Division through France, June 1944*, Pan Books, London, edition 2009

Hees, Arie-Jan van; *'Green On!' – A Detailed Survey of the British Parachute Re-supply Sorties during Operation 'Market Garden' 18–25 September, 1944*, AJ van Hees, Eijsden, The Netherlands, 2004

Houlton, Johnnie; *Spitfire Strikes – A New Zealand Fighter Pilot's Story*, John Murray, London, 1985

Jones, Geoffrey; *Attacker – The Hudson and Its Flyers*, William Kimber, London, 1980

Kemp, Paul; *U-Boats Destroyed – German Submarine Losses in the World Wars*, Arms and Armour Press, London, 1997

King, J Norby; *Green Kiwi versus German Eagle*, J Norby King, Tauranga, 1991

Luck, Hans von; *Panzer Commander – The Memoirs of Hans von Luck*, Cassell, London, 1989

Manson, Jock; *United in Effort – The Story of No. 53 Squadron, RAF 1916–76*, Air-Britain (Historians), Tunbridge Wells, 1997

Martyn, Errol W; *For Your Tomorrow – A Record of New Zealanders Who Have Died While Serving with the RNZAF and Allied Air Services since 1915*, Volumes 1–3, Volplane Press, Christchurch, 1998–2008

Merrick, KA; *Flights of the Forgotten – Special Duties Operations in World War Two*, Arms and Armour Press, London, 1989

Middlebrook, Martin and Everitt, Chris; *The Bomber Command War Diaries*, Midland Publishing, East Shilton, Leicester, revised edition 1996

Mitchell, Alan; *New Zealanders in the Air War*, George Harrap, London, 1945

Mondey, David; *British Aircraft of World War II*, Chancellor Press, London, 1994

Morris, Gerard S; *Spitfire – The New Zealand Story*, Reed Books, Auckland, 2000

Orange, Vincent; *Ensor's Endeavour – A Biography of Wing Commander Mick Ensor*, Grub St, London, 1994

Orman, Ken G; *I Was Born Lucky*, Dorset Enterprises, Wellington, 2009

Price, Dr Alfred; *Aggressors – Patrol Aircraft vs. Submarine*, Airlife Publishing, Ramsbury, Wiltshire, 1991

Reek, Harry; *Airborne Drops*, self-published booklet, England, 2005

Roberts, Mervyn; *Drop Zone*, self published, Pleasant Point, undated

Scott, Desmond; *Typhoon Pilot*, Leo Cooper, London, 1982

Seth, Ronald; *Lion with Blue Wings – The Story of the Glider Pilot Regiment 1942–1945*, Victor Gollancz Ltd, London, 1951

Shores, Christopher and Thomas, Chris; *2nd Tactical Air Force*, Volumes 1-3, Ian Allan Publishing, Hersham, Surrey, 2004–06

Sortehaug, Paul; *The Wild Winds*, self published, Dunedin, 1998
Spooner, Captain A (Tony); *In Full Flight*, Macdonald & Co, London, 1965
Spooner, Tony; *Coastal Ace – The Biography of Squadron Leader Terence Malcolm Bulloch*, William Kimber, London, 1986
Spurdle, Bob; *The Blue Arena*, William Kimber, London, 1986
Stitt, Robert M; *Boeing B-17 Fortress in RAF Coastal Command Service*, Stratus s.c., Sandomierz, Poland, 2010
Thompson, HL; *New Zealanders with the Royal Air Force,* Volumes I–III, War History Branch, Department of Internal Affairs, Wellington, 1953–59
Tunnicliffe, Don; *From Bunnies to Beaufighters*, Alan Tunnicliffe, Christchurch, 1990
Walters, Anne-Marie; *Moondrop to Gascony*, Macmillan, London, 1946
Williams, Dennis; *Stirlings in Action with the Airborne Forces – Air Support for SAS and and Resistance Operations during WWII*, Pen and Sword Aviation, Barnsley, South Yorkshire, 2008
Wood, Wing Commander DH; *A Noble Pair of Brothers – A History of No. 38 Group*, self published, UK, 1996

ABBREVIATIONS

2TAF	2nd Tactical Air Force
ADGB	Air Defence Great Britain
ADU	Aerodrome Defence Unit
CO	Commanding Officer
(C) OTU	(Coastal) Operational Training Unit
DC	Depth Charge
DZ	Drop/Dropping Zone
ETA	Estimated Time of Arrival
FFI	Forces Française de l'Intérieur (French Force of the Interior: the armed branch of the French Resistance)
GCI	Ground Controlled Interception
G-H	Blind bombing device
HCU	Heavy Conversion Unit
HSL	High Speed Launch
H2S	Radar carried by RAF bombers
IFF	Identification, Friend or Foe
LCT	Landing Craft Tank
LFS	Lancaster Finishing School
LNSF	Light Night Striking Force (RAF)
LZ	Landing Zone
MREU	Missing Research and Enquiry Unit
ORB	Operations Record Book
OTU	Operational Training Unit
PFF	Pathfinder Force
PLE	Prudent Limit of Endurance
PPI	Position Plan Indicator
SAS	Special Air Service
SIS	Secret Intelligence Service
SOE	Special Operations Executive
U/S	Unserviceable
WOp/AG	Wireless Operator–Air Gunner

INDEX OF NZ AIRCREW
(and selected others)

Ranks listed here are those held at the end of World War II. So too are decorations but they do include awards announced in the first year or two of peace for events during the war. All those listed are members of the Royal New Zealand Air Force (RNZAF) unless otherwise specified.

- † Denotes those who lost their lives
- ♦ Denotes brothers
- ★ Denotes bar to decoration

ABBREVIATIONS

AIR FORCE RANKS

ACM	Air Chief Marshal
AM	Air Marshal
AVM	Air Vice-Marshal
Air Cdre	Air Commodore
Gp Capt	Group Captain
Wg Cdr	Wing Commander
Sqn Ldr	Squadron Leader
Flt Lt	Flight Lieutenant
Flg Off	Flying Officer
Plt Off	Pilot Officer
Wt Off	Warrant Officer
Flt Sgt	Flight Sergeant
Sgt	Sergeant
LAC	Leading Aircraftman

OTHERS

RAF	Royal Air Force
RAFVR	Royal Air Force Volunteer Reserve
RAAF	Royal Australian Air Force
RCAF	Royal Canadian Air Force
RNZAF	Royal New Zealand Air Force
RNZN	Royal New Zealand Navy
SAAF	South African Air Force
WAAF	Women's Auxiliary Air Force
FAA	Fleet Air Arm

AWARDS AND HONOURS

VC	Victoria Cross
GCB	Knight Grand Cross, Order of the Bath
KBE	Knight, Order of the British Empire
CBE	Commander, Order of the British Empire
OBE	Officer, Order of the British Empire
MBE	Member, Order of the British Empire
DSO	Distinguished Service Order
DFC	Distinguished Flying Cross
AFC	Air Force Cross
GM	George Medal
MM	Military Medal
DFM	Distinguished Flying Medal
mid	Mention in Dispatches
(bbc)	Battle of Britain Clasp
(pff)	Pathfinder Force Badge
cvsa	Commendation for Valuable Service in the Air

INDEX

Adamson, Sgt JWM, RAF 291–92
Aitken, Wg Cdr RF, RAF – OBE, mid (3) 177
Anderson, Flg Off WE – DFC 340–45
Andrews, Flg Off EC 328
† Andrews, Flg Off W 268
Appleton, Flt Lt LJ 267
♦ Archibald, Flg Off DD 96
♦ Archibald, Flt Lt J 93–97
† Armstrong, Plt Off JW 64–67, 70
† Arnold, Flt Lt WR 274
† Atkinson, Flt Sgt EHF 2, 22, 24–26

Bailey, Flg Off FE – DFC 357
† Baker, Wg Cdr RW – DFC, mid 316
Balfour, Flg Off JDK 274
Barclay, Flt Lt WJML – DFC, DFM (pff) 9, 64
Barley, Flt Lt HJ – DFC 186–88, 222–24, 247–49
† Barron, Wg Cdr JF – DSO★, DFC, DFM 68–69
† Barton, Wt Off BG 57–58

Baveystock, Flt Lt L, RAF – DSO, DFC★, DFM 5–6, 51–56, 113, 115–20
† Bebarfald, Flg Off BA 22, 200–2, 210–14
Beckett, Flt Lt VL, RAF 30–31
Beeson, Flg Off WCJ, RAF 91–92
♦ Bell, Flt Lt WP – DFC, mid 22, 138–44, 268
†♦ Bell, Plt Off RP 139
† Blaikie, Flg Off IA – DFM 128
† Blance, Plt Off IE 87
† Bonisch, Plt Off LL 70–71
† Boocock, Flg Off W 76
† Bowling, Flt Sgt CB
† Braddock, Wt Off RJ 128, 135, 138
† Brain, Flg Off WWD 22, 126
Bretherton, Flt Lt BJF – DFC 10–12, 46–47, 49
† Brierley, Wt Off TB 210, 215–16
Brough, Sqn Ldr ET – DFC 189–91
Brown, Plt Off LJS – MM 12–13, 153, 155–62

Bulloch, Sqn Ldr TM, RAF – DSO★, DFC★ 321–23, 350
Burgess, Flt Sgt PN 59–61
† Burman, Wt Off DC 192

Calvert, Sqn Ldr RO – DFC★★, mid 85–86, 89–90
Carey, Flt Lt JCL, RAF 167–69
Carter, Wt Off D – DFM 105–9
† Chalmers, Plt Off JC 3, 37–40
Checketts, Wg Cdr JM – DSO, DFC, Silver Star (US), Cross of Valour (Pol) 16, 148
Cheshire, Gr Capt GL RAF – VC, DSO★★, DFC, mid 8, 33, 64, 90
Chesterton, Flt Lt GH, RAF 219–20
Christian, Wt Off HJ 172–75
Clark, Wt Off RT 12, 164–67
† Climo, Flt Sgt FWP 87
Clouston, Gr Capt AE, RAF – DSO, DFC, AFC★, mid, bbc 139, 252, 327–28, 361–64
† Clouston, Sqn Ldr JG 40–41
Cochrane, Sqn Ldr AWG, DSO, DFC★★, (pff) 194
† Collender, Plt Off RG 74
Collins, Wt Off AJ,
Cook, Flt Lt DN 167–71, 210
† Cook, Flt Sgt SA 165
Corcoran Wt/Off J 205, 207
† Couchman, Flt Sgt LN 64–66, 70
† Couper, Plt Off NB 205–7
Cox, Flt Lt FA – cvsa 22, 27
† Crampton, Flg Off HT 73
† Croudis, Flt Sgt P 156, 219
Curtis, Flg Off J 182–85
† Curtis, Flt Sgt KG 185

†♦ Dale, Flg Off JA 272
†♦ Dale, Plt Off TW 272
† Dall, Flg Off DJ – DFC 297
Daniell, Sqn Ldr RD – DFC, AFC, Flying Cross (Neth) 6–7, 45–46, 220–22

Davies, Flt Lt GS – DFC 292–93
† Davies, Flt Sgt SH 85
Dawber, Flg Off JE 137

Dawe, Plt Off DM 168
† Dillon, Flg Off MF 64–68, 70
† Donaghy, Flt Sgt TR 70–71
† Donnelley, Flg Off NW 79
† Dudding, Wt Off K 85
Duder, Wg Cdr DH, RAF – DSO, DFC 18, 135

Eagleson, Flg Off OD – DFC 296, 300–4
† Eckhold, Flg Off MC 76
† Egley, Flg Off RA – DFC 260
Ensor, Wg Cdr MA – DSO★, DFC★ 315–21, 324–29, 337, 359–60
Evans, Flt Lt AR – DFC 267
Evans, Flt Sgt FEO 128–29

Fairhall, Flt Lt GWL 168
† Fauvel Flt LT SF 165
Fittall, Flt Lt VC – DFC 145
† Fittock, Flg Off LJS 179–80
Frizell, Sqn Ldr TFP, RAAF – DFC 101–4

Gapes, Flg Off JD 293
Gay, Flt Lt CS – DFC 150–55
Gibb, Sqn Ldr DS – DFC mid 168, 216, 218
Gibson, Sqn Ldr JAA, RAF – DSO, DFC (bbc) 260–61
† Grant, Flg Off DI 79
† Green, Plt Off WJ 64–66, 70
† Green, Flg Off WR – DFC 79–80
Greenough, Flt Sgt CC 293
Greig, Wt Off CFJ 87
Griffin, Flg Off CR – mid 86
Grocott, Flt Lt J 312–13
† Gutzewitz, Flg Off JL 274–76

† Hall–Jones, Flg Off FW 335
Hammond, Wg Cdr DH – DSO, DFC★ 254, 256
† Harden, Plt Off RC 192
Harris, Ft Lt TP 231–35, 258
† Harrison, Wg Cdr GE, RAF – DFC 214–16
Haugh, Wt Off JW 179–80
Hawker Flt Lt DE – DFC 85–87
Hay, Wt Off RE 172–75
† Heays, Flt Sgt IR 357–59
Helean, Flg Off NJA 12, 149–50
Hender, Sqn Ldr WCK – mid (photograph only)
Herbert, Flt Lt SID 84
Herring, Wt Off JE 225–28, 258
Hill, Wt Off LG 165
Hitchcock, Flt Lt EH 4, 41–45
† Hollard, Plt Off MC 79–80
Holmes, Sqn Ldr HG, RAF – DFC★ 324, 338
† Houghton, Flt Sgt EG 84
Houlton, Sqn Ldr JA – DFC 16, 270
† Hunniford, Flt Sgt WB 127
Hurse, Wt Off AW, RAAF – CGM 71–73

Insull, Flt Lt EJ – DFC (US) 3, 36–37, 162–63

Jameson, Flt Lt GE – DSO, DFC 241–43
Jameson, Gr Capt PG, RAF – DSO, DFC★, mid (5), (bbc), War Cross (Norway), Cdr Order of Orange Nassau (Neth), Silver Star (US) 261
† Jenkins, Flt Sgt FFA 87
† Joblin, Flt Lt GR – DFC 77–78, 81, 84–93
Judson, Flt Lt WG – DFC 243–45

† Kain, Flg Off EJ, RAF – DFC, mid 98
† Kalka, Flg Off WA 266–68
Kay, Flt Lt JH – DFC 22

Kay, Sqn Ldr JR – DFC 324
† Kearney, Sgt JE, RAF 95
Kearns, Sqn Ldr RSD – DSO, DFC, DFM (pff) 9, 64
† Kennedy, Flt Lt GM – (pff) 56–57
† Kilgour, Flg Off LAA 22, 126–27, 219
Kilpatrick, Flt Lt MA – DFC 284, 286–87
King, Flt Lt AT – DFC 9, 30, 32, 138–40
King, Flt JN 270
Kirk, Flt Sgt AC 87
Knapman, Flt Lt TS – DFC 9, 32
Knewstubb, Flg Off AH 116–17

Langley, Flg Off ML – CGM 251–53
Layne, Flt Lt BEH 360
Lee, Wg Cdr DH, RAF – DFC 225
Le Long, Flt Lt RE – DFC★ 10, 33–34, 236–38
Lennon, Flt Lt JW – DFC (pff) 85–87
†♦ Lewis, Plt Off RD, RAF – DFM 182–85
†♦ Lewis, Flt Sgt WR, RAF 182
Lindsay, Flg Off RA – BEM, (pff) 290
Lock, Flt Lt IF – DFC (US) 9, 32
Longhurst, Wt Off WD 225, 229–31
† Lord, Flt Lt DSA, RAF – VC, DFC 202–3
Lucas, Wg Cdr FJ – DFC★, mid 191

McCabe, Flt Lt OJ 238–40
McCardle, Fl Lt CW – mid 71–73
† McCracken, Plt Off RU 316
† Macdonald, Plt Off AJ 322
MacDonald, Flt Lt JS 100–01, 104
† MacDonald, Flg Off WH 70
† Macduff, Flg Off RD 129–30
† McGregor, Flt Lt R 130
† McKenzie, Flt Sgt JMT 71
McLaren, Flg Off JA, RAFVR – DFC 10, 33, 236
† McRae, Flg Off JK 85

Mann, Flg Off DH – DFC 255
Manser, Flg Off LT, RAFVR – VC 55–56
Mart, Flt Lt WG – DFC 298
† Matheson, Flg Off AA – DFM 245–46
† Mathewson, Wt Off DM 210, 215–16
Max, Wg Cdr RD, RNZAF/RAF – DSO, DFC, CdeG (Fr) 279
Mercier, Flg Off JD – DFC, (pff) 273
† Mewa, Flt Lt A 191
Millar, Wt Off PH 312–13
† Miller, Flt Sgt JS 71
Mills, Flg Off HJ – DFM 357
Mitchell, Flt Lt IR – DFC 324, 338
† Mitchell, Wt Off OJ 294–96
† Moosman, Wt Off MC 364–65
† Morgan, Plt Off KF 128
Mortimer, Flt Lt JE – DFC 12, 145–49
Mullinder, Flt Lt TLW 243
Munro, S/L JL – DSO, DFC 8–9, 32–33

† Nelson, Sgt PG 313–14
† Newton, Wg Cdr RJ – DFC, mid 269
† Norriss, Plt Off GA 216

O'Brien, Flg Off LP 274, 276
† O'Kane, Wt Off RA 57–58
Orman, Flt Lt KG – DFC★ 271, 276–84, 290

Park, ACM Sir Keith R, RAF – GCB, KBE, MC★, DFC, CdeG (Fr), Legion of Merit (US) 146, 177
† Park, Plt Off NM – DFM 146
† Paterson, Pl Off GW 128–29
Patterson, Sqn Ldr IC, RAF/RNZAF – DSO, mid 319, 321–24, 329–33, 337
†♦ Pepper, Flt Sgt DR 84
†♦ Pepper, Flt Sgt TB 84
Perks, Flt Lt RS – DFC 28–29, 81

Petersen, Flg Off WJ 290–91
Peterson, Wt Off LHF 168
† Pettit, Sqn Ldr WR, RCAF – OBE, DFC 22, 24–26
† Pettitt, Flg Off IA 252
Poole, Flt Lt HA – DFC 324, 333–40, 349
† Potts, Flt Sgt TC 85
Pugh, Flt Lt AGC 328

Reader, Flg Off RF 28–30, 128, 134–35
Reece, Flt Lt F 316, 318, 324
Reese, Flg Off BG 86
Reevely, Flt Lt WD – DFC 1–2, 17–19, 21
Reid, Flt Lt JW, RAFVR/RNZAF – mid 300
† Richardson, Flt Sgt GS 105–6, 109–12
Riddell, Flg Off IC 116–120
Robb, Wt Off FG 9
Roberts, Wt Off MA 172–75
† Robinson, Plt Off EG 22, 128–34
† Rodgers, Flg Off AO 77
Rouse Flt Lt CG – mid 22, 123–24, 208
Runciman, Sqn Ldr WJ – AFC, DFM, mid 194
† Rundle, Plt Off JR 37–38

† Sampson, Flt Sgt DJ 156
Saunders, Flg Off AK – DFC, Air Medal (US) 50–51, 176–81, 194
Saunders, AVM Sir HWL, RAF – KBE, CB, DFC★, MC, MM 239
Schrader, Wg Cdr WE – DFC★ 145
Scott, Gr Capt DJ – DSO, OBE. DFC★, CdeG (Fr & Belg), Cdr Netherlands Orange Nassau 48–49, 194
† Scott, Sgt FAJ 164–65
† Searell, Plt Off LP 128
Short, Flg Off SJ 295

Siegert, Flt Lt CL – DFC 22, 200, 217–20, 258
† Sinclair, Flt Sgt GA 85
Smith, Flg Off KA 303
Somerville, Flt Lt RB 139
† Souter, Flt Sgt AJP 362–64
Sparks, Flt Lt WA 225–28, 258–59
Spooner, Wg Cdr A, RAF – DSO, DFC 356, 358–59
Spotswood, Wg Cdr D, RAF – DSO, DFC, mid (2) (later Marshal of the RAF) 327
Spurdle, Sqn Ldr RL, RNZAF/RAF – DFC★, mid, (bbc) 4–5, 49–50, 258, 261–65
Stableford, Flg Off BAH 225, 228–29
Stafford, Flt Lt JH – DFC 300
† Stafford, Flt Sgt KV 74
† Stead, Flt Lt AB – DFC 269–70
† Steel, Flg Off MJ 35–36, 97–98
† Sterling, Plt Off JDK 269
Stirling, Flt Lt W – DFC 291–92
† Stokes, Flt Lt NAD 87
† Strang, Flg Off CR 29,
Stuart, Flg Off LB 274–76
Sutherland, Flg Off NW – DFC 22–23, 27, 122–25, 207–9, 217, 258

Tacon, Wg Cdr EW, RAF – DSO, DFC★, AFC 254
Tait, Flg Off RS – DFC 271, 284, 286–87
† Taylor-Cannon, Sqn Ldr KG – DFC★ 145, 193, 294
Thomson, Wt Off IRWR – DFC 357–58
Thomson, Plt Off WJ 218–19
† Trafford, Flg Off GR 194
†♦ Trainor, Wt Off IW 128–34
†♦ Trainor, Sgt T, NZ Army 133–34
† Trolove, Plt Off PN 322
Tunnicliffe, Flg Off DM – DFC 249–56
Turnbull, Flg Off BW – DFC 349–56

Twaddle, Flg Off AA 269
† Umbers, Sqn Ldr AE – DFC★ 193, 267
† Uru, Plt Off HW 128, 135–38

† Vercoe, Flt Sgt PN 84
Vincent, Flg Off REG 22, 123,

Waddy, Sqn Ldr ID – DFC 191–192, 194
Wallwork, Staff Sgt JH, Glider Plt Rgmt – DFM 19
† Walters, Flt Sgt HG 185
† Walters, Flg Off JW – DFC, (pff) 69
† Watts, Wg Cdr SD – DSO, DFC, mid 245–46
Wells, Wg Cdr EP – DSO, DFC★ (bbc) 5
Whincop, Flt Lt G – CdeG (Fr) 243
White Flt Lt LSM – DFC 270
White, Flg Off MR 292
† Whitehouse, Flg Off KO 85
† Whittleston, Plt Off RJ 272
† Whyte, Flg Off J 345–49
† Williams, Wt Off JLT – DFM (pff) 99
Wilson, Flt Lt JG – mid 194, 296–300
† Wood, Flt Sgt JH 277
Woodman, Flg Off BW – DFC 234, 304–7
† Wright, Plt Off JAS 252

† Yarwood, Plt Off MJ 22, 210, 212–13
† Young, Flg Off HS 192

Zillwood, Flt Lt AHR – DFC 72–73

GENERAL INDEX

Air Sea Rescue (ASR) 142–44, 176–85, 237
aircraft
  Albacore 331–32, 333
  Albemarle 49, 127, 200
  Anson 10, 322–23, 335
  B-17 Fortress 180, 278–79, 311, 322–23, 349, 352
  B-24 Liberator 55, 57–58, 96, 105–13, 117, 156, 180, 311, 327–28, 333, 339–42, 344, 350–57, 359, 362, 364
  B-25 Mitchell 3, 22, 106, 123, 180, 183–84, 191, 357
  Beaufighter 106, 116–17, 241, 243, 249–54
  Blenheim 139, 182, 277, 316–18, 335–36, 357
  Blohm and Voss 138 238
  Boston 3, 39–40, 41, 145–46
  Breda 88 338
  Buckner (Bu) 131 306
  Catalina 54, 101, 106, 112
  Dakota 6, 7, 27, 45–6, 175, 186–87, 198–202, 209–11, 220–25, 228–29, 249, 257, 259, 262
  Defiant 178
  Dornier 24s 237–38
  Dornier 217 242
  Fiesler Storch 300
  Fortress *see* B-17 Fortress
  FW 190 146–47, 168, 191, 209, 217–19, 294, 306
  Halifax 1–2, 11, 18, 19, 21, 27, 28, 30, 34, 46–48, 56–57, 62, 65–66, 68, 81–83, 85, 89, 122, 128–30, 134, 140, 172–73, 199–200, 248, 257, 269, 274, 278, 290–93, 311, 316
  Hampden 106, 116–17, 225–26
  Harvard 304
  Heinkel 111 306
  Heinkel 219 246
  Hudson 57, 128, 313–14, 316, 318–33, 336, 338, 349
  Hurricane 84, 189, 194, 261, 304
  Junkers (Ju)
  Ju 88 16, 24, 163, 236, 240–42, 248, 265, 338, 359–64
  Ju 188 236–37, 240
  Lancaster 7, 9, 31, 34–35, 36–37, 56–57, 65–66, 68–74, 76–99, 140, 162–65, 168, 180, 186, 226, 247–48, 269, 273–74, 277–79, 282–93, 364
  Liberator *see* B-24 Liberator
  Lysander 149, 177–78
  Manchester 55–56, 85
  Marauder 146, 180
  Martlet 332, 333
  Messerschmitt (Me)
  Me 109 168, 209, 211–12, 265, 269, 294
  Me 110 134, 247–48, 357–58, 361, 363
  Me 210 33
  Me 410 33–34
  Mitchell *see* B-25 Mitchell
  Mosquito 10, 29, 33–34, 56, 62, 64, 65, 82–83, 90, 123, 179, 183, 191, 194, 236–46, 288, 360
  Mustang 191, 204, 211, 269, 285, 287, 298
  P-38 Lightning 41
  Sea Otter 176, 178, 180–81
  Seafire 270
  Siebel 204 306
  Spitfire 12, 16, 40, 49
  Stirling 2, 7, 9, 17, 23–27, 31, 32, 37–9, 46, 59–61, 70, 122–37, 140–44, 150–52, 155–57, 167–69, 172, 198–203, 205, 208–18, 221, 223–25, 229–34, 248, 257–59, 262, 268–69, 272, 278, 284–85, 291–92

Sunderland 5, 51–54, 101–4, 111, 113, 115, 117–20, 311, 357, 360
Tempest 191, 193–94, 211, 260–61, 266–67, 294–301, 307
Thunderbolt 204, 226
Torbeau 254
Typhoon 12, 17, 149, 169, 186, 188–94, 204–5, 211, 217, 244, 260, 262, 264–65, 296–97, 300–3, 306–7
Uru *see* Heinkel
Ventura 22–23, 123–24, 138, 156, 183, 213, 216
Walrus 176–78
Wellington 17, 82, 128, 134, 249, 278, 311, 346
Whitley 82, 162, 172, 312

airfields/bases
 Abbotsinch 322
 Aldergrove 349
 B2 (Bazenville) 249
 B5 (Camilly) 240
 Ballykelly 106, 334, 339
 Beaulieu 327, 362
 Benbecula 349
 Biggin Hill 146
 Bircham Newton 316, 318, 322, 335, 349
 Blakehill Farm 186, 220, 228
 Blida 338
 Boscombe Down 72
 Boxhill 305
 Bradwell Bay 10, 239
 Breighton 274
 Castle Archdale 117
 Celle 305
 Chedburgh 9, 37, 140, 284, 140, 284
 Chivenor 335, 346
 Colerne 240–41
 Coltishall 237
 Coningsby 57
 Cranwell 336
 Dallachy 256
 Davidstow Moor 346
 Detling 5, 335
 Deurne 305
 Diest 305
 Down Ampney 221
 Driffield 85
 Dunholme Lodge 77
 Dunsfold 183, 185, 191
 Dyce 306
 East Kirkby 78, 84, 88–90
 East Leicester 124, 130, 140
 Elsham Wolds 65, 68, 94
 Eshott 305
 Fairford 2, 21, 23–24, 59, 124, 130, 141, 155, 167, 200–1, 210, 214, 218, 220, 224, 259
 Fassberg 300, 303, 305
 Feltwell 279
 Finmere 182–83
 Fiskerton 77
 Ford 125
 Friston 177, 179
 Grave 305
 Harrowfield 317, 336
 Hartford Bridge 3, 183
 Harwell 205, 207, 224
 Helmond 260–61
 Hurn 141
 Keevil 136, 226, 231, 233–34
 Kirmington 77
 Kristiansand 306
 Langham 250, 252, 254
 Leuchars 117, 252, 336
 Lissett 66, 293
 Ludford Magna 35, 97–98
 Manston 10, 34, 237–38, 260
 Martlesham Heath 178
 Melsbroek 185
 Mepal 70, 273, 287
 Mildenhall 3, 17, 36–37, 151, 162
 Montrose 322
 North Coates 254
 North Weald 296, 305
 Odiham 38
 Ophoven 305
 Pembroke Dock 51, 54

Pennfield Ridge 22, 123, 138, 156, 183, 213, 216
Peterhead 177
Portreath 11
Quackenbruek 297
Sawbridgeworth 5
Scampton 88–89
Shepherd's Grove 233
Shoreham-on-Sea 50, 178, 181
Sleap 172
Snaith 274
Squires Gate 335
St Eval 32, 58, 317, 320, 327, 328, 336–37, 349, 358, 364
Stoney Cross 22, 123, 231
Stornoway 320–21, 336
Stradishall 278, 280, 284
Swanton Morley 41
Tafaraoui 321, 329
Taieri 177, 182, 284, 304, 333, 335
Tain 106, 109, 112, 346
Tangmere 45, 192
Tarrant Rushton 1, 11, 12, 18, 30, 46, 155–56, 175
Thorney Island 340, 342–43, 356–57
Tilstock 23, 124, 172, 225
Tuddenham 151, 280, 284
Turnberry 116
Twente 305
Volkel 260, 268
Waterbeach 273
Westhampnett 177
Wethersfield 233–34
Whenuapai 276, 346
Wick 106, 117, 322
Wigram 66, 177, 252, 335
Witchford 273
Woodbridge 74, 201
Amiens 65–66, 68
Andelst 212, 215
Angers 36
Antwerp 166–67, 196, 305
Anzac Wing 252–53
Arctic convoys 310

Ardennes 14, 266, 280
Arnhem 21, 22, 49, 61, 123, 124, 144, 167–70, 173, 195–235, 249, 257, 258, 262, 269
Atlantic 51, 58, 101, 103–4, 107, 114–17, 240, 261, 308–16, 320, 323–24, 338, 345, 349–53, 356–7, 359, 361–2
Aulnoye-Aymeries 65–66
Ault 33–34

Baden 136–37
Bahamas 106, 328, 334, 339, 357
Baltic Sea 29, 237–38, 303, 328
bases *see* airfields/bases
Battle of the Atlantic 308–9
Battle of Britain 4, 41, 114, 261, 304, 306, 365
Battle of the River Plate 16
Bay of Biscay 11, 51, 55, 87, 115, 118, 120, 268, 313, 318, 320, 328, 336–37, 340–41, 344, 350, 357, 359, 361–63
Belgium 12, 14, 16, 36, 56, 62–65, 89, 128–30, 164–66, 185, 188, 196, 199, 207, 211, 220, 222, 233, 259, 280, 293, 305
Bell Block 66
Belsen 299, 303
Berlin 17, 26, 63, 81, 89, 245, 248, 288
blind bombing 31–2, 279, 282–83, 285, 286
Blitzkreig 74
Bomber Command 8, 18, 23, 29, 34, 36, 54–56, 62–99, 116, 140, 156, 196, 215, 236, 246, 249, 271–72, 279, 285–86, 288–89, 292, 297, 316–18, 357, 361
Bordeaux 12, 37, 115, 157–58, 341, 346
Boulogne 8, 36
Bremen 17
Brest 115, 336, 341, 360
British Army
    1st Airborne Division 197, 200, 210, 224

2nd Battalion, Oxfordshire and
  Buckinghamshire Light Infantry
  19–20
6th Airborne Division 1–2, 18, 20, 27,
  59, 258
7th Light Infantry Parachute Battalion
  26
11th Armoured Division 265
156 Parachute Battalion 170
Brunswick 90
Buer plant 273
Bulbasket 124–25, 141–42

Caen 2, 17, 18–21, 37, 46, 56–57, 59, 78,
  131, 134, 141, 183, 187, 190, 213,
  232, 240–42
Canada
  training in 10, 28, 56–57, 76, 88, 96,
    106, 116, 123, 134, 138–40, 145,
    212, 216, 225, 231, 284, 304, 321,
    346, 357
Cap d'Antifer 8
Cap Gris Nez 36
Caribbean 308, 310, 314
Castelnau-sur-l'Auvignon 160–62
casualties 15, 19, 26, 44, 62, 63, 65–66,
  70, 73–80, 83–90, 98–99, 123,
  126–29, 161, 190–91, 198, 208,
  210–11, 216–17, 221, 252, 272–73,
  277, 282, 289, 292–93, 309–10, 315,
  335, 349, 365
  Dresden 289
  friendly fire *see* friendly fire
  U-boats 308–9, 347, 356
'chaff' 8
Chambly 36
Chartres 41, 88, 183, 248
Chemnitz 288, 292–93
Cherbourg 10, 142–44, 188, 196, 245
Coastal Command 18, 54, 101, 105, 109,
  112–13, 116–17, 309, 311, 316, 318,
  321–22, 327, 335, 339–40, 342–43,
  350, 356–57, 361
Cologne 55, 85, 247–48, 273, 285, 292

Coulommiers 236–37
Creeping Line Ahead (CLA) search
  pattern 51–52, 107

Dambusters 7
Darmstadt 99
Den Helder 249, 254
depth charges 51, 53, 100–11, 119, 313,
  315, 320–21, 324–25, 327, 329–31,
  337, 342, 344, 347, 351–55
Detling Wing 5
Dieppe 147, 180, 237, 253
Dijon 124, 129, 134
Dives-Sur-Mer 26
Dog Beach 15, 42, 44
Dresden 287–92
Dreux 70–71
Druten 205, 207
Dunkirk 14
Dutch Resistance 169–71, 173–75, 198,
  210, 212

E-boats 253, 317, 336
Easy Beach 44
Eindhoven 168, 196, 220, 227, 265,
  305
Emmerich-Wesel 257
Enigma 315, 343
Epinal 93–94, 96
Essen 247, 277, 280–81
Eureka-Rebecca system 122, 142
Evreux 10, 33

Falaise 172, 186–94
Ferry Command 321
flak 2, 13, 16, 24–25, 28, 33–34, 37, 39–
  40, 45–46, 48, 55, 65, 67, 69–72,
  82, 85–86, 89–91, 98, 104–11, 125,
  128–30, 134–36, 142–43, 150, 152,
  157, 168–69, 173, 183–84, 189–94,
  199–202, 205, 207, 209–13, 217–18,
  221–31, 237–38, 251–52, 254,
  257–58, 260, 262–63, 267, 272, 274,
  276–77, 281–83, 285, 287, 289–90,

292, 297, 301, 306, 320, 342, 344, 346, 353, 364
Flensburg Peninsula 237–38
Fox Beach 15
Frankfurt 17, 74, 97, 155
French Forces of the Interior (FFI) 150, 245
French Resistance 12–13, 23, 26, 87, 94, 121–22, 125, 127, 129, 136, 141, 145, 148–49, 150, 151–53, 156, 159–61, 163, 166, 172, 219, 232
Friedrichshafen 36
friendly fire 16, 38, 41, 73, 266–70, 293
  casualties *see* casualties
Frisian Islands 246, 253–54

G-H aid 31–2, 279, 282–83, 285, 286
Gander 323, 324
Gee set (navigation aid) 281–82
Gelsenkirchen 273, 286
German Army
  7th Army 186–88
  Herman Goering Division 60–61
  Panzer Divisions 21, 159, 198–99
Gestapo 12, 155, 158, 164, 166–67
Ghent 65, 230
Gibraltar 56, 162, 320–21, 329, 333, 337–38, 362–63
Gien 151
Gironde Estuary 37
Givors 73, 87
Glider Pilot Regiment 18, 198, 262
gliders 257–59, 263–64
  Hamilcar 11, 47–48, 49, 257
  Horsa 7, 11–12, 17–21, 30, 47, 49, 201–2, 207, 257, 259, 262
  towing 2, 10–11, 21, 23, 47, 49, 59, 124, 130, 140–41, 162, 172, 186, 198, 200, 202, 207, 222, 232, 259, 277
  Wacos 11, 259
Gold Beach 15, 45
Graffigny-Chemin 126–27
Grave 197, 305

Ground Controlled Interception (GCI) 42, 45

Hamburg 8, 36, 85, 193, 289, 299, 305
Hanover 17
Heavy Conversion Units (HCUs) 364
  1663 66
  1665 23, 124–25, 225
Hedgehog bombs 352
Heligoland 253, 319
Holland 14, 29, 124, 164, 173, 188, 192, 195–235, 246, 260–61, 268, 273, 290, 297, 305, 317, 320
Holten synthetic-oil plant 272
Homberg 273–74
Houndsworth 124–25

Iceland 106, 114, 117, 314, 350–51, 353

Juno Beach 15

Karlsruhe 36, 293
Kiel 17, 86, 90, 237, 303, 308
Krupp Treibstoff plant 274, 276–77, 291

La Pallice 115, 341
Landing Craft Tank (LCT) 4, 41–43, 45
Laon 65, 70
Le Havre 8, 37, 40, 125, 243
Le Mans 68–69
Leigh Light 339, 341, 344
Leipzig 66, 284, 288, 291
Lens 70, 73
letters to families 66–68, 127, 132–33, 219–20, 230, 275, 316–18, 358–59
Leuna oil works 284
Light Night Striking Force (LNSF) 245
Lille 17
Lisieux 129, 131, 242
Locust light tanks 257
Lorient 40, 114–15, 314, 340, 341, 343, 352
Louvain 36
Lubeck 294, 297, 301, 303

Luftwaffe 14–15, 16, 75, 199, 245, 258, 282, 286, 297, 300, 302–3, 306, 361

Maas 197A, 216, 266, 268
Mailly-le-Camp 63, 79, 90
Malta 146, 356
Maquis *see* French Resistance
marking targets 64
Mediterranean 308, 321, 329, 333, 337–38
Meerbeck plant 273
Merlin 10, 285
Milice 158, 159
Missing Research and Enquiry Service 131–32
Mortain 188, 190
Munich 38, 90, 365

Nancy 84–85, 94, 98, 126
Nantes 36, 71, 244, 336
Narvik 109, 113
Nassau 339, 357
New Zealand Army
  28 (Maori) Battalion 133
Normandy 1–2, 8, 10, 12, 25, 27–30, 34, 49, 59, 62, 70–71, 78, 83, 87, 115, 123–24, 127–29, 131, 134, 141–42, 144, 159, 168, 186–87, 190, 196, 199, 204, 213, 218–19, 231–32, 240–41, 243, 249, 268, 286
  landing 6, 14–20, 23, 37, 41–48, 51, 127, 145, 215, 244
North Africa 11, 21, 222, 248, 321, 337, 356, 360
Norway 102–5, 107–9, 115, 117, 124, 130, 144, 173, 209, 228, 234, 251, 253, 256, 261, 306, 319, 323, 328
Nuremberg 63, 89, 365

Oboe radio navigation system 31
Omaha Beach 4, 15–17, 41–42, 45
Ontario 96, 132, 304
Oosterbeek 170, 197–98, 201, 216
Operation Cobra 188
Operation Cork 52

Operation Coup de Main 17, 21
Operation Derange 341
Operation Gain 126
Operation Glimmer 7–8, 9, 31–2
Operation Goodwood 78
Operation Mallard 2, 27, 45–46, 49, 59
Operation Market Garden 196, 199–201, 207, 209, 220, 231
Operation Musketry 340–41
Operation Overlord 14, 16, 52
Operation Pegasus 1 169–71
Operation Pegasus II 171
Operation Percussion 341
Operation Rupert 126
Operation Seaslug 341
Operation Taxable 7, 9, 31, 32–3
Operation Thunderclap 288, 293
Operation Tonga 2, 11, 22–23, 27–8, 30
Operation Torch 337
Operation Varsity 173, 257–58, 260
Operation Wash 126
Operation Wheelwright 157, 158–59
Operational Training Units (OTUs) 9, 39, 57, 102, 123, 134, 139, 162, 172, 183, 278, 284, 292, 327–28, 335, 339, 357
Orne River 18, 20, 27, 48
Ostend 202, 253
Osterfeld 286–87

paratroopers 2, 7, 21, 23–27, 59, 124–26, 130–31, 141, 168–71, 172, 186, 200, 219, 232, 257, 263
Paris 62, 70, 74, 79, 88, 94, 142, 149, 151, 155, 162, 187, 236, 293
Pas de Calais 8, 31, 64, 70
pathfinders 56–57, 65, 69, 77, 82, 200, 219, 290
Pegasus Bridge 1, 19, 26
petroleum industry targets (Germany) 271–93
Plougoumelen 135–36
Poitiers 23, 124
Prestwick 323, 324

prisoners of war (POWs) 12, 24, 26, 28,
40–42, 60, 68, 71, 82–83, 87, 92,
132–33, 151–52, 155, 159, 167, 184,
192–94, 198, 203, 216, 228, 243,
254, 274–75, 293, 301–2, 313, 315

Quebec 304

radar 41–45, 51, 311, 319, 341
  countermeasures 8, 31
  H2S 75, 279–80
radio-jamming transmitters 35
rail targets 62–65, 73–75, 90, 244, 269,
  285–86
Ranger patrol 237
Ranville 30
Reims 70, 74, 79, 128
rescues 50–51, 97, 104–5, 112, 142–44,
  176–85, 255, 309, 317, 361
Revigny-sur-Ornain 74–76
Reykjavik 106–7, 351, 353
Rhine 81, 97, 123–24, 144, 162, 167,
  169–73, 196–97, 203, 205, 209–10,
  222, 224, 227–28, 231, 234–35, 249,
  257–65, 275, 305
Rodeo 40
Rouen 10, 33, 191
Royal Air Force (RAF)
  2nd Tactical Air Force (2TAF) 64, 183,
    199, 204–5, 211, 269, 303, 306
  Commands
    Bomber *see* Bomber Command
    Coastal *see* Coastal Command
    Ferry *see* Ferry Command
    Transport *see* Transport Command
  Groups
    1 75, 288
    2 41, 140
    3 17, 70, 140, 156, 272, 274, 279,
      282, 285–86, 288, 291
    4 274
    5 77, 90, 116, 288
    6 288
    8 288

    38 1–2, 21, 22, 27, 122–23, 126, 136,
      140, 156, 168, 199, 200, 204, 210,
      215, 224, 232–34, 257, 262
    46 7, 27, 46, 186, 199, 200, 204, 210,
      224, 228, 234, 257
    60 (Signals) 4, 41
    83 305
    84 48
    100 272
  Squadrons
    3 261
    7 69
    15 69, 84, 261
    33 297
    44 186, 247, 248
    48 6, 45, 221
    49 77–78, 79
    50 55, 85
    51 274
    53 57–58, 314, 340, 344, 356
    56 18, 261
    57 88–90, 99
    59 352, 355
    65 40
    74 4, 192
    75 (NZ) 12, 69–70, 85, 87, 99, 164–
      65, 168, 191, 248, 269, 272–74,
      277, 279, 285–87, 293, 328
    76 18, 28, 30, 81
    78 274
    80 5, 49, 260–61
    83 56–57, 99
    86 55, 105, 106, 112–13, 328
    88 3, 39–40
    90 150–51, 156, 283
    98 183, 191
    101 35, 90, 97, 99
    102 291
    103 64, 65, 68, 76, 77, 94
    115 69, 269, 273, 283, 291–92
    120 112, 334, 339, 350–51
    122 146
    125 241
    126 146

GENERAL INDEX

130 (Punjab) 5, 304–6
132 177, 189, 192, 297
137 191, 260
138 128–29, 130
143 254
149 17
156 77
158 64–66, 293
159 96
161 128
164 191, 194
166 77
172 346
180 183, 185
181 260
182 189, 191
186 278–80, 282, 305
190 2, 21–23, 27, 124, 126, 141, 155, 162, 168, 200, 208–11, 216–17, 219–20, 224–25, 258, 280
196 65, 168, 225
198 48, 297
199 269, 272
201 5–6, 51, 54, 102, 115–17, 120, 334, 360
206 322, 349
210 112
214 37, 39, 278
218 7–9, 30, 31–2, 140
220 322, 352
222 297, 298
224 268, 327, 328, 359, 362–64
226 3, 183
233 7, 186–87, 220–22, 228, 249
245 192
268 269
269 322
271 221
274 261
277 50–51, 178–79
295 10–11, 200, 205
296 127
298 1, 11, 18, 20, 28, 30, 128–30, 134–35

299 22, 123–24, 136, 138, 229–34, 258
311 (Czech) 55
320 (Dutch) 183–84
342 (Lorraine) 3, 39
401 269
403 (RCAF) 180
423 (RCAF) 102
437 (RCAF – Husky) 220, 228
455 117, 252, 254
466 85
467 79
485 (NZ) 12, 16, 145–46, 148, 269–70
486 (NZ) 12, 149, 193–94, 261, 266, 294, 296–97, 300
487 (NZ) 123, 183, 243
488 (NZ) 239–41
489 (NZ) 106, 116–17, 249, 252–54, 256
490 (NZ) 101, 104
500 (County of Kent) 137, 316–17, 320–21, 329, 331, 333–35, 337–38, 349
501 261
513 61
514 73, 273–74
547 345–48
550 76–77
570 200, 224
575 224
576 94, 96
591 (Antrim) Parachute 24
605 (County of Warwick) 10, 236
609 48
612 312
616 177
617 7–9, 31–3, 64, 90
619 77–79
620 2, 12, 21–26, 27, 59, 61, 128, 130, 132–34, 140–42, 155, 168–69, 200, 208, 210, 224–25
622 3, 36, 84, 85, 162
625 65

630 78, 80–81, 84–90
635 290
644 1, 11, 18, 20, 46–47, 172
692 29, 245
Wings
  122 261
  123 48
  124 191, 260
  137 3
  139 183
Royal Navy 16, 55, 309, 356
  Support Group 2 341
Ruhr Valley 7, 17, 29, 80, 85, 192, 195, 201, 226, 247, 269, 273–74, 286, 291
Runnymede 29, 40, 58, 69, 112, 127, 130, 180, 185, 191–93, 246, 272, 275, 345, 348, 364
Russelsheim 97–99

Sagan 92, 151, 155
Saint Quentin 70, 149
Sale, Morocco 11
sappers 24–25, 30, 171
Scheldt Estuary 195–96
Schweinfurt 90
Ships
  Alsterufer 55
  Awatea 315–16, 321
  Cap Ancona 303
  HMS *Ajax* 16
  HMS *Barham* 329
  HMS *Black Prince* 16
  HMS *Eagle* 189
  HMS *Erne* 326
  HMS *Formidable* 331
  HMS *Furious* 146
  HMS *Glorious* 261
  HMS *Lapwing* 113
  HMS *Lark* 113
  HMS *Onslow* 268
  HMS *Orwell* 36
  HMS *Wilton* 331, 333
  Matsonia 182
  Mauretania 139

  Orkan 348
  Piako 114
  Port Victor 114
  Queen Elizabeth 278
  Scharnhorst 323
  Tainui 322
  Tamaroa 349
  Uruguay 216
  USS *Leedstown* 329
  Tirpitz 109, 113
Sindelfingen 91–92
Somme Estuary 33, 78, 147
sonar buoys 339–40
Sortehaug 267
Special Air Service (SAS) 26, 122–29, 131, 134, 141–42, 144, 151, 158, 269
Special Operations Executive (SOE) 21, 70, 159, 160
  drop codes 23, 173
  flights 121–44, 151, 173, 209, 213, 215, 218, 228, 231–34
Sperrbrechers 252–53
St Andre-de-l'Eure 10, 33–34
St Lo 142, 188
St Nazaire 317–18, 336, 341
St Vith 266, 280–81
Stuttgart 81–87, 90, 93–94
Supreme Headquarters Allied Expeditionary Force (SHAEF) 124
Sword Beach 15, 20

T-5 Zaunkonog homing torpedo 353
Ta 152 294–96
Tergnier 65
Tetrarch light tank 47–48
Tilburg 165, 216
Torpex 321, 324
Toulouse 90, 158–59
Tours 65
Trans-Atlantic Ferry Pool *see* Ferry Command
Transport Command 249
Trappes 62, 162

Trinidad 313–14
Troyes 77, 79, 129

U-boats 6, 15, 51–54, 57–58, 100–20, 308–65
  U-107 113–15, 117–20
  U-135 352
  U-170 341–42
  U-187 351
  U-206 313
  U-259 321, 325–26
  U-317 105, 107
  U-331 329–33
  U-391 57
  U-458 321
  U-459 346–47
  U-505 313–15
  U-535 341–43
  U-536 341–42
  U-540 353–56
  U-549 346
  U-579 328
  U-609 351
  U-624 352
  U-675 100–2
  U-762 352
  U-955 51–54, 113
  U-968 105–6, 109–10, 113
  U-1008 328
U-tanker 346
Union Rheinische synthetic plant 273
United States Army 187–88, 268–69, 310–11
  1st Infantry Division 15
  21st Army Group 195
  29th Infantry Division 15
  82nd Airborne 197
  101st Airborne 196
  Eighth Airforce 64, 285
  Radar Unit 15082 42, 45
Utah Beach 15

Varennes 150
Venlo 245–46
Vichy France 151, 158

Waal 167–68, 197, 205, 207, 212, 230
Wesel 257, 264
Wilhelmshaven 17
'window' 8

Yevres 88

Zetten 215, 216
Zuider Zee 246, 254

ABOUT THE AUTHOR

Max Lambert spent most of his working life with the New Zealand Press Association Wellington, and reported for the news agency from Sydney (1969–71), from Washington (1975–80) and from the Antarctic in the summer of 1974–75. He co-authored *The Wahine Disaster* in 1968 and wrote *November Gold*, an account of New Zealand horses in the Melbourne Cup, in 1985 before *Night after Night* (2005) and *Day after Day* (2011). He and his wife have two adult daughters and live in Wellington.

Contact him at maxlambert@paradise.net.nz

www.ingramcontent.com/pod-product-compliance
Lightning Source LLC
Chambersburg PA
CBHW031234100526
44583CB00050B/586